Frontiers of Political Economy

Frontiers of Political Economy

GUGLIELMO CARCHEDI

VERSO

London · New York

First published by Verso 1991

Verso

UK: 6 Meard Street, London W1F 0EG
USA: 388 Atlantic Ave, Brooklyn, NY 11217

Verso is the imprint of New Left Books

British Library Cataloguing in Publication Data
A catalogue record for this book is available from the British Library

Library of Congress Cataloging-in-Publication Data
A catalogue record for this book is available from the Library of Congress

ISBN: 978-1-86091-566-9

Typeset by BP Integraphics Ltd, Bath, Avon

Printed in the United States

Contents

Foreword   ix

Chapter 1   A Few Words on Method   1

   1.1   An Example   1
   1.2   Some Basic Concepts   3

Chapter 2   Production as a Social Process   7

   2.1   Marx's Analysis of the Production Process   7
   2.2   Braverman and the Labour Process Debate   14
   2.3   Elements of a Theory of Material and Mental Labour 18
   2.4   The Dialectics of the Production of Value   28
   2.5   Agents of Production and Classes under Modern
       Capitalism   32
   2.6   The Social Production of Knowledge   41

Chapter 3   Social Distribution through Price Formation   55

   3.1   Individual and Social Values: Preliminary Remarks 55
   3.2   Market Values   57
   3.3   Production Prices without Technological Competition 68
   3.4   Production Prices with Technological Competition   73
   3.5   The Dynamics of the Transformation Procedure   87
   3.6   The Transformation Debate   90
   3.7   The Complete Notion of Production Prices   98
   3.8   Some Further Aspects of a Marxist Theory of Prices 106
   3.9   The Law of Value in the National Context   117

Chapter 4   Recent Controversies on the Law of Value   125

   4.1   The Formation and Distribution of Value   125

4.2	The Reduction of Skilled to Unskilled Labour	130
4.3	Joint Production	134
4.4	Destruction of Value	137
4.5	Okishio and the Fall in the Rate of Profit	139
4.6	Productivity, Exploitation and Redistribution of Value	141
4.7	Abstract Labour versus Standard of Value	146

Chapter 5 Growth, Crises, Inflation and Crashes — 153

5.1	The Fall in the Rate of Profit: Causes and Nature	153
5.2	The Fall in the Rate of Profit, Crises of Profitability and of Realization	161
5.3	Crises, Inflation and Stagflation	163
5.4	Alternative Marxist Interpretations of Crises	179
5.5	The Cyclical Nature of Production Crises	189
5.6	Financial Crises and Stock Exchange Crashes	201
5.7	The Fallacy of the Multiplier	210

Chapter 6 (Neo-)Ricardian and (Neo-)Marxist Views of International Prices, Specialization and Exploitation — 217

6.1	Ricardo and Comparative Advantages	217
6.2	Marx on International Market Values	220
6.3	Emmanuel's "Narrow" Unequal Exchange	222
6.4	The Neo-Ricardian Production Prices and Unequal Exchange	225

Chapter 7 Production and Distribution as Worldwide Processes — 231

7.1	Oligopoly Capitalism versus Free Competition Capitalism	231
7.2	The International Equalization of Oligopolistic Profit Rates	236
7.3	International Wage Zones	240
7.4	International Production Prices in Value Terms	243
7.5	Rates of Exchange and International Production Prices in Money Terms	246
7.6	Depreciation and Appreciation	251
7.7	Unequal Exchange between Capitalist and Non-capitalist Systems	259
7.8	International (Super-)Exploitation	261
7.9	Exploitation, Inflation and Rates of Exchange in the Dominated Countries	263

Chapter 8 Two Contemporary Problems — 275

8.1	International Production Prices and the Current Monetary Crisis	275

CONTENTS

8.2 Is the Theory of Comparative Advantages Compatible with
Socialist Development?   282

Appendix   The Method of Social Research   291

A Dialectics   291
B Laws and Tendencies   299

Bibliography   307

Index   321

Foreword

There seems nowadays to be an inverse relationship between the degree of mathematical and statistical proficiency reached by our students of economics and their awareness that economic life is a specific form of social life. The reason for this situation is not difficult to find. Mainstream economics has been turned into a byzantine theoretical fabric based on fictional assumptions and obsessed with static equilibria. Dynamics is misconceived as the study of a logical (that is, mathematical) path between two sets of equations. Techniques have been emptied of their social dimension, as if they had been devised in a world devoid of social content. Empty mathematical formalism, as opposed to concern with the real (that is, social) nature of the economic system, has become the object of inquiry. In short, economics has been turned into a branch (a sort of poor cousin) of mathematics.

This work carries a different set of assumptions. Its thesis, in a nutshell, is that production, exchange and consumption, the object of economics, are historically specific social processes; and that the relations in which people engage when they produce, exchange and consume are historically specific social relations. Thus, economics is first and foremost a social science, a science which studies historically specific social phenomena. As such, it must be based on real assumptions (or abstractions of real world phenomena), must be concerned with real world problems, and must study the real (and contradictory) forces which change an inherently dynamic (because contradictory) situation into another one. This is the approach which must be pursued by political economy.

Political economy must reappropriate social reality. It cannot but, at the same time, squarely challenge orthodox economics and question its method of inquiry, the relevance of its problems and the usefulness of its results. This work is thus addressed to all those who, disappointed by conventional and formalistic economic theory, wish to turn to a more realistic and substantive approach.

ix

This reappropriation of social reality, however, is not free from challenges. To begin with, most contemporary political economists accept the "modern" method of inquiry and frame of reference of orthodox economics. They seem to be unaware that political economy must rely on the dialectical method of social inquiry, rather than on mathematics and statistics. These latter are important tools but should be only auxiliary devices to the former. It is only by adopting a dialectical perspective that insight into the complex and contradictory nature of contemporary economic reality can be gained: from the labour process to the production and commercialization of knowledge; from the production of value to its redistribution through the formation of prices; from the de-skilling of qualified labour to the destruction of value; from joint production to the production of means of destruction; from technological innovations to crises, inflation and stagflation; from comparative advantages to unequal exchange; from international prices to rates of exchange, devaluation and revaluation; from international competition to the current monetary crisis. This book, then, stresses that, in order to understand the economy, and thus society – or better said, in order to understand the economy as society – it is not necessary to have mathematical skills. To understand real social processes, one must understand and apply the dialectical method of social inquiry, independently of whether these processes can be analysed by using mathematical or statistical tools.

But the choice of a proper method of social inquiry is not sufficient. This method must be actually applied to analyse present-day social dynamics, the contemporary concrete features of social reality. Of these, three stand out particularly vividly. To begin with, an increasing proportion of economic agents is employed to generate the knowledge needed to produce material goods, rather than being directly engaged in their production. Second, under modern conditions, production and distribution are truly international, rather than being activities which cross the national borders only in the form of international trade. Third, in the contemporary economy, the basic units of economic activity are modern oligopolies, rather than free competition capitals. In spite of these macroscopic changes, political economy has been blind to the need to develop a theory of mental labour (and of the conditions under which mental labour is productive of value) and, on the whole, has scored very low in its efforts to extend value analysis both to the international level and to oligopolistic reality. Yet these are the themes which must delimit the new frontiers of political economy and which will allow us conceptually to recompose the seemingly unrelated pieces of the contemporary economic mosaic.

The following pages, then, represent an attempt to inquire into the dialectics of value, prices and exploitation in the contemporary world economy. They have been written to be accessible to students of social sciences, including students of economics. They aim at forming economists as social scientists, rather than social engineers; as skilful analysts of social reality, rather than experts in the manipulation and application of mathematical and statistical techniques.

But an analysis of modern reality cannot disregard alternative analyses and contemporary debates. Thus, this work surveys the most important recent controversies in the field. The aim is twofold. First of all, debates often force the participants to sharpen their theoretical tools. Some of the results of these debates have certainly been beneficial to political economy and have been incorporated into this work. Second, the aim is to familiarize the reader with ongoing controversies which often, and quite unnecessarily, are couched in a jargon incomprehensible to "non-specialists".

In making no concessions to the current mood in economic theory and in purposely avoiding the use of mathematics, I have been guided by two considerations. From the point of view of exposition, I want to encourage those readers who might be put off by mathematical and statistical tools. From the point of view of inquiry I want to avoid the danger that concern with casting reality in mathematical models and with the formal consistency of those models replaces the analysis of real economic life, of its changing forms and of its processes of reproduction and supersession. This book, then, relies on verbal exposition. But reliance on verbal, rather than on mathematical, exposition does not necessarily make the reading easier. The reader will have to apply himself or herself with as much dedication as if this book had been fully couched in mathematical formulae. But then, as we know, there is no royal road to science.

I should like to express my gratitude for useful comments to my students at the University of Amsterdam. The following colleagues were kind enough to discuss parts of my manuscript at various stages (in alphabetical order): Chris Arthur, Bruno Carchedi, Trevor Evans, Alan Freeman, Paolo Giussani, Werner de Haan, David Laibman, Paul Mattick Jr., Fred Moseley, Gianfranco Pala, Roald Ramer and Geert Reuten. I also benefited from discussions with staff members of the University of Havana in March–April 1989 and in November–December 1991, and with staff members of the University of Poznan in November 1989. Needless to say, responsibility for the final result is mine alone.

G. Carchedi
Faculty of Economics, University of Amsterdam

1

A Few Words on Method

1.1 An Example

This work is built upon the dialectical method of research. The first question, then, which must be addressed is: what is dialectics? As a first step towards an unambiguous answer we can say that dialectics is a specific way to look at, and make sense out of, reality. If this is so, the question becomes: How do we see reality when we think dialectically? Since, in what follows, the focus will be on the notion of dialectics to be found in Marx,[1] our initial question (What is dialectics?) becomes: How do we see reality when we think in terms of Marxian dialectics?[2]

Consider, to begin with, an example. Suppose a car maker plans the production of a new model and thus has to fix the price at which that car will be sold. From the point of view of the capitalist, the fixing of the price depends on a large number of factors which basically can be reduced to two orders of consideration. First, the capitalist must make a realistic estimate of how much it would cost to produce that particular type of car. Second, the capitalist must make a realistic estimate of how many cars of that particular type can be sold at a certain price. This price must be higher than that car's cost of production. The difference is the capitalist's estimated future profit. If this latter is considered to be sufficient, the production of that car will get the green light.

This is how the capitalist perceives reality. However, in reality that price is determined by a social process rather than by these computations. Consider first the fixing of the cost of production of that car. Given certain qualities of the product aimed at, the capitalist has a choice of inputs and possibly of techniques. As far as techniques are concerned, the capitalist will choose those techniques which will minimize his or her costs. For example, s/he can choose between three levels of factory automation: Computer Integrated Manufacturing (CIM), Flexible Manufacturing Systems (FMS) and Cell Manufacturing (CM).[3]

But all other capitalists will reason likewise. Thus, if the pace of techno-logical innovation is relatively slow or if the number of producers of a certain commodity is relatively great (free competition), at any given moment the bulk of the products will be made by using the same technique, that which minimizes costs (or maximizes productivity). This is then the average in the sense of modal technique. The modal productivity in that branch is then that of the modal technique. If technological change is relatively rapid or if the number of producers of a certain commodity is relatively small (oligopolistic competition), there might be no modal technique, only an average in the sense of mean.

This implies that at any given time some capitalists will have already introduced new and more efficient techniques than the average (either the mode or the mean) and other capitalists will have been left behind in the technological race. For example, at the moment, CIM seems not to be suitable for the majority of enterprises. The issue is whether FMS or CM will become the modal, or commonly used technique (Garnett, 1988). A similar reasoning applies to inputs, given that the choice of a technique implies the choice of the inputs to be used.

These deviations from the average (either the mode or the mean) only prove the existence of the average, that is, that the choice of both tech-niques and inputs is socially determined. Hypothetically, the capitalist might want to use extravagant and costly production techniques or inputs. The market, however, will be quick to point out this mistake. It will either choose the competitors' products, thus paying a price which only covers the average costs, or it will offer to pay only that much for that capitalist's cars.

But the social determination of price fixing does not stop here. The capitalist invests in car production only if there are no opportunities to make higher profits in other branches. If the capitalists are free to move to (invest in) other branches, this capital movement between branches will tendentially equalize the rates of profit in all branches. The price realized by the average productivity capitalists, then, tenden-tially incorporates the average rate of profit in that economy. This means that those capitalists who have used better techniques or cheaper inputs tendentially make higher than average profits and those capitalists who have used more expensive inputs or less efficient techniques tendentially make less than average profits.

Therefore, the price the consumers are willing to pay for that product does not necessarily coincide with the price the capitalist had hoped to realize. Nor does it necessarily coincide with the *individual value* of that commodity, which is the value of the inputs used plus the extra value actually produced during the production of that commodity (and which is not known to the capitalist). The price society is willing to pay is the *social value* of that commodity. The individual value and the social value of a commodity do not necessarily coincide.

This means that the price of that car has a double aspect. On the one hand, it is an individual value and as such it is determined by the specific conditions of that particular production process. On the other hand it is a social value, the price society is willing to pay. The social value is the modification of the individual value.

We can now see what the relation is between individual and social values. Since commodities must be sold in order to realize their value, their individual values can realize themselves only as social values, as modified individual values. Or, individual values are only potentially social values, which realize themselves as actual social values. They do that at the moment of sale, that is, through exchange; or, the instant they realize themselves, they modify each other.

This example contains all the elements we need to understand dialectically the process of price formation. First, the individual value of commodities is determined by the structure of the production processes (in short, the structure of production). This structure determines the value of the inputs at the beginning of the production process and the extra value produced during the production process. Second, given that what is produced must be sold and that therefore the price society is willing to pay can be different from the individual values of the commodities, these individual values can realize themselves only as social values by influencing and modifying each other. Third, both individual and social values are part of reality (in this case, price formation); or, reality is not only what has realized itself (prices, or social values), it is also what exists only potentially (individual values).

1.2 Some Basic Concepts

It is now possible to provide a sketch of the method to be employed in this work. I shall single out only those features which are strictly necessary for the following chapters.

Let us begin with the notion of the *dialectical view of social reality*. This is a view that stresses:

1. that social reality is formed by both actually realized and potentially existing social phenomena;
2. that both categories of phenomena are tied by a relation of mutual interdependence, or *determination in the last instance*. This means that some realized social phenomena are determinant and others are deter-

mined in the sense that some potential social phenomena have realized themselves as conditions of either reproduction (in the same or in a modified form) or of supersession (radical change) of the determinant phenomena; in symbols,

$$A => B$$

indicates the determination in the last instance of B by A, that is, that B is a condition either of reproduction or of supersession of A;

3. that it is through their mutual interaction that the realized instances (both determinant and determined) take on (and thus modify) their concrete features;

4. that all social phenomena are constantly subjected to movement, that is, not only to change from a realized form to another realized form (as has just been said) but also to change from a potential to a realized state and vice versa, and from being a condition of reproduction to being a condition of supersession (and vice versa) of the phenomena which have determined them.

This view thus stresses the dynamic nature of reality (in our case, social reality), that is, its being in constant movement. This movement, however, is not chaotic. Rather, it is a *tendential movement*, a movement regulated by tendencies and counter-tendencies. The tendencies are primary in the sense that they are the state towards which the counter-tendencies gravitate and the counter-tendencies are secondary in the sense that they are deviations from the tendency.

I distinguish between two major types of tendency. Given the present movement of reality, its future tendential state, or *future tendency*, is the hypothetical situation of what reality would be like at some point in the future if only the tendency were operative. Given the same present movement of reality, the *present tendency* is the hypothetical situation of what reality would be like now, again if only the tendency were operative.

This work will make ample use of the distinction between three types of present tendencies and counter-tendencies. I shall call a *tendency of the first type* a movement towards a point or an area in which most realized phenomena are clustered. The counter-tendency is given by those phenomena which are not found in that point or area but which gravitate towards it. For example, within a nation, the wages of a certain category of labourers tend towards a certain level because most of them are actually paid that level. But there are also labourers paid more or less than that tendential level because of specific, but transitional, circumstances. Both the tendency and the counter-tendencies are realized at the same time.

4

By a *tendency of the second type* I mean a cyclical movement showing the alternate realization of first the tendency and then the counter-tendency. When the tendency realizes itself, the counter-tendency is present only in a potential state. The movement of the rate of profit is a case in point. When this rate falls, it is the tendency which predominates and which thus realizes itself; when this rate rises, it is the counter-tendency which predominates and which realizes itself.

Finally, in a *tendency of the third type* the tendency does not realize itself at all: only the counter-tendency does. Or, only the movement around the tendency (and not the tendency itself) is observable. This is the case of the formation of a tendentially equalized rate of profit. Only the fluctuations of the different capitalists' rate of profit around a mean are observable.[4]

To conclude, I shall state the *general methodological principle* which will inform the analysis of economic phenomena in terms of dialectical analysis: only those concepts and procedures which either reflect, or facilitate the observation of, *real* processes, that is, processes in concrete reality, will be relevant. Alternative, and often conflicting, concepts and procedures will be either accepted or rejected on the basis of this principle. The real process forming the foundation of economic life is the production process. Thus it is from an analysis of this process that economic theory must start.

This chapter has dealt only with those aspects of method which are strictly necessary to understand the following pages. It is, however, utterly insufficient to grasp the dialectical method of social research. The reader interested in a brief, but adequate for the purposes of this volume, exposition of that method is referred to the Appendix at the end of this volume. For a more detailed treatment, the reader can consult Carchedi, 1987a.

Notes

1. Dialectical thinking is present both in Western and in Eastern philosophies. For a useful discussion of dialectics in the Western tradition, see Oiserman, 1979.

2. Actually, Marx never wrote a treatise on dialectics. That notion is only implicitly contained in his works. Thus, any reconstruction of the Marxian notion of dialectics is inevitably also an interpretation of it. This holds for Engels's *Anti-Dühring* (1970) and *The Dialectics of Nature* (1976), the first treatises on dialectics. This holds also for the interpretation submitted here. In this interpretation, dialectics is a (socially determined) way to see, or to *interpret*, reality. For Engels, on the other hand, dialectics is inherent in nature and dialectical thinking is a *reflection* in thought of the dialectics of nature. It should be stressed that, contrary to the purely philosophical notions of dialectics, the interpretation submitted in this work is meant to be a tool of social research and social action. Thus, it should be evaluated in these terms.

3. CIM

is a total system. This involves customer orders arriving electronically and an integrated-computer system running the production operation from start of assembly to final dispatch.

FMS involves the computer-linking of several production or assembly machines, usually with an automated handling system.

The simplest form of automation is known as cell manufacturing. Each cell is made up of one or two cutting machines connected to a robot or simple handling equipment. The cells are programmed by computer but operate separately from everything else in the factory. (Garnett, 1988).

4. All these three types of tendency hold the principle that the choice of some element of reality as the tendency rather than as the counter-tendency reflects our conception of reality. This choice is itself a hypothesis whose validity must be checked through a process of verification. See Carchedi, 1987a; Appendix to ch. 3.

2

Production as a Social Process

2.1 Marx's Analysis of the Production Process

Economics is the science of production, exchange and consumption. But something has to be produced before it can be exchanged and consumed. It is for this reason that the analysis of the production process occupies a pivotal position in Marx's economic theory.

2.1.1 The capitalist production process

In order to reproduce themselves, people must transform objects with a certain use into different objects with a different use. In other words, they must transform existing use values into new use values. Thus, a *use value* is anything which satisfies needs and is given by both the particular characteristics (physical, chemical, etc.) of the commodity being exchanged and by the needs of those who exchange the commodity, "whether they spring from the stomach or from fancy" (Marx, 1967a, p.35). The transformation of use values is the *labour process*, which is the basis of all societies. This process can be represented as follows

$$LPr = U \rightarrow U*$$

where LPr stands for labour process, U for a use value, U* for a different use value and where $\rightarrow$ symbolizes the transformation of U into U*. The transformation of iron, plastic, rubber, etc. into a car is a clear example of the production of a new use value.

The labour process takes on special features according to the specific nature of each society. Under capitalism, products are produced only inasmuch as they are a source of profit. Or, the capitalist production process is first of all production for and of profit.[1] Thus the capitalist production process has a double nature. On the one hand it is a labour process, a transformation of use values; on the other hand it is production of profit, of surplus value, and thus it is a *surplus value producing process*.

Production of profit means that the capitalists do not invest their money (capital) in order to produce for their own consumption nor simply to provide consumers with useful things (use values). What is produced by their labourers must be converted into money, sold on the market. The capitalist is thus interested in the product's use value only inasmuch as that use value can be sold, exchanged on the market first for money and then for other commodities. In other words, the capitalist is interested in the product's use value only inasmuch as it has (is) an *exchange value*. The exchange value is thus the quantity of other commodities for which a certain quantity of that commodity is exchanged.

In its turn, exchange value is important for the capitalists only inasmuch as they can realize a profit. It follows that (a) a product must have both a use value and an exchange value and (b) that exchange value, when converted into money, must be greater than the quantity of money initially invested by the capitalist at the beginning of the production process. Figure 2.1 summarizes this process.

Figure 2.1 The capitalist production process as a whole

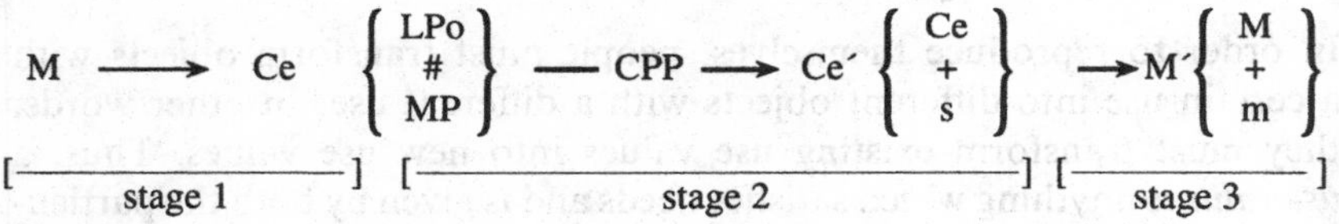

$$M \longrightarrow Ce \left\{ \begin{array}{c} LPo \\ \# \\ MP \end{array} \right\} — CPP \longrightarrow Ce' \left\{ \begin{array}{c} Ce \\ + \\ s \end{array} \right\} \rightarrow M' \left\{ \begin{array}{c} M \\ + \\ m \end{array} \right\}$$

[————— stage 1 —————] [————————— stage 2 —————————] [————— stage 3 —————]

In stage 1 the capitalist advances money (M) in order to buy commodities, here considered only as exchange values (C indicates commodity and Ce indicates the exchange value of a commodity). This is a transformation (symbolized by →) of money into commodities. The commodities bought are of two types: labour power (LPo) and means of production (MP). Consider first labour power. Under capitalism, use values are produced by labourers (those who transform use values) with means of production which do not belong to them. Since they do not own the means of production, they have to sell their capacity to labour, or *labour power*, to the owners of the means of production, the capitalists. Consequently, their labour power is bought and sold on the labour market, that is, it is a commodity. The *means of production* include both the objects of

8

labour (that which has to be transformed) and the instruments of labour (the means with which to operate the transformation).

Stage 1 is a *formal transformation* since there is no transformation of use values: the use value of the means of production is not changed through their purchase.

In stage 2, the capitalist combines both means of production and labour power into the production process proper (the combination being indicated by #). This is a *real transformation*, a transformation of use values. In fact, at the end of this process, the use value of the product is different from the use value of the means of production (this is not shown in this figure). Also the product, or commodity, has an exchange value greater than the exchange value of both the means of production and labour power: it is equal to the initial value, Ce, plus an extra value, s; or, $Ce' = Ce + s$.

In stage 3 the capitalists sell this product, realize the product's exchange value, and receive a quantity of money (M') which is equal to the initial one (M) plus an extra m. M is the monetary form of the value initially advanced, m is the monetary form of surplus value. This too is a formal transformation, given that the use value of the product is not changed through sale.

The question now is: In which of the three stages of the capitalist production process as a whole is surplus value (s, in Figure 2.1) created? It cannot be either stage 1 or stage 3, that is, it cannot be purchase and sale. In fact, if equal values are exchanged, no value is created. If different values are exchanged, the more value that is obtained by the seller, the less is left to the buyer, and vice versa. Or, stages 1 and 3 can account for the redistribution of value, not for the creation of new value. Thus surplus value must come from stage 2, the production process proper. This process is summarized in Figure 2.2.

Let us explain Figure 2.2. The capitalist buys both the means of produc-

Figure 2.2 The capitalist production process proper

9

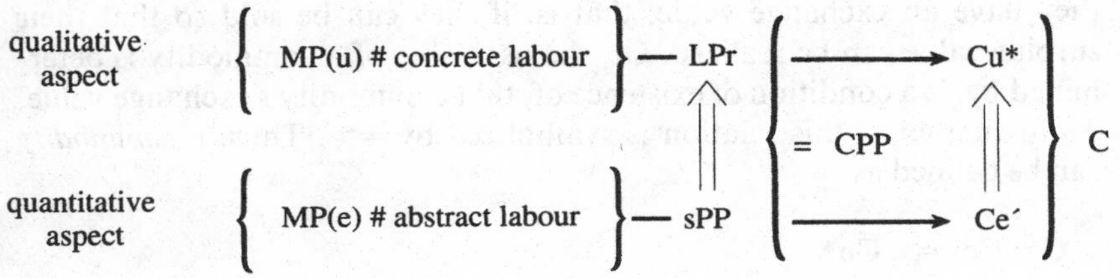

tion and the labourers' labour power. The capitalist then combines these two elements of the production process (this is symbolized by #) by setting the labourers to work. The labour power, or the potential capacity to labour, is transformed into *labour*, the actual expenditure of human energy.

Labour is always of a specific type. To begin with, it is *concrete* (in the sense of specific) labour. It is its action on the means of production which creates the specific aspects of a commodity, its use value. The labour of a carpenter is different from that of a cobbler and this is why they produce different use values, and thus different commodities. Here, the means of production are considered as having specific qualities, as specific necessary additions to labour, in short as use values. This is symbolized as MP(u). The combination of the means of production as use values and concrete labour is the labour process (LPr), the qualitative aspect of the production process. The labour process creates the new, *different*, use value, or the commodity as new use value (Cu*).

But commodities must be exchanged on the market, that is, they must be equalized in order to be comparable. For this to happen, their specific features must be disregarded and only their quantitative aspect must be taken into consideration. That which makes exchange possible cannot therefore be the action of concrete labour, since concrete labour is what differentiates commodities. What makes exchange possible is the action of labour in general, of the expenditure of human energy in the abstract; in short of abstract labour. *Abstract* labour is thus the expenditure of human energy disregarding its specific characteristics. Seen from this angle, (abstract) labour is applied to the means of production seen not as specific instruments and objects of labour, but as exchange values, as depositories of exchange value, or MP(e). The combination of abstract labour and of the means of production thus considered is the surplus value producing process (sPP) which is the production process seen in its quantitative aspect. This process creates the new, *greater*, exchange value of a commodity (Ce').

Which of the two aspects of production is more important? For the capitalist, the use value of commodities is important only inasmuch as they have an exchange value, that is, if they can be sold so that their surplus value can be realized. Or, the use value of a commodity is determined by, is a condition of existence of, that commodity's exchange value. As in chapter 1, this relation is symbolized by =>. Thus, a *commodity* can be defined as

$$C = Ce' \Rightarrow Cu*$$

and, for the same reason, the capitalist production process (CPP) can be succinctly depicted as

$$CPP = sPP => LPr$$

where sPP is the surplus value producing process and LPr is the labour process.

2.1.2 The origin of surplus value

Let us now consider the question as to how surplus value is created. In the process of production, labour acts upon the means of production. As abstract labour it creates exchange value. Thus each moment of abstract labour is at the same time creation of new value. As concrete labour it transforms the use value of the means of production. The concrete aspects of the means of production disappear only to re-emerge as a new use value, that of the product. At the same time, through concrete labour, the means of production are consumed, that is, their exchange value diminishes as the process is carried out. This exchange value, however, does not vanish. It re-emerges as the exchange value of the product. Thus, each moment of concrete labour is at the same time both a transformation of use values and a transfer of exchange value (the exchange value of the means of production) to the product. Or, as far as the formation of the exchange value of the product is concerned, each moment of labour is both the transfer of value of the means of production through concrete labour and the creation of new value through abstract labour.

But capitalists invest in labour power and means of production in order to get a greater exchange value when the product is sold. If the process of production stopped at the point where the new value created is equal to the exchange value of labour power, there would be no surplus value and thus no profit. Given that the value of the means of production has been transferred to the product, the product would have the same value as the value originally advanced. As seen above, sale of the product at a higher value would not explain the creation of surplus value, it would only explain the redistribution of already existing value. The question then is: How can we explain the creation of surplus value if we assume that products are exchanged at their value?

The answer requires that we elucidate two concepts we have not dealt with yet. The first is the *exchange value of labour power*. This is given, similarly to all other commodities, by the labour socially necessary to produce it. In this particular case, this is the labour socially necessary to produce what the average labourers and their families need to reproduce themselves. This is the socially, not biologically, determined subsistence minimum.[2]

But labour power has also a use value. If the capitalist must make

11

a profit, s/he must force the labourers to labour for a time longer than the time necessary for the reproduction of their labour power; or, the capitalist must force the labourers to work beyond the point at which they have created a value equal to that of their labour power. Every moment of labour after that point creates new value which can be appropriated by the capitalist.

Thus, the *use value of labour power* is its ability to create more exchange value than its own exchange value. This difference is called *surplus value* (which, for the purposes of this chapter, can be equated with profit) and is the exchange value appropriated by the capitalists. *Exploitation* is the production by the labourers of value which is appropriated by the capitalists. Under capitalism the labourers cannot produce "useful" things and thus the means for their own subsistence without being, at the same time, exploited by the capitalists.

It should be stressed that exploitation has nothing to do with paying the labourers less than the value of their labour power. The assumption, on the contrary, is that the full exchange value of labour power is paid. Rather, exploitation derives from the fact that labour power can produce more exchange value than its own exchange value. However, exploitation is hidden by the fact that the wages and salaries the labourers receive for their labour power are sufficient to sustain them for the entire working day. This creates the illusion that wages and salaries are the payment for the labour provided during the entire working day.

There is another important, and related, aspect which must be mentioned. The exchange value produced by the labourers is not the same for all labourers. Other things being equal, skilled labourers produce more value than unskilled labourers. As Marx puts it, skilled labour power "being of higher value, its consumption is labour of a higher class, labour that creates in equal times proportionally higher values than unskilled labour does" (Marx, 1967a, p. 197). To see this, consider again the production process. The expenditure of labour power, when considered as concrete labour, transforms the use value of the means of production and thus transfers their exchange value to that of the product. Only what already exists can be transferred, nothing more and nothing less. This exchange value is thus constant, it does not vary in the course of the production process.

Things are different when the expenditure of labour power is considered as abstract labour. It then creates new value, and thus it can create more value than its own value. Thus the exchange value of labour power is not transferred to the product (if this were the case only the value of labour power could be transferred, as is the case for the means of production) but is produced anew together with more value (surplus value) than its own value.

The value of the skilled labourers' labour power is greater than that of the unskilled labourers, due for example to higher costs for education and training. Therefore, the unskilled labourer produces anew a lower value (that of his or her labour power plus surplus value) than that produced anew by the skilled labourer. Or, labour power creates value in proportion to the value (and thus to the level of skills) it has. For example, if the labourers must produce as much surplus value as the value of their labour power, an unskilled labourer whose labour power is equal to, say, 5 hours of social labour produces a new value equal to $5 + 5 = 10$ in the same period of time; in the same period of time a skilled labourer whose labour power is equal to 10 hours of social labour produces a new value equal to $10 + 10 = 20$.[3]

Since labour power is the only value-producing commodity, the capital invested in it emerges at the end of the production process enlarged. The relationship between the value entering, and the capital leaving, the production process is variable. Thus the capital invested in the purchase of labour power is called *variable capital*. The capital used to purchase the means of production, on the other hand, does not change in size. Its value is only transferred to the product. Therefore, this capital is called *constant capital*. It follows that the value of a commodity can be decomposed into the sum of constant capital, plus variable capital plus surplus value. Or

$$V = c + v + s$$

where c is constant capital, v is variable capital, s is surplus value and V is the value of the commodity.[4]

The relation between surplus value and variable capital is called the *rate of surplus value*. This rate can be increased in two ways. We say that *absolute* surplus value has increased when, given the value of labour power, the length of the working day and/or the speed and intensity of labour is increased. We say that *relative* surplus value has increased when, given the speed and intensity of labour and the length of the working day, the value of labour power is decreased, basically through a productivity increase in the branches producing the means of subsistence (wage goods).[5]

2.1.3 Social and technical division of labour

Two points should be made before closing this section. First, in a capitalist society a number of different production processes co-exist. However, in this work only the determinant one, the capitalist production process, will be considered. Second, this process is not an undifferentiated unity but is internally structured through the capitalist division of labour. The *social division of labour* indicates that the societal labour process is subdivided into a number of different branches of production (or different labour processes) producing different commodities. But the objects of labour might go through a series of transformations (the different parts of the labour process) before the new commodity emerges. How do we know that these intermediate transformations do not produce new commodities? Since under capitalism a commodity is such only inasmuch as it can be exchanged on the market (sold), a series of transformations ends with a new commodity when the outcome of the transformation is ready to be exchanged (sold).

It has been said that the objects of labour undergo a series of transformations before emerging as the new commodity. An important difference between the capitalist production process and previous production processes is that, while the medieval artisan made the whole product and thus engaged in all the transformations, the modern labourer makes only a part of it, and very often a very small part. The labour process is thus subdivided into a number of positions (jobs), that is, it has been subjected to the *technical division of labour*. Consequently, the product is the outcome of the combined effort of a great number of labourers, subdivided into different categories (jobs), each performing a different task.

2.2 Braverman and the Labour Process Debate

After Marx's death, a certain orthodox interpretation of the production process gained widespread circulation in Marxism. In this view, production is based on a type of technology which is class neutral: technology's development is due to its inner laws of development and therefore does not carry the class content of the society which has produced it. At most, so this interpretation goes, a certain type of science and technology can be misused for the benefit of a few rather than used for the benefit of all. In this view, therefore, it would be sufficient to abolish the surplus value producing process (and thus exploitation and the capitalists as a class) while retaining the present labour process (which is based on the present technologies and technical division of labour) in order to use science, technology and more generally the productive forces for the benefit of all. Lenin's view of Taylorism, and of its applicability to a socialist society, rests on this technological conception.

This dominant view ignores what Marx has called the *collective labourer*, that great number of individuals collectively producing the whole of the product but individually producing only a small part of it. This view ignores the fact that capitalist production relations shape not only the surplus value producing process but also the labour process itself. Under capitalism, the fragmentation of positions within the labour process is such that it becomes impossible for the individual labourers to develop themselves, to develop all aspects (instead of only some aspects) of their personality through their productive activity. This view, then, cannot see that a socialist society must not only abolish the surplus value producing process (exploitation): it must also radically change the labour process in its capitalist shape and the technical division of labour inherent in it.

The orthodox interpretation greatly reduces the potential for social critique offered by Marx's analysis of the labour process under capitalism. This potential was rediscovered, and the orthodox interpretation challenged, towards the end of the 1960s in the wake of anti-authoritarian social movements critical not only of capitalism but also of "realized socialism". It is within this context that the social and political matrix of the "labour process debate" – the debate that followed the publication of H. Braverman's *Labor and Monopoly Capital* (1974) – can be understood.[6]

Braverman sticks closely to Marx's original analysis of the widespread erosion of skills (deskilling) under the impact of the introduction of modern techniques. But he goes further. He updates it by applying it not only to the factory floor but also to the office (to the so-called white-collar workers). Also, he adds a new dimension to that analysis by focusing on managerial strategies of control. He argues that Taylorism is not only a particularly important managerial method but actually "the" method under monopoly capitalism for the organization of the labour process, with its attendant deskilling and control of labour. In Braverman's view, Taylorism is essentially both the separation of conception and execution, that is, of manual and mental labour, and the monopoly of the knowledge of the labour process by management. Moreover, he relates changes in the labour process to changes in the composition of monopoly capitalism's class structure, placing particular emphasis on the process of proletarianization.

Braverman emphasizes some of the most vital aspects of Marxism. However, there are four strands of criticism which can be directed at his approach. The first is perhaps the most damaging one. This is that Braverman fails not only to account for, but also to incorporate into his analysis, the role of workers' resistance in shaping the labour process (Elger, 1979). Closely related to this is the point that Braverman focuses on an idealized view of labour (Cutler, 1978). But, it is argued, the loss of craft does not necessarily imply the loss of the ability of the workers to resist the rule of capital. Recent history shows that semi-skilled and unskilled workers can be the spearhead of workers' resistance. Also, deskilling

15

should be seen as a tendency and not as an absolute law. The same forces which deskill existing jobs create, at the same time, new skilled jobs (Carchedi, 1975).

The second strand of critique focuses on forms of management and control. While Braverman's attempt to relate scientific management to the monopolistic phase of capitalism is widely appreciated, the point has been raised that Taylorism is only one of the forms of control management devises to subdue labour (Edwards, 1979). For example, Friedman (1977) argues that the main form of workers' domination is not direct control but "responsible autonomy" or the identification of the workers with the aims of the firm and the consequent reduction of direct supervision to a minimum. Other examples are work "humanization" schemes and quality control schemes. However, it can be objected that direct control does remain a very powerful way to subordinate labour. In any case, it is sterile to argue for the absolute priority of one way of control over another. Capital devises forms of control which it uses according to the context of the situation both inside and outside the workplace. Moreover, managerial methods emphasizing motivation are not incompatible with methods of direct control and both methods can be used at the same time.

A third strand of criticism focuses on Braverman's (and, it is argued, Marx's) disregard of the "organization of consent". Burawoy (1979) is the main protagonist of this view. Burawoy argues that it is the labour process itself, rather than factors outside it (like, e.g. ideology), which creates consent by constituting the workers as individuals rather than as members of a class. In short, the labour process manufactures both commodities and consent. This critique is problematic. Workers do develop forms of resistance against capital, like co-operation and solidarity also on the shopfloor, in different forms, in different degrees and at different times (Lippert, 1978; Fennel, 1976). Where then do these forms of resistance come from if they do not come from the point of production? More fruitful seems to be an analysis which inquires into the structural factors which constrain the rise of antagonistic forms of consciousness, as for example the performance of the function of capital by strata of the working class (Carchedi, 1975; Carter, 1985). Further, it is unlikely, to say the least, that external factors (e.g. the educational system, the mass media, etc.) have only a very limited role in shaping class consciousness.

The last strand of criticism is the feminist one. This critique, especially in its "radical" version, is directed not only against Braverman but also, and first of all, against Marx and the Marxist conceptual apparatus. The point is made that Braverman (and Marx) unduly emphasized wage labour and the homogenization of labour due to the process of deskilling and proletarianization and that consequently he failed to recognize the emergence of separate labour markets, job allocations, systems of rewards, etc. for men and women. Braverman, it is argued, goes further than Marx in emphasizing the sexual division of labour but still remains within the theoretical limits of that conceptual apparatus. For example, Braverman sees the extended participation of women as a further extension of the process of homogenization of labour. Also, he does not discuss the role of the family in the production of labour power nor does he extend the labour process perspective to the analysis of domestic activities. He thus fails to theorize the exploitation of women by men both within the family and within capitalist production relations. The counter-argument is that, while the feminist critique has forced Marxism to abandon its restricted focus, there is reason to believe that Marxist categories can be used to analyse patriarchal relations and their intertwining with capitalist production relations.

While some elements of the critique directed at Braverman are valid, Braverman's critics share a fundamental weakness of their own. Contrary to Braverman himself, they do not theorize the labour process as one aspect of the capitalist production process, as the other side of the production of and for profit. Almost without exception, the surplus value (or valorization) process is disregarded. Yet this is the *determinant* aspect of the capitalist production process.[7] To disregard it is to make an error opposite to, but equally as misleading as, the one made by orthodox Marxism, which exclusively focused on the valorization process. Emphasis is placed on control and, sometimes, on workers' resistance. However, since the labour process is not seen as an aspect of the capitalist production process, the other aspect being the process of creation of value, control is not tied to surplus value creation. Thus, in spite of superficial similarities, the notion of control in the labour process debate differs substantially from Marx's notion of function of capital, or work of control (see 2.5.2 below).

In spite of their differences, both Braverman and his critics share two major and strictly related lacunae. The first is the lack of development and application of a dialectical method to understand both labour and the production process. This is the cause of the second lacuna, the lack of inquiry into what mental labour is both in general and in capitalist societies. Consequently, we are left without a theory of mental labour and of the conditions under which it is productive of surplus value. This is a very serious drawback in a type of society which increasingly relies on mental labour. The remainder of this chapter will attempt partly to fill these lacunae.

2.3 Elements of a Theory of Material and Mental Labour[8]

One of the most important differences between the capitalism of Marx's time and modern capitalism is the increasing importance and commercialization of knowledge. Knowledge, incorporated in innovations, has always been a most important element of capitalist competition. The difference is that vast numbers of agents are now engaged in the production of science and techniques and that this production is increasingly commercialized, that is, either carried out by business as "in-house" research,[9] as a business in itself,[10] or directly or indirectly influenced by business. For example, universities increasingly adopt a more commercial approach to their research by seeking research contracts with industry, by patenting inventions, by licensing technologies, by forming joint ventures with the business world and by offering training courses for industry. These are also, at the same time, so many ways in which the production of knowledge is influenced and steered by business. Governments too shift funds to research of more strategic value to business.

This raises the problem of intellectual property. As an article in the *Financial Times* reports, "US business claims to have lost $24bn in 1986 from piracy of patents, illegal copying of microchip design and software and counterfeiting" (Dullforce, 1988). Intellectual property is actually the capitalist's property, the outcome of other people's intellectual labour. It is through this appropriation that the capitalists enrich themselves. There are then two difficult questions which need to be addressed. First, what is mental labour? And, second, under what conditions is mental labour productive of value? The former question is tackled in this section, the latter in the next section. For reasons of exposition, this section has been subdivided into four subsections.

2.3.1 Material and mental transformations as conceptual building blocks of labour

No matter how one chooses to define it, human labour is always conscious activity. More precisely, the transformation of material objects, or *material transformation*, both requires some previous knowledge of that transformation (no matter how vague, tentative, hypothetical or incomplete that pre-figurative knowledge might be) and causes new knowledge of that material transformation to emerge. Alternatively, the transformation of existing knowledge, or *mental transformation*, both requires some material objects (even though they might only be pencil and paper) and causes their transformation (consumption). In short, material transformations necessarily require mental transformations, production of knowledge, and mental transformations necessarily require material transformations; or, labour is always a combination of material and mental transformations.

Even if, in reality, material and mental transformations do not exist separately, it is possible to *examine* them independently of each other. In fact, the *objects* of transformation differ: they are material objects in the case of material transformations and knowledge in the case of mental transformations. Or, to use Marx's terminology (Marx, 1973), the object of the former process of transformation is the real concrete (material reality, as it exists independently from our perception of it[11]), while the object of the latter process is knowledge. We are therefore justified in analysing these two types of transformations separately. We are also justified in making material and mental transformations the *conceptual* building blocks of the notion of labour. Let us then examine these two types of transformations.

Material transformations are the transformation of material objects into different material objects. Since the use of the new material objects is different from the use of the old objects (and this is the purpose of the transformation), we can say that a material transformation is the transformation of a material use value into a different material use value. In symbols

$$MAT = MAU \rightarrow MAU*$$

where MAT stands for material transformation, MAU means material use value, MAU* indicates a new material use value and $\rightarrow$ symbolizes the transformative process which changes MAU into MAU*. The transformed material use value is the outcome of the incorporation of the labourer's concrete, or specific, labour (and, through this, of the use value of the instruments of transformation) into the use value of the objects of labour.

It should be mentioned that there is also a material transformation, a change in the material use value, when existing material use values are prevented from deteriorating. Thus storage and maintenance too are a transformation of material use values because without them the use value of a material object would either diminish or disappear. Even though the material qualities of a use value remain the same, in reality there has been a change, the incorporation in the material use value preserved of the concrete labour and instruments of storage and maintenance. Without them MAU would not be MAU any more; with them it becomes MAU*.

Let us now consider mental transformation, which is the production, or rather the transformation, of knowledge. *Knowledge* is any perception of material and social reality. Thus it encompasses science, superstition, art, etc. Conceptually (and thus neither chronologically nor psychologically), the transformation of knowledge can be separated into two steps. The first is observation, which – to begin with – is sensory perception, perception of the real concrete through our senses. But observation is not independent of social conditioning, it is socially filtered. The "filter" is given by the mental producers' previous knowledge and social practice. Thus, *observation* is the socially filtered sensory perception of the real concrete. The result of observation is the *imagined concrete*, a "chaotic conception of reality" (Marx, 1973, p. 100).

The second step is *conception*. Once observation has given the real concrete a mental shape, this imagined concrete is transformed by the conscious application of the previous knowledge of reality. The outcome is the *concrete-in-thought*, which, compared to the imagined concrete, is a more structured view of reality. As we shall see in a moment, the concrete-in-thought, or transformed knowledge, can be either new knowledge or the re-confirmation of the validity of the already existing knowledge, it can be either production of new knowledge or reproduction of existing knowledge.

Even though analytically we can separate observation from conception, in practice this is not possible. A mental transformation is always both observation and conception, that is, it is the transformation, with the aid of material instruments, of the socially filtered sensory perception of the real concrete and of the already existing knowledge of the real concrete. As a short-cut, if we focus only on the change undergone by knowledge, the process of mental transformation can be depicted as

$$MET = K \rightarrow K*$$

where MET means mental transformation, K existing knowledge and K* transformed (both new and re-confirmed) knowledge.

We have seen that knowledge is any perception of material reality. The *use value of knowledge* is thus its ability to relate to material reality.[12] Then *old knowledge* is any knowledge which allows us to relate to material reality in the same way, while *new knowledge* is any knowledge which allows us to relate to material reality in a different way. New knowledge, then, also includes the refutation of old knowledge, since "to refute is not simply to deny but to find relevant grounds for such rejection" (Arthur, 1986, p. 51). Similarly, the re-confirmation of the validity of old knowledge is transformation of knowledge (K*) because it is the old knowledge plus the re-confirmation of its validity. The reproduction of old knowledge can be compared to the storage and maintenance of material use values, which as we have seen is also a transformation of MAU into MAU*.

There are at least two important differences between material and mental transformations. The first is that existing knowledge (K) is both an object and an instrument of transformation. In material transformations, on the other hand, there is always a strict separation between objects and instruments of transformation (something which does not preclude the transformed objects of a certain transformation from becoming instruments of the *following* material transformation). The second is that in material transformations there is always a logical as well as a chronological separation between production and consumption. In mental transformations, on the other hand, the separation is only analytical. A person engaged in conception both transforms knowledge (production) and incorporates it in his or her labour power (consumption). The non-materiality of the product imposes a chronological contemporaneity of production and consumption.

But we are not interested in the transformation of knowledge for its own sake, we are interested in it inasmuch as we can conceptualize what a mental use value is. In other words, what is a mental use value and how does it differ from knowledge? A *mental use value* is a *specific* type of knowledge, that type of knowledge which is functional for the transformation, immediately or mediately, of material reality.[13] Thus, the transformation of knowledge needed for the destruction of material use values or for dealing with them without transforming them (e.g. purchase and sale) is not a mental use value.[14] In symbols, the mental transformation which produces a mental use value can be represented as

$$MET = K \rightarrow MEU*$$

where K can be any type of knowledge (including a previous mental use value, or MEU) and MEU* is either new knowledge or re-confirmed knowledge functional for the transformation of material use values.[15]

The use value of knowledge is not the same as a mental use value. As we have seen, the use value of knowledge is its ability to relate to material reality. A mental use value, on the other hand, is that specific type of knowledge which allows us to relate to material reality in a specific sense, by allowing us to transform material use values into new ones. Similarly to what has been said above, there is production, transformation, of a mental use value when either new knowledge is produced or old knowledge is reproduced which, immediately or mediately, allows us to transform material use values. In both cases, knowledge allows us to change material reality either in the same way or in a new, different way.

21

2.3.2 What are material and mental labour processes?

As stressed above, material and mental transformations can only exist conjointly, as elements of a labour process; or, material and mental transformations *must* combine in a labour process.

The labour process in its general form, that is, in the form common to all types of society, is the transformation of use values (both material and mental) into new use values (also both material and mental) through the application of concrete labour. The labour process has been represented as follows:

$$LPr = U \rightarrow U^*$$

where LPr is the labour process, U now explicitly indicates both the material use values and knowledge to be transformed and U* indicates both the transformed material use values and knowledge.

If material and mental transformations always exist conjointly, the question becomes that of specifying the nature of the relation binding them. This relation is one of dialectical determination, as expounded in chapter 1. In fact, this relation conceptualizes these transformations' mutual existential interdependence in the sense that either material transformations are determined by (are conditions of existence or supersession of) mental transformations or vice versa. Second, this relation accounts for material and mental labour as specific forms of combination of material and mental transformations. In fact, by assigning the determinant role to either one or the other type of transformation, we can theorize material and mental labour processes as specific forms of combinations of material and mental transformations.

Thus, a *material labour process* is a process in which material transformations are determinant. There are mental transformations but they are determined by the transformation of material use values. In short,

$$MAT => MET$$

where MAT and MET stand for material and mental transformations respectively and => indicates determination.

A *mental labour process*, on the other hand, is a process in which it is the mental transformations which are determinant. There is transformation of material use values but this is determined by the production of knowledge in the sense that it is (a) the consumption of the material aids to the production of knowledge and (b) for some labour processes, their transformation into the material depositories of knowledge (as, for example, the physical qualities of a book).[16] In short,

$$MET => MAT$$

2.3.3 How can we recognize material and mental labour processes?

If the labour process always has a double nature (it is always a dialectical relation between material and mental transformations) we need a criterion on the basis of which to judge when the labour process is material or mental, that is, when it is the material or the mental transformations which are determinant.

If either one or the other of these two types of transformation is determinant, the product will also have a double nature in which either the material aspect or the mental one will be determinant. Therefore, we can trace back the nature of the labour process by considering the product. Usually the determinant aspect of a product is empirically given. Thus in the production of a car it is the material aspect which is empirically given (and on this basis we know that the production process is a material one) and in the production of a concert it is the mental aspect which is empirically apparent (something which allows us to know that in this production process it is the mental aspect which is determinant).

However, this rule is not always accurate. The rule which allows us to allocate the determinant role to either the material or the mental transformations within a labour process is given by whether *the determinant aim of the individual labour process, as socially validated at the moment of exchange,* is a material use value or knowledge. In short, the nature of the labour process is revealed by whether the product is exchanged primarily because of its material qualities or because of its knowledge content. For example, a book would appear to be the product of a material labour process. However, the book is produced and exchanged primarily because of its knowledge content and the material transformations (the book must be clearly printed, graphically attractive, with as few printing mistakes as possible, etc.) are important but subordinate to the knowledge content carried by the book. The same applies to the labour process producing a game or a toy or a shop's signboard. These are all examples of mental labour processes, that is, of mental products for which a material shell is needed.

The principle submitted above stresses both the individual aim and social validation. The former element stresses the subjective, and the latter element stresses the objective, aspects of production. The former, the individual aspect, implies that the same person making the same thing can engage either in a material or in a mental labour process. If I make shoes as a form of art I engage in a mental labour process; that is, the fact that those shoes can be used as shoes is secondary. What is of primary importance, the aim of my activity, is the transformation of knowledge. The social use of those shoes resides in their knowledge content and it is because of this knowledge content that they will be exchanged. If, on the other hand, I make the same shoes because I want to create a material object which can be worn by human feet, no matter how beautiful that object might be, then I engage in a material labour process. The shoes are exchanged as material use values, as shoes. The conception needed to make them, no matter how beautiful they may be, is determined by the material transformations.

This should not be read to imply that the intention, the aim of the producer, is the only determinant of the nature of the labour process. If this were so, a serious element of indeterminacy would be introduced since it would be difficult to know what the aim of the producer has been simply by looking at the nature of the product. Moreover, the individual aim of the producer could clash with the use aimed at by the consumer at the moment of exchange. However, the material or mental nature of a labour process is also determined by social validation.

In a system in which products are made in order to be exchanged, individual production must be validated as social production, as socially useful production: the product of the individual producer (be it a person or an enterprise) must pass the final examination by society. Or, in a system in which products are exchanged (bought and sold), the realization of a use value takes place *after* the moment of exchange; however, *the moment of exchange is the moment at which the use value is validated not only as such but also as either material or mental*. That is, this is the moment at which the buyers show whether they are interested in that use value either primarily because of its material qualities or because of its knowledge content.

Thus, *individual production* creates the material and mental qualities as well as the *individual nature* of a use value but exchange must validate the *social nature* of that use value. Or, individual production takes on a social character, becomes social production, only at the moment of its social validation, that is, when the product is exchanged on the market. It is at that moment that the *potential social* production (i.e. individual production) becomes *realized social* production. From a practical point of view, therefore, we need only know the social validation of the product in order to know the social nature of the labour process.

Notice that it is social, not anomalous, validation that counts. Consider the case of shoes being bought by a competing producer in order to copy some technical or aesthetic features. Here the determinant aim of production is a material use value while the primary aim of the consumer at the moment of exchange is its knowledge content. Is this then a material or a mental labour process? The answer is that it is a material labour process. In fact, *it is the general, social validation of the use value* as revealed at the moment of exchange which should be looked at. Thus it does not matter whether somebody buys those shoes as shoes or as an object of study. The fact is that they have been produced as shoes, because of their physical qualities, and that their normal, social use is perceived to be as shoes. This anomalous validation does not change the labour process from a material into a mental one. Similarly, I can buy a book as combustion material and not because of the knowledge it carries. However, this anomalous validation does not change the process which has produced that book into a material one.

Thus social production is the social form taken by individual production. This implies that the latter might realize itself at the social level, as socially validated production, in a modified form.[17] If the aim of the labour process, or the determinant transformation, has been a material (respectively mental) transformation and if exchange validates the nature of the labour process (and thus of the product) as material (respectively mental), the individual nature of production realizes itself as its social nature. The individual and social aspects coincide. Conversely, if the determinant transformation (aim of) the labour process has been a material (respectively mental) transformation but exchange validates that product for its knowledge content (respectively material qualities), individual production realizes itself at the social level in a modified form. In this case, the material (respectively mental) nature of individual production has been changed, at the moment of exchange, into its opposite. In this case too all we need to know for practical purposes is the social realization of that use value.[18]

2.3.4 What is material and mental labour?

The answer to this question follows logically from the analysis submitted above. Labour is material or mental according to whether the determinant transformations are material or mental, that is, according to whether the social validation of the principal aim of that labour is a transformation of material use values or of knowledge. We should distinguish between the case in which the transforming agent performs the whole of the labour process and the case in which s/he performs only a part of it.

In the former case, the transforming agent carries out material or mental labour according to the nature of the labour process in which s/he is engaged. Shoes are made and sold primarily because of their material qualities, that is, the aim of the process of transformation is a material use value. Therefore, a cobbler carries out material labour. This, to repeat, does not mean that s/he does not engage in mental transformations. Rather, those mental transformations are determined by the material ones and not vice versa, the knowledge produced in that labour process (which, as pointed out above, can be either different from, or a reconfirmation of, the initial knowledge) is a consequence of the need to produce a material use value. On the other hand, a shoemaker who makes models of shoes used in the Middle Ages and sells them to a museum for a historical exhibition, engages in a mental labour process and thus in mental labour. Here the material transformations are determined by the mental ones.

As we have seen, however, under capitalism the typical production process is not carried out by one individual but is fragmented in a number of, sometimes very large, positions. In this case, both the material transformations and the mental ones are carried out collectively, by what Marx calls the collective labourer. In a shoe factory, for example, there are workers who physically transform leather, glue, etc. into shoes. Each one of these workers carries out only a fraction of the whole process. They perform material labour within a material labour process. On the other hand, that labour process also needs, say, shoe designers who engage in the conception of shoes. They carry out mental labour within a material labour process.

The former category of agents is engaged in material labour because they carry out collectively the material transformations needed by that labour process. The latter category of agents carry out mental labour for similar reasons. Again, each one of those agents is engaged in both material and mental transformations. But material labourers are such because, in their positions (jobs), it is the material transformations which are determinant, and this – in its turn – is so because those positions are a part of the collective material transformation needed by that labour process. Mental labourers are such because in their positions the mental transformations are determinant and this – in its turn – is so because their positions are part of the collective conception needed by that labour process. In short, a certain position can be seen as requiring either material or mental labour only after it has been placed within the context of that labour process's technical division of labour.

Thus to work at the assembly line means to perform material labour not because those agents do not think (of course they do), nor because they wear a blue overall, nor because they "work with their hands", but because they are part of the collective transformation of material use values within that labour process. The researchers employed by a research and development enterprise perform mental labour not because they do not use their hands (of course they do) nor because they wear a white overall, nor because their labour is expenditure of "nervous" (as opposed to "physical") energy, but because they are part of the collective conception, transformation of knowledge, within that labour process.

It is also possible for the same labour to be either material or mental. Consider a newspaper. In this mental labour process there are mental labourers (e.g. the journalists) and material labourers (e.g. those operating the printing machines). These are clear examples of mental and material labour. What about a typist whose task is simply to type the journalists' articles? Taken in itself, this position is material labour. In fact, the aim of this labour is to give somebody else's conception a material shell. Of course, the typist too engages in conception. But the typist's conception is secondary (determined) since it is needed only inasmuch as s/he can give a material shell to another person's conception. In this job, what counts is not what the typist thinks but what s/he transforms physically (white paper into typed paper). The typist's conception is obviously needed but it is needed only because s/he must engage in a material transformation. However, from the point of view of the labour process, that position is part of the collective transformation of knowledge. Or, when placed within the context of that labour process's technical division of labour, that typist performs mental labour, albeit a very dequalified one. Suppose now that a supervisor asks the same person to type the technical instructions which s/he used to impart orally to those operating the printing machines. Now the typist performs material labour because his/her labour has become part of the collective transformation of material use values.

Thus, within the societal labour process, it is the social division of labour which structures the individual labour processes into material and mental processes; and, within each of these individual labour processes, it is the technical division of labour which structures the individual transformations into material and mental labour.

Throughout I have used the term "material" and not "manual" labour. It is impossible, both analytically and empirically, to draw a distinction between expenditure of physical energy (manual labour) and expenditure of mental energy, or between blue-collar and white-collar work, or between other similarly dubious categories. But it is possible and advisable to operate a distinction between material and mental *transformations* by looking at the objects of transformation; between material and mental *labour processes* by looking at the determinant type of transformation within each labour process after the labour process has been placed within the social division of labour and after social validation has been taken into account; between material and mental *labour* when the agent performs *the whole labour process* by considering the determinant aspect of the labour process; and between material and mental labour when the agent performs only *a fraction of the labour process* by looking at the determinant transformation within that position after that position has been placed within that labour process's technical division of labour.

2.4 The Dialectics of the Production of Value

We now come to the question as to when labour is productive in a capitalist sense, that is, when it is production of (surplus) value.[19] This is a question of great importance for a theory of economic growth and crises. Two conditions must be satisfied. First, labour must be carried out under capitalist production relations. Second, labour must perform real transformations (Marx, 1967a, p. 188). These latter are processes in which old material use values and knowledge are changed into new material and mental use values. In what follows, a distinction is made between labour processes and labourers.

2.4.1 Productive and unproductive labour processes

In the case of material labour processes there must be a transformation of the use value of the material objects of labour into a different use value, that of the product; or, there must be a *real material labour process*. At the same time, this labour process must be carried out within capitalist production relations, by labourers working for capitalists. If these two conditions are satisfied, this labour process is productive of value. The mental transformations needed for this process are determined by the material ones.

It should be recalled that the transformation of material use values does not necessarily imply a change in their physical characteristics. Any labour process which affects a use value by either preventing its deterioration (e.g. storage) or bringing it to a place where it can be a use value (transportation) should be regarded as being a real material transformation and thus the material basis for the production of value. But any labour process which does not affect the use value of a material object, such as purchase and sale, banking, insurance, etc. should be regarded as a formal transformation and thus unproductive. This is a *formal material labour process* which can produce neither value nor surplus value.

As for mental labour processes, the first condition is that there must be a production of a mental use value, that is, of knowledge which allows us to transform old material use values into new ones. But, due to the social division of labour, mental labour processes are only rarely immediately tied to material transformations. How do we know then whether the knowledge produced is determined by real material transformations, that it allows us to transform material use values into new material use values? Of course, if knowledge is immediately determined by either formal material transformations or the destruction of use values, there is no production of mental use values and there can be no production of (surplus) value. Moreover, if knowledge is immediately determined by the work of control (which, as we shall see, is non-labour), it cannot produce a use value since only labour can do that. In these cases, there is production of knowledge but not of mental use values. But, mostly, there is no imme- diate determination of knowledge. How do we know then whether this knowledge is a mental use value?

The problem is solved by looking at it from a different angle. Let us consider again labour power. We have seen above that its use value is its ability to create more exchange value than its own exchange value. This is the *capitalist* nature of the use value of labour power. But, in general, labour power's use value is its ability to change all other use values into new use values. It is because of this that labour power cannot have a definite form. Since, under capitalism, the production of use values is only a means for the production of exchange value, the use value of labour power becomes, as we said above, the ability to create surplus value through the transformation of use values.

Consider now the production of knowledge. This has a special feature. Whenever mental labourers produce new knowledge they at *the same time* consume it, that is, incorporate it into their labour power. They become more knowledgeable, more skilled labourers. Their labour power has been changed because these labourers can now change material reality in novel ways (even though successive processes of production of know- ledge might still be necessary to reach the stage where material use values will be finally transformed). At the same time, their labour power has increased in value and thus can create more (exchange) value than pre- viously. The *use value of labour power has been changed* both in its general and in its capitalist nature. It is in this sense that the production of new knowledge not immediately functional for the transformation of material use values is none the less determined by material transformations in a mediated way, in the sense that the production of new knowledge changes the ability to engage in future material transformations.

The same holds for the reproduction of old knowledge which also is production of a mental use value. Even though the capacity to transform use values remains the same, there has been a change in the use value of labour power because its use value (and thus its exchange value) has been preserved. Similarly to the work of storage and maintenance of material use values (which changes a material use value by preserving it, that is, by preventing its deterioration), the reproduction of old know- ledge changes the use value of labour power by preserving it, by preventing its deterioration. It is through the preservation of the ability to transform material use values (in the same way) that the reproduction of old know- ledge allows us to change material reality. It preserves our ability to change material use values, that is, it allows us to transform them again in the same way. The production of a mental use value is thus a *real mental labour process*.

Therefore, there is production of value (a mental labour process is productive in a capitalist sense) when knowledge is produced under capitalist production relations *unless* that knowledge is *directly* determined by (is a condition of existence of) either (a) formal transformations, and in this case we have a *formal mental labour process* as in the case of advertising, (b) the work of control (and in this case those mental transformations, by being directly determined by non-labour, cannot be regarded as constituting a mental *labour* process), or (c) destruction of use values.

2.4.2 Productive and unproductive labourers

Up to now, I have dealt with the conditions for material and mental labour processes to be capitalistically productive. Let us now consider the internal structure of both productive and unproductive labour processes (independently of whether they are material or mental) in terms of what kind of labourers participate in each of them.

Consider first a productive labour process. Here we have productive labourers, those who engage in real (material and mental) transformations, as well as unproductive labourers, those engaged in formal transformations, such as selling the products and purchasing materials. Strictly speaking, these latter labourers are not exploited. Yet they too work longer than the time necessary to produce their labour power. We can thus say that they are subjected to *economic oppression*. Moreover, given that profits must be made, there are also non-labourers, those whose task is the control of the labourers and who expropriate surplus value from the productive workers and surplus labour from the unproductive ones. Thus not all agents in a capitalist productive process are productive. The value and surplus value produced in that process are the result of the action of only one category of agents, those who, through their concrete labour, change the material and mental characteristics of the objects and instruments of labour into a different use value, that of the product. It is through their concrete labour that the value of the means of production is transferred to that of the product and it is through their abstract labour that first the value of their labour power and then surplus value are created.

What is the role of the unproductive labourers? They do not transform use values. Therefore, neither does their concrete labour transfer the value of the means of production used by them to that of the product, nor does their abstract labour create new value. Thus, the value of the means of production they use as well as the value of their labour power simply vanish. The reconstitution of these two elements of value must then come from the surplus value produced by the productive labourers. The same applies for the non-labourers.

Consider next an unproductive labour process, for example a supermarket or an advertising agency. Here too there are both unproductive labourers (e.g. salespersons) and productive labourers (e.g. those engaged in the maintenance of the buildings or in the transportation of the sold goods). Moreover, here too there are non-labourers, those who perform the work of control either because they are capitalists or because they do it on behalf of the capitalists. This means that the value of the buildings, equipment, etc. used by the unproductive labourers, as well as the value of the labour power, vanishes and must be reconstituted through the appropriation of surplus value produced in the capitalist productive processes (that is, based on real transformations). This takes place through the price mechanism to be explained in the next chapter. The same applies to the value of the buildings, equipment, etc. used by the non-labourers as well as to the value of their labour power and to the surplus value appropriated by the capitalist as profit. In short, the capitalist operating a labour process based on formal transformations must appropriate from the productive spheres of the economy (a) the value of the building, equipment, etc. used by both unproductive labourers and non-labourers, (b) the value of the labour power of these two categories of agents and (c) the surplus value.

However, not all the value of the instruments of labour and of labour power as well as not all surplus value is appropriated from the productive branches. In fact, productive labourers also participate in this labour process. Take, for example, those engaged in maintenance. They do not change the material characteristics of the means and objects of labour but act upon those use values by preventing their deterioration. By so doing they maintain the exchange value already created. Therefore, they transfer the value of the instruments of labour employed by (or, inasmuch as these instruments are employed by) them to the objects of labour and produce both the value of their labour power and surplus value.[20]

To conclude, the productive labourers are subjected to exploitation in the strict sense (since they produce value and surplus value). As seen above, this is measured by the *rate of exploitation* or *rate of surplus value*, which is equal to surplus value divided by variable capital. But the unproductive labourers do not produce value and surplus value and thus cannot be exploited. They are economically oppressed, their economic oppression is measured by the *rate of economic oppression*, which is the ratio between the surplus labour and the necessary labour (wages and salaries of the unproductive labourers).[21]

2.5 Agents of Production and Classes under Modern Capitalism

Up to now, it has been assumed that the participants in the capitalist production process are the owners of the means of production and the labourers, these latter being both productive and unproductive, both mental and material. While this is true for all stages of capitalism, in each stage the agents of production take on specific forms. This holds also for the present stage.

2.5.1 Ownership relations

Let us distinguish between two types of ownership. *Legal ownership* refers to juridical ownership. Real ownership refers to the power somebody has over the object of ownership. As far as the means of production are concerned, *real ownership* refers to the power to buy, sell and put them to use as one wishes, in short to dispose of them. Under capitalism, there is private, rather than collective, or self-managed, ownership of the means of production. Legal ownership and real ownership do not necessarily (and often do not) co-exist within the same person. This is the case with the ownership of joint stock companies.[22] Since in what follows the focus will be on production relations, in the remainder of this chapter ownership will refer to real ownership.

Historically, the ownership of the means of production belonged to a single person or at most to the members of a family. Also, there was no reason to differentiate between ownership, as defined above, and *possession*, that is, the control over the means of production. But now possession can be delegated to a specific category of agents of capital, the top managers, or chief executive officers (CEOs). They have the power to buy, sell and put to use the means of production on behalf of, and thus under the control of, the owners. Possession, then, can also be seen as dependent ownership and the possessors as dependent owners. Owners and possessors exercise conjointly the real ownership of the means of production. The latter are delegated that ownership by the former and the former are those who can delegate, but are not delegated, that ownership.

Usually, the means of production have been implicitly assumed to be the means of material production. But this conceptualization is unnecessarily restrictive. Here, I shall consider three other objects of ownership.

First, as Marx says, those who own the means of material production also own the *means of mental production*. As we shall see in 2.6.2, this means that the class owning the means of material production also has the power to define and solve the problems arising from production, and thus problems in the natural sciences, to its own advantage. Differently from other cases of delegation, this power not only can, but actually must, be delegated to a specific group of labourers, the mental labourers. Thus the owners of the means of material production own the means of mental production because they have the power to delegate to mental labourers the definition and solution of problems for their own (the owners') benefit.

Second, the owners of the (material and mental) means of production also have the ownership of *surplus labour*. This means that they have the power to appropriate the fruits of surplus labour[23] and thus to decide upon its further use (for example either consumption, e.g. dividends, or investment). This power too can be delegated by the owners to the top managers.

Third, and last, the owners of the (material and mental) means of production can buy, use as they wish (of course, within the legal limits) and terminate the use, or dispose of, the *labour power* of other people. The owners of the means of production, then, by buying labour power, become the owners of that labour power, but only for the time specified in the labour contract.[24] Therefore they can delegate the ownership of labour power both to top managers and, as we shall see, to other agents who neither own nor possess the means of production. This is all summarized in Figure 2.3.

In the material production process, the relation between the ownership of the means of material production and the other three objects of ownership is one of dialectical determination. This means that the former calls into existence the latter as conditions of its own existence and reproduction. Or, the power to dispose of the means of material production requires the power to dispose of labour power, to have labourers define and solve problems to one's own advantage and to appropriate the fruits of surplus labour. A similar point can be made for the mental production process.

Figure 2.3 Ownership relations

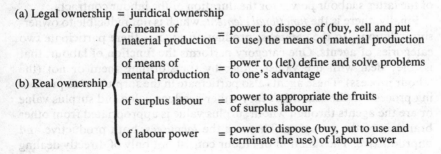

(a) Legal ownership = juridical ownership

(b) Real ownership
- of means of material production = power to dispose of (buy, sell and put to use) the means of material production
- of means of mental production = power to (let) define and solve problems to one's advantage
- of surplus labour = power to appropriate the fruits of surplus labour
- of labour power = power to dispose (buy, put to use and terminate the use) of labour power

Here, there is a relation of dialectical determination between the owner-ship of the means of mental production and the other three elements.

2.5.2 Production relations

These notions allow us to define the capitalist production relations, that is, the relations in which people (agents of production) engage when parti-cipating in the production process.

Consider first the material production process.[25] In it, the production relations are first of all relations between the owners, the possessors and the non-owners of the means of material production. But this, the *material ownership*, determines four other elements of production relations.

The first element is *mental ownership*. For the relation between owners and non-owners of the means of material production to reproduce itself, the separation is needed between material labourers (those whose determin-ant function is to transform material reality for the owners of the means of material production) and mental labourers (those whose determinant function is to transform the knowledge of material reality on behalf, and to the advantage, of the owners of the means of material production). The mental labourers are the non-owners of the means of mental produc-tion.

The second element is *ownership of surplus labour*.[26] Under any social system, labourers have to labour longer than the time needed for their immediate reproduction. Under capitalism they cannot appropriate the fruits of their surplus labour because they lack the ownership of the means of production. From this point of view, the agents of production are either the owners of surplus labour, those who can appropriate the fruits of other people's surplus labour, and the non-owners of surplus labour, those who cannot appropriate the fruits of their own surplus labour.

The third element is the *ownership of labour power*. On the labour mar-ket, buyers and sellers of labour power meet each other. After the former have bought the latter's labour power, the former acquire the ownership of the latter's labour power for the duration of the labour contract.

Finally, there is the *functional element*, which is not reducible to owner-ship relations. In the capitalist production process there participate two categories of agents. One category performs the function of labour, that is, they deal with use values either by transforming them or not (the labour process). These agents also participate in the surplus value produc-ing process, in the sense that they either produce value and surplus value or are the agents through whom surplus value is appropriated from other branches of the economy. They are the *labourers*, both productive and unproductive. The function of labour consist not only of directly dealing with use values; it also encompasses the work of co-ordination and unity necessary in each complex labour process. Thus there are those who co-ordinate the labour process, the *co-ordinators*, and the *co-ordinated*. Given the complexity of the labour process, many co-ordinators are also, in their turn, co-ordinated.

The second category of agents engages only in the surplus value produc-ing process in the sense that they perform the function of capital, or work of control. They are the *non-labourers*. The work of control[27] goes from forcing the labourers to perform their function for a time longer than that required for their reproduction to making them internalize the need to do that, through a continuum of intermediate combinations of force and persuasion, coercion and consent, repression and co-option.[28] The function of capital, which used to be carried out only by the capitalists, is now delegated both to top managers and to agents who neither own nor possess the means of production: managers and supervisors. The difference between managers and supervisors is that the former are dele-gated the ownership of (both labourers' and non-labourers') labour power while the latter are not, and thus are not delegated any ownership what-soever. But both categories are non-labourers.[29]

The non-labourers, by performing the work of control on productive labourers, expropriate surplus value. But if they do not own the means of production, they cannot appropriate it. They are the *ex*propriators but not the *ap*propriators. Thus, under modern conditions, to conceptua-lize *exploitation* one must consider not only the ownership element (both of the means of production and of surplus value) but also the functional element. If labourers engage in non-transformative labour, if they are unproductive, they are economically oppressed. This means that they perform non-transformative labour for a time longer than the time needed to reconstitute their labour power. In this section what will be said about exploitation will also hold for economic oppression and the former term will be used also to include the latter.

Given the complexity of the surplus value producing process, many agents (in principle, all agents except the real owners) who perform the function of capital are also the object of the work of control. Or, there are different levels of work of control, from the highest ones, which can be performed by the owners and top managers, to the lowest ones which are performed by the foremen and first-line supervisors.[30] It follows that the controllers who are themselves controlled are expropriated of surplus non-labour, that is, labour time needed to perform the function of capital in excess of the labour time needed to reconstitute their labour power. Both unproductive labour and non-labour cannot create surplus value but are channels through which the owner can appropriate, through the price mechanism, surplus value produced by other agents (Carchedi, 1977, 1983, 1987a).

Under modern capitalism, given the technical division of labour, both the individual labourers and the individual non-labourers are organized in a complex structure. To understand this, let us distinguish among three categories of agents. Category 1 is made up of all those who own and/or possess the means of production (ultimate owners and dependent owners) and who either perform only the function of capital or also the function of labour. Category 2 is made up of all those who neither own nor possess the means of production and who either perform only the function of capital or also the function of labour (managers and supervisors). Category 3 is made up of all those who neither own nor possess the means of production and only perform the function of labour. The *collective labourer* is, then, made up of all those who perform the function of labour, by category 3 and by categories 1 and 2, but only inasmuch as they perform the function of labour. Similarly, the *global non-labourer* is made up of all those who collectively perform the function of capital, by categories 1 and 2 but only inasmuch as they perform the function of capital. In functional terms, production relations are relations between the collective labourer and the global non-labourer.

Non-labour, just as labour, can be either material or mental. The criterion to make this distinction changes according to whether the work of control is performed on labourers or on other non-labourers. In the former case, non-labour is either material or mental according to the nature of the labour controlled. In the latter case, the controlled non-labour can be part of the production of knowledge needed to devise and perform the function of capital or of the actual performance of that function. The former is mental non-labour, the latter is material non-labour. Thus the mental non-labourers are those who participate in the work of control of the mental labourers as well as those who produce the knowledge needed for the work of control. The material non-labourers are those who participate in the work of control of material labourers as well as those who carry out (without producing the knowledge necessary for) the function of capital on other non-labourers. This is all summarized in Figure 2.4.

Five important points will now be mentioned to conclude this subsection. First, it is now possible to distinguish the four different types of agents of capital. The *ultimate owners* have the ultimate ownership of the means of production. The dependent owners, or *possessors*, are delegated the ownership of the means of production and thus the ownership of labour power and of surplus labour plus the performance of the function of capital (with or without the performance of the function of labour, usually in the form of the work of co-ordination of the labour process). The *managers* are delegated from the top managers the ownership of labour power and the performance of the function of capital

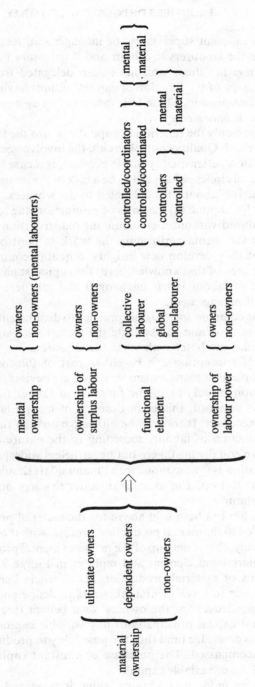

Figure 2.4 Capitalist production relations in material production

(they apply different supervisory, or management, techniques to coerce or convince the labourers to labour and if necessary fire them). Finally, the *supervisors* are those who have been delegated from the managers the performance of the function of capital without having been delegated any form of ownership. These four categories of agents of capital constitute the *private bureaucracy*.

Second, not only the function of capital but also the function of labour can be delegated. Quality control circles, the involvement of the labourers in striving for a better quality of the product, is a case in point. Through quality control circles, what used to be a task of the managers (as members of the collective labourer) is delegated to the workers. There are several advantages for capital: (a) the costs of production due to waste and rejection are reduced without a concomitant redistribution of the economic gain, (b) fewer agents performing the work of control are needed, (c) inasmuch as they develop new insights in quality control, the labourers are expropriated of that knowledge, (d) the capitalist nature of the technical division of labour is left unchanged and (e) there is no increase in workers' self-management.

Third, it is common sociological practice to distinguish between conception and execution and to associate the former with what the agents of capital do and the latter with what the labourers do. This is mistaken. The work of conception can be either part of the function of capital (if, for example, new management strategies are devised, this is an example of mental non-labour) or of the function of labour (if, for example, a prototype is designed, this is an example of mental labour). The same holds for execution. It too can be either part of the function of capital or of the function of labour, according to the nature of the task to be executed. An equally mistaken, but nevertheless widespread, assumption is that execution is synonymous with "manual" (it should be said "material") labour. But one can execute an order to carry out either material or mental labour.

Fourth, what has been said above for the material production process can be applied to the mental production process, with the proper modifications. Basically, the ownership of the means of mental production becomes here the determinant element and replaces in Figure 2.4 the ownership of the means of material production. The owners here are those who have the power to force mental labourers to define and solve problems (produce knowledge) for the owners' own benefit (see 2.6 below). The owners invest capital principally to buy variable capital because it is in this that the knowledge (and thus the possibility to produce further knowledge) is encompassed. The purchase of constant capital is determined by the purchase of variable capital.

Fifth, under modern conditions, value is produced not only by the working class but also by all other agents who are part of the collective labourer, inasmuch as they perform transformative labour, either material or mental. Surplus value is extracted not only by the capitalist class but also by all other agents of capital, inasmuch as they perform that function. But this surplus value is appropriated only by the capitalist class.

2.5.3 Class relations

We can now provide the basic elements for the identification of classes under modern capitalism in terms of production relations. The *capitalist class* is made up of both the (ultimate) owners and the possessors (dependent capitalists). Together they have the power to decide what to produce, how to produce it and for whom. In other words, this class is made up of all those who have the power to dispose of the means of production and thus also to dispose of labour power, to appropriate the fruits of surplus labour and to force or convince labourers to produce a knowledge functional for capitalist domination and thus for the reproduction of the capitalist production relations.

It could be objected that the possessors, or top managers, cannot be part of the capitalist class because they are paid a wage, rather then living off dividends and interests. But this argument ignores (1) that an agent's class position must be determined first of all in terms of production, rather than distribution, relations and (2) that the top managers' wages are not related to the value of their labour power and thus hide the appropriation of surplus value, even though not in the form of dividends and interests.[31] The wage relation on the one hand hides the top managers' class position as capitalists but on the other hand makes the dependent nature of that position clear. It is when their own labour power is disposed of that the nature of the dependent capitalists' position becomes clear. For example, "with profits shrinking and no recovery in sight" several Wall Street investment houses can no longer justify the staff they built during the 1980s. "As a result, executives who once did the firing are now being fired" (Eichenwald, 1990).

The capitalist class analysed by Marx, which has survived as small capitals dominated by oligopolies, has both the legal and the real ownership of the means of production, performs the function of capital individually (rather than the global function of capital) and the function of labour (usually in the form of co-ordination and unity of the labour process).

Under modern capitalism, the capitalist class is structured first of all as owners and possessors. The former can be a person, some persons, a family or a group who, either through legal ownership of the means of production (e.g. majority holder) or not, has that power. The owner can own the money capital which has been initially invested but can also have acquired real ownership through a subsequent purchase of stocks. The possessors can be top managers in a privately owned enterprise or in a state owned enterprise. In the latter case, their position is dependent upon those who hold ultimate political power.[32] Thus ownership can be delegated both by the private ultimate owners or by the holders of ultimate political power. Second, the capitalist class participates in the performance of the global function of capital. Third, this class can, but does not necessarily, perform the function of collective labour.

The *working class* consists of all those who perform only the function of collective labour while at the same time neither owning nor possessing the means of production. The notion of working class submitted here stresses its internal structure as material and mental labourers, as co-ordinators and co-ordinated and as productive and unproductive labourers. This notion differs from the orthodox Marxist one which disregards mental labour and which considers the distinction between productive and unproductive (material) labourers as the distinction between working class and middle class. This point is very important. It allows us to reveal the erroneousness of the thesis that the working class is dwindling in size. This conclusion can be reached only if one persists in seeing the working class as urban, material and productive labourers rather than all labourers (urban or not) engaged in material and mental, productive and unproductive, activities.

The same thesis is put forward in numerous sociological works where it is submitted that under modern capitalism the service sector grows at the expense of the productive ones (and thus of the working class). But the category "services" only confuses matters and should be dropped. "A service is nothing more than the useful effect of a use value, be it of a commodity, or be it of labour" (Marx, 1967a, p. 192). Therefore, "services" encompasses productive labour (hotels, entertainment), unproductive labour (advertising, market research) and non-labour (conception and sale of new management techniques). Therefore, inasmuch as the growth of the service sector implies the growth of productive and unproductive labour, the working class actually grows, even though in a different form.

The "dwindling working class" thesis is even more off the mark if one refers to the decreasing number of labourers. In this connection one should mention the collective labourer, that is, the working class plus all those who perform both the function of labour and the function of capital, independently of whether they own or possess the means of production or not, but only inasmuch as they perform the function of labour.

The new *middle class* consists of managers and supervisors, both when they only perform the global function of capital and when they also perform the function of the collective labourer. The new middle class is by its very nature an unstable class. This means that technological changes constantly reduce the function of capital performed by this class and enlarge the function of the collective labourer. This is the process of proletarianization, the objective substratum which, under favourable political and ideological conditions, causes the emergence of this class as an ally of the working class (Carchedi, 1977, ch. 4). But this is a tendential movement, since technological innovations create new positions and thus new forms of work of control. This is summarized in Figure 2.5, where the sign + indicates either ownership or performance of one of the two functions, the sign – indicates the contrary, and the downward-aimed arrows indicate delegation.

This chapter has provided the basic notions for an identification of social classes in terms of production relations. While it is not possible to extend this analysis here to take into consideration other factors, cursory mention can be made of how the class structure is modified when the state enters the picture. The ultimate owners of the means of production, the top managers (both within private and state owned enterprises) and the holders of ultimate political power are the main constituents of the *bourgeoisie*. The middle class (managers and supervisors) and all those in the state apparatus who are delegated political power in order to ensure the reproduction of the system[33] are the *petty bourgeoisie*. Finally, the *labouring classes* are all those who either participate in real or formal labour processes, independently of whether they are hired by capital (the collective labourer) or not (artisans, independent peasants, employees of state-owned enterprises, etc.).

2.6 The Social Production of Knowledge

Up to now, the production of knowledge has been seen from the point of view of the individual producer of knowledge (mental labourer). This, however, is insufficient to inquire into the social, class determination of knowledge, that is, into how knowledge produced by individuals can be class determined. Class determination of knowledge means that the knowledge is a condition of reproduction or of supersession of classes and thus a condition of ideological domination of classes upon each other.

2.6.1 Social knowledge and social classes

It has been submitted in the previous section that to own the means of mental production means having the power to define and solve problems to one's own advantage. This proposition must now be argued for. To this end, we must enunciate the basic materialist epistemological principle:

41

Figure 2.5 The identification of classes in terms of production relations

Classes	Agents of capital	Elements of production relations				
		Ownership of the means of production	Ownership of surplus labour	Ownership of labour power	Global function of capital	Function of the collective labourer
Capitalist class	Ultimate owners	+	+	+	+	+
		↓	↓	↓	↓	↓
	Top managers	+	+	+	+	+
				↓	↓	↓
Middle class	Managers	–	–	+	+	+
					↓	↓
	Supervisors	–	–	–	+	+
						↓
Working class		–	–	–	–	+

only those who transform reality (both material and social) can gain knowledge of it.

Let us point out right away that this holds only on the societal level, at the level of classes. It does not hold at the level of individuals, given the fragmentation of the societal production process in material and mental labour processes, and given the fragmentation of each of these two types of processes into material and mental labour. But, at the level of classes, of the entities which transform reality at the societal level by participating in the societal production process, it is material transformations which determine knowledge. Two important points follow from this. First, only those classes which transform reality can gain knowledge of it. Second, given that classes are carriers of different aspects of production relations, the knowledge of a certain reality produced by a certain class must necessarily be different from the knowledge of the same reality produced by another class. This could not be otherwise, if knowledge is to be both a cognitive instrument and an element of (ideological) class domination. The only exception is given by the trans-class and trans-epochal elements of knowledge, to be discussed further below.

But how can a class produce knowledge if only individuals (alone or in groups, it does not matter) can concretely do that? The answer is that all individuals carrying the same aspects of production relations, and thus objectively belonging to the same class, potentially share the same view of reality. Given the primacy attributed in this view to production relations, and thus to classes in terms of production relations, this becomes the primary aspect of a Marxist epistemology. Also, given that different classes have different interests, the working class's view of social reality is functional for the supersession of the system while the view of the capitalist class is functional for its reproduction. These views, however, are formless, potential views. They can become concrete only through the mental production of each concrete individual.

This should not be read as if an undifferentiated class knowledge already existed before it is fragmented into, and appears as, individual knowledge. Rather, the emphasis in this interpretation is on the fact that if all other determinants of individual knowledge could be removed (and, with them, the concrete features of individual forms of knowledge) only the most important (shapeless) element, that of being determined by the class position of the individual producers of knowledge, that is, that of being functional for class domination, would remain.[34]

But of course, each individual's concrete view of reality is formed by an infinite variety of individual, concrete factors. This means that this formless class knowledge emerges at the individual level as a great number of individual forms of that knowledge. These individual forms share one important feature, that of being class determined and thus, no matter which concrete form they take, of being potential conditions of reproduction or of supersession of the class to which the individual producer of knowledge belongs objectively. These, then, are potential forms of concrete, class-determined, social knowledge. This latter is a form of knowledge which is accepted by a sufficient number of people to become a social phenomenon, a phenomenon relevant at the level of society rather than only at the level of the individuals. The logical passage is from potential, shapeless, individual knowledge to concrete, realized, individual knowledge and, given that this also is potential social knowledge, to realized, concrete, social knowledge.

But not all these individual forms of knowledge become social phenomena. Actually, this is the case only for a few of them. The next question, then, is: How and why do these few individual forms of knowledge become the socially realized form of knowledge? The answer rests on the above-mentioned point that classes create their own view of reality (knowledge) as a condition of their own reproduction or supersession and thus of their domination upon each other. Thus they constantly try to impose their own view of reality upon each other. The way they do this is through the reciprocal incorporation and penetration by the individual producers of knowledge of each other's mental productions. This means that producers of knowledge, who objectively belong to a certain class and whose mental production is functional for that class's domination over other classes, can incorporate elements of a different class-determined knowledge up to the point where the class nature of their mental production undergoes a radical change.

To sum up, the process of production of class-determined knowledge through the mental production of individuals can be summarized in three logically, but not chronologically, separable steps. The first is the process of *individual internalization* in which the individual producers of knowledge, each in his/her own way, internalize and give concrete form to the undifferentiated class-determined knowledge. The second is the process of *reciprocal penetration*, in which the individual forms of knowledge reciprocally incorporate and penetrate each other in a struggle to become the socially accepted one(s). The third is the process of *social realization*, in which large numbers of individual forms of knowledge are recomposed into just some socially realized (accepted) forms. This presupposes a whole system of material and non-material (e.g. status) rewards and a system of institutions through which the mental producers are stimulated to produce knowledge by competing with, and prevailing upon, each other.

2.6.2 Natural and social sciences

We can now be more specific as to the class determination of knowledge by distinguishing between natural and social sciences and by considering

44

how the capitalist class, the working class and the new middle class produce their own form of these two types of science.

Consider first natural sciences. Here we face a strange situation. If
only those who transform reality can develop their own knowledge of
it, then under capitalism it is the collective labourer (and not only the
working class) which collectively transforms natural reality. The global
non-labourer is there only to perform the work of control and thus engages
neither in the material transformation of reality nor in developing its
own view of it. However, since the collective labourer does not own the
means of material production, it does not own the *means of mental production* either. This means that the collective labourer must solve problems
defined as such by the capitalist class, framed within its perspective and
solved for its benefit.[35] Or, the collective labourer can and does produce
a view of material reality, but this view is functional for the domination
of the collective labourer itself (and thus of the working class) by the
global non-labourer (and thus by the capitalist class). This explains why
under capitalism only one type of natural science (even though in several
and sometimes opposite realizations) can emerge: that type which is functional for the domination of the working class by the capitalist class.[36]
This also explains why the global non-labourer, and thus the capitalist
class, cannot produce the knowledge functional for the transformation
of material reality and *must* delegate this task to mental labourers.

The same applies to the new middle class. It too does not own the
means of production and inasmuch as it performs the function of labour
it belongs to the collective labourer which produces a type of natural
science, together with the working class, functional for its own domination
by the global non-labourer and thus by the capitalist class.

But how can the collective labourer be forced and/or persuaded to
produce a form of knowledge functional for its own domination by the
capitalist class? This is possible because, first, the individual mental
labourers (e.g. scientists) are separated from material labour; second, they
are subjected to specific forms of the work of control, and, third, through
the technical division of labour within the process of production of knowledge, they only have a limited, partial and isolated exposure to the collective process of the production of knowledge. The recomposition of these
partial elements of knowledge into a body of knowledge can then be
functional for the labourers' domination by the capitalists. It is in this
way that the point of view of the capitalist class can be imposed by the
global non-labourer on the individual producers of knowledge and thus
that the collective labourer's ability to work out its own collective view
of reality (both to pose its own problems and to solve them to its own
advantage) is destroyed. A firm's advertisement in the *International Herald
Tribune* of November 6, 1990, claimed: "We put fantasy to work", some-

thing which, in the light of what has been said above, should be taken quite literally. The meaning of this was clarified by revealing that that firm is busy with "solving problems most people have yet to imagine". We now know what this implies: "most people" cannot imagine, or formulate, those problems because of the separation between material and mental labour, and if that separation were superseded they would formulate totally different problems.

The situation changes completely when we consider the social sciences, a case dealt with briefly here and only for the sake of completeness. In this case, it is not necessary for a class to own the means of material production in order to participate in social transformations. Each class can then produce its own knowledge of social reality and transformations. While this process of knowledge formation has its own specific traits, only one will be mentioned here. Given that different classes do produce their own, and irreconcilable, views of social reality, which is the one which potentially at least can fit reality? The answer rests on the privileged epistemological role assigned to the working class. In fact, this class has an objective interest in the supersession of this system and thus in discovering its laws of motion and fundamental contradictions. The capitalist class, on the other hand, has an objective interest in the reproduction of the capitalist system and thus has no objective interest in discovering those fundamental laws and contradictions. It can thus at most develop views and techniques aimed at the continued reproduction of the system but cannot penetrate its essence.

The new middle class too can and does develop its own view of social reality but, given the spurious nature of the production relations on which this class rests, the knowledge it develops is either functional for the domination of the capitalist class over the working class or vice versa, according to the relation of force between the two classes.

This points to an important difference concerning the production of knowledge. In the natural sciences, only one type of class-determined science (even if in different concrete forms) can be produced on behalf of the capitalist class, and this is produced by the whole of the collective labourer. In the social sciences different (class-determined) types of social sciences can and do emerge: it is not the collective labourer but classes which produce social knowledge. Thus the knowledge needed for the supersession of the capitalist system stems from the working class and not from the collective labourer.

2.6.3 Trans-epochal and trans-class elements of knowledge

At this point, a threefold objection could be raised. The thesis submitted here is that natural sciences and techniques are class-determined in the

46

sense that only that type functional for capitalist domination can take (many) concrete form(s). But if this is so, first, how is it possible that (elements of) these sciences and techniques can also be used by other classes to resist that domination? Second, how is it possible that (elements of) these sciences and techniques can be used for the advantage of all classes (and not only of the capitalist class)? And third, how is it possible that (elements of) sciences and techniques developed in pre-capitalist societies can not only still have cognitive value but also can still be used as elements of class domination under capitalism? The first two objections concern the issue of the trans-class elements of knowledge, the third concerns the issue of the trans-epochal elements of knowledge.

Consider the first question, the possibility that science and techniques can be used both for capitalist domination and to resist that domination. This can be explained if we recall that science and technology are determined by contradictory production relations. Therefore, they have a contradictory nature too. Some dominant elements characterize them as functional for capitalist domination. But some other, non-dominant elements (perhaps present only in a potential state) can have the opposite function of resisting that domination and contributing to the supersession of the capitalist system; or, science and technology are almost never pure forms of domination of one class over the other. But, and this is the important point, both the possibility to use them for capitalist domination and the possibility to use them to resist that domination are class-determined. The measure in which the non-dominant elements are present, and thus the possibility to use those sciences and techniques to resist capitalist domination, varies from case to case.

For example, I have argued elsewhere that computer and information technology show their class nature by fostering

(1) a mechanical and formalized way of reasoning (as opposed to a substantive and dialectical one), (2) the production of only a quantifiable and technical knowledge (as opposed to a qualitative knowledge based upon an experience of socio-political decision-making processes) and (3) a passive and individualized use of that knowledge (as opposed to an active and social one).

This does not exclude the computer being used to resist capitalist domination in a number of ways (Carchedi, 1987a, p. 242). But "it should never be forgotten" that these alternative possibilities "are secondary features of the computer, and that its main function is that of being an instrument for the domination of the labourer by the non-labourer" (Carchedi, 1987a, p. 243).

Consider now the second question, the possibility that (elements of) science and technique born as a condition of domination of the bourgeoisie can be used for the benefit of all classes. Medicine is an often quoted example. The argument here is similar to that submitted above. Given that science and techniques are determined by contradictory production relations, they too have a contradictory nature. It is because of this that they can be beneficial to all classes and not only to the capitalist class.

A cure for cancer benefits everybody. However, the functionality for capitalist domination is revealed by two factors. First, the process of production of that knowledge rests upon (a) a capitalist technical division of labour, (b) the performance of the function of capital within that production of knowledge and (c) the division between material and mental labour also within that process. Second, the success in solving a problem (a cure) legitimizes this type of science as the only possible one and thus implicitly forecloses the possibility to develop an alternative type of science which would be the outcome of a different type of society (for example, one in which the social causes of cancer would be eliminated). Ultimately, then, it legitimizes this type of society. The positive use of that knowledge does not take away the negative features of the process through which that knowledge has been produced.[37] Another example is given by genetic manipulation which, while offering opportunities to cure and prevent sickness, threatens to transform life itself into a source of profit and life forms into forms functional for the production of profit.

Finally, we come to the third question, the possibility that some elements of knowledge developed in previous societies can still be used in this society not only as cognitive elements but also as elements of class domination. The point here is twofold. First, these trans-epochal elements of knowledge acquire a new meaning when immersed in a new cultural class context (a new society) and thus cannot be considered to be the same. A similar point is made by P. Mattick Jr., in dealing with "the allegedly trans-cultural" phenomenon of cleansing rituals: "It is what differentiates the two rituals that gives them sociological interest, what gives them, that is, the meanings they have for the members of the cultures concerned" (1986, p. 35). Second, not all elements of knowledge can be incorporated in the new cultural class context. Only those which, having acquired this new meaning, can be functional for class domination in the new context, can become trans-epochal elements of knowledge. These elements of knowledge too can be functional for the domination of one class over the other in various measures and thus, as mentioned above, can be used also to resist capital domination.

The concept of numbers is a case in point. For the ancient Greeks, numbers were numbers of something, collections of entities, and thus could not be abstract numbers. Their function was that of counting things. Being collections of concrete things, they could be represented by dots which, in their turn, could be arranged in geometrical shapes. The ancient

Greeks therefore had the notion of triangular, square, etc. numbers. This is an absurdity for us. We think of numbers as abstract entities. This change in perception took place in the sixteenth century and was canonized by the Dutch mathematician Simon Stevin. It was made necessary by the fact that at that time the function of numbers was changing. The need had arisen for numbers to be used not only to count (as for the ancient Greeks) but also to measure. In its turn, this need was due to the fact that, in the sixteenth century, measurement had become necessary to grasp ballistics, navigation and the use of machinery. But these, as Hessen shows in his classical study of the social determination of Newton's theory, were fundamental problems to be solved for capitalism to rise and develop (Carchedi, 1983, pp. 17–19).[38] To sum up, the trans-epochal and trans-class elements of science and techniques can and should be explained on the basis of their being class-determined rather than of their supposed class neutrality.

This chapter has charted the path from labour to value. This path had to wind through territories largely unexplored by orthodox economics, the sociological and epistemological dimension of the production of value. The next task is to inquire into the objective laws which regulate the distribution of value through price formation.

Notes

1. Production *of* profit indicates the objective feature of the capitalist production process. Production *for* profit indicates that this objective need has been internalized by the capitalist who is thus the agent of capital.

2. Emphasis should be placed on the term "socially". What people deem necessary for the maintenance of the labourer and his or her family (the value of labour power) changes within a society over time and between societies. It is in this sense that the exchange value of labour power is socially determined. The determination of the value of labour power is further discussed in 4.1.4 below.

3. H.J. Sherman submits that "the labor expended in 'producing' (educating) the more skilled workers ... is greater than that expended in producing an ordinary worker; and therefore, he passes on to the product a greater value per hour" (1979, pp. 260–61). The term "passes on" is confusing since it could be interpreted as either "transfers" or "creates".

4. The notion that the labourers replace the value of constant capital in the first hours, create the value of labour power in the next hours and create surplus value in the last hours is the object of vehement criticism by Marx. This notion was made famous by Senior in 1836 and is at the basis of the capitalists' (and bourgeois economists') recurrent claim that the reduction of the working day by the last hour(s) would wipe out profits. Let us suppose a working day of 12 hours in which a value of 120 is produced as follows:

$$80c + 20v + 20s = 120V$$

According to Senior, the labourers create the value of constant capital in the first 8 hours, the value of variable capital in the next 2 hours and surplus value in the last 2 hours. If, then, the working day is reduced from 12 to 10 hours, there is no production of surplus value any more.

Consider now Marx's calculation. The rate of surplus value is 20s/20v = 100%. Then, 6 hours are needed to reproduce the value of labour power (20v) and 6 hours are needed to create surplus value (20s). Each hour of work transfers 80c/12 = 6.66c to the product and creates a new value equal to 40/12 = 3.33. If the working day is reduced to 10 hours, only 4 hours are left for the production of surplus value, that is, 4 × 3.33s = 13.32s is created. The rate of surplus value falls to 13.32s/20v = 66.6% and not to zero.

5. The value of labour power increases due to acquired skills. Usually the skilled labourer produces different goods than those produced by the unskilled labourer. But it is also possible that the skill consists in being able to work more quickly or more intensively.

6. The literature is enormous. For a good introduction to the labour process debate see Thompson, 1983. See also Carchedi, 1987a; Glegg, Boreham and Dow, 1986.

7. A similar point is made, but within a different perspective, by S. Cohen, 1987.

8. This and the following section rely heavily on Carchedi, 1987a, ch. 3, section 2, and ch. 4. See also Carchedi, 1989. Some formulations have been improved.

9. In Japan and in the United States, in-house research in industry accounts for about 35% and 15–20% respectively of total national expenditures on basic research (Brainard, 1988, p. 21).

10. In 1989, in the EEC, contract research organizations (which develop new technologies for other companies, both large and small and medium-sized) totalled 129 for a combined turnover of £863m (Fishlock, 1989).

11. In fact, the real concrete is given by both material and social reality. However, the focus in what follows will be on material reality in order to contrast it to our perception of it and to limit the scope of this chapter. Carchedi (1987a) deals with both aspects of the real concrete.

12. In fact, we should say: its ability to relate to the material and social world, to the real concrete (see note 11). Here, however, I focus only on the relation between material and mental transformations.

13. Instead of saying that knowledge is functional for the transformation of material reality, we could use a more precise formulation and say that knowledge is determined, in the sense explained in chapter 1, by material transformations. This less exact formulation is sufficient for the present purposes. Subsection 2.4.1 below will return to this point and submit a criterion which allows us to ascertain when a mental transformation is determined by material transformations either in a direct, or in a mediated, way.

14. We shall see in 2.5.2 that there is no production of mental use values also when knowledge is produced which is directly functional for the work of control.

15. The fact that the "input", K, of the present MET need not be a MEU accounts for the possibility that a type of knowledge which – as the output of the previous MET – was devised for, say, military purposes, can now be used in the present MET as an input for the production of knowledge functional for the transformation (rather than the destruction) of material reality, that is, for a MEU*.

16. There is no inconsistency between this notion of material and mental labour processes and the principle that, within a materialist theory of knowledge, material transformations are always determinant. The ultimate generation of knowledge by material transformations does not imply at all that in the actual combination of material and mental transformations the former are always determinant. Due to the social division of labour, the societal labour process splits into a variety of individual labour processes, some of which are material and others mental. But knowledge is always ultimately determined by material transformations.

17. The relation between individual and social production is similar to that between individual and social values as analysed further in chapter 3. There is no relation of determination between individual and social production; rather, the latter is the socially realized form of the former through, and at the moment of, exchange.

18. The fact that some objects (e.g. beautiful shoes), originally born as the result of a material labour process, might later be appreciated as works of art does not change

the material nature of the labour process which has produced them and which has been validated at the moment those shoes have been exchanged on the market.

19. For a more detailed treatment of what follows see Carchedi, 1987a, ch. 4, section 3.

20. In my previous writings, I have taken a different view on this point which I now consider to be incorrect.

21. In this connection, one should mention the notion of exploitation entertained by rational choice, or neo-classical, or analytical, or game-theoretic, or no-nonsense Marxism. John Roemer is the best known representative of this approach. I shall briefly refer to one of Roemer's articles which has the advantage of setting forth the basic themes of this notion in a non-mathematical fashion. Roemer rejects the notion of exploitation as appropriation of surplus value. Instead, he submits that "a group is conceived of as exploited if it has some *conditionally feasible alternative* under which its members would be better off". In terms of game theory, a coalition of agents "can either participate or withdraw from the economy" so that "if a coalition can do better for its members by withdrawing, then it is exploited". Conversely, this must imply that there is another coalition of agents which would do worse if the first coalition withdrew from this situation. What if "two people disagree on whether a particular group is exploited in some situation"? In this case, "they should specify the payoff or reward that each coalition would receive by withdrawing under hypothetical conditions" (Roemer, 1982, p. 276).

So many objections can be made to this approach, that one does not know where to begin (for some of these objections, see Lebowitz, 1988; Locke Anderson and Thompson, 1988; Kieve, 1988). For the present purposes it is sufficient to mention that *no objective* criterion is offered for deciding whether one group is exploited or not. In fact, the specification of the "hypothetically feasible alternative" and thus of the withdrawal rules is purely arbitrary. Moreover, different people can think up different "hypothetically feasible alternatives" and thus adopt different withdrawal rules. Which principle shall tell us which alternative and thus which withdrawal rule are to be preferred? So much for an approach which prides itself for having "reconstructed" Marxism on a "rigorous" basis. Attempts to apply this approach to sociology, and in particular to class theory (see, e.g., Wright, 1985), do not fare any better (for a critique, see Carchedi, 1986b).

22. Under a system of joint stock companies, the real ownership of the means of material production usually belongs to the majority holders. But it is possible that a situation arises in which no one has a clear majority. However, this can only be an occasional and temporary situation since such a prolonged period would hamper the functioning of the enterprise. An example is given by the Italian chemical joint venture Enimont, one of the world's top ten chemical groups. Eighty per cent of its shares are held in equal parts by Montedison and ENI, which, at the time of writing, are fighting for its control (*International Herald Tribune*, 10–11 November, 1990).

23. I use here the term "surplus labour" to refer to the surplus labour performed both by productive and by unproductive labourers (the latter is surplus value).

24. Under capitalism, the labourers are the owners of their own labour power, which they must sell in order to reproduce themselves. But, once this labour power has been sold, that is, once the labourers enter into production relations with the capitalists, it is the latter who become the owners, but only for the time covered by the labour contract, of the labourers' labour power.

25. The analysis that follows also holds for the societal production relations, since the material aspects of the societal production process are always determinant vis-à-vis the mental ones.

26. See note 23.

27. I refer to "labour" to indicate the activity of labourers only and to "work" to indicate the activity of non-labourers as well.

28. We should distinguish between the function of capital, which is work, an *activity*, and that aspect of the real ownership of labour power which is the *power* to use labour power as one wishes. A person can have no power to use other people's labour power as s/he wishes and yet either force or persuade them to work on behalf of those who have that power.

29. More explicitly, I distinguish between two *modes of control*, external and internalized. Thus the work of control consists not only of coercing but also of convincing. These two modes take a variety of concrete *forms of control* (management strategies) which are always a combination of coercion and persuasion. Coercion always needs some degree of participation and internalization always needs an element, no matter how small, of coercion. Edwards (1979, p. 131) distinguishes between technical and bureaucratic control. But these are not modes of control. They are two concrete forms taken by the two general modes (external and internalized control). For example, of the elements of bureaucratic control, wage scales are closer to participation and internalization while work rules are closer to coercion. Management strategies change continuously, due to the introduction of new production processes and/or to political needs, something which can lead to some positions losing the function of capital and some others losing the function of labour (Carchedi, 1977; Carter, 1985; p. 119).

As I have pointed out (1977), the ideal for the capitalists is that the workers totally internalize control and thus control themselves and each other. In this case, they perform both the function of capital and the function of labour at the same time. But from the point of view of their economic significance, inasmuch as they engage in the (real or formal) transformation of use values, they are labourers, whether they engage in each other's control or not.

30. Given that those who perform the function of capital can, but do not necessarily, also perform the function of labour, in functional terms an agent can be either (1) supervisor and co-ordinator, (2) supervisor and co-ordinated, (3) supervised and co-ordinator and (4) supervised and co-ordinated.

31. The argument that top managers deserve a higher salary because their work is more important, requires more responsibility, etc. than other work, rests on circular reasoning. There is no way to show that their work is more important except by arguing that the proof of its greater importance is that it is better paid. But this is just what has to be shown. This argument is simply a rationalization of the inequality inherent in capitalist production relations. The top managers participate in the exercise of power deriving from the (delegated) real ownership of the means of production and can thus participate in the appropriation of surplus value (labour).

32. For the purposes of this work, ultimate political power can be defined as the power to hire and fire those to whom real ownership of the means of production has been delegated in state-owned enterprises. This power refers only to those dependent capitalists who are directly dependent upon the politicians. Or, ultimate political power is the power to delegate real ownership to the highest representatives of capital within state-owned enterprises. The fact that some ultimate capitalists (e.g. some powerful industrialists or financiers) can influence or even determine the nomination of those holding ultimate political power only means that the dependent capitalists are directly dependent upon the holders of political power but indirectly and ultimately dependent upon the holders of ultimate economic ownership.

33. "In order to" refers to the objective function, not to the conscious motives behind the delegation of political power.

34. I should like to thank Paul Mattick Jr. for pointing out to me, in a private correspondence, that my formulation of this point in my 1987 book was couched in terms which could be misread as submitting a metaphysical view.

35. The famous quotation reads:

The class which has the means of material production at its disposal, has control at the same time over the means of mental production, so that, thereby, generally speaking, the ideas of those who lack the means of mental production are subject to it. (K. Marx and F. Engels, *The German Ideology*, 1970, p. 64).

Here I have attempted to interpret the sense of this quotation in a way consonant with Marx's theory.

36. The same argument can be made *mutatis mutandis* for sectors of the collective labourer which are subjected to specific forms of domination. An example would be women medical

researchers working within a patriarchal scientific system and thus accepting a patriarchal definition of medical problems (e.g. infertility), framed within a patriarchal perspective and solved for the benefit of men, irrespective of the class to which they objectively belong. On the relation between class domination and specific forms of domination within the collective labourer, and thus on the relation between class struggle and social movements, see Carchedi, 1977, ch. 6.

37. Here I disregard the fact that often the class determination of knowledge is revealed by the fact that, as pointed out above, the problem itself is defined by, framed within the perspective of, and solved for the benefit of the capitalist class.

38. A related argument is that the trans-epochal elements of knowledge, once they have acquired a new meaning in the new epoch, carry the ideological values of that epoch and thus of the classes characterizing that epoch. This is another way in which they become functional for the reproduction or supersession of that new socio-economic system. When elements of knowledge functional for the domination of one class (e.g. the capitalist class) over the other classes within a socio-economic system are imposed on other socio-economic systems, that class's domination is extended also on these other systems. For example, A. J. Bishop (1990) argues that Western mathematics is "one of the most powerful weapons in the imposition of Western culture" on colonized countries.

Social Distribution through Price Formation

3.1 Individual and Social Values: Preliminary Remarks

We have seen in chapter 2 that the value of a commodity is given by the abstract labour which has been necessary to produce it, or "the labour-time that the article in each individual case costs the producer" (Marx, 1967a, p. 317). This is the *individual value* of that commodity.[1]

But society not only produces value: it also distributes it, assigning a certain value to each commodity at the moment of exchange. This is a fraction of the total value produced by that society, that is, of the total abstract labour expended under capitalist relations of production and producing – as concrete labour – use values, both material and mental. Of course, society is not an individual and thus does not consciously decide what a commodity should realize. It is the objective process of competition which will "decide" what a commodity is worth. This is its social value. This social value manifests itself as money, that is, money is the necessary form of appearance of social value.

The *social value* of a commodity depends both on the structure of production and on social demand. The *structure of production* of a certain branch is given by (a) the number, (b) the size and (c) the level of productivity of the capitals invested in that branch. The structure of production of an economy is then given by the structure of production of all its branches as connected to each other through (a) commodity movement and (b) capital movement. At any given moment the structure of production determines both the supply of a certain commodity and the average productivity, that is, the labour time necessary to produce it under normal (average) conditions of productivity. The structure of production is changed by technological competition, which changes the level of productivity of capitals, and by capital movement, which changes the number and size of the capitals which have attained each level of productivity.

The *social demand* for a commodity is determined by how much the consumers are willing to spend (demand), and are able to spend (purchasing power), on that commodity. The social demand for that commodity depends upon the distribution of social demand among all branches. A change in the social value is determined by a change in the structure of production, and thus by technological competition and capital movement, and by the concomitant change in the distribution of social demand.

The social value of a commodity is also its *purchasing power*, and thus the purchasing power of the commodity's owner, since the owner can only buy what s/he realizes from that commodity's sale. The owners of the means of production derive their purchasing power from the sale of the product, the non-owners from the sale of their labour power.

The all-important point for the purposes of this chapter is that there is no reason to assume that the fraction of total labour which a commodity has cost (the individual value) and the fraction of total labour society is willing to assign it (the social value), coincide. Consequently, individual values must be transformed into social values. The process of price formation is the process of transformation of individual values into social values.

The social value can take several forms according to the *level of abstraction*, that is, according to the aspects of reality we choose to consider. At the more concrete level of abstraction, there are money prices, prices which can be empirically observed. These prices express in terms of money the market prices, or the value actually realized by commodities. The market prices, in their turn, are fluctuations around tendential prices. These latter can be either market values, if there is no capital mobility between the different branches of an economy, or prices of production, if this mobility does exist. Money prices, market prices, production prices and market values are all different forms taken by the social value of commodities; they are all transformed individual values. This is shown in Figure 3.1, where → indicates transformation.

Figure 3.1 Values and prices

	VALUE DIMENSION		MONEY DIMENSION
	Tendential values	*Realized values*	
Individual values {	→ Production prices →	Market prices →	Money prices
	→ Market values	→ Market prices →	Money prices

The process of price formation summarized in Figure 3.1 constitutes the hub of this chapter. Let us begin by inquiring into how individual values are transformed into market values.

3.2 Market Values

The market value

> on the one hand ... is to be viewed as the average value of commodities produced in a single sphere and, on the other, as the individual value of the commodities produced under average conditions of their respective sphere and forming the bulk of the production of that sphere. (Marx, 1967c, p. 178)

It is clear that here Marx uses the term "average" not in the sense of "mean" but in the sense of "mode" or "modal group", that is, as the value around which, or the class in which, the values of commodities tend to be more heavily concentrated. If this is kept in mind, there is no harm in using the term average.

3.2.1 Productivity and organic composition of capital

The process through which the market value arises is technological competition among capitals within a sphere of production. To understand its nature, we should look at Marx's notion of *organic composition of capital* (from now on, OCC). The OCC has a double nature, so to speak. On the one hand it depicts a value relation, it is a *value composition of capital*. From this point of view it depicts the relation between the value invested in constant capital and the value invested in variable capital. On the other hand, it is a technical relation. From this point of view it depicts the relation between the quantity and quality of specific types of machines, buildings, etc., on the one hand, and the quantity of labourers, with specific types of skill, who operate those means of production, on the other. This is the *technical composition of capital*. In short, "the value-composition of capital, inasmuch as it is determined by, and reflects, its technical composition is called the organic composition of capital" (Marx, 1967c, pp. 145–6).

This allows us to see the relation between technological competition and OCC. An increased efficiency (or productivity) within a certain branch means an increased output of use values per unit of capital invested in that branch. This is made possible by the introduction in that branch of more efficient technologies, of more "capital intensive" techniques,

57

and thus by a higher OCC per unit of capital (Marx, 1967a, p. 622). This means that the value per unit of output of these products falls while the OCC increases. Thus *increased efficiency* (productivity) is not simply a *reduction of the value per unit of output* but, rather, it is such a decrease as a result of an *increase in the physical output per unit of capital invested* due to the introduction of "labour saving" techniques, that is, *due to* techniques which require a *higher OCC* per unit of capital.

For example, in the textile industry we can witness "changes paralleling those which ushered in the Industrial Revolution in Britain 200 years ago". In weaving, "shuttleless looms . . . have greatly increased the speed of weaving". In spinning, "friction spinning machinery produces yarn at the rate of 300 metres a minute, compared with the 150 metres a minute that is the norm with established techniques of rotary spinning". In dyeing and finishing, "sophisticated control systems are required to monitor the various stages in the addition of dyes and other chemicals to fabrics". In the design of new clothes, "computer-aided design is playing a part" while "other advances are taking place in the area of carding machines". Some progress has even been made "in linking the use of robots to automatic sewing machines". Moreover, research and development will have to be stepped up and new technologies are expected to be even more expensive (Marsh, 1987).

There are at least two points with regard to productivity which should be mentioned. First, productivity is here a measure of units of output per unit of capital, considered as the sum of its constant and variable parts. The standard notion used in business literature is obtained by dividing units of output by units of input. The advantage of the notion submitted here is that it makes it possible to see the positive relation between an increase in productivity and an increase in the percentage share of constant capital (or a percentage decrease in variable capital) in a unit of capital, that is between an increase in productivity and an increase in OCC.

Second, productivity is a physical measure. It thus applies typically to material labour. This notion can be applied to mental labour, but only inasmuch as (a) the knowledge produced is incorporated in physical entities (newspapers, pupils, etc.) and (b) that incorporation is immediate, it does not go through intermediate steps. If there are such intermediate steps, it is impossible to determine its effects on productivity. For example, it would be wrong to measure the productivity of product designers in terms of the number of prototypes completed. In fact, "designing an item to make production smoother will improve the efficiency of the entire plant" but "if such a design takes twice as long to complete as a simpler approach, it certainly does not mean that the engineer is less productive" (Chew, 1988, pp. 115–16).

3.2.2 The tendency of the OCC to rise

While technological competition and thus technological improvements can lead to an increased OCC, it is also possible that more productive technologies might be less, rather than more, "capital intensive". There would seem to be then no clear relationship between increased OCC and higher efficiency. Actually, such a relationship does exist.[2]

Consider the semiconductor industry. Here, companies must continuously invest in Research and Development (R & D) programmes and engage in capital investments. Those unable to do so "do not survive more than one or two product generations" (Ferguson, 1988, pp. 58–9). This is the tendency, as indicated by the fact that, in the 1974–84 period, capital expenditure in this branch has risen from 6% of revenue in both Japan and the US to 28% in Japan and 20% in the US. This leads to increased productivity in the production, and thus to lower prices of, semiconductors. At the same time, they become increasingly powerful.

The counter-tendency is given by the cheapening of capital goods due to technological innovations. In this case, as a consequence of the lower costs and technological improvement of semiconductors, personal computers (of which semiconductors are an essential component) become cheaper and more powerful. This lowers the OCC ("barriers to entry") in certain sectors based on machining.

But this is only a counter-tendency, a temporary obstacle, so to speak, to the realization of the tendency. In fact, the tendency reappears within the counter-tendency as soon as this latter has become manifested. In the computer industry itself, capital expenditures are increasing. It now seems that

the entire information technology sector is headed towards a single, wide technology base dominated by micro-electronics, systems architecture, software, and flexible mass manufacturing. Cost structures will be dominated by the initial and fixed costs of R & D, capital investment and marketing. Marginal and direct labor costs will decline to *negligible* levels. (Ferguson, 1988, p. 59; emphasis added, G.C.)

Against this background, we can now properly understand the nature of the law of the tendential increase in the OCC. This is not an argument for a secular trend, for a secular increase in the OCC. Rather, since a tendency cannot exist without its counter-tendencies, we can observe the co-existence of both tendency (in some branches) and counter-tendencies (in others) and again the reappearance of the tendency within the counter-tendency as soon as the latter (the branches where the OCC has fallen) realizes itself. Seen like this, this is a tendency of the first type. If data on the OCC are aggregated for all branches (both branches where the OCC is increasing and where it is decreasing), then data show a tendency of the second type, that is, the temporal succession of increases and decreases in the OCC, according to whether the tendency or the counter-tendencies are stronger at any specific moment. This movement, far from being a sign of the unpredictability of the relation between increased efficiency and level of OCC (see, e.g., Pasinetti, 1981, p. 188), clearly depicts one of the fundamental laws of movement of the system.

What empirical evidence is there to support this thesis? When estimates of the OCC are examined statistics can be found which either support or reject the thesis of the increase in the OCC.[3] Is there then a reason why we can confidently choose figures supporting, rather than rejecting, the thesis of the tendential increase in the OCC? There is. But then this thesis must be correctly interpreted, that is, it must be seen as a tendential increase in the ratio of constant to variable capital due to the tendential mechanization and automation of production, distribution and exchange, and thus to the tendential replacement of men and women by machines.[4] In short, higher OCC and higher unemployment are two sides of the same coin.

Estimates of the OCC in specific countries are hard to come by. What one can find are substitutes, as for example estimates of the ratio of the stock of capital per employed. This ratio, even though a pale indication of the OCC, is a good enough indicator for the present purposes.[5] Column (a) of Table 3.1 gives the figures of the stock of capital per employed in the ten countries of the European Community (EUR 10), where 1960 is equal to 100, and columns (b) to (g) give the rate of unemployment in selected countries.

Comparison of column (a) with columns (b) through (g) in Table 3.1 leaves no doubt as to the direction of the movement. Equally eloquent are international data on total unemployment for the OECD countries: this was 8 million in 1973 and had reached 30 million in 1987 after having peaked at 32 million in 1983. Total unemployment continues to increase, even though with a fluctuating movement. The role of information techno-logy in this process has been momentous. As a recent survey put it, so far information technology "has been used to reduce production costs" but its widespread adoption "has contributed more to unemployment than to growth" (UNCTC, 1988, pp. 47–8). Only one illustration will suffice: "in Fiat's factories the first generation of automation cut manning levels by half" (*The Economist*, May 21, 1988, p. 81).

3.2.3 Technological competition and modal techniques

Technological competition within branches leads to the introduction of new and more efficient techniques by some capitalists. In order to be competitive, the other capitalists have to adopt those techniques as well.

Table 3.1 Stock of capital per employed (a) and
unemployment rates (b) to (g)

Year	EUR 10	US	UK	WG	France	Italy	Canada
	(a)	(b)	(c)	(d)	(e)	(f)	(g)
1967	130,6	3.8	2.2	2.1	1.0	3.5	4.1
1968	136,1	3.6	2.3	1.5	1.3	3.5	4.8
1969	140,7	3.5	2.1	0.7	1.6	3.4	4.7
1970	146,1	4.9	2.3	0.5	1.7	3.1	5.9
1971	152,5	6.0	3.0	0.7	2.1	3.1	6.4
1972	158,9	5.6	3.4	1.0	2.3	3.6	6.4
1973	164,1	4.9	3.5	1.1	2.2	2.3	5.6
1974	170,0	5.6	2.5	2.7	2.3	2.9	5.4
1975	176,4	8.5	3.9	4.8	4.0	3.3	7.1
1976	182,1	7.7	5.4	4.7	4.2	3.7	7.2
1977	186,8	6.9	6.8	3.6	5.2	7.1	8.1
1978	191,2	5.9	6.1	3.5	5.2	7.1	8.3
1979	195,3	5.7	5.5	3.2	5.9	7.5	7.4
1980	200,7	7.0	6.9	3.0	6.3	7.4	7.5
1981	208,2	7.5	10.9	4.4	7.3	8.3	7.5
1982	215,2	9.7	11.0	6.7	8.0	9.1	11.1
1983	221,8	9.6	11.6	8.2	8.4	9.8	11.9
1984	226,6	7.5	11.7	8.2	9.9	10.3	11.3
1985		7.2	11.9	8.3	10.2	10.6	10.5
1986		7.0	12.0	8.0	10.2	11.0	9.2
1987		6.2	11.7	7.2	10.2	11.2	9.2

Source: (a) Mortensen, 1984, pp. 62–7; (b) to (g) various issues of OECD *Economic Outlook* and OECD *Main Economic Indicators.*

For a time, these are the commonly used (modal) techniques. But while the bulk of the producers use these techniques, on the one hand some producers have not yet adopted them and, on the other hand, new inventions are already being introduced in the production process. Thus the general adoption of a certain technique does not exclude that, at any given point in time, some capitalists have already introduced new, and yet more advanced, techniques and some other capitalists have fallen behind in the technological race. It follows that, under the coercion of competition, the bulk of commodities is produced by the modal capitals, that is, the bulk of the production units is clustered in a modal category. It is this modal category which determines the social value of commodities.[6]

At this juncture, let us mention parenthetically two points. First, technological competition is such that capitals compete not only by introducing new techniques to produce the same good but also by producing substitutes of that good. Inasmuch as commodities compete as substitutes, they can be aggregated as one type of commodity and constitute one branch.

Secondly, under conditions of rapid technological change, enterprises can use different techniques at the same time. The process through which a technique becomes modal, that is, through which the bulk of commodities is produced with that technique, is thus a gradual one. An example is provided by the experience of a small engineering company:

> In one corner of the factory stands a numerically controlled machine tool bought in the early 1970s which is controlled by a perforated paper tape and which the operator loads by hand with the appropriate drill bit or cutting tool.
> Nearby is a mid-1970s version of the same piece of equipment which is computer numerically controlled. It has a programmable memory capable of running several different machine programs and an automatic tool change.
> The latest stage in [this] automation drive stands on another part of the shop floor; it has a flexible machining centre with a series of work tables which permit the operator to set up several rough castings for machining. This allows him to carry out other tasks while the centre selects the correct tool from the 80 in its magazine.
> [This company] is one of a growing number of small companies in Britain to computerize its manufacturing operations. Two thousand small companies (employing between 10 and 99 people) – equivalent to 11 per cent of manufacturing companies of this size range in Britain – had introduced CAD/CAM by the end of 1986. (Batchelor, 1988)

It is thus not necessary to assume that the bulk of enterprises only uses the modal technique and that the remaining part only uses either less or more advanced techniques.[7]

The process of diffusion of techniques and the emergence of the modal one can be better understood by using the so-called S-curve,[8] as in Chart 3.1. In phase A, the introductory phase, a certain technique is emerging. In phase B, the growth phase, it is adopted by an increasing number of capitalists. In phase C, the maturity phase, it is adopted by the maximum number of firms, which is not necessarily 100% of all firms. In phase D the technique begins to be abandoned in favour of other, more efficient, ones.

At any given moment there is a technique which has become the modal one (except for a particular case to be discussed shortly) and which has reached or is reaching phase C. Other competing techniques are emerging (phase A), are spreading (phase B), have reached their maximum expansion without having become the modal one (phase C), or are starting to disappear.

It is possible that during a certain period no technique is modal because this is a period of transition in which two or perhaps more techniques produce approximately the same quantity of a certain product. In this case, the tendency towards a modal technique, a tendency of the first type, changes into a tendency towards a mean technique, one of the third type. The realized modal technique changes into an unrealized mean tech-

Chart 3.1   The diffusion of a technique

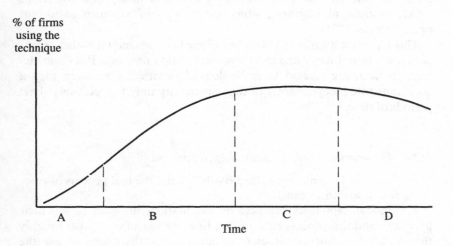

nique towards which the realized techniques tend by overtaking each other in terms of efficiency and thus in terms of the quantity of products produced by each of them. But this change, important as it is, has no relevant theoretical consequences for the present purposes. It is also possible that the unrealized mean technology, a tendency of the third type, changes again into a tendency of the first type if one of the competing technologies gains again the upper hand and produces the bulk of the commodities.

The choice of the modal[9] technique, or production process, is influenced not only by technological changes in the branches producing its instruments of labour but also by at least three other factors. First, the technology in a certain branch is changed by technological developments in those branches which produce its objects of labour. Biotechnology provides a particularly important example. As a result of developments in the biotechnology branches, their products become interchangeable inputs for other branches, e.g. food and beverages. For example, at the beginning of the 1980s, the US soda producers switched from beet sugar, imported from the Philippines, to maize (of which the US is the largest world producer) as a sweetener (Ruivenkamp, p. 7).[10]

Second, the choice of the modal production process can be influenced by technological developments outside that branch and affecting the use and/or the price of that product. For example, in the competitive struggle between conventional 35 millimetre cameras and instant cameras, the declining popularity of instant photography can be explained not only by "the advent of easy-to-use, relatively inexpensive 35 millimetre cameras" but also by "the proliferation of one-hour film processing shops which produce photographs which may cost half as much as instant prints" (Sims, 1988).

Third, the question as to which technique becomes modal is also dependent upon brand-name and extensive distribution network. But these factors, in turn, are related to technological superiority and can play a dominant role independently of that superiority only for relatively short periods of time.

3.2.4 The market value as a tendential concept

How do we find the market value? By theorizing the real process of price competition within a branch.

The modal capitalists compete on the market, in order to sell their products, and this process ensures that those products are sold at roughly the same price. But the other (non-modal) capitalists tend to ask the same price too. If there is sufficient demand for all products to be sold, capitals with above mode productivity have no reason to lower their price and capitals with below mode productivity must sell their commodities at this price. If demand and supply do not coincide, price competition and supply adjustments will tend to bring supply in line with demand, so that all commodities are tendentially sold (I disregard crises of realization). In short, tendentially, all commodities are sold and their price tends towards the price realized by the modal ones, that is, the price realized by the commodities produced under modal conditions of productivity. It is because of this assumption that the market value is a *tendential* concept.

This means that the computation of the market value must be carried out under the $D = S$ *assumption*, that is, under the assumption that social demand is such that *all commodities are sold* at their social (market) value, *at the price realized by the modal commodities so that capitals with different levels of productivity tendentially realize different rates of profit.*[11] In Marx's words,

> For a commodity to be sold at its market value, i.e. proportionally to the necessary social labour contained in it, the total quantity of social labour used in producing the total mass of this commodity must correspond to the quantity of the social want for it, i.e. the effective social want. (Marx, 1967c, p. 192; see also pp. 178 and 185)

Or, in order to determine the level of the market value, we must abstract from discrepancies between social demand and supply.

3.2.5 *The computation of the market value*

It follows from what has been said above that, in order to compute the market value we must first compute the individual value of the modal commodities and then consider whether social demand is such for the modal commodities (and thus for all commodities) to realize that value or not. If it is not, both modal and non-modal commodities must realize a modified value. Consider Table 3.2 which depicts three capitals within the same branch, where c is constant capital, v is variable capital, s is surplus value, V is the value produced by each unit of capital, O is the output per unit of capital, V/O is the individual value per unit of output, VTR/C is the value tendentially realized per unit of capital, and VTR/O is the value tendentially realized per unit of output, or market value per unit of output. In this table these three capitals are assumed to constitute the whole branch and capital I is assumed to produce the bulk of those commodities. Here, capital I is not shown to be the modal one (its output would have had to be much larger than that of the other two capitals). A more detailed picture would show three (or more) categories such as $I_A \ldots I_H$, $II_I \ldots II_M$, $III_N \ldots III_Z$ where the output of the capitals in category $I_A \ldots I_H$ would represent the bulk of that branch's commodities and where for each capital the total capital invested would be shown.[12] This would be a more detailed picture of reality but a simple model as in Table 3.2 has all the elements necessary to depict the real process under consideration while, at the same time, conveniently showing them at a glance. Also, in this and the following tables, by value is meant hours of homogeneous labour, that is, after skilled labour has been reduced to unskilled labour and after more or less than average intensity labour has been reduced to its average intensity (for the rationale behind this assumption, see 3.7.4 below). Since value manifests itself as money, c, v, s, V, etc. can also be expressed in money terms.

By assumption, in Table 3.2 the individual value of the modal commodity is the value of the unit of output of capital I, $120/100 = 1.2$. Under the assumption that the market value coincides with the individual value

Table 3.2 The formation of the market value

Capital	c	v	s	V	O	V/O	VTR/C	VTR/O
I	\multicolumn{4}{l}{$80 + 20 + 20 = 120$}	100	1.2000	112.50	1.125
II				$85 + 15 + 15 = 115$	130	0.8846	146.25	1.125
III				$75 + 25 + 25 = 125$	90	1.3889	101.25	1.125
Total				$240 + 60 + 60 = 360$	320		360.00	

FRONTIERS OF POLITICAL ECONOMY

of the modal commodities, capital I realizes 100 × 1.2 = 120; capital II realizes 130 × 1.2 = 156; and capital III realizes 90 × 1.2 = 108. In this case, the value realized is 384 (120 + 156 + 108) which is bigger than 360, the value produced. To realize 384 there must be a transfer of purchasing power from other branches.

But such an outcome can only be accidental. Suppose that only the value produced can be realized in that branch. To see how much value each capital tendentially realizes under this distributional constraint in Table 3.2, a *distributional ratio* equal to 360/384 = 0.9375 must be applied. Then, the value realized per unit of output (VTR/O) falls to 1.2 × 0.9375 = 1.125. This is the market value per unit of output (see the last column of Table 3.2). The three capitals then tendentially realize the values given in the VTR/C column, 100 × 1.125 = 112.5, 130 × 1.125 = 146.25 and 90 × 1.125 = 101.25. The three rates of profit are 12.50%, 46.25% and 1.25%. This is the tendential reward for the most efficient capital (II) and the penalty for the less efficient one (III). In terms of value, there is a transfer of value from capitals I (112.5 − 120 = −7.5) and III (101.25 − 125 = −23.75) for a total of 31.25 to capital II (146.25 − 115 = 31.25). Now the total value realized (112.5 + 146.25 + 101.25) is equal to the total value available for distribution (360), all commodities are sold at a value (1.125) equal to the value realized by the modal commodity, and the capitals which are more (less) efficient that the modal ones realize a higher (lower) rate of profit than that of the modal capitals.

3.2.6 Weak and strong demand

The previous subsection has shown that the size of the market value depends upon whether transfers of (and thus changes in) social demand are allowed or not. This would seem to contradict what was said in subsection 3.2.4, that to find the market value we have to abstract from changes in demand, or fluctuations of demand around supply. It would seem then that we both need to take into account shifts in social demand and abstract from them. However, this is not the case.

Consider two branches, A and B, where – given a certain level of supply – there is sufficient social demand (demand and purchasing power) for all commodities *a* and *b* to be sold at a price equal to the individual value of the modal ones.

Suppose now that the social demand for *a* increases, while supply remains unchanged: *a*'s price increases too. But then *b*'s price must decrease. If purchasers, due to this shift in relative prices, return to the previous pattern of demand, prices will return to the old level. This is a *weak* or *self-correcting* change in social demand. In this case the market

66

value has not changed, but there has been a fluctuation of the market price of a and b around their market value. The fluctuation of demand around supply has not created a new axis around which the market prices can fluctuate (Marx, 1967c, pp. 180–81).

But it is also possible that an increase in the social demand for, and the price of, a does not discourage the purchase of a and that the concomitant decrease in the social demand and price of b does not encourage the purchase of b. The need for a and b can still be satisfied, but at different price levels. In this case, the market value has risen in A and fallen in B. The modal commodities realize more than their individual value in A and less in B. This is a *strong* or *non self-correcting* change in social demand. A new centre of gravity has been created around which the market prices fluctuate.[13]

In short, the changes in demand which determine the level of the market value (non self-correcting changes) are not the changes in demand (self-correcting changes) we have to abstract from in order to determine that level and which determine the market prices.

Thus the D = S assumption means not only that there is sufficient social demand for all commodities to be sold at a price equal to the price realized by the modal commodities (something which implies that we take into account strong changes in social demand) but also that we disregard weak changes in social demand.

3.2.7 The market value defined

To sum up, the *market value per unit of output* is the value realized by (and not necessarily the individual value of) the modal commodities. Its level, or magnitude, is determined (a) by the structure of production (which determines the individual values of the modal commodities), (b) by the distribution of social demand among branches (which can cause deviations of the value realized by the modal commodities – and thus by all commodities – from their individual value due to non self-correcting changes in the distribution of social demand) and (c) under the tendential condition that all commodities are sold when their price equals this social value, and disregarding the self-correcting differences between demand and supply.[14]

3.2.8 Market value and transfer of value

Table 3.2 shows that *capitals* are rewarded in terms of transfer of value for the introduction of new techniques. But the reward in terms of value is not perceived by *capitalists*. They are only interested in prices and profits, in the fact that within a given time period they are now producing more physical units per unit of capital invested and that they can sell them at a money price that brings in larger money profits. This larger production, or this larger money profit, is what motivates the capitalist to invest in capital intensive techniques. But at the level of value, the discrepancy between the individual value of a commodity and the value it realizes is what causes an appropriation of value from other capitalists. Thus, for capital II, $1.125 > 0.8846$. The opposite holds for the less efficient capitals (for capital I, $1.2 > 1.125$, and for capital III, $1.3889 > 1.125$).

Through the price mechanism, the more productive capitals can appropriate more value than the value produced by their workers and increase the tendentially realized rate of profit as well as, once we drop the D = S condition, the actually realized rate of profit. This creates the *illusion* that dead labour, or constant capital, creates value, whereas constant capital is only the means through which value is appropriated from other, less productive, capitals.

3.3 Production Prices without Technological Competition

Today, technological competition is important not so much because it leads to the formation of market values, that is, not because it takes place in the absence of capital movements among branches. Rather, this form of competition is important because it leads to the emergence of modal techniques (and thus productivities) in an economic scenario characterized by capital movements and thus by the emergence of a tendentially equalized rate of profit.

As Marx points out, "capital withdraws from a sphere with a low rate of profit and invades others, which yield a higher profit" (1967c, p. 195). For example, after the 1983-4 boom in the world microchip market, the 1985-6 slump, caused by too high investments in the boom period, meant "major losses in the semiconductor divisions of Japanese electronics companies" and drove most US chipmakers out of the important memory-chip market (*International Herald Tribune*, March 11–12, 1989). It is through this real constant and reciprocal overtaking in terms of profitability and the concomitant movement of capital that the tendency emerges towards the equalization of the rates of profit between branches, that is, towards the formation of the price of production. This concept reflects the fact that under capitalism profits

are not distributed in proportion to the surplus value produced in each special sphere of production, but rather in proportion to the mass of the capital employed in each sphere, so that equal masses of capital, whatever their

68

composition, receive equal aliquot shares of the total surplus value produced by the total social capital. (Marx, 1967c, p. 194)

Notice that the capital invested comprises not only the capital necessary for production proper but also the capital needed for research and development, for the purchase of the means of production and of labour power, and for the sale of the products (e.g. advertising). Actually, in some branches research and development and advertising represent a much larger proportion of total capital invested than production proper. For example, Heineken, the Dutch beer producer, is a self-proclaimed "marketing company with a production facility" (*The Economist*, December 24, 1988, p. 97).

3.3.1 Productivity, capital movements and profitability

Capital movement between branches is tied to technological competition within branches, which raises the actually realized rate of profit of the innovative capitals. Other capitalists within the same branch will introduce the advanced technology too and a new structure of productivities, including a new modal productivity, will emerge. Assuming a transfer of value is allowed from other branches, this change in the structure of productivities will raise the actually realized rate of profit of that branch. Capital movement to that branch will follow.

Notice that this *productivity* increase is relative to the previous level of productivity in that branch, *not* relative to the level of productivity in other branches. This latter is a meaningless comparison. However, levels of *profitability* can be compared both within and between branches. Thus an increase in a branch's productivity also means an increase in its profitability both relative to its previous profitability and to that of other branches. Inasmuch as capitalists in other branches have a lower realized rate of profit than capitalists in this branch, these higher realized rates of profit will cause a flow of capital from other branches into this branch.

Of course, there is no immediate transfer of capital (except for financial capital, where huge amounts of money capital can be transferred with the speed of a telephone call). The difference in rates of profit must be large enough to justify de-investing in one branch and investing in the other branch where the rate of profit is higher. Sometimes the costs of moving to another branch are very high. These and other costs enter the capitalist's computation of the rates of profit differentials. Only if differences in the rates of profit are sufficiently large in the opinion of the capitalist, will capital movements ensue.

Capital movement between branches does not necessarily imply disinvesting in some branches and investing in other branches. Profits reaped in some branches can be invested in other, more profitable, ones. This process is facilitated by the fact that large corporations are usually active in different branches (and nations). This process too leads to a tendential equalization of the rates of profit among branches. Thus, "Heinz has fed some of its profits from other markets into Japan for the past 20 years: its tomato ketchup has not reaped its success, but Ore Ida frozen potatoes have become a market leader there" (*The Economist*, December 24, 1988, p. 97).

3.3.2 The price of production: first approximation

Let us now reproduce in Table 3.3 one of Marx's numerical examples of the transformation of individual values into the price of production per unit of capital (Marx, 1967c, p. 164), where the three spheres of production are assumed to constitute the whole of the economy and where the average organic composition of capital $(240/60 = 4)$ coincides with that of branch I $(80/20 = 4)$.[15] In the Table c is constant capital; v is variable capital; s is surplus value; V is the individual value produced by a unit of capital in each branch and is equal to $c + v + s$; PrPr(C) is the price of production per unit of capital, or value tendentially realized by one unit of capital; OCC is the organic composition of capital and is equal to c/v; O means output, and PrPr(O) is the price of production per unit of output, or value tendentially realized by one unit of output.

To find the *price of production per unit of capital* we must first of all compute the average rate of profit, p. This is equal to the total surplus value divided by the total constant and variable capital $(60/300 = 20\%)$. Then, PrPr(C) is equal to $c + v + p$ (see the PrPr(C) column in Table 3.3).[16] This is equal to 120 for all three branches. By dividing 120 by the output in each branch we find the *prices of production per unit of output*, or tendentially realized prices (see the PrPr(O) column in Table 3.3). Actually realized prices are then fluctuations around these tendential values.

Social demand – which, it will be recalled, encompasses both the willingness (demand) and the ability (purchasing power) to buy – seems to play no role here. However, as mentioned above, the realization of social values

Table 3.3 Marx's tendential equalization of the rates of profit

	c	v	s	V	PrPr(C)	PrPr(C)–V	OCC	O	PrPr(O)
Branch I	80 + 20 + 20 = 120				120	0	4	100	1.2
Branch II	90 + 10 + 10 = 110				120	+10	9	120	1.0
Branch III	70 + 30 + 30 = 130				120	−10	2.3	130	0.92
Total	240 + 60 + 60 = 360				360	0			

– or the value society assigns individual commodities at the moment of, and through, exchange – depends also on social demand. Thus, in Table 3.3, the assumption is that all products of the three branches are sold and that the price they realize is such that all three branches realize the average rate of profit. In other words, the meaning of the $D = S$ *assumption* in this context is that *social demand is such that all commodities are sold at the price realized by the modal ones and that these prices are such that all branches (and thus all capitals) realize the average rate of profit.*

The price of production is a *tendential* concept in a specific, dynamic sense. Given a certain structure of production, the rates of profit would be equal only if the distribution of social demand among branches would be such that $D = S$. But this can only be a chance event. Since demand is not equal to supply, or since capitals do not realize the same, average, rate of profit, technological innovations and capital movements ensue, thus changing the structure of production. But this change affects the distribution of social demand, and a further change in the structure of production follows. The price of production is a continuously changing point towards which the structure of production and the distribution of social demand tend in their interplay, without ever being able to reach it.

Thus the tendential nature of production prices does not reside in capitals moving towards a point at which they all *produce* (as opposed to realize) the same surplus value per unit of capital. This would imply an equalization of the OCCs across branches, which is an unwarranted hypothesis. Neither does that tendential nature reside in the structure of production and the distribution of social demand converging towards an equilibrium point at which all capitals realize the same rate of profit. Rather, the structure of production and the distribution of social demand continuously chase each other, as it were, thus constantly changing the point towards which they tend, rather than converging towards a static point.

How do we find, then, the price of production if it is constantly changing? Given a certain structure of production, we compute the average rate of profit, and thus the price of production, and then we assume that $D = S$. Or, the $D = S$ assumption gives us the tendential distribution of social demand at that particular instant, the distribution which makes it possible for all capitalists to realize the average rate of profit deriving from that particular structure of production. This is how Table 3.3 should be interpreted. This table depicts a purely hypothetical outcome of a movement at which the structure of production and the distribution of social demand have modified each other in such a way that all capitals realize the average rate of profit. Its usefulness is purely didactic and does not depict a static, or equilibrium, point of convergence.

At this juncture, a new aspect arises. If, as we do in this chapter, a national economy is considered, weak changes in social demand among its branches do not affect the total value to be realized in that economy and thus do not change the price of production. However, strong changes in social demand do affect the production prices. There are two cases to be considered.

First, if we disregard transfers of value to and from other economies, we assume that only the value produced in that economy can be realized there. Strong changes affect the actually realized rates of profit and these, in their turn, cause capital movements across branches. While the total capital invested remains the same, the value and surplus value produced is modified because, when a unit of capital moves from one branch to another, it changes its OCC and thus the surplus value produced. If the sum of constant and variable capital remains the same (100) but surplus value changes, the average rate of profit changes too and so do the prices of production both per unit of capital and per unit of output.

Second, if we allow for international transfers of value, weak changes only cause oscillations of market prices around the international price of production, due to the self-correcting nature of those changes (see chapter 7). But strong changes in demand across national boundaries do change the value realized within a nation. If we assume no international capital mobility, the hierarchy of national average rates of profit is not tendentially equalized into an international one and strong changes in demand for the products of a nation affect its price of production. Thus, in Table 3.3, the price of production per unit of capital is 120 not only because of the D = S assumption but also because of the implicit assumption that the international distribution of social demand is such that only the value produced in that economy can be realized there. If we assume international capital mobility, there emerges, tendentially, an international average rate of profit. Strong shifts in social demand change this average by causing capital movements and thus investments with different OCC and surplus value produced per unit of capital.

3.3.3 Unequal exchange: first approximation

Table 3.3 shows the transfer of value inherent in the exchange of the different commodities produced with different organic compositions of capital when the rates of profit are equalized, that is, under the assumption of capital mobility. If, given that structure of production, social demand is such that all capitals can realize the average rate of profit, branch II gains value at the expense of branch III. But if each percentage unit of capital invested tendentially realizes the same profit while having different OCCs, it follows that units of capital (representing branches, as I shall argue shortly) with lower than average OCC (which produce more value) have to lose some value to units of capital with higher than average OCC. Higher than average OCC branches must appropriate value from lower than average OCC branches.

Let us call this transfer of value *unequal exchange* (from now on UE). Branch II produces an individual value equal to 110 and tendentially realizes a value of 120, while branch III produces a value of 130 but tendentially realizes a value equal to 120. Tendentially, the product of branch II is exchanged for more value than its own individual value, that of branch III for less value; or, the branch with higher organic composition of capital (II) produces less value per unit of capital invested than the branch with lower organic composition (III) and appropriates part of the value produced by the latter through the formation of the price of production, that is, through the tendential equalization of the rates of profit. The branch with an OCC equal to the average OCC tendentially realizes the value it produces, which is also the price of production per unit of capital.[17]

3.3.4 Which real situations do market values and prices of production tendentially depict?

The market value and the price of production correspond to two different situations. If we do not assume capital mobility between branches, all commodities within a branch tendentially realize the same market value per unit of output so that capitals with different levels of efficiency (and thus OCC) tendentially realize different rates of profit.

If we do assume capital mobility between branches, the social value is given by the equalization of the rate of profit. As long as capital is not sufficiently mobile, the social value is given by the market value. But, as soon as it can be observed that branches constantly overtake each other in terms of profitability, we can assume that capital has become sufficiently mobile to justify a tendential equalization of the rates of profit. In this case, the social value is the price of production. In the former case, the individual values are transformed into market values. In the latter case, they (and not the market values!) are transformed into prices of production. There is, of course, the formation of modal production processes in each branch, but these do not yield market values.

3.4 Production Prices with Technological Competition

Section 3.3 has dealt with the formation of production prices on the assumption of a uniform technology in each branch. This is a valid assumption only as a first approximation. We must now relax this assumption and inquire into the formation of production prices under conditions of technological competition within branches.

3.4.1 Modal capitals and the average rate of profit

Marx pays only passing attention to this matter. However, it is clear that, for him, the formation of the price of production (the equalization of the rates of profit) also entails surplus profit for the most efficient capitals in any particular sphere of production:

> Our analysis has revealed how the market value (*and everything said concerning it applies with the appropriate modifications to the price of production*) embraces a surplus profit for those who produce in any particular sphere of production under the most favourable conditions. (Marx, 1967c, p. 198; emphasis added)

Marx does not elaborate on this point but this is perfectly consistent with a system of competition which, as we have seen, rewards capitalists for the introduction of new techniques.

But if the more efficient capitals realize a higher than average rate of profit, and the less efficient capitals realize a lower than average rate of profit, then *only modal capitals*, capitals with modal productivity, *tendentially realize the average rate of profit* while capitals above or below mode in their respective spheres tendentially realize more or less than the average rate of profit. This, I submit, is why in Table 3.3 branches (which realize the average rate of profit) must be represented by modal capitals.

The alternative to this thesis is that all capitals, and not only the modal ones, tendentially realize the average rate of profit. This hypothesis is rejected here not only because it contradicts Marx's textual evidence (in itself an insufficient motivation) but also because of a very important reason.

One of the theses of this work is that Marx's law of value is also a theory of relative prices. But a theory explaining why commodity *a* exchanges for a multiple of commodity *b* must be a theory which explains why tendentially *any a* exchanges for a multiple of *any b*. This implies that all commodities within a branch should tendentially realize the *same* value. But the equalization within a branch of the rates of profit of capitals with different levels of productivity implies that, tendentially, the commodities of the less efficient capitals realize more than, and the commodities of the more efficient capitals realize less than, the value realized by the commodities produced by the capital with modal productivity.[18]

The assumption that tendentially all commodities within a branch realize the same value could be made to co-exist with the assumption that tendentially all capitals realize the same rate of profit only if we assumed that all capitals within a branch used the same technology. The argument supporting this assumption could be that, due to technological competition, all capitals within a branch tend to adopt the same technique and that this real movement warrants the hypothesis of technological uniformity within branches as a tendential situation. But, if – as we do here – we want to inquire into the distribution of value, we must take *production as given* and find out the tendential distribution in order to understand the real distribution as a deviation from this tendency. If, on the other hand, we wanted to inquire into the tendential production structure, we would have to equalize the OCCs within branches (but could not equalize the OCCs of the different branches). Moreover, following the distinction made in chapter 1 between present and future tendencies, the equalization of the OCCs within branches would result in all producers using (a) the present modal level of productivity, if we wanted to find out the present tendency, and (b) the present highest level of productivity, if we wanted to find out the future tendency.

3.4.2 The price of production: second approximation

The question then is: how is the computation of the price of production affected by the introduction of non-modal capitals? Again, the answer must be sought in the real movement. If both modal and non-modal capitals are free to invest in other branches' modal and non-modal techniques, if all capitals constantly overtake each other in terms of profitability, then all capitals participate in the tendential equalization of the rates of profit. But, if within each branch the bulk of the commodities (the modal commodity) is produced with a similar technique which is adopted by the bulk of the capitalists (the modal capitalists), and if the price of all commodities in a branch is determined by the price of the modal commodity,[19] then it is the modal producers who must realize the average rate of profit, while the above and below mode producers must realize more and less than that average.[20]

It follows that in order to compute the price of production under conditions of technological competition within branches, the following four requirements must be satisfied: (a) the rates of profit of all capitals must be equalized into an average, (b) only modal capitals must realize this average; (c) all commodities within a branch must realize the same value and, (d) non-modal capitals must realize a rate of profit proportional to their level of productivity, relative to the productivity of modal capitals in their branch.

These requirements can be satisfied only if in each branch each com-

Table 3.4 Prices of production before technological change

	I below mode	II modal	III above mode
Branch A			
V	$75c+25v+25s = 125$	$80c+20v+20s = 120$	$85c+15v+15s = 115$
O	90	100	110
VTR	108	120	132
VTR−V	−17	0	+17
Branch B			
V	$85c+15v+15s = 115$	$90c+10v+10s = 110$	$95c+5v+5s = 105$
O	50	60	70
VTR	100	120	140
VTR−V	−15	+10	+35
Branch C			
V	$65c+35v+35s = 135$	$70c+30v+30s = 130$	$75c+25v+25s = 125$
O	120	130	140
VTR	110.8	120	129.2
VTR−V	−24.2	−10	+4.2

modity tendentially realizes a value equal to the price of production per unit of capital, computed on all capitals, divided by the output of the modal capital in that branch. This is the price of production per unit of output, or socially necessary labour time, at this level of abstraction. The $D = S$ assumption now means that *social demand is such that all commodities are sold at the price realized by the modal commodities* (which also are the commodities produced under average conditions of profitability) *and that these prices are such that all modal capitals realize the average rate of profit* (or – as we shall see shortly – a modification of it, due to strong changes in social demand among nations) *so that above and below mode capitals tendentially realize more or less than that average.*

To depict this, consider Table 3.4 in which each branch (A, B and C) is made up of three capitals (I, II and III). As in Table 3.3, for our purposes it is sufficient to show only one modal capitalist per branch. A more detailed example would only modify the numerical results while leaving the substance of the argument unchanged.

In Table 3.4 V stands for the value produced per unit of capital invested, or individual value; O is the output, also per unit of capital invested; VTR is the value tendentially realized by a unit of capital under conditions of capital mobility across branches, and VTR-V is the transfer of value associated with the formation of VTR, or unequal exchange (UE).

The computational procedure is as follows. We compute first the average rate of profit for all capitals. We then compute the value tendentially realized by a unit of modal capital by adding to the constant and variable capital of that modal unit the average rate of profit. This is the price of production per unit of capital. We then divide this value by the output of that unit of modal capital in order to arrive at the value tendentially realized by the modal commodity in that branch (which is also the commodity produced under average conditions of profitability). This is the price of production per unit of output; it is also the value tendentially realized by all other commodities. Subsequently we multiply this value by the output of the non-modal capitals. The result is a higher than average rate of profit for capitals with a level of productivity higher than the mode in their branch and vice versa a lower than average rate of profit for the less productive capitals.

Let us apply this procedure to Table 3.4. The average rate of profit is determined by the c, v and s of all capitals and is, in this example, equal to $180/900 = 20\%$. Thus the rate of profit tendentially realized by the three modal capitals must be 20% and the price of production per unit of capital is 120. The price of the commodities in each branch is the value of the commodities produced under conditions of average profitability, or $120/100 = 1.2$ for A, $120/60 = 2$ for B and $120/130 = 0.923$ for C. Thus, the value tendentially realized by all capitals is equal to these prices times their own output; this is the VTR line. For example, capital BI realizes the value tendentially realized by the commodities produced by BII (the modal capital, which tendentially also realizes the average rate of profit) times its own output, or $2 \times 50 = 100$. The consequent loss of value, or $VTR - V$, is $100 - 115 = -15$. The total value produced is 1080 which is equal to the total value available for redistribution, that is, $(1.2 \times 300) + (2 \times 180) + (0.923 \times 390) = 1080$.

If a nation is considered in isolation, the value available for redistribution is the value produced in that nation. If that nation is considered in the context of the world economy, transfers of value from or to other countries due to strong discrepancies between demand and supply among nations must be allowed to influence the price of production. If the international distribution of social demand is given, the price of production is affected by the distributional constraint which – if needed – adjusts the value realized by the commodities produced under conditions of average profitability, and thus the value tendentially realized by all commodities, to a level consistent with the value available for redistribution in the economy as a whole. In Table 3.4, on the assumption of no transfer of social demand from or to other nations, there is no need to apply a distributional ratio.[21]

An important conclusion can now be reached. If only modal capitals are considered (as in Table 3.3), the social value of a unit of capital is also automatically the price of production per unit of capital. But if also non-modal capitals are considered (as in Table 3.4), *the price of production is the social value of modal capitals only.* Non-modal capitals too have a social value (VTR) but this is not the price of production.

It is important to realize that the theorization of production prices, and thus the computational procedure chosen, depends upon the concrete situation hypothesized. We have seen how both theorization and computation change when we shift from the hypothesis that only modal capitals are operative to the hypothesis that the structure of production within branches is differentiated into levels of productivity around a modal one. But there is a third alternative which must be considered.

In the case of rapid technological innovation in which no technique has emerged as the modal one, or in moments of transition from one modal technique to another one, or in the case of oligopolistic competition in which no oligopoly (or group of oligopolies) produces the bulk of commodities,[22] we cannot hypothesize a modal technique. Two important theoretical consequences follow. First, the average technique is not a modal any more but a *mean*, a statistical quantity which does not realize itself because no capital has that average level of productivity. Some capitals might accidentally and temporarily have a mean productivity, but this, as all accidents are, is a theoretically unimportant case. Second, given that all capitals are free to move across branches and to introduce new technologies, all capitals participate in the tendential equalization of the rates of profit. But this average is not realized by any capital, not even tendentially. Tendentially, capitals can only realize more or less than the average rate of profit, according to whether their productivity is more or less than the average (mean) in their branch.

The computational procedure changes as follows. Consider again Table 3.4. Now, this table must be seen as if each branch were made up of three categories of capital with different levels of productivity, no capital having a modal productivity any more. All capitals must participate in the tendential equalization of all rates of profit, while no capital can tendentially realize this average rate: only rates of profit below and above this average can tendentially be realized. Suppose that capitals I in branches A, B and C invest two units of capital and that capitals II and III invest only one unit in all three branches. The average rate of profit is now 255/1200 = 21.25% and the price of production per unit of capital is computed by adding this average rate of profit to a unit of capital, that is, 121.25. The mean productivities are

(90 + 90 + 100 + 110)/4 = 97.5 in A
(50 + 50 + 60 + 70)/4 = 57.5 in B and
(120 + 120 + 130 + 140)/4 = 127.5 in C

and the prices of production per unit of output are

121.25/97.5 = 1.24 in A
121.25/57.5 = 2.11 in B
121.25/127.5 = 0.95 in C

Multiplication of these prices by the outputs of the individual capitals gives us the value and the rate of profit they tendentially realize. Also, multiplication of these prices by the total quantity produced in each branch gives the total value appropriated by each branch. In this example, this value is 485. By multiplying this value by 3 we obtain 1455 which is also the value actually produced in all three branches. Again, there is no need to apply a distributional ratio.

From now on, this work will assume modal techniques. However, the conclusions to be reached under this assumption will usually hold, aside from changes in numerical results, also under the hypothesis of mean techniques. This latter hypothesis will be mentioned only when it affects significantly the results of the inquiry. But the analysis of the process of price formation remains the same, no matter which hypothesis is chosen.

3.4.3 Unequal exchange: second approximation

The notion of unequal exchange can now be accurately defined. *Unequal exchange* is the various capitals' loss or gain of value when all modal capitals tendentially realize the average rate of profit, that is, when all commodities tendentially realize the value realized by the commodities produced under average conditions of profitability in their branch. If the distribution of social demand among nations is such that modal capitals tendentially realize this unmodified average rate of profit, those modal capitals whose OCC is equal to the average OCC realize the value they produce. Those modal capitals whose OCC is lower than that average realize less, and those modal capitals whose OCC is higher than that average realize more, than the value they produce. As G. Kay appropriately puts it, "equal exchange plays no fundamental part in Marxism ... the law of value presupposes unequal exchange" (Kay, 1979, pp. 60 and 61).[23]

The production prices per unit of output are *tendential absolute prices*. They indicate how much of the total abstract labour is appropriated through the sale of a particular commodity. Once they are found, we can compute the *tendential relative prices* or the relation between absolute prices. It is possible that absolute prices change while relative prices do not. For example, in moving from Table 3.4 to Table 3.5, the production price per unit of capital changes from 120 to 117.3. However, relative prices do not change, since all modal capitals realize equally less. The production prices per unit of output vary but relative prices of commodities do not.

This presupposes that D = S. If this assumption is dropped, we consider market prices, the deviations from (fluctuations around) the price of production per unit of output due to weak changes in demand among nations as well as within nations. In this case, the transfer of value and thus UE will be modified too. But in order to understand this transfer of value, the actual UE, we must first of all have gained knowledge of UE under tendential conditions, since the former is only a modification of the latter. This real transfer of value gives us the *realized absolute prices*, or market prices, in value terms.[24] From them, we compute the *realized relative prices*.

To sum up, Marx's theory of production prices presupposes both capital mobility across branches and free technological competition. Since Marx explicitly considers only modal capitals (see Table 3.3), each branch must be represented by a modal capital so that the equalization of the three branches' rates of profit does not pose the problem of which capitals within branches realize that average rate. Once we extend this analysis and introduce below and above mode capitals in each branch, the equalization of the rates of profit explicitly becomes the equalization of all capitals' rates of profit while tendentially only modal capitals realize that average rate. Tendentially, above mode capitals realize a higher, and below mode capitals realize a lower, rate of profit.[25] Finally, if the average technique is not a mode but a mean, all rates of profit are equalized into an average which is not realized by any capital. All capitals tendentially realize either more or less than that average according to whether their productivity is higher or lower than the (unrealized) mean in their branch.

3.4.4 Technological change and price changes

Against this background, we can now examine the effects of technological change on prices. Here, I shall consider how technological changes modify both the surplus value produced and its distribution among capitals under the assumption that the value of inputs (constant and variable capital) is not affected by this change. In sections 3.6 and 3.7 below I shall also consider how technological change affects the value of inputs.

Consider capital BI in Table 3.4. This capital invests 100 but tendentially realizes 100 and does not make any profits. Naturally, it will switch to a more productive technique or move to another branch. Suppose it opts for the former alternative and adopts the modal production process (that of capital BII), which has an OCC = 90/10 and an output per unit of capital invested equal to 60. The situation changes as depicted in Table 3.5.

Table 3.5 Prices of production after technical change

	capital I	capital II	capital III
Branch A	below mode	modal	above mode
V	$75c+25v+25s = 125$	$80c+20v+20s = 120$	$85c+15v+15s = 115$
O	90	100	110
VTR	105.5	117.3	129
VTR − V	−19.5	−2.7	+14
Branch B	modal	modal	above mode
V	$90c+10v+10s = 110$	$90c+10v+10s = 110$	$95c+5v+5s = 105$
O	60	60	70
VTR	117.3	117.3	136.8
VTR − V	+7.3	+7.3	+31.8
Branch C	below mode	modal	above mode
V	$65c+35v+35s = 135$	$70c+30v+30s = 130$	$75c+25v+25s = 125$
O	120	130	140
VTR	108.2	117.3	126.3
VTR − V	−26.8	−12.7	+1.3

Total constant capital is 725, total variable capital is 175 and total surplus value is also 175. The OCC is $725/175 = 4.14$ and the average rate of profit is $175/900 = 19.44\%$. The average rate of profit falls because the new modal capital BI has an OCC (9) higher than the previous average (4), so that the new average OCC is also higher (4.14). The value of the commodities produced under average conditions of profitability is then

$119.44/100 = 1.1944$ for A
$119.44/60 = 1.9907$ for B and
$119.44/130 = 0.9188$ for C

The value which would be realized on the basis of these prices is then $1.1944 \times 300 = 358.33$ for A, $1.9907 \times 190 = 378.23$ for B and $0.9188 \times 390 = 358.33$. The total is 1095. Let us assume that the distribution of social demand among nations is such that only the value produced in that nation can be realized there. In this case, there is no equality any more between the value produced and thus realizable in that nation (1075) and the value which would be realized if all commodities realized the individual value of the modal ones (1095). Then, assuming that all commodities realize uniformly less, a distributional ratio equal to $1075/1095 = 0.9817$ must be applied. The production prices per unit of output become then

0.9817 × 1.1944 = 1.1725 for A
0.9817 × 1.9907 = 1.9543 for B and
0.9817 × 0.9188 = 0.9 for C

Multiplication of these prices by the output of both modal and non-modal capitals gives the value tendentially realized (the VTR line). Subtraction of the value actually produced from the value tendentially realized (the VTR-V line) gives the UE inherent in the formation of production prices. For example, the VTR for AI is the price of production per unit of output in A (1.1725) times the output of capital AI (90), or 105.5. The (negative) transfer of value, or VTR-V, is 105.5 − 125 = − 19.5. The average rate of profit for modal capitals is 19.44% without distributional constraint, and 17.3% if that constraint is applied. Below and above mode capitals realize less and more than that average.[26]

3.4.5 Nine important aspects of the model

There are nine aspects which should be stressed.[27]

First, modal capitals (AII, BII, CII in Table 3.4 plus BI in Table 3.5) tendentially realize the average rate of profit. However, these capitals might not have the average OCC and thus there might be a discrepancy between value produced and value realized by modal capitals even when they realize the average rate of profit. In Table 3.5, AII and CII tendentially realize respectively 2.7 and 12.7 less than their workers produce because their OCC (respectively, 4 and 2.33) is below the average (4.14). Capital BII, on the other hand, tendentially realizes 7.3 more than its labourers produce because its OCC (9) is higher than the average one. Yet, all three capitals tendentially realize the average rate of profit. It is also possible for the structure of productivities to be such that a modal capital has the average OCC (capital AII in Table 3.4). In this case, that capital realizes the average rate of profit because of its modal character and the value produced because of its OCC.

Second, only modal capitals tendentially realize either the same, more, or less than the value they produce according to whether their OCC is equal to, higher, or lower than the average OCC. The same does not hold for capitals which are above or below mode. For example, in Table 3.4, capital BI has an OCC (85/15 = 5.67) higher than the average OCC (4) and yet loses value to other capitals. Similarly, in Table 3.5, capital CIII has an OCC (75/25 = 3) lower than the average OCC (4.14) and yet gains value from other capitals (+1.3). This is so because non-modal capitals realize value according to the level of their productivity relative to the modal one rather than according to the level of their OCC (as modal capitals do).

Third, these tables show how technological competition within branches causes a transfer of value within branches as well as between branches. In fact, before technological change (Table 3.4), BI loses 15 while after technological change (Table 3.5) BI gains 7.3, that is, a value of 22.3 must come from other capitals. AI goes from a loss of 17 to a loss of 19.5; or, 2.5 comes from AI. Similarly, 2.7 comes from AII, 3 comes from AIII, 2.7 from BII, 3.2 from BIII, 2.6 from CI, 2.7 from CII and 2.9 from CIII. The total is 22.3. Thus the value appropriated by the capital which has increased its productivity is appropriated not only from the capitals in the same branch but also from capitals in other branches. This means that capitalists become aware of the need to compete not only through technological innovations and capital movements but also for purchasing power with capitalists in other branches. This awareness is more developed under oligopoly capitalism than under free competition capitalism, given that oligopolies invest in several different branches (see chapter 7).

Fourth, in Table 3.5, when BI adopts the modal productivity, the average rate of profit for modal capitals falls to 19.44% before the application of the distributional ratio and to 17.3% after that application. This is a general rule, since to adopt a more efficient technique means to increase the OCC. No matter which capital increases its productivity (and thus its OCC), the average rate of profit must fall, unless of course transfer of value is allowed from other branches or nations.

Fifth, technological change in one branch brings about a change in the price of production per unit of capital and thus in the prices of production per unit of output of *all* commodities. This means that, if – in Tables 3.4 and 3.5 – branch A produces means of production, B means of subsistence and C luxury goods, technological change in any of these branches affects the price of production – and thus the value tendentially realized by commodities – in both that branch and the other branches. In particular, technological change in the branch producing luxury goods brings about a change in the value realized also by the means of production and by the means of subsistence, independently of whether these luxury goods re-enter the production process as inputs or not.

This shows the erroneousness of the neo-Ricardian position on this point. In this theory, a distinction is made between basic and non-basic goods: the former enter into the production of all commodities, the latter do not. The former "have an essential part in the determination of prices and the rate of profits, while non-basics have none" (Sraffa, 1960, p. 54). This is wrong, as it can easily be seen if we assume that capital BI in Table 3.4 produces a non-basic. A change in its production process (Table 3.5) brings about a change in the value realized by all other commodities. The difference between basics and non-basics is another, it has to do with the *next* production process. The former goods re-enter the next production process as inputs at the new value and thus are the transmission belt through which value changes in the previous production process are carried into the next one. Non-basics cannot have this function, by definition. As far as these goods are concerned, value changes are limited to this production and realization process.

Sixth, what has been said about technological change within a branch and its effects on the appropriation of value between and within branches can be repeated *tout court* for the case of capital movement across branches. When a capital moves to another branch, it adopts by definition a new technology and thus a different OCC. This affects the average rate of profit and the transfer of value between and within branches, just as in the case of technological change within a branch. The difference is that the effect of a capital moving across branches need not be a lower average rate of profit. That average can also either increase or remain unchanged. For example, in Table 3.4 capital AI realizes a tendential rate of profit equal to 8%. If it moves to CI, where it can realize a higher rate of profit (10.8%), it moves to a lower OCC technique thus causing an increase in the average rate of profit.

Seventh, within branches, higher OCCs indicate higher physical productivity (efficiency) and thus a higher tendential profitability due to a transfer of value from other capitals both in that branch and in other branches. But between branches different OCCs cannot indicate different levels of productivity, given that different branches produce by definition different use values.[28] If we compare capitals in different branches, we cannot assume that higher OCCs indicate higher profitability. Therefore, we cannot assume that capitals necessarily move from low to high OCC techniques in different branches.

Suppose that in Table 3.3 branch III (the low OCC branch) actually realizes a higher rate of profit than the other two branches due to a strong shift in social demand. The actual appropriation of value is by the low and from the high OCC branches. Due to these rates of profit differentials, capital moves from higher to lower OCC branches. As supply increases in III and decreases in the other two branches, prices fall in the former and rise in the latter branches. The appropriation of value decreases. At first, surplus value is still appropriated, then no surplus value is appropriated, and finally surplus value is lost until when, tendentially, branch III loses sufficient surplus value for all branches to realize a new, average, rate of profit. If we now suppose that initially it is branch II (the high OCC branch) which has a higher realized rate of profit, the actual appropriation of value is by the high and from the low OCC branches. Capital moves from lower to higher OCC branches. This movement causes a decrease in the price of branch II's product and the surplus value appropriated by this branch falls. The actual appropriation of value by II decreases to the level at which, tendentially, all capitals realize the new average rate of profit. This implies no change in social demand.

To sum up, the appropriation of value inherent in the equalization of the rates of profit is always from low by high OCC capitals *only* for modal capitals. For non-modal capitals, that appropriation can also go in the opposite direction (see point 2 above). But the capitals searching for higher rates of profit, that is, the movement determining the equalization of the profit rates, can go either from low to high OCC techniques or vice versa. This holds both for non-modal and for modal capitals. It follows that it is wrong to argue, as even some Marxists do, that the rationality of the capitalist system resides in the fact that capital moves from low OCC techniques to high OCC techniques *across* branches, or that it tends to invest in labour saving branches (technologies) and thus to increase productivity. It is only within branches that capital tends to "save", or to expel, labour and then only when this is a source of higher profits. The equalization of the rates of profit does not reward the branches with higher OCC; rather it is simply the tendential result of capital movement. Capital movement cannot be associated with technological "progress".

Eighth, prices (the prices of production per unit of output) change continuously with changes in the productivity in any capital, as can be seen when capital BI shifts from a non-modal technique in Table 3.4 to a modal technique in Table 3.5. Each individual productivity change affects prices, even though it might take substantial changes in productivity for them to have visible effects on the price structure. This means it is wrong to assume that under conditions of free competition individual capitals have no effect on prices. This is so only apparently, at the empirical level. Marxist analysis shows that one of the fundamental tenets of bourgeois economics is simply wrong.

Ninth, productivity changes can determine a change in the prices of production also because they can cause a change from a modal to a mean productivity (and vice versa). Whether this change occurs or not, the prices of production are a sort of moving target around which the market prices constantly fluctuate.

3.4.6 *Capital movement and partial external exchange*

It has been submitted above that the tendential equalization of the rates of profit is due to free capital movement. In fact, it is only by moving to where higher rates of profit can be realized that capitals (here, for the sake of simplicity, modal capitals) tendentially realize an average rate of profit. But what is the role of free *commodity* movement within this theory?

It is often believed that the condition for the equalization of the profit rates and thus for the formation of production prices is the freedom of movement of commodities, rather than of capital. But, assuming a certain distribution of social demand, if branch A realizes a higher rate of profit than branch B, it will continue doing so in the absence of capital movement from B to A, that is, in the absence of a mechanism which increases supply, and thus decreases prices and profits in A and reduces supply, and increases prices and profits, in B. It is unrestrained capital movement, not free commodity circulation, which is the cause of the tendential equalization of the profit rates and thus of the formation of production prices.

But suppose that not all commodities can be sold across branches. Let us assume that, while all capitals in A and B are free to move across branches, a certain quantity of the product of A, $a1$, must be sold within A and the other quantity, $a2$, must be sold to B. The same holds for the product of B, which is subdivided into $b1$, to be sold internally, and $b2$, which must be sold to A. Let us call this case *partial external exchange* to distinguish it from the case of *full external exchange*, which has been implicitly assumed up to now. In this case, all capitals must realize the same rate of profit, that is, there must be a transfer of value from one branch to another. Suppose that branch A appropriates value from branch B. The specific feature of this case is that this transfer of value must take place through the partial exchange of $a2$ and $b2$. This means that $a2$ must fetch a price higher, and that $b2$ must fetch a price lower, than in the case of full exchange. Commodities $a1$ and $b1$ can only realize their own value. Thus there arise *two prices for the same commodity*, internal and external prices. All capitalists in A sell a part of $a1$ to each other for $a1$'s individual value and a part of $a2$ to B's capitalists for a price (higher than $a2$'s individual value) such that all capitalists in A realize the average rate of profit. Similarly, all capitalists in B sell a part of $b1$ to each other at $b1$'s individual value and a part of $b2$ to A's capitalists at a price (lower than $b2$'s individual value) such that all capitalists in B realize the average rate of profit.

The emergence of two prices for each type of commodity would seem to contradict the principle enunciated in 3.4.1 above according to which all commodities of the same type must tendentially realize the same value. But this principle rests on the assumption that the circulation of commodities between A and B is not limited, that is, that any a can be exchanged for any b. It is precisely this assumption which is relaxed under the hypothesis of partial external exchange. However, all $a1$s must be sold at the same price and all $a2$s must also be sold for the same price, even though the price at which the $a1$s are sold differs from the price realized by the $a2$s. Capital mobility causes the equalization of all capitals' rates of profit and partial external exchange causes two prices for the same commodity to arise, according to whether it is sold internally or externally. The combination of these two conditions requires that these two prices are such that all capitals tendentially realize the average rate of profit. Or, the role of free and full commodity circulation is that of ensuring the equalization of each commodity's price. Partial external exchange excludes the *a*s and *b*s exchanged internally from the process of transfer of value implicit in the formation of production prices.

3.5 The Dynamics of the Transformation Procedure

We can now properly grasp Marx's transformation procedure, the transformation of individual values into prices of production, through the tendential equalization of the rates of profit, as exemplified in Table 3.3.

It should be clear by now that Table 3.3 does not show the actual, or actually realized, situation. This is a common mistake made far too often by Marxist writers as betrayed by the opinion that rates of profit above or below the average are temporary phenomena which will disappear as soon as all these rates of profit differentials will be actually equalized.[29] According to this view, then, the price of production is an empirical reality. But this view does not correspond to the way things actually are: the prices of production per unit of output do not realize themselves as such, they realize themselves only as market prices constantly fluctuating around the prices of production.

It should also be clear that Table 3.3 does not imply a static, equilibrium analysis either. It does depict a situation of *no* capital movement, since all (modal) capitals realize the average rate of profit. They have no incentive to move. But this is not an equilibrium point towards which reality tends. Rather, it is a tendential point of a hypothetical situation extracted from the real situation only for didactic purposes. This calls for a brief discussion of the fundamental difference between a static, or equilibrium, and a dynamic, or dialectical, method of analysis.

If we start from the hypothesis that capital movements can only be understood as deviations from a state of capital immobility towards which reality tends, we employ a static method in which equilibrium informs the whole of the analysis. In this view, to understand disequilibrium we have first of all to understand equilibrium; or, we theorize equilibrium in order to understand lack of equilibrium. This is an obviously absurd, and yet commonly and a-critically accepted, procedure (similar to the Weberian ideal type). The opposite procedure starts from a theorization of lack of equilibrium in order to understand lack of equilibrium, an obviously correct procedure. The way lack of equilibrium in the real world is dialectically perceived is by theorizing reality in terms of tendencies and counter-tendencies. Once this is done, we can focus only on the former as a didactic device.

The *starting point of the inquiry* has been that, in reality, there are both modal capitals (a tendency of the first type) and non-modal capitals (its counter-tendency) and that commodities are not sold at their price of production (a tendency of the third type) but at their market prices (the counter-tendency which reveals the presence of the tendency). In the course of the inquiry the double assumption has been made of both a tendential structure of production (only modal capitals) and of a tendential distribution of social demand (all commodities realize their price of production and these prices are such that all modal capitals realize the average rate of profit). Under these conditions, tendential prices are formed in the absence of capital movement. This is the *result of the inquiry*. Its usefulness resides in the fact that it depicts the simplest case of the redistribution of value inherent in price formation. This is shown in Table 3.3. Thus what is taken to be the normal case is in fact only a very specific case, important only as a heuristic device towards an understanding of a more realistic picture of reality.

Given its simplicity, this result has been chosen as the *starting point of exposition*. We first assume both a tendential structure of production and a tendential distribution, as in Table 3.3. Having understood the price mechanism under these hypothetical conditions (and thus under conditions of no capital movements), we enrich this table by first taking into consideration non-modal capitals, that is, the real structure of production. This is done in Tables 3.4 and 3.5. We now see that under the hypothesis of tendential distribution, that is, of tendential prices, modal capitals tendentially realize the average rate of profit and non-modal capitals tendentially realize a different rate of profit, consonant with their level of productivity. Since there are different tendential rates of profit, capitals move across branches in search of higher profits. Thus *tendential prices, differently from equilibrium prices, are inherently dynamic*; that is, at these prices there is neither capital immobility nor lack of technological innovations. Even if, by chance, $D = S$, that is, even if modal capitals realized the prices of production, these latter would be immediately changed by the action of both modal and below mode capitals searching for higher profits. In short, it is only the exposition, not the analysis, which starts from a situation of no capital movement. The method of inquiry is dynamic and the very opposite of equilibrium analysis. Between a notion of capital immobility as the state towards which reality moves and a notion of capital immobility as a hypothetical case useful only for didactic purposes there is a sea of difference.

If we now drop the $D = S$ hypothesis, we must distinguish between price changes caused by strong changes in social demand and those caused by weak changes in social demand. The former are non self-correcting, the latter are self-correcting (see 3.2.6). The latter cause the fluctuations around the production prices, they are the cause of the actually realized prices, or market prices. Being self-correcting, they could be considered to be similar to price fluctuations in equilibrium analysis. But this similarity is purely formal. Weak changes in social demand do cause *self-correcting* price changes but these latter fluctuate *around non self-correcting* price changes (the changes in the production prices which are the result of non self-correcting changes in the structure of production, of the concomitant non self-correcting, or strong, changes in social demand and thus of the interrelationship between these two types of non self-correcting changes). It is because of this reason, because they are self-correcting fluctuations around non self-correcting price movements (movements in the production prices), that *self-correcting* price fluctuations do not tend towards equilibrium, that they are *not the same as self-equilibrating* price changes. Market prices are part of a dynamic price theory, based on the notion that the economy is endemically in disequilibrium and tends, as we shall see in chapter 5, towards a point where disequilibrium manifests itself as a crisis.

In equilibrium analysis, on the other hand, demand changes can either cause a change in supply or not. The latter are similar to self-correcting price changes due to weak changes in social demand. In case changes in demand do cause changes in supply, a distinction is made between the short-run period, in which supply is adjusted to the new level of demand by increasing or decreasing the utilization of the existing production capacity, and the long-run period, in which production capacity is either increased or decreased, according to the new level of demand. In both cases, in equilibrium analysis, supply adjusts to the new level of demand and reaches a new equilibrium level. Put differently, equilibrium price analysis is static because the only type of movement is a movement around a static situation. Movement does not touch the essence of reality. Stasis is primary, movement is secondary, and equilibrium is the regulatory principle of price formation. However, in reality, strong changes in social demand cause changes in the structure of production and these in their turn cause changes in social demand in a continuous interaction and modification in which the notion of equilibrium has no meaning.

The dogma that the economy tends towards equilibrium, that is, that changes in demand cause equilibrating changes in supply and that, if demand and supply were really in equilibrium, capital movements would stop, has no scientific value whatsoever. Unfortunately it has shaped, and continues to shape, the minds of generations of economists who, because of this dogma, cannot understand that changes in demand cause non self-equilibrating changes in supply (and vice versa) and that, even if supply and demand were fortuitously equal, capital movement and technological innovations would immediately upset this situation.

3.6 The Transformation Debate

As we have seen in Table 3.3, Marx transforms individual values into prices of production by adding to constant capital and variable capital of the modal capitals the average rate of profit. This procedure has been the object of much misunderstanding and debate since von Böhm-Bawerk's critique of the third volume of *Capital* in 1896 (1973). This section reviews the two most influential lines of critique, the circularity and the infinite regression critiques, both of neo-Ricardian matrix.

In itself, the neo-Ricardian critique is weak. However, a review of its arguments is important both because it has been accepted as valid by a vast number of authors and because the discussion of those arguments will provide an opportunity for the clarification of two important points. First, I shall set out in detail the dialectical nature of Marx's procedure, since it is my conviction that it is impossible to properly understand Marx's transformation procedure unless one gains a firm grasp of its dialectical nature. Second, I shall discuss the effects of technological change on the value of those products which have already entered the following production process as inputs.

3.6.1 The circularity critique

This is perhaps the best-known line of critique. It was originated by von Böhm-Bawerk in 1896 (1973) which, with the reply by Hilferding (1973) and the contribution by von Bortkiewicz (1973), was brought to the attention of a wide readership in the Anglo-Saxon world by Sweezy's classical work (1942). Basically, the circularity critique argues that, in the computation of the prices of production, "the capitalists' outlays on constant and variable capital are left exactly as they were in the value scheme; in other words, the constant capital and the variable capital used in production are still used in value terms" (Sweezy, 1942, p. 115). This has been formulated in modern terminology as follows: inputs are expressed as values (individual values, in our terminology) but outputs are expressed as prices of production. This is a logical flaw, since the same commodity is bought as an input and sold as an output at the same price.

In terms of Table 3.3, branch I sells its products at 120 (the price of production) but these products are bought at their not yet transformed value, for 80 by branch I, for 90 by branch II and for 70 by branch

III. These products are sold at 120 but bought at 240. This discrepancy, it is argued, is due to a logical inconsistency in Marx's transformation procedure, since in that procedure the same commodities are bought as inputs at their (not yet transformed) values but sold as outputs at their price of production (transformed value). By far the most influential solution to this problem is that offered by von Bortkiewicz (1973).

Von Bortkiewicz's solution, reduced to its essentials, assumes a situation of simple reproduction, given the three sectors of Table 3.3:

$$c_1 + v_1 + s_1 = V_1$$
$$c_2 + v_2 + s_2 = V_2$$
$$c_3 + v_3 + s_3 = V_3$$

where c, v, s and V are respectively the constant capital, variable capital, surplus value and total value of each branch and where each of the subscript numerals refers to each branch. If demand equals supply

$$c_1 + v_1 + s_1 = V_1 = c_1 + c_2 + c_3$$
$$c_2 + v_2 + s_2 = V_2 = v_1 + v_2 + v_3$$
$$c_3 + v_3 + s_3 = V_3 = s_1 + s_2 + s_3$$

The assumption is then made that with the transformation of values into prices of production the price of the products of branch I becomes x times greater than their value, that of the products of branch II y times and that of the products of branch III z times. If we call the average rate of profit in price terms r, then the model of simple reproduction transformed in prices of production becomes

$$c_1x + v_1y + r(c_1x + v_1y) = (c_1 + c_2 + c_3)x$$
$$c_2x + v_2y + r(c_2x + v_2y) = (v_1 + v_2 + v_3)y$$
$$c_3x + v_3y + r(c_3x + v_3y) = (s_1 + s_2 + s_3)z$$

Von Bortkiewicz thus obtains three equations with four unknowns (x, y, z and r). In terms of mathematics, to solve this system we must supply a fourth equation. In terms of economics, this means that we must choose between two equally undesirable solutions. Either we assume, as the fourth equation, that the total of prices equals the total of values, but then the equality between surplus value and profits is not respected any more; or our fourth equation is the equality of the total of profits and the total of surplus value, but then the total of prices and of values does not coincide any more. The two equalities do not hold, in general, at the same time.[30] After von Bortkiewicz many other authors have worked out improved, or more complete, equally "consistent" solutions which, however, all share the same characteristic of severing either the equality between prices and values or that between surplus value and profits.

The consequences are far reaching. If the former equality does not hold, it makes no sense any more to speak of "transformation" of values into prices. If the latter equality does not hold, profits no longer necessarily come from surplus value and the theory of exploitation is dealt a fatal blow. Both conclusions are very grave for the Marxist theory of value. However, there is no reason to be concerned. What we have here is a pseudo-problem.

3.6.2 The fallacy of the circularity critique

Let us assume that the output of a certain process immediately enters a new production process as an input. Labour power is temporarily excluded from the present discussion because of its specific feature of not being the product of a capitalist production process. It will be dealt with later on. Here, only the inputs and outputs of capitalist production processes are considered. Therefore, outputs can be both means of production and means of subsistence, while inputs can only be means of production. Thus a commodity which is both an input and an output must be a means of production. The discussion that follows will focus on means of production, unless differently stated.

Suppose that A is the output of a process P_1 which starts at time t_0 and ends at t_1 and also an input of a process P_2 which starts at t_1 and ends at t_2 and which results in the production of B. This is depicted in Figure 3.2.

Here, the social value of A *as an output* is tendentially realized at t_1 and is thus expressed as its price of production at that moment. Therefore A is sold as an output of P_1 and bought as an input of P_2 at that price. There has been a production of value and of surplus value during the $t_0 - t_1$ period and a redistribution of that surplus value at the moment

Figure 3.2 The chronological sequence of two production processes

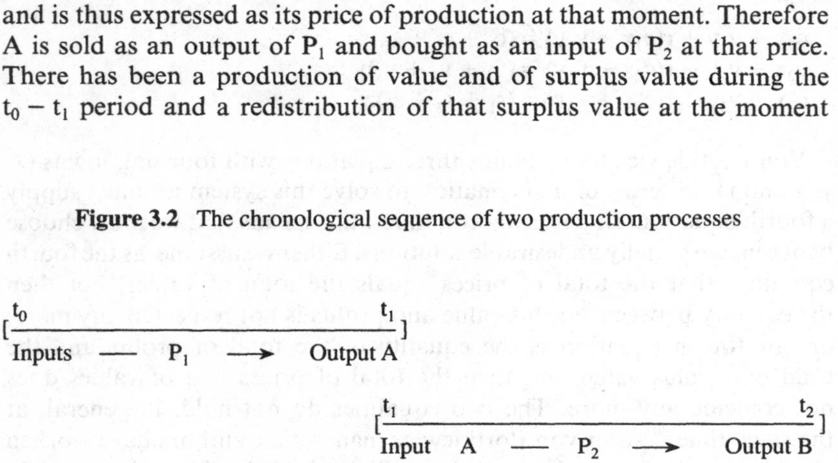

92

t_1. Now a new process starts and A enters P_2 as an input. The product of P_2, B, tendentially realizes its social value at t_2. The question now is: will the social value of A *as an input* of P_2 remain the same or will it not instantaneously change at the moment it enters the new production process P_2?

Suppose that the producer of B has used a greater quantity, or a more expensive quality, of A than is socially necessary, that is, needed by B's modal production process. As far as A is concerned, the value of B is given only by the socially necessary quantity and quality of A. The real process which ensures this is, of course, capitalist (price) competition. What the market tendentially gives the producer of B is not only a rate of profit proportional to his or her productivity (the average rate of profit, it will be recalled, is tendentially realized only by modal capitals) but also the average value of A, the average value of the inputs. As Marx puts it:

> Though the capitalists have a hobby, and use a gold instead of a steel spindle, yet the only labour that counts for anything in the value of the yarn is that which would be required to produce a steel spindle, because no more is necessary under the given social conditions. (Marx, 1967a, p. 188)

This case is similar to the one in which B's producer uses the socially necessary quantity and quality of A, but A's modal production process changes between t_1 and t_2. Here too, the value of A going into the value of B is not the value at which A has been bought at t_1 but the value A has at time t_2. If, in this period, A has become either cheaper or more expensive, the value of B will accordingly be either reduced or increased. Again, this will be brought about by capitalist (price) competition.

Once the transformation process is seen as a real process, and thus as a sequence of real processes, it becomes clear that the social value of A as an output of P_1 enters the new production process P_2 as the individual value of A as an input. But the social value of A as an input of B will be determined only at the moment of exchange of B, at t_2. *At t_1, A has both a social value* (the value at which it is bought and sold, that is, the price of production) *as the output of P_1 and an individual value* (the potential social value which will realize itself only at t_2) *as an input of P_2.* Thus the moment at which A tendentially realizes its social value as an output (t_1) is not the moment at which it realizes its social value as an input (t_2).

In short, individual values are only potentially social values and tendentially realize themselves as social values only at the moment of exchange. This holds both for the social value of outputs, which tendentially realize themselves at the moment at which they are exchanged, and for the social value of inputs, which tendentially realize themselves at the moment the

Figure 3.3 The superimposition of two production processes

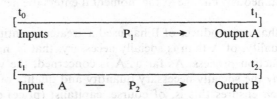

output of which they are inputs realizes itself.

The mistake inherent in the circularity critique is thus clear. This approach collapses two periods ($t_0 - t_1$ and $t_1 - t_2$) into just one, as Figure 3.3 makes clear.

Since two production processes and two moments of realization are collapsed into one, the illusion is created that, in Marx's transformation procedure, A is exchanged at both its social value and at its individual value at t_1. But only the social value of A as an output tendentially realizes itself at t_1; its social value as an input tendentially realizes itself at t_2. The individual value of A does *not* realize itself as such, it realizes itself only as social value, and thus either at t_1 (as an output) or at t_2 (as an input). Or, the individual values are the *potential*, not yet realized, social values and the prices of production are the tendentially *realized* social values, the average form taken by the individual values at the moment of, and through, exchange. The *individual value* is thus the value a commodity has before being sold, including the value it has immediately after production.

The circularity critique thus makes a double mistake. On the one hand it considers as a chronological sequence what in fact is a chronologically contemporaneous process (the realization of individual values as social values). On the other hand, it considers as a chronologically contemporaneous process what is in fact a chronological sequence (the realization of the social value of A as an output and as an input). In reality, however, the value of A can appear only in its tendentially realized, social form and the moment of its realization as an output is different from the moment of its realization as an input. Consequently, the value of the inputs in Table 3.3 cannot be their individual value. In short, c and v appear in Table 3.3 as already transformed values, as production prices of the previous production process which are also the individual values of the inputs of the new production process.[31]

To sum up, the circularity critique shows a remarkable ignorance of

Marxist methodology. It does not see the dialectical nature of the relation between individual and social values. It does not see that the value of a commodity does not realize itself first as an individual value (of the commodity as an input) and then as a social value (of the same commodity as an output). Rather, individual values realize themselves *as* social values so that a commodity, as an output, realizes its social value at the moment of its sale and, as an input, realizes its social value at the moment of the sale of the output of which that particular commodity is an input. The dialectics of the realization of value is, in the last analysis, the transformation of individual values into social values at the moment of exchange, that is, at the end of that production process; their transformation back into individual values when those products enter a new production process as inputs; and their transformation anew into social values when the output of which they are inputs is exchanged (sold).

The question which remains to be answered concerns the practical relevance of the change in the individual value of the inputs in the period during which they are transformed into the output. If all the social value of the means of production is transferred to the value of the product in just one production process, it is unlikely that the individual value of these inputs diverges from their social value, due to changes in the branch of production producing them. But if the means of production are used for more production processes, the individual value of these means of production can diverge from their social value during the period starting with the beginning of the first production period and ending with the termination of the last production period using those means of production. The longer this period, the more likely a change in the value of the means of production, that is, a difference between their individual and their social value as inputs. One striking example is provided by IBM, which – under the pressure of competition – cut its computer workstation prices, on May 8, 1991, by up to 60% (Kehoe, 1991). Those capitalists who had paid $130,000 for a machine which is now sold for $52,500 will be able to charge only this last amount for the remainder of that machine's life cycle.

But, more importantly, as we have seen above, a productivity change in *any* capital (for example, BI in Table 3.5) causes a change in the social value of all commodities (since it changes the price of production per unit of capital and thus per unit of output). It follows that, quantitatively, the individual value of all inputs equals their social value *only in the case of lack of technological change in the whole economy*, rather than only in the branches producing those inputs. This quantitative equality is then just a theoretical curiosity. Moreover, even if there were a quantitative equality, there would still be a qualitative difference between the individual and the social value of the inputs and thus a qualitative transformation of the former into the latter at the moment of the output's sale.[32]

3.6.3 The infinite regression critique

But, it is argued, if the inputs (A in the case of P_2 in Figure 3.2) are expressed as realized, social value, if they are prices of production, then to compute the price of production of A we must go back to the previous production process which produced A and from there to the previous one, thus falling into infinite regression. As J. Robinson put it:

> the constant capital was produced in the past by labour-time working with then pre-existing constant capital and so on, *ad infinitum* backwards. It therefore cannot be reduced simply to a number of labour hours that can be added to the net value of the current year. And there is no advantage in trying to do so. (Robinson, 1972, p. 202)

It does not take much to see that, if this critique were sound, it would mean the bankruptcy not only of Marx's transformation procedure but also of social science in all its versions, including the neo-Ricardian one. This critique, in fact, would have to apply to any social phenomenon inasmuch as it is determined by other phenomena, both present and past. Social sciences, then, would become an endless quest for the starting point of the inquiry. Fortunately, however, our predicament is not as gloomy as Marx's critics incautiously represent it. The reason is that the choice of the starting point depends upon the scope and purpose of our research. If we want to determine the value of B, then it is perfectly justified to take the value of A as given. If, for whatever reasons, we wanted to determine the value of A as well, we would have to take the value of its inputs as given. Infinite regression is a figment of neo-Ricardian imagination.

The neo-Ricardian theorists think they can escape their own critique by computing the labour contents of physical inputs through the "reduction to dated quantities of labour", that is, through "an operation by which in the equation of a commodity the different means of production used are replaced with a series of quantities of labour, each with its appropriate 'date'" (Sraffa, 1960, p. 34). For example, the "reduction equation" of product A has the following form (Sraffa, 1960, p. 35):

$$L_aw + L_{a1}w(1 + r) + \ldots + L_{an}w(1 + r)^n = Ap_a$$

Here, the first term (L_aw) indicates the labour expended in the production of commodity A times the wage paid to it. The second term, $L_{a1}w(1 + r)$, indicates the inputs expressed in labour terms. Since these inputs have been the product of labour in the previous period, they are equal to the labour needed to produce those inputs in the previous period times the wage ($L_{a1}w$) plus the rate of profit on these inputs so computed (r times $L_{a1}w$). By so doing, we can compute the inputs needed to produce those inputs two production periods ago, and so on. The term $L_{an}w(1 + r)^n$ indicates the inputs expressed in labour terms in the nth period back in time plus the rate of profit on those inputs so computed.

But this procedure is far from being immune from the "infinite regression" critique. Sraffa seems to think that the further back we go, the smaller will be the "commodity residue", that is, that part of the inputs expressed in physical terms, and thus the bigger will be that part of the inputs expressed in labour terms. In this case, the question becomes one of "how far the reduction need be pushed in order to obtain a given degree of approximation" (Sraffa, 1960). The point, however, is that it is simply not true that the "commodity residue" becomes smaller as we retrace the labour content of the physical inputs in the more and more distant production processes. Every time we make such a step back we compute the labour content not of a *decreasing physical residue of the inputs of this process but of the physical inputs of the previous production process*. And this means quite simply that this procedure too falls into the "infinite regression" trap. In any case, even if this method did find smaller and smaller physical residues, or greater and greater labour contents, of the means of production, this quantity would not be the social value of the means of production as inputs: this is given by their cost of reproduction at the time the output is sold.

3.6.4 A last misunderstanding

Occasionally, the objection is raised that in Table 3.3 the value of the outputs does not correspond with the value of the inputs needed for the production process to start anew on the same scale. For example, branch I produces and realizes a value of 120. This is its output which becomes the inputs of all three branches in the next production process. However, the inputs must have a social value of 240. Branch I, then, produces less than what is needed by the economy for the next production process. This, of course, has nothing to do with the transformation problem. This quantitative inconsistency is due to the fact that each branch is represented by one unit of capital instead of displaying the actual, or absolute, amount of capital invested. It is clear then that, given that structure of the economy, branch I would have to employ more units of capital per each unit of capital invested by the other two branches. To take another example, let us suppose the following two sectors:

I $73.3c + 26.7v + 26.7s = 126.7$

II $\underline{60.0c + 40.0v + 40.0s = 140.0}$

    133.3c   66.7v   66.7s   266.7

where sector I produces means of production and sector II produces means of consumption. After the equalization of the profit rates, each sector realizes 133.3. Sector I realizes a value of 133.3 for its means of production which also is approximately the social value of the means of production needed by both sectors in the next production process $(73.3 + 60)$. Similarly, sector II realizes a value of 133.3 for its means of consumption and this also is approximately the social value of the means of consumption needed by both sectors in the next production process $(66.7 + 66.7)$.

3.7 The Complete Notion of Production Price

It follows from 3.6.2 that (a) given a certain output, the social value of the inputs is their cost of reproduction at the time the output is sold (time t_2 in Figure 3.2) and (b) this cost of reproduction is the price of production of similar inputs, also at the time the output is sold.

3.7.1 Individual and social values

We can now sum up Marx's notion of the individual and social value of a commodity.

1. The individual value of a commodity is the value it has before being sold, but after production. Therefore, its computation must be carried out immediately before sale.

2. The social value of a commodity, or price of production per unit of output, is the value society assigns to it at the moment of sale. Therefore, its computation must be carried out at that moment.

A commodity can be either an input or an output. In both cases, it has both an individual and a social value. Therefore:

3. The individual value of an input is equal to the price which has been paid for it. This, at this level of analysis, is its price of production per unit of output when it is bought.

4. The individual value of an output is equal to the individual value of its inputs plus the surplus value actually generated during its production.

5. The social value of an input is its cost of reproduction, or the price

of production per unit of output of similar inputs, at the time the output is sold.

6. The social value of an output is the value of the modal commodity, or the price of production per unit of output. This is equal to the price of production per unit of capital divided by the modal output. In its turn, the price of production per unit of capital is equal to the social value of the inputs used by the modal producer plus the average rate of profit. If this commodity enters the next production process as an input, this social value becomes the individual value of the same commodity as an input (see point 3).

A point of clarification can now be made. We have seen in chapter 2 that labour is always both concrete and abstract. Concrete labour transfers the value of the means of production to the product. This is their individual value, their price of production at the time they are sold. For example, if a machine's price of production is equal to 100,000 and if each hour of concrete labour consumes one hundredth of that machine's use value (if that machine is completely used up in a thousand hours), each hour of concrete labour transfers a value of one hundred to the product. However, at the time of the output's sale, the value of the means of production counts as their cost of reproduction. If there is a discrepancy between individual and social value, those capitalists whose means of production have lost (or gained) value lose (or gain) value to (from) other capitalists when the products are exchanged (sold). It is through this redistribution of value among capitalists that the individual value of the means of production is transformed into their social value.

Abstract labour creates new value, first the value of labour power and then surplus value. Since the value of labour power is the value of the means of subsistence, the individual value of labour power as an input is the price of production of the socially necessary means of subsistence at the time labour power is bought. The social value of labour power as an input is the cost of reproduction of the means of subsistence at the time the output is sold. It should be recalled that labour power differs from other commodities in that the quantity and quality of the means of subsistence change in accord with what society deems necessary for the labourers to reproduce themselves. Thus the individual value of labour power as an input is modified not only by changes in the cost of reproduction of that basket of wage goods but also by changes in the composition of that basket at the time the product is sold. This is the value which must be created by abstract labour before it can create surplus value. If the individual value of labour power as an input differs from its social value, there is a redistribution of the newly created value between the value of labour power and surplus value. It is through this redistribution between capitalists and labourers that the individual value of labour power is transformed into its social value.

It follows that, contrary to what is commonly believed, the redistribution of value inherent in the sale of the product, or the transformation of individual into social values, encompasses not only the redistribution of surplus value among capitalists as a result of the tendential equalization of the rates of profit. It also encompasses (a) a change in the value of the means of production, if their individual value as inputs differs from their social value; and (b) a change in the value of labour power, if the individual value of a basket of wage goods at the time labour power is bought differs from the social value of a possibly modified basket of wage goods at the time the product is sold. The former is a redistribution of value among capitalists, the latter is a redistribution between capitalists and labourers. *The transformation process, or the process of price formation, is a redistribution of value affecting all three components of a commodity's value*, not only the surplus value created during its production. It is not only a process of redistribution of surplus value among capitalists; it is also a process of redistribution of value both among capitalists and between capitalists and labourers.

3.7.2 Two common misunderstandings

It is commonly believed that for Marx the individual value is the value embodied in a commodity, meaning the labour which has been actually needed to produce it, and that the social value of that commodity should be equal to this individual value. In other words, the value realized by a commodity (a part of societal labour) should be equal to the value actually created during its production (the labour actually expended). Nothing could be further from the truth.

First of all, *individual values are not values embodied*. It is impossible to compute the labour actually needed to produce the means of production and of subsistence without falling into the backward *ad infinitum* trap. The individual value of the inputs is already transformed: it is the price of production of the means of production and the social value of labour power (which depends on the price of production of the means of subsistence considered as necessary for the reproduction of labour power) at the time they enter the production process. Value embodied is not only a notion alien to Marxist price theory, it is also a quantity which cannot be known. However, if value embodied cannot be known, the individual and social value *can* be known and measured, once we start from a given social value of the means of production and of labour power. The other critique, that value is a metaphysical concept because "it cannot be observed" (Sawyer, 1989, p. 226), can be easily disposed of once we realize that, for example, electricity is not observable either and yet is anything but a metaphysical concept. Second, the individual value is equal to the social value only by way of exception. This is the case of those modal capitals which have an OCC equal to the average (e.g. capital AII in Table 3.4), if the change in the value of the means of production and of labour power as a consequence of the equalization of the profit rates is disregarded.

One reason for commonly identifying Marx's notion of individual value with that of labour embodied might be that traditionally the term "value embodied" has been used to translate two quite different concepts. On the one hand, Marx uses expressions such as "Wertding", "verkörperter Wert", "Wertkörper", or simply "Körper" to indicate the physical body in which labour is materialized. These terms are translated as "value embodied". For example, in discussing the exchange of two commodities, 20 yards of linen for one coat, Marx points out that they exchange in that proportion because the value of 20 yards of linen is equal to that of one coat. The linen is the relative form of value, the coat the equivalent form of value. The coat is "the mode of existence" of the value of the linen, its "value embodied" (Marx, 1967a, p. 50). The coat "as equivalent of the linen ... counts ... as embodied value, as *body* that is value" (p. 51, emphasis added, G.C.). Or, "the value of the commodity linen is expressed by the *bodily form* of the commodity coat" (p. 52, emphasis added, G.C.); "the *use value* coat, as opposed to the linen, figures as an embodiment of value" (p. 56, emphasis added, G.C.); "*use value* becomes the form of manifestation, the phenomenal form, of its opposite, value" (ibid., emphasis added, G.C.), it is the "incarnation of abstract human labour" (p. 76), "the form of manifestation of the value of commodities" (p. 89), etc.

In short, in all these cases, the translation "value embodied" is used to refer to the *use value* which serves as the embodiment of a certain quantity of exchange value, not to the *exchange value* contained in that use value. For this latter concept Marx uses other terms, such as "enthalten" (contained) labour. But these terms too have been translated as "embodied labour". It is the combining of these two opposite meanings in the term "value embodied" which is one of the likely sources of confusion.[33]

A second mistaken belief is that production prices are the labour socially necessary to *produce* commodities, that is, only by the structure of production. Again, this is wrong. Production prices are determined both by the structure of production and by the distribution of (strong shifts in) social demand. As 4.7.1 below will make clear, the notion that production prices are solely determined by socially necessary labour time, understood as only technically determined, is a Ricardian, rather than a Marxist, one. In other words, *the socially necessary labour time is not found directly by computing how many hours are technically needed by the modal producers.* This would exclude the role played by social demand. Rather, it is given by the equalization of the rates of profit into an average rate which is tendentially realized only by the modal producers. This presupposes the active role of social demand, inherent in the D = S assumption. Once this computation has been carried out, it is possible to compute how many hours of labour are expended for the production of, and are appropriated by, each commodity. This computation will be carried out in 3.7.4. Here it suffices to stress that it is this socially necessary labour time (or price of production in labour terms) per unit of output which explains why a certain use value, which incorporates a certain socially necessary labour time, is exchanged for a multiple (or a fraction) of a different use value which incorporates the same socially necessary labour time.

3.7.3 What is value?

Often one runs into expressions such as surplus value being "produced by labour" (Castells, 1980, p. 45), as labour being "the substance of value", etc. Used in a figurative sense, these expressions are acceptable. However, taken a-critically, they can be used to support an idea of value as being something endowed with a reality of its own, possibly even a physical reality. This interpretation is mistaken and rests on a confusion between concrete and abstract labour, between use value and (exchange) value.

Let us recall, from chapter 2, that labour is both concrete and abstract. As concrete labour, it creates new use values. In this sense, the use of the term "creates" is justified. But labour is also abstract, in the sense of expenditure of human energy, irrespective of the specific tasks performed. In this sense we cannot say that (abstract) labour creates (exchange) value. Value is *not* created by (abstract) labour. Value *is* labour; it is abstract labour performed under capitalist production relations and which must express itself as money. Moreover, if the distinction between productive and unproductive labour is introduced, we must add the further specification that value is abstract labour transforming, as concrete labour, use values. Value is the product of labour *power*, or the expenditure of labour power as abstract labour.

Put in different words, value is a category developed to understand the production of wealth *for* the capitalist class *by* the labourers. Value is a historically specific and thus a *socially specific* concept. This holds both for individual and for social value, for value both before and after it is redistributed through the price mechanism, since value expresses a relationship between classes typical of a specific historical period. Ultimately, value expresses the fact that capitalism is first and foremost the appropriation of labour (when the labourers do not own the means of production but are the owners of their own labour-power) and that the production of use values is only a means for such an appropriation.

Notice that abstract labour is a category of thought which corresponds to something real, to the expenditure of human energy irrespective of the specific forms of activity carried out (concrete labours). The abstraction from these specific forms of activity is made in order to focus on what all these forms have in common, e.g. consumption of proteins, calories, etc., in order to focus on a real process. The concept of abstract labour, therefore, is different from the concept of, say, fruit. This latter merely serves to subsume under one category different objects, such as peaches and melons. The concept of fruit has no reality of its own (there is no such thing as fruit). The concept of abstract labour, on the contrary, does have a reality of its own, that part of reality we focus on when we analyse the exertion of human energy without taking into consideration its specific forms. Abstract labour must manifest itself as social value, as value quantitatively transformed, at the moment of exchange, but it already exists at the level of production. Actually, it can manifest itself at the level of exchange only because it exists before being exchanged.

An alternative interpretation (generally referred to as the "value-form" interpretation) stresses that it is the act of exchange which reduces the different use values to a common ground, that of also being (having) exchange value (see, e.g., Reuten, 1988, p. 52). In this view, abstract labour "constitutes itself at the moment of", or "is grounded in", exchange. This view denies reality to abstract labour before exchange and reduces Marx's notion of abstract labour, a concept Marx grounds in production, to an abstraction with no reality of its own (just like the notion of fruit). It follows that individual values are denied reality and only social values are said to exist. The transformation "problem" then vanishes but with it also vanishes the possibility to develop a Marxist price theory, which is based solely on that transformation.

One more point must be made in this connection. The abstract labour which goes into the value of a product is not only the labour carried out in the present production period but is also the abstract labour carried out in the previous period. This latter is incorporated in this period's means of production. As we have seen in this chapter, the value transferred to the value of this period's product counts as the abstract labour which would be socially necessary to produce the means of production at the moment the product is sold and, as we have seen in chapter 2, this value is transferred through *concrete* labour. Or, the labour which is value (abstract labour) is not the same as the labour which transfers value (concrete labour). This is another reason why the value of a product cannot be said to be created by abstract labour. Even if value were created by abstract labour, it would be the new value which is so created: the other part of the product's value is transferred by concrete labour.

If all these qualifications are kept in mind, the expressions "value is created by abstract labour" and "labour is the substance of value" can be used as convenient, but imprecise, short-cuts.

3.7.4 Production price and socially necessary labour time

It has been submitted above that the socially necessary labour time (SNLT) can be found only after the rates of profit have been equalized. Let us now engage in this computation. First of all, to hold that value is abstract labour (with the above-mentioned qualifications) does not imply that the total *new* value is equal to the total number of hours actually worked. In fact, hours of higher than average intensity or of skilled labour create more value than hours of average intensity or of unskilled labour. Yet value can be measured in terms of labour hours once above or below intensity labour is reduced to average intensity labour and skilled labour is reduced to unskilled labour. For example, given a certain average intensity of labour, one hour of labour of double intensity is equal to two hours of labour of average intensity. Or, given the value of the unskilled labourers' labour power, one hour of skilled labour expended by a labour power whose value is twice the value of unskilled labour's labour power, is equal to two hours of unskilled labour and counts as (because is) twice as much value. Both the value produced by different levels of intensity and the value produced by different levels of skills can be quantified: the former by measuring e.g. the rapidity of certain movements, the latter by measuring the value of labour power. In the previous pages as well as in what follows, therefore, the computation assumes homogeneous hours, hours of unskilled labour of average intensity.

Let us begin by computing the *individual* value of a commodity in terms of labour hours, starting from money quantities. We know the total value produced in the previous period expressed in money (M_0) and the price of production of the means of production also expressed in money (PP_0). The percentage of the latter relative to the former, then, is $z = PP_0/M_0$. If we know the total of homogeneous labour hours expended in the previous period (TL_0), the SNLT incorporated in these inputs is z times TL_0. This computation applies also to labour power. Its value is given by the price of production of those goods (of a certain quantity and quality) deemed necessary for the reproduction of the labourers at the time labour power is bought. Let us call the price of production of these goods in money terms PL_0. Then, for labour power $y = PL_0/M_0$. By multiplying y by TL_0, we obtain the SNLT incorporated in the wage goods. This is also the number of homogeneous labour hours the labourers have to work in order to reproduce the value of their labour power. Given the length of the working day, the remaining labour hours are surplus labour expended to produce that commodity. By adding these three components, we obtain the individual value of the commodity in terms of labour.

Let us now compute the *social* value of that commodity also in terms of labour, under the simplifying assumption that the SNLT incorporated in the inputs does not change. Since we know the average rate of profit in terms of money, we know the surplus value realized (s*) by that commodity, also in terms of money. This is a percentage of total value (M_1), again in terms of money, or $j = s*/M_1$. Since we also know the total labour expended in this period (TL_1), the surplus labour corresponding to s* is j times TL_1. By adding this number to the SNLT incorporated in the inputs, we get the labour time socially necessary to produce that commodity. The difference between the labour time incorporated in the commodity before and after the equalization of the rates of profit gives the gain or loss of labour inherent in the price mechanism, or unequal exchange of labour. Under the assumption of capital mobility, the labour time socially necessary to produce a commodity is its price of production.

3.7.5 Value and full automation

What has been said above allows us to understand why machines do not produce value. If value is abstract labour performed by labourers under capitalist relations of production, the less labour is expended the less value is created, by definition. This becomes clear in the hypothetical case of a fully automated economy. In this case, machines could not create value or surplus value, they could only transform use values. In fact, the non-owners of the means of production would cease to exist as labourers and capitalists could sell their different products (use values) only to each other. But then value, the expenditure of labour by a class for another class, would cease to exist. Capitalists would cease to exist too and would become producers of use values both for their own consumption and for exchange. Since value is a socially specific concept, based on the existence of two categories of agents of production, if one category, the labourers, disappears, the other category, the capitalists and their agents, disappears too: the owners of the means of production cease to be capitalists and become independent producers. The advent of a fully automated economy would mean the end of capitalism, but it would not necessarily mark the birth of socialism.

3.8 Some Further Aspects of a Marxist Theory of Prices

The approach outlined above rests on a number of simplifying assumptions. Some of them can now be relaxed. Sections 3.6 and 3.7 have already
dropped the assumption that technological change does not affect the
value of the inputs before the output is sold. Let us now consider some
further cases.

3.8.1 Production prices and purchasing power

In Table 3.3, after the equalization of the profit rates, all three branches
sell their output for the same price (120), independently of its individual
value. All three branches have sufficient purchasing power to buy each
other's products. But this is only so by chance. For example, in Table
3.5, branches A and C sell their product at 351.8 but branch B sells
its output at 371.4. In this case, for sufficient purchasing power to be
generated, the former two branches have to invest more than one unit
of capital per each unit of capital invested by branch B. This chapter
will not examine the question as to whether sufficient purchasing power
is generated by each branch after that purchasing power has been redistributed through the price mechanism. Here, it is sufficient to compute the
production prices under the assumption that each capital invests only
one unit of capital.

3.8.2 Production prices and absolute values

Up to now production prices have been computed on percentage values,
that is, the sum of c and v has always been assumed to be equal to
100. Let us now consider the computation of production prices when
c and v are absolute values. Take the example in Table 3.6 depicting
three branches represented by three modal capitals. The average rate of
profit is $120/760 = 15.8\%$. Tendentially, each branch (modal capital) must
realize 15.8 per unit of capital. Or, given that branches A, B, and C

Table 3.6 Production prices computed on absolute values

	c	v	s	V	Output
Branch A	270	20	20	310	50
Branch B	200	40	40	280	60
Branch C	170	60	60	290	70
Total	640	120	120	880	

invest respectively 2.9, 2.4 and 2.3 units of capital, tendentially the *surplus value* realized by each branch is

A $15.8 \times 2.9 = 45.82$
B $15.8 \times 2.4 = 37.92$
C $15.8 \times 2.3 = 36.34.$

The total is $45.82 + 37.92 + 36.34 = 120$, or the total surplus value available for redistribution. Tendentially, the *total value* realized by each branch is

A $270 + 20 + 45.82 = 335.82$
B $200 + 40 + 37.92 = 277.92$
C $170 + 60 + 36.34 = 266.34.$

The total is $335.82 + 277.92 + 266.34 = 880$, or the total value available for redistribution. Tendentially, the value realized by each type of commodity is

A $335.82/50 = 6.72$
B $277.92/60 = 4.63$
C $266.34/70 = 3.80$

Now the $D = S$ assumption means that social demand is such that all commodities are sold at a price at which each modal capital tendentially realizes a profit equal to the average rate of profit *times the units of capital invested*. Below and above mode capitals (not shown in Table 3.6) realize less and more than this average rate of profit by selling their output at the prices just computed. If the value to be realized differs from the value available for redistribution, a distributional ratio must be applied. The assumption that all capitals invest one unit of capital is thus a simplification of reality which can be easily removed without affecting the results. It is for this reason that it has been made and it is for the same reason that it will be retained in the remainder of this work.

3.8.3 Production prices and capital used

Another assumption which has been made throughout this chapter is that all the constant capital is used in the production process. Usually, however, constant capital is subdivided into constant *circulating* capital (e.g. raw materials), which is used up in one production cycle, and constant *fixed* capital (e.g. buildings and machinery) which is used in more than one production process. Let us then consider the computation of the production prices under these conditions. Consider the example in Table

Table 3.7 Production prices computed on capital used

	K	c	v	s	V^k	V^c	Output
Branch A	270	180	20	20	310	220	50
Branch B	200	160	40	40	280	240	60
Branch C	170	140	60	60	290	260	70
Total	640	480	120	120	880	720	

3.7, where K indicates the total constant capital invested, c indicates only that part of constant capital used to produce that output, V^k is the value of the output when all constant capital (K) is used up, and V^c is the value of the product when only a part of constant capital (c) is used up. Here the average rate of profit is again $s/(K + v) = 120/(760) = 15.8\%$. The use of K rather than c in the denominator reflects the fact that, even though only c is used in the present production process, K is needed to activate v and to produce s. This is perceived by the capitalists, whose decision to invest in one branch rather than another depends on the rate of profit they make on the total capital invested $(K + v)$. It is this consideration which determines capital mobility across branches. The tendential situation in which all capitals realize the same rate of profit must then be computed on the total capital invested by each capitalist, and not only on the capital used in that production process.

However, if only part of the constant capital invested is used (c), modal capitalists can charge for their products only the constant and variable capital actually used $(c + v)$. Thus, each branch realizes $(c + v)$ plus the average rate of profit, computed on total capital, times the units of capital invested. If p^* is the average rate of profit computed as total surplus value divided by total $(K + v)$, and u is the units of capital invested, the value tendentially realized by each branch, here represented by a modal capital, is

$c + v + (p^* . u)$

and the value tendentially realized in each branch is

A   realizes $180 + 20 + 45.82 = 245.82$
B   realizes $160 + 40 + 37.92 = 237.92$
C   realizes $140 + 60 + 36.34 = 236.34$

for a total of 720, which is equal to V^c. The prices tendentially realized by each commodity are $245.82/50 = 4.92$ for A; $237.92/60 = 3.96$ for B and $236.34/70 = 3.38$ for C. Again, non-modal capitals within branches are not shown here but can be easily introduced along the lines suggested above.

The specific feature of this case is that, in order to arrive at the price of production, the rate of profit is computed on the total capital *invested*, and this rate of profit (multiplied by the units of capital invested) is added to the capital *used* in the production process. But whether the whole or only part of the capital invested is used, the rate of profit which guides the capitalists to move to those branches where the realized rate of profit is higher is the one computed by dividing the profit they realize by the total capital they have invested.

As in the previous subsection, the hypothesis that only part of constant capital is used in a certain production cycle, that is, that not only circulating capital but also fixed capital is used, can be dropped without altering the results reached in this chapter. The simple case in which all capital is circulating capital is thus to be preferred for didactic reasons and will be kept throughout this work.

3.8.4 Production prices and simple reproduction

A third assumption implicit in this chapter is that the whole product of a branch is sold to other branches. In reality, however, only a part of the commodities produced by a branch is exchanged for the commodities produced by other branches. The other part is exchanged within that branch, as in the case of innovative chip producers selling their (cheaper) chips to other chip producers to be used as means of production. It could be argued that, at high levels of disaggregation of the economy, very few commodities are sold within the branches which have produced them and thus that this case is practically irrelevant. This might be true. But the theoretical problem remains. Moreover, if this case is extended from the national to the international scene, and thus if international branches are considered (see chapter 7) the problem takes on empirical relevance as well.

The proportion of the output a branch can sell to other branches is variable. However, if we look for the conditions under which an economy reproduces itself, this proportion is not arbitrary but technically determined, that is, determined by the techniques used in each branch. We can distinguish between two cases. The first is *simple reproduction*. This is the case in which all surplus value is consumed by the capitalists instead of being (partly) reinvested. The second case is *expanded reproduction*. This is the case in which surplus value is partly consumed by the capitalists, partly used as additional constant capital and partly used as additional variable capital. Due to the reinvested parts of the surplus value, the production cycle can begin again on an extended scale. In this subsection I shall consider simple reproduction and in 3.8.5 I shall deal with expanded reproduction.

Consider sectors A and B, making up the whole of the economy,[34] and producing respectively means of production (*a*) and means of consumption (*b*):

Sector A $\quad c_1 + v_1 + s_1 = V_1$ means of production
Sector B $\quad c_2 + v_2 + s_2 = V_2$ means of consumption

V_1 is the total value produced by A and incorporated in the means of production. Of these, a part (c_1, in value terms) is acquired by the capitalists in A (as means of production to produce means of production) and a part ($v_1 + s_1$) is sold to the capitalists of B (as means of production to produce means of consumption). V_2 is the total value produced in B and is incorporated in means of consumption. Of these, a part (c_2, in value terms) is exchanged for the means of production acquired from A and becomes the means of consumption of both the capitalists and the workers of A. The other part ($v_2 + s_2$) is used by the capitalists and labourers of B as their own means of consumption. The *general* condition for simple reproduction, or *proportionality requirement* between the two sectors, as determined by the production techniques, is that a certain quantity of means of production with an individual value of $v_1 + s_1$ is exchanged for a certain quantity of means of consumption with an individual value of c_2, or

$$c_2 = v_1 + s_1$$

The question then is: what are the prices of the commodities incorporating c_2 and $v_1 + s_1$? While Marx dealt with this question by implicitly assuming capital immobility, modern conditions require that we make the opposite assumption, capital mobility. Under this assumption, these prices are the price of production. Consider the following example:

A $\quad$ 80c + [20v + 20s] = 120V $\quad$ output 120*a* $\quad$ Number of producers 120A

B $\quad$ [60c] + 40v + 40s = 140V $\quad$ output 140*b* $\quad$ Number of producers 140B

Following a procedure applied by Marx, "the various component parts of the value of the product" are "represented by corresponding proportional parts of the product itself" (Marx, 1967a, p. 222). Thus, for example, 80c in branch A is represented by 80*a*. The terms within brackets indicate the values and thus the use values that must be exchanged between sectors. Here, an individual value of 40 incorporated in 40*a* must be

110

exchanged for 60b, incorporating an individual value of 60.

The specific aspect of this situation is that, if the proportionality requirement is to be maintained, 120A can sell only 40a to B. They cannot
offer, by hypothesis, the other 80a to B; these must be sold internally.
For a similar reason, 140B must sell 60b externally and 80b internally.
This case is easily dealt with if we recall the discussion on partial external
exchange in 3.4.6.

Under the assumption of capital mobility, if we drop the implicit
assumption that capitals invest only in their own branch, the rates of
profit must be equalized into an average rate, that is, both sectors must
realize a value of 130. This means that sector A must gain a value of
10 and sector B must lose the same value. However, given that only
40a can be sold externally, a value of 10 can be appropriated from B
through the sale of only 40a. Similarly, for branch B, a value of 10 is
lost through the sale of only 60b. This implies that 40a must be sold
at $50/40 = 1.25$ each and that 60b must be sold at $50/60 = 0.83$ each. But
in sector A, only a value of 80 is available to purchase 80a and similarly
in sector B only the same value is available to purchase 80b. Thus in
sector A, 120A sell 80a internally at 1 each but 40a externally at 1.25.
Similarly, in sector B, 140B sell 80b internally at 1 each but 60b externally
at 0.83. Thus all capitals realize the same, average rate of profit by selling
their commodities internally at a *different price* than the price realized
for the same commodities sold externally.[35]

Now, the $D = S$ *assumption* means that the distribution of social demand
is such that the technically determined quantity of means of production
corresponding to $v_1 + s_1$ is demanded by and sold to B, and the technically
determined quantity of means of consumption corresponding to c_2 is
demanded by and sold to A, at prices (different from the internal prices)
such that all capitals tendentially realize the same rate of profit. Put differently, the proportionality requirement under conditions of capital
mobility means that a technologically determined quantity of means of
consumption, whose individual value is c_2, must be exchanged for a technologically determined quantity of means of production, whose individual
value is $v_1 + s_1$, at prices (different from their individual values) at which
the rates of profit of all capitals are equalized. As in the previous two
sections, the hypothesis that only a part of the output is exchanged can
be disregarded if the aim is to inquire into the essential elements of the
process of price formation.

3.8.5 Production prices and expanded reproduction

In the previous section, the assumption has been made that capitalists
consume unproductively all the surplus value realized. However, capitals

must constantly attempt to grow, to re-invest part of the surplus value as additional constant capital and variable capital. This is expanded reproduction. Given two sectors, A, producing means of production (*a*), and B, producing means of consumption (*b*), expanded reproduction is depicted as follows:

A $c_1 + v_1 + c_1' + v_1' + s_1$
B $c_2 + v_2 + c_2' + v_2' + s_2$

where c' stands for additional constant capital, v' for additional variable capital and s for the surplus value consumed unproductively. Given that c_1 and c_1' are exchanged within A, the part of means of production sold to B is $v_1 + v_1' + s_1$. Given that v_2, v_2' and s_2 are exchanged within B, the part of means of consumption sold to A is $c_2 + c_2'$. Thus, the proportionality requirement under the condition of capital mobility is

$$c_2 + c_2' = v_1 + v_1' + s_1$$

which means that a definite quantity of means of consumption, whose individual value is $c_2 + c_2'$, must be exchanged for a definite quantity of means of production, whose individual value is $v_1 + v_1' + s_1$, at prices (different from their individual values) at which the rates of profit of all capitals are equalized. Having found out the quantities which must be exchanged externally and the transfer of value needed for the equalization of the profit rates, the computation of the production prices follows easily from 3.8.4.

3.8.6 Production prices and luxuries

The production of luxuries can be theorized either by assuming that all sectors, including luxuries, exchange the totality of their products with each other, and in this case Tables 3.3, 3.4 and 3.5 apply; or by assuming that a part of the output in all sectors is exchanged internally. Let us consider first simple reproduction. In Table 3.8, L, or luxury goods, is added to the two basic reproductive sectors producing means of production (A) and means of consumption for the labourers (B). O means output

Table 3.8 External exchange and production of luxuries

		O	N	Use values exchanged		
A	$90c + 10v + 10s = 110V$	$110a$	$110A$	$90a + [10a] + [10a]$		
B	$80c + 20v + 20s = 120V$	$120b$	$120B$	$[80b]$	$+ 20b + [20b]$	
L	$70c + 30v + 30s = 130V$	$130l$	$130L$	$[70l]$	$+ [30l] + 30l$	

and N means the number of producers. The column "use values exchanged" is explained below.

In this case, L produces luxury goods which can be bought only by capitalists in A, B and L and which can only be purchased with surplus value. But L needs both means of production and means of consumption for its labourers. Thus,

$90a = 90c_1$ are exchanged internally as means of production in A
$10a = 10v_1$ are exchanged for means of consumption, for $80b$
$10a = 10s_1$ are exchanged for luxuries, for $70l$

$80b = 80c_2$ are exchanged for means of production, for $10a$
$20b = 20v_2$ are exchanged internally as means of consumption
$20b = 20s_2$ are exchanged for luxuries, for $30l$

$70l = 70c_3$ are exchanged for means of production, for $10a$
$30l = 30v_3$ are exchanged for means of consumption, for $20b$
$30l = 30s_3$ are exchanged internally as luxuries

This is summarized in the column "use values exchanged", in which the units of outputs to be exchanged under conditions of simple reproduction are placed within brackets and vertically one above the other. More generally, the proportionality conditions are

(1) $v_1 = c_2$
(2) $s_1 = c_3$
(3) $s_2 = v_3$

It has been said above that the products of L can be bought only by capitalists in A, B and L, that is,

(4) $c_3 + v_3 + s_3 = s_1 + s_2 + s_3$

which can also be derived by adding conditions (2) and (3), thus obtaining $s_1 + s_2 = c_3 + v_3$, and by adding to both sides s_3.

We can now compute external prices. All three branches must realize a value of 120. Thus $20a$ must be sold at $30/20 = 1.5$ each, $100b$ must be sold at 1 each and $100l$ must be sold at $90/100 = 0.9$ each. These are the external prices under the assumption that only one unit of capital per branch is invested.[36] Simple reproduction can continue indefinitely on the basis of a tendential equalization of the profit rates among branches, one of which produces luxury goods, as long as in each branch each capital keeps investing the same constant and variable capital and sells its output, according to the technically determined proportionality requirement, at the same internal and external prices.

The production of luxuries is thought, by some authors, to be inflationary because luxuries are not reproductive goods (do not re-enter the production process). A result of this section is that there is nothing inherently inflationary in the production of luxuries.

Consider now expanded reproduction, or

A $\quad c_1 + v_1 + c_1' + v_1' + s_1$
B $\quad c_2 + v_2 + c_2' + v_2' + s_2$
L $\quad c_3 + v_3 + c_3' + v_3' + s_3$

Sector A sells means of production to B $(v_1 + v_1')$ in order to buy means of consumption $(c_2 + c_2')$ and to L (s_1) in order to buy luxuries $(c_3 + c_3')$. Sector B sells means of consumption to A $(c_2 + c_2')$ in order to buy means of production $(v_1 + v_1')$ and to L (s_2) in order to buy luxuries $(v_3 + v_3')$. Sector L sells luxuries to A $(c_3 + c_3')$ in order to buy means of production (s_1) and to B $(v_3 + v_3')$ in order to buy means of consumption (s_2). The proportionality conditions, then, are

(1) $\quad v_1 + v_1' = c_2 + c_2'$
(2) $\quad s_1 = c_3 + c_3'$
(3) $\quad s_2 = v_3 + v_3'$

Similarly to the case of simple reproduction, if we add conditions (2) and (3) and if we add s_3 to both terms, we get

(4) $\quad s_1 + s_2 + s_3 = c_3 + v_3 + c_3' + v_3' + s_3$

that is, the condition that the output of sector L can be bought with that part of surplus value which is unproductively consumed in all three sectors. Conditions (1), (2) and (3) allow us to carry out the computation of the production prices along the lines sketched above.

3.8.7 Production prices and rates of exploitation[37]

Up to now we have assumed that the wage rates and rates of exploitation are the same throughout the economy. But suppose that different capitals in the same branch, or different branches of the same nation or different nations have different wage rates and rates of exploitation. How does this new element affect the theorization and computation of the price of production? Let us take, for example, the case of different rates of exploitation between branches (the results to be reached are also valid

Table 3.9   Value produced under labour mobility and labour immobility

	(1) Labour immobility	(2) Labour mobility
A	90c+10v+20s = 120V	90c+25v+30s = 145V
B	60c+40v+40s = 140V	60c+25v+30s = 115V
Total	260V	260V

for differences within branches and between nations). Let us avail ourselves of the numerical example in Table 3.9.

In this table, branch A can impose a rate of exploitation double that of branch B. In A, this rate is 20/10 = 200% while in B it is 40/40 = 100%. Now we must distinguish between two cases: either there is labour mobility between branches (and this is the assumption when a national economy is considered) or not (and this can be the case in the international economy, as will be explained in chapter 7). Let us first examine the case of labour mobility.

(a) Within a nation, labour moves where conditions are more favourable to it and less favourable to capital. This real movement allows us to assume a tendential equalization of wage rates and rates of exploitation. Clearly, then, the tendential situation will be characterized by an average wage rate and rate of exploitation. The former is (10 + 40)/2 = 25. If the same total quantity of value (260) is to be produced, the value produced by both branches is given in column 2 of Table 3.9. The average rate of exploitation, then, is 60/50 = 120%. This mathematical operation is justified because it depicts the tendential outcome of a real movement, *labour* mobility.

Once *capital* mobility comes into the picture, the rates of profit are equalized into an average 60/200 = 30%. Recalling what has been said in 3.8.2 above and given that A invests 1.15 units of capital and B invests 0.85 units, the value realized by these two branches is given in Table 3.10. In this case, the average rate of profit is 30% and the tendential transfer of value is + 4.5 for A and – 4.5 for B.

Table 3.10   Production prices: labour mobility

	(1) Production prices	UE
A	(90+25)+(1.15×30) = 115+34.5 = 149.5	149.5−145 = +4.5
B	(60+25)+(0.85×30) = 85+25.5 = 110.5	110.5−115 = −4.5

Table 3.11   Production prices: labour immobility

	(1) Production prices	UE
A	$90c+10v+30s = 130$	$130-120 = +10$
B	$60c+40v+30s = 130$	$130-140 = -10$

(b) Now take the case of lack of labour mobility. Here, the real movement does not any longer justify the assumption of an equalized wage
rate and rate of exploitation. If labourers in A are prevented from moving
to B, they will have to accept lower wages and a higher rate of exploitation
than in B. Now there are tendentially two rates of exploitation, but this
does not affect the computation of the price of production. In fact, inasmuch as lower wages and higher rates of exploitation result in higher
rates of profit, capital moves to those branches where the rates of profit
are higher, thus equalizing the extra surplus value and thus the rates
of profit. Or, in spite of labour immobility and thus of tendentially different wage rates and rates of surplus value, there emerges an average rate
of profit which in this case is again equal to $60/200 = 30\%$. This is shown
in Table 3.11. Here, the average rate of profit has not changed (it is
still 30%) but the transfer of value is $+10$ (instead of $+4.5$) for A and
-10 (instead of -4.5) for B.

(c) To sum up, capital mobility is the only prerequisite for an average
rate of profit to emerge, whether there is labour mobility or not. However,
the price of production changes according to whether labour is mobile
or not and, more generally, according to whether wages and rates of
exploitation can be equalized or not.[38]

3.8.8 The two components of UE

In Marx's transformation procedure, based on the assumption of an average (equalized) rate of exploitation, there is appropriation of surplus value
(UE) by the high OCC branch from the low OCC branch. This, as we
have seen in 3.4.5, point 7, holds only for modal capitals. Let us retain
this assumption.

If we now assume different rates of exploitation, the extra surplus value
is redistributed among branches, whether we assume labour mobility or
not, due to capital mobility. If we assume labour mobility, as Marx does,
we tendentially equalize the rates of exploitation and then we fall back
into Marx's case of different OCCs and equal rates of surplus value.
This assumption is warranted within a nation and this is why Marx can
safely assume that the wage rates and rates of surplus value are equal

in all branches. If we do not assume labour mobility, we cannot equalize wage rates and rates of exploitation and then, if the rates of profit are equalized, there must be a transfer of value from the high rates of exploitation to the low rates of exploitation branches.

It follows that, if we assume tendentially different rates of exploitation (labour immobility), the equalization of the rates of profit needed to compute the price of production implies *a double transfer of value: from low OCC to high OCC branches and from high rates of surplus value to low rates of surplus value branches*. It is the combined effect of these two factors which decides which branch appropriates value and which loses it. In the example above, it is branch A, the high OCC branch, which appropriates value $(130 - 120 = +10)$ from B, the low OCC branch. But once we introduce labour immobility, this is only accidentally so. Had branch A produced a surplus value equal to, say, 60, the average rate of profit would have been $(60 + 40)/200 = 50\%$, both branches would have realized 150V, and branch A (the high OCC branch) would have realized 50s instead of 60s, thus losing 10 to branch B (the low OCC branch).

To sum up, if the rates of profit are to be equalized, a certain capital appropriates surplus value from another one if it produces less surplus value, either because it has a higher OCC or because it has a lower rate of exploitation. But it should be stressed that in both cases the appropriation of value goes from capitals to capitals and not from workers to workers.

3.9 The Law of Value in the National Context

We can now properly understand the nature of the Marxist law of value. In all societies what has been produced must be distributed among the members of that society, if that society is to reproduce itself. The laws governing production and distribution change from society to society. The *Marxist law of value* theorizes the laws governing production, distribution and consumption in, and thus the economic reproduction of, the capitalist system.

As far as production is concerned, the basic claim of the Marxist labour theory of value is that only labour produces value. In his analysis of the capitalist production process, Marx shows that each moment of labour is both concrete and abstract labour. Concrete labour (or labour of a specific kind) transforms the means and objects of labour as use values into new use values (the product) and thus transfers their exchange value to that of the product. Abstract labour creates new value. Up to a certain point, the value newly created equals the value of the labour power employed. From that point on, extra, or surplus, value is produced. This is the value appropriated by the capitalist class. It is in this sense that the labourers are exploited, expropriated of a part of the value they produce. In short, then, the law of value states that value is labour expended under capitalist relations of production and that the producers of value cannot produce their means of subsistence without being, at the same time, exploited.

The value produced within a production unit is not necessarily the value appropriated by it (by that capitalist). Rather, the value produced by all productive (of value) units is redistributed. Aside from the value appropriated by the state (e.g. taxes) it is important to note that not all capitalist enterprises are productive of surplus value. This is the issue of unproductive labour (see chapter 2). Or, there are capitalist enterprises where there is no transformation of use values, that is, where concrete labour does not transform the objects of labour into new use values (e.g. commercial enterprises). The profits these enterprises make are then value appropriated from the sector of the economy where value (and thus surplus value) is produced. Similarly, the extra profits made by the more efficient capitals are also appropriated from other capitals.

How does this happen? Through the price mechanism. This mechanism redistributes the value produced among all capitalist units, both productive and not. That part of the Marxist labour theory of value which deals with this aspect is the Marxist price theory. This theorizes the objective laws regulating the distribution of value through exchange.[39]

To the great disappointment of the critics of Marx's transformation procedure, the relationship between production and distribution is *not* one of equality. This relation cannot be one in which the value realized is equal to the value embodied (see 3.7.2). But this relation cannot be one of *equal exchange* either, one in which the individual value of a commodity coincides with its social value. Equal exchange applies only to the very specific case of modal capitals with an OCC equal to the average, under the double assumption (a) that there are no strong shifts in social demand causing quantitative changes in the surplus value to be realized and (b) that there is no quantitative change in the individual value of the inputs. Thus, equal exchange is a sub-case (the exception) of unequal exchange (the norm). This latter is the difference between the individual and the social value of commodities and can be caused by a difference in any of the three components of a commodity's value (see 3.7.1). This is then the *complete notion of unequal exchange*. This notion is already implicit in volume 1 of *Capital*. Throughout this volume, Marx never tires of repeating that "that which determines the magnitude of the value of any article is ... the labour-time socially necessary for its production" (Marx, 1967a, p. 39). There is then absolutely no contradiction between volume 1 of *Capital*, where Marx would have assumed individual

118

values (or, even worse, value embodied), and volume 3 of the same work, where he would have moved to social values, or production prices. Volume 1 assumes already transformed prices, volume 3 explains the transformation process. Marx's price theory is perfectly consistent.

The alternative price theories are no match for the Marxist one. For the neo-classical theory, the equilibrium price is determined by the intersection of a sector's supply and demand curves.[40] But in order to construct the demand and supply curves, we must *postulate* a series of possible prices, including the equilibrium one. Thus the demand and supply curves do not really determine, or explain the formation of, the equilibrium price; they only "find out" or "select" which one of the pre-given possible prices is the equilibrium one. This attempt to explain price formation thus falls into circular reasoning. Marxist price theory, on the other hand, does not presuppose prices, or social values. It *presupposes individual values* and *explains the formation of social values*, (prices), *as a transformation* of individual into social values.[41]

The neo-Ricardian theory of prices and distribution presents a different type of problem. Here, prices are given by the solution of a system of simultaneous equations depicting production techniques in terms of physical inputs and outputs. The advantage of this procedure, it is held, is that the price of a commodity as an input is equal to its price as an output. This, as seen above, would solve the "transformation problem". Yet not only is there no transformation problem, the identity of input prices and output prices, or stationary prices, abstracts from technological change and thus results in a static price theory. Marx's approach, on the contrary, incorporates technological change in its price theory since it considers competing techniques within a branch and the possibility of technological change between the beginning and the end of the production process.

Finally, there is the post-Keynesian theory of prices. This theory holds that oligopolies set their prices above normal production costs, or "the costs which would apply at some standard, or expected, rate of capacity utilization if the economy were on its secular (or long-run) growth path" (Kenyon, 1979, p. 40). This margin above normal production costs is the "mark-up", which is a level of retained profits required by the firm's planned investment expenditures. This is a theory of how oligopolies set their prices, a behavioural theory, and not of price formation for the economy as a whole. In terms of price formation, there is no reason to assume, given oligopolistic competition, that oligopolies will actually realize what they hope to realize. Moreover, normal production costs are both unknown to the oligopolies and irrelevant to them, since they, like all capitalists, are interested in the actual, not the normal, production costs.

Marx's price theory, therefore, is not only perfectly consistent, it is the only one explaining the objective process of price formation in a non-circular and dynamic way.

Notes

1. This is a first, restricted notion of individual value. We shall see in 3.6.2 that this notion fits into a more general one of individual value as the value a commodity has before being sold.

2. We disregard, of course, the case in which an increased OCC does not lead to increased efficiency because mistakes are made. Consider the following example. As *Business Week* reports,

> In 1979, General Motors was making huge profits and building well over half of the cars produced by U.S. carmakers. In a bid to become even more dominant, GM announced plans to spend $40 billion over seven years on new technology, new plants and new cars. (Hampton and Norman, 1987, p. 45)

The plan, however, did not work. "Eight years and some $60 billion later, Ford and Chrysler are not the ones in trouble. GM is." (Hampton and Norman, 1987). What went wrong? An ill-conceived management reorganization and other factors played a part. But mostly, an increase in OCC neither reflected increased productivity ("a lot of equipment did not work or didn't work as expected") nor produced commodities which met the public's demand.

3. Even Marxists question the validity of the rise in the OCC. See, for example, Sweezy, 1987, pp.43–4. Sweezy's argument relies heavily on Gillman's figures. See M. Cogoy's critique of Gillman in Cogoy, 1987(b), pp. 67–8. J. Weeks stresses the failure of Marx's critics correctly to operationalize constant capital in the computation of the OCC. Usually only the fixed, and not the circulating, part of constant capital is considered. Obviously, this reduces the numerator and thus the OCC (Weeks, 1977, p. 287).

4. To show the increase in the OCC, we do not need to know whether there is an increase of the same or of different means of production. For a different view, see Giussani (1988, pp. 23–4).

5. There are estimates of the OCC carried out according to Marxist criteria; see, in chapter 5, the studies by Moseley (1988a and 1988b), Wolff (1986) and Reati (1989). But they are very few, cover very few countries and are carried out according to different methodologies. It is for this reason that I have chosen the stock of capital per employed for a group of countries as a measure of their OCC. These estimates are not carried out according to Marxist criteria but have the advantage of covering many countries and of being methodologically homogeneous.

6. The social value of a commodity can also be theorized as the value of the commodity produced either under the least favourable or under the most favourable conditions. The former is a Ricardian notion which does not fit within the Marxist framework. The latter is a neo-Ricardian notion which is advanced on the basis of the fact that capitalists choose the most efficient technique, not the average productivity one (Howard and King, 1985, p. 156). On the face of it, this argument seems to be reasonable. However, while all capitalists aim at the most productive technique, not all of them can introduce it at the same time. Usually, at any given point in time there is an average production technique together with above-mode and below-mode ones. The neo-Ricardian choice is needed to avoid the anomalies of joint production, as the neo-Ricardians see it; that is, the possibility of negative value and negative surplus value. But this is a neo-Ricardian problem, not a Marxist one; see 4.3.2 below.

7. There are two ways to measure the diffusion of a technique and thus to determine which is the modal one. They are: the proportion of firms using it and the share of output it accounts for. Under free competition, if we assume that each enterprise uses only one

technique, the bulk of the products is accounted for by the bulk of the capitalist enterprises which roughly use the same technique. If we assume that enterprises use different techniques, it is the share of output which defines the technique as the modal one. This point will be discussed in 7.2.1 under oligopolistic competition.

8. Adapted from Edquist and Jacobsson, 1988, pp. 11–14

9. In this work, "modal technique" and "modal production process" are used interchangeably. It should be stressed, however, that modal techniques emerge not only in production but also in exchange and distribution. Everything said about modal technologies in production applies just as well to exchange and distribution.

10. In the US, more than 50 per cent of maize is produced by only two enterprises, Pioneer-Hi-Bred and Dekobalb Pfizer.

11. For the complete notion of D = S see the end of 3.2.6 below.

12. I assume, for the sake of simplicity, that each enterprise only uses one technique. But, as seen above, an enterprise can use more than one technique. This element can be taken into account without changing the outcome of the analysis.

13. Of course these price changes, due to different levels of demand and purchasing power, might in their turn affect the level of supply by increasing (or decreasing) the existing rate of capacity utilization (operating rates) or by increasing (or decreasing) productive capacity (e.g. by building new, or closing down, plants). This will change the market value, due to changes in supply. But when discussing the effects of social demand on the social value, we take the level of supply as given.

14. There is no contradiction between a supposedly "technological theory of market value" and a "demand and supply theory of market value", as Itoh and Yokokawa submit (1979, p. 105). Indart correctly points out that "the supply and demand issue has been, in fact, thoroughly considered and coherently incorporated into the theory of value by Marx" (1987–88, p. 467). Indart's approach, however, differs from the one submitted here.

15. This table rests on several assumptions. They will be explained in section 3.8 below.

16. When c and v are absolute values, the price of production is equal to $c + v + p(c + v)$. When c and v are percentage values, as in this work, the formula becomes $c + v + p$.

17. This notion of unequal exchange is implicit in Marx's analysis of the price of production even though Marx does not use the term "unequal exchange". This concept of unequal exchange should not be confused with Emmanuel's, to be discussed in chapter 6, section 3.

18. Suppose, for example, that in Table 3.2 all capitals realized the same rate of profit, $60/300 = 20\%$. Capital I would then have to sell its commodities at $100 \times 1.2 = 120$, capital II at $130 \times 0.9231 = 120$ and capital III at $90 \times 1.3333 = 120$.

19. The case in which there are no modal commodities will be discussed shortly.

20. Notice that all capitals participate in capital movement. This is the reason why we cannot hypothesize two (or more) average rates of profit. If, on the other hand, some capitals were definitely excluded from capital movement (as in 3.8.4 and 3.8.5 below), we would have to hypothesize a separate average rate of profit for this particular category.

21. The reader should remember that the assumption here is that there is no capital mobility among nations.

22. Oligopolistic competition will be discussed in chapter 7. It is mentioned here for the sake of completeness.

23. This notion of unequal exchange is adequate for the time being. A complete notion will be found in 3.9.

24. Prices in money terms will be discussed in chapters 5 and 7.

25. In Table 3.4 each modal capital tendentially realizes the average rate of profit while each capital below mode realizes a lower than average rate of profit (8% for AI, 0% for BI and 10.8% for CI) and each capital above mode realizes a higher than average rate of profit (32% for AIII, 40% for BIII and 29.2% for CIII).

26. Notice that the rates of profit after application of the distributional constraint are found by applying the distributional ratio to the prices of production per unit of output. Multiplication of these adjusted prices by the different levels of output gives the different values tendentially realized and thus the different tendential profit rates. It would be incorrect

to apply the distributional ratio to the unadjusted rate of profit, since the result would not respect the distributional constraint. For example, we have seen that in Table 3.5 the average rate of profit for modal capitals is 17.3%. We would have reached a different result if we had applied the distributional ratio to the modal rate of profit: $0.9817 \times 19.44 = 19.08\%$. Only the application of 17.3% for modal capitals and of the other rates of profit arrived at in a similar manner can ensure the equality between value available for redistribution and value to be redistributed.

27. As mentioned above, what follows applies to the hypothesis of both modal and mean productivities, with the proper computational modifications.

28. Many authors do not seem to have seen this point. Even Mandel, for example, thinks that two branches, or Departments, can be compared in terms of productivity: "This equalization of the average productivity of the two large Departments, i.e. of the average organic composition of capital, is part of the very essence of automation" (1975, p. 191). This thesis is untenable. There is neither an equalization of productivities between branches (and even less between Departments), since such a comparison is possible only within branches, nor an equalization of the OCCs, since branches use, by definition, different techniques and thus different technical compositions of capital and organic compositions of capital. "It may be possible, to a degree, to average the organic composition of capital within a particular industry; but this cannot be done between totally different spheres of production" (Mattick, 1969, p. 41).

29. This point is also made by Bryan (1986, p. 210).

30. For a discussion of the conditions under which both equalities hold, see Salama, 1975, p. 159.

31. A slightly different version of the circularity critique stresses that if in volume III of *Capital* c and v are bought as inputs at their individual value and sold as outputs at their price of production, the same logical inconsistency must apply to volume I of *Capital*. But, and this agrees completely with the interpretation submitted here, in volume I too Marx considers the value of the inputs as already transformed. I shall cite only one of the many quotations which support my argument. In considering the value of the cotton needed to spin yarn, Marx says

We have no need at present to investigate the value of this cotton for our capitalist has, we will assume, bought it *at its full value* ... In this price, the labour required for the production of the cotton is always expressed *in terms of the average labour of society*. (Marx, 1967a, pp. 186-7; emphasis added)

32. There have been many reactions to the circularity critique. Yaffe (1975), Baumol (1974), Rubin (1972), Shaikh (1977), Gernstein (1976), Fine (1983) and Fine and Harris (1979) are discussed in Carchedi, 1987a, ch. c5. Foley (1986, p. 104) submits that there are in Marx's work two definitions, rather than only one, of the value of labour power: "as concrete labour embodied in the commodities workers consume" and "as the amount of abstract social labour workers receive in wages for 1 hour of labour power". The transformation procedure would then hold if we chose the latter definition. But the circularity critique should not be countered by creating an artificial separation in Marx's notion of labour power. Itoh (1976, p. 338) seems to move in the same direction as the approach submitted here by stressing that the transformed values show "the result, not the starting condition of exchanges" and that c and v reappear again "in the following period", as inputs of the following production process. However, Itoh does not develop these points. Recently, a very good collection of articles has been edited by Mandel and Freeman (1984). Aside from specific differences, these contributions and the approach submitted here are broadly complementary. Kliman and McGlone (1988) agree on the validity of the method submitted here but argue that my distinction between realized social values (tendentially, prices of production) and potential social values (individual values) "denies the actuality of values as distinct from prices" (Kliman and McGlone, p. 78). Unfortunately this is a misreading of my position. In the dialectical view submitted here, potential social phenomena are just as "actual" (real), as realized social phenomena. Finally, for an important but relatively undiscussed paper, broadly consistent with the theses submitted here, see P. Mattick Jr., 1981.

33. I should like to thank Werner de Haan for bringing this point to my attention.

34. Since this is the highest level of aggregation, the quantity of goods exchanged within branches is the highest possible.

35. Notice that each capital in A sells 80/120 = 66.7% of its product internally at 1 per unit of output and 40/120 = 33.3% to B at 1.25 per unit of output. It would be wrong to assume that 80 capitals sell only internally and 40 capitals sell only externally. Similarly for each capital in B.

36. It is because only one unit of capital is invested in each branch that in Table 3.8 the $c_3 + v_3 + s_3 = s_1 + s_2 + s_3$ condition is not respected. Therefore, the purchasing power of the three branches is either excessive (branch B realizes 100 but needs $15 + 27 = 42$ and branch L realizes 90 but needs $15 + 20 = 35$) or insufficient (branch A realizes 30 but needs $80 + 63 = 143$). A different numerical example could be thought of in which the three branches invest more than one unit of capital so that sufficient purchasing power is generated for all branches to buy the technically determined use values at a price at which each of the three branches as a whole realizes the average rate of profit.

37. The results reached in this section are different from those reached in Carchedi, 1988, pp. 43–6. That work should be regarded as a first attempt to come to terms with some of the problems dealt with here.

38. The computation of the price of production with different wages and rates of exploitation is of practical importance when it is not realistic to assume a tendential equalization of these factors, as in the case of different nations (actually, wage zones, as chapter 7 will argue) and of women, immigrants, coloured people, etc. within a nation.

39. P. Mattick's opinion that the "problem of individual price determination was of no real interest to Marx" (Mattick, 1969, p. 47; see also Mattick, 1972, passim) unnecessarily restricts the field of application of the Marxist theory of value. Much worse is P. Sweezy's opinion that

in so far as the problems which are posed for solution are concerned with the behavior of the disparate elements of the economic system (price of individual commodities, profits of particular capitalists, the combination of productive factors in the individual firms, etc.), there seems to be no doubt that value calculation is of little assistance. Orthodox economists ... have developed a kind of price theory which is more useful in this sphere than anything to be found in Marx or his followers. (Sweezy, 1942; p. 129)

40. I refer, of course, to the partial equilibrium version. For a critique of the general equilibrium version, see Guerrien, 1989.

41. There is no circularity in positing some prices (of inputs) in order to arrive at some other prices (of outputs), as long as one explains the process through which the former are transformed into the latter. Rather, circularity means to postulate what one wants to explain. The neo-classical theory postulates the *same* price it wants to explain. Thus, contrary to Marx's approach, its attempt to explain prices cannot escape circular reasoning.

4

Recent Controversies on
the Law of Value

4.1 The Formation and Distribution of Value

Besides the attack on Marx's transformation procedure (see 3.6) and the critique that Marx's price theory is based both on equal exchange and on unequal exchange (see 3.9), many objections have been raised against his theory of production and distribution. In this section I shall review the three most common lines of critique.[1]

4.1.1 Prices are determined by chance, not by abstract labour

Marx points out that, if two different things are comparable, they must be equal to a third thing which is common to both of them and on the basis of which they can be compared (exchanged in definite quantities). But this, the critics argue, is not necessarily so, exchange could also be ruled by chance. What the critics fail to realize is that this principle applies not to sporadic acts of exchange where, as Marx is well aware, the proportions in which products are exchanged "are at first quite a matter of chance" (Marx, 1967a, p. 86) but to a system of general exchange with relatively stable ratios of exchange. It is this relative stability which compels us to presuppose a common thing (abstract labour) whose relative stability (labour time socially necessary) explains the relative stability of the exchange ratios, of the proportions in which products are exchanged.

4.1.2 Prices can be determined by abstract labour as well as by other qualities

Some critics are willing to concede that two different things can have something in common if they must be compared but argue that abstract

125

labour is not the only thing two different commodities have in common. There are many more candidates for this role.

A first category is given by physical inputs: any physical input (e.g. coal), it is argued, would do just as well (or as badly) (see, e.g., Hodgson, 1981 and Cohen, 1981). Marx's answer is that the common substance, and thus the unit of measure of all commodities cannot be a specific characteristic (coal in its specific features). The specific properties are exactly what differentiate commodities from each other. Coal as a material with a certain colour, atomic structure, etc. might be common (directly or indirectly) to all (other) commodities but the various quantities of coal's specific features (qualities) are exactly what makes commodities different from each other. To function as a unit of measure, coal must equalize, rather than differentiate, commodities. But this is only possible if the specific features of coal are abstracted from, that is, if coal is considered as abstract labour.

A related point is the attempt to show that "labour power as a commodity is not unique in its magical property of producing more value than it embodies" (Roemer, 1982, p. 273) and to prove that corn too (or any other commodity) can be exploited. This is useless in understanding the question as to who labours for whom, or in understanding human history. But, the critics add, somehow sensing that they have produced yet another cranky idea, if one is interested "in studying the history of people and not of corn ... we could classify producers as corn exploited if the amount of corn value they command through goods they purchase is less than the amount of corn they contribute to production" (Roemer, 1982, p. 274). But this argument has been convincingly refuted by Marx, as shown above: to reduce all other commodities to corn, we must abstract from its physical characteristics and we are back to abstract labour.

A second, and related category comprises only one candidate: utility. This, and not abstract labour, would be the substance of value (von Böhm-Bawerk, 1973, p. 74). One answer to this critique is provided by the "value-form" approach which submits that abstract labour "has no substantial existence apart from the value form, money" (Eldred, 1984, p. 136). This position, however, denies the labour theory of value its ability to explain price formation in terms of abstract labour time (Gleicher, 1985, p. 151; 1985–6, p. 467). But this ability is precisely the strength of the Marxist approach, as chapter 3 has shown.

The real objection to the notion that utility is the element common to all commodities and thus the essence of value is another. Utility is the most abstract, the most general notion indicating that each commodity has its own specific use, is useful for something in its own specific way, and not that all commodities share a common type of utility, are useful for the same purpose in the same way. *Utility is thus the most general concept of what makes things different.* As such, it cannot be used to indicate a feature things have in common. What the neo-classical economists do not seem to realize is that, by holding that utility is what is common to all commodities, they in fact submit that what is common to all commodities is that they are all different.

A third, and final category, encompasses all other qualities which might be common to different commodities. Von Böhm-Bawerk mentions "the property of being scarce in proportion to demand", that they are "subject to demand and supply", that "they are appropriated" and that "they are natural products" (von Böhm-Bawerk, 1973). All these elements can easily be accounted for within the frame of the Marxist labour theory of value. But many other features can be found which are common to all commodities and which, according to the critics, have the same right to be regarded as the substance of value.

In this respect, G. Kay (1979, p. 51) aptly points out that abstract labour can be regarded as being the substance of value because it can explain the ratios in which the different commodities exchange for each other. This is not the case for other qualities shared by all commodities. For example, all commodities are in orbit around the sun. If one wants to argue that this property is the substance of value, let him or her show that exchange ratios can be explained on this basis. Moreover, the labour theory of value is the theory of the collective labourer and as such it aims at inquiring into who labours for whom. From this point of view, the choice of labour as the substance of value is a necessary one.

To support the thesis that labour is not (necessarily) the source of value, it has also been submitted that a capitalist, commodity-producing society could exist without labour. This would be the case for a fully automated economy in which the "capitalists" produce for, and sell to, each other. The "working class" would be unemployed and living on charity (Hodgson, 1980, p. 259). This argument has already been disposed of in 3.7.5, this hypothesis is inconsistent with capitalism.

4.1.3 Not all prices are determined by the socially necessary labour time

This is true, but is no objection to the theory submitted here. The socially necessary labour time discussed in chapter 3 is the social value, or production price, of capitalist commodities only. A commodity, however, is not necessarily produced under capitalist conditions. For a product to be a commodity it is sufficient that it is produced for sale, or not for one's own consumption. A commodity becomes a capitalist commodity when it is also produced by labourers for the capitalists; when it incorporates, as a use value, value and surplus value. There are five possibilities, as follows.

First, some goods (e.g. the products of independent farmers or artisans) are produced by labour not expended under capitalist relations of production, but similar goods are capitalistically produced. These goods incorporate abstract labour which is not value. However, this labour counts as if it had been expended under capitalist relations of production as soon as these products are sold on the capitalist market.[2] By being exchanged on this market, these commodities become capitalist commodities and thus obtain the same price as the same (or similar) products which are capitalistically produced (and exchanged). This case is similar to direct barter, which is explicitly mentioned by Marx. The two bartered articles "are not as yet commodities, but become so *only by the act of barter*" (Marx, 1967a, p. 87; emphasis added).

Second, some goods are gifts of nature (e.g. natural products) for which no labour has been expended. If the same things are also produced by capitalist enterprises, their price is determined in the same way as the above category. They are exchanged as if they were capitalist commodities. Here there is an additional requirement, besides their being exchanged on the capitalist market, they "must be the property of some individual whose claim over them is recognized and substantiated socially" (Kay, 1979, p. 49).

Third, some other goods are gifts of nature (e.g. land) which cannot be produced by capitalist production processes or are produced only by non-capitalist labour processes. In this case no social term of comparison is available. Their price, similarly to the price of a monopoly's products, cannot be determined by the law of value and is determined by the "purchaser's eagerness to buy and ability to pay" (Marx, 1967c, p. 775).

Fourth, some "goods" are neither the products of labour nor real things. Marx mentions conscience and honour, but class allegiance is also a good example. They might have a price but then this price is based on an imaginary value, as imaginary as the "commodity" itself.

In the two former cases, there are objective criteria (in terms of socially necessary labour time), albeit indirect ones, to determine the price of non-capitalist commodities. In the latter two cases, there are no such objective criteria. Thus the labour theory of value explains what is typical of capitalism, the price of capitalist commodities and of those non-capitalist commodities which are also capitalistically produced (and which become capitalist commodities when they enter the sphere of capitalist realization). The theory does not explain the price of non-capitalist commodities when such a capitalist term of reference is lacking.

This, however, should not be a cause of concern. In fact, the realm of reality which is not explained by the labour theory of value is only marginal to capitalism. Moreover, the elements which can be drawn upon to explain the price of non-capitalist commodities, like scarcity, relations of power, etc. can only be understood within the frame of a capitalist, commodity-producing society. Or, "the logic of Marx's position that we can only analyze the exchange of non [capitalist, G.C.] commodities once we have analyzed [capitalist, G.C.] commodities stands its ground with ease" (Kay, 1979, p. 50).

4.1.4 A specific case: labour power

The fifth case is a particularly important example which has been singled out by the critics: labour power. This is a commodity and yet, it is argued, it is not capitalistically produced. What has been said above allows us to see the emptiness of this critique. If labour power is not a capitalist commodity, its price cannot be its price of production; its price is then determined differently. This is all there is to it. However, labour power deserves particular attention because of the specificity of its price determination. Four aspects will be mentioned here.

First, we have seen above that the value of labour power is given by the price of production of those commodities (both material and mental) which society deems necessary for the labourers' reproduction. This is a socially, not a biologically, determined subsistence minimum. Second, this implicitly assumes that all the means of subsistence are capitalist commodities, that all labour going into the production of labour power is labour performed under capitalist production relations. But this is not so, as the particularly important example of domestic labour shows. This, and other similar types of labour, is not value and thus, while contributing to the formation of labour power as a use value, does not contribute to the formation of its (exchange) value.

Third, the social value of labour power is also influenced by the state. The state appropriates part of the value initially accrued to the several classes and redistributes it in the form of services, subsidies, etc. Ultimately, both the quantity of value appropriated from each class and the quantity of value redistributed to each class depend on the power relations among classes. The value of labour power, then, can be assessed only after this complex system of appropriation and redistribution has been taken into account. This is a further aspect of the social nature of the subsistence minimum. While this topic cannot be further pursued here, it is important to mention that recent studies of national accounts in value terms have shown that the quantity of value appropriated from the working class is either equal to or (especially in times of crises) less than the quantity of value redistributed to it (see Bartelheimer and Wolf,

1985; Guerrero, 1990a, 1990b).

Fourth, what has been said above holds for the value of labour power in general. But different types of agents have different types of skills. Given that each level of skills needs a certain (degree of) education and training, the values of those different types of agents' labour power are different. This means that unskilled labourers need less value to reproduce themselves than skilled labourers. The question is: why should skilled labourers receive a higher value (that of their labour power, as wage) not only in the period immediately following the sale of their newly formed labour power but also in following periods? Recall from chapter 3 that every time a commodity is sold, it is sold at its social value; this is also its individual value as an input of the next production process. In the case of labour power, this value is the social value of the means of subsistence (including the skills, education and training) deemed as socially necessary for the reproduction of labour power at the time labour power is sold. Or, the social value of labour power as an output, its individual value as an input, includes training, education, etc. at the time labour power is sold. In other words, the cost of acquiring those skills is a required part of the value of labour power not because those skills have been acquired years ago but because they would be necessary if that labour power had to be produced now. It follows that there is inherent in the wage system the reproduction of not only the collective labourer but also of the different levels of wages.

4.2 The Reduction of Skilled to Unskilled Labour

The critique of the labour theory of value has also focused on the reduction of skilled to unskilled labour. In one of the most quoted passages on this point, Marx says

> Skilled labour counts only as simple labour intensified, or rather, as multiplied simple labour, a given quantity of skilled being considered equal to a greater quantity of simple labour. Experience shows that this reduction is constantly being made. A commodity may be the product of the most skilled labour but its value, by equating it to the product of simple unskilled labour, represents a definite quantity of the latter labour alone. The different proportions in which the different sorts of labour are reduced to unskilled labour as their standard, are established by a social process that goes on behind the back of the producers and, consequently, appear to be fixed by custom. (Marx, 1967a, p. 44)

As in the transformation debate, it was von Böhm-Bawerk who first outlined the classical features of the critique. Von Böhm-Bawerk submits that "the real subject of inquiry is the exchange relations of commodities" and asks himself "why, for instance, a statuette which has cost a sculptor one day's labor should exchange for a cart of stones which has cost a stone-breaker five days' labor". His answer is that, according to Marx,

> the exchange relation is this, and no other, because one day of sculptor's work is reducible exactly to five days of unskilled work. And why is it reducible to exactly five days? Because experience shows that it is so reduced by a social process. And what is this social process? The same process that has to be explained, that very process by means of which the product of one day of sculptor's labor has been made equal to the value of the product of five days of common labor. (von Böhm-Bawerk, 1973, pp. 83–4)

In short, von Böhm-Bawerk argues that the process which reduces skilled to unskilled labour (in modern literature, this is commonly referred to as deskilling) remains unexplained.

If Marx had offered no explanation of the process of deskilling, the critique would have been well taken. But the contrast between Marx's position and von Böhm-Bawerk's rendering of it is so vivid that one is left with the suspicion of malicious reading. Marx does explain not only how and why labourers with different levels of skill produce different quantities of value (which in their turn explain exchange relations) but also the process which reduces skilled to unskilled labour.

4.2.1 The value of an agent's labour power and deskilling

The social value of labour power has been determined in 4.1.4. But labour power can be either an output (of a non-capitalist production process) or an input (of a capitalist production process). The social value of labour power as an output is the social value of the means of reproduction deemed necessary at the moment labour power is sold. This is also its individual value as an input of a capitalist production process. Let us now consider its social value as an input of this process. This is the social value of those means of subsistence which society deems necessary for the repro-duction of labour power at the time the output is sold. As in all other types of commodities, the individual and the social value of labour power as an input differ, due to technological change in any branch of the econ-omy (see last paragraph of 3.6.2). For example, due to productivity increases, the price of production of the means of subsistence decreases, thus reducing the value of labour power. This latter has been devalued.

But, as we have seen above, to different levels of skills there correspond different values of labour power. Another form of devaluation of labour power arises when fewer skills are required to perform a certain task. To see this, we must introduce the concept of *value required:*[3] to occupy a certain position (to perform a certain task) an agent must acquire certain skills; this, in turn determines the social value of labour power of that agent, other things being equal. Or, a position requires a certain value of labour power for an agent to perform that task.

For example, if four years of university education are needed to become a chemist and if it takes a certain student eight years to take that degree, the value of his or her labour power is based on four, and not eight, years of university education. The reason for this is that the value required is determined by four, and not by eight, years. Or, the level of university education needed to train a chemist might drop from four to three years because, say, certain skills have been incorporated in certain machines. In this case, the social value of a chemist's labour power (including that of the chemists who had to study four years under the old university system) falls accordingly: the value required by the position occupied by the agent of production has fallen. It is also possible that, while the value required by a position does not change, that position is filled by an agent whose labour power has a value higher than that required by that position. For example, if a chemist has duly completed his or her university training in four years, but if s/he can find employment only as (fills the position of) a chemical technician, for whose formation only two years of training are needed, then the social value of that chemist's labour power corresponds to two, and not four, years of training.

Moreover, not only the collective labourer but also the global non-labourer participate in the production process (see 2.5). Individual non-labourers too must acquire specific skills, and this acquisition is a further specific element which determines the value required by that position. This does not hold, however, for the dependent capitalists, whose salary is independent of the value of their labour power. Finally, there are specific categories of agents who, independently of the function performed in the production process, are important from an ideological and political point of view for the reproduction of the subordination and exploitation of the collective labourer. The performance of this function also requires specific "skills" and these too contribute to the determination of the value required by those positions.

In short, while the *social* value of labour power *in general* is determined by the social value of the means of reproduction which all labourers need (whether this social value is completely determined by the law of value or not does not matter), the *social* value of the labour power of a *specific* agent is determined by the value required by the position occupied by that agent. This is the social value of the means of reproduction which all labourers must be able to buy plus the social value of the means of reproduction specific to that particular position and needed to acquire those specific skills, plus an extra portion of value if these agents' task also implies their being functional for the political and ideological subordination of the collective labourer. Thus, inasmuch as the social value of a certain product depends on the social value of labour power needed to produce it, it is the social value of that particular labour power, as determined above, which must enter the computation. This having been said, in what follows I shall only focus on the technical skills needed to perform the different tasks making up the collective labourer.

We can now understand the social process which reduces skilled to unskilled labour. Due to the introduction of new techniques in the labour process, the level of skills required of an agent is lowered. The value of his or her labour power is then devalued. We can refer to this process as *devaluation* (of labour power) *through dequalification* (of skills). It is this process which reduces skilled to unskilled labour and thus (at least as far as the value of labour power is concerned) alters the exchange relations between the commodities of which those different types of labour power are an input. It is this real process which justifies the theoretical reduction of skilled to unskilled labour, or the expression of the former as a multiple of the latter.

Notice that devaluation through dequalification is different from the devaluation of labour power resulting from the cheapening of the (culturally determined) means of subsistence. The latter cheapens the labour power of all labourers, since it affects means of subsistence used by all labourers; the former cheapens the labour power of specific types of labourers, since it affects the value needed to produce specific levels of skills and training.

The process of devaluation through dequalification is a constant tendency in capitalist production, due to the constant need capitalists have to reduce the level of wages. On the other hand, the same techniques create new, and qualified positions (the counter-tendency) which, in their turn, are soon subjected to dequalification.[4] Dequalification, or the reduction of skilled to unskilled labour, is thus a tendential movement. This tendency is of the first type since at any moment in time we can observe both the tendency (the dequalification of certain positions and thus the devaluation of the agents' labour power) and the counter-tendency (the creation of new, qualified positions for which agents with a high value of labour power are needed).[5]

4.2.2 Labour homogenization and wage equalization

The point which emerges from this discussion is that the tendential process of wage equalization is a consequence of the tendential process of labour homogenization. The former is apparently purely a market phenomenon and has deep roots in the tendential devaluation of labour power due to the constant tendency towards the deskilling of labour. This is why to take wage differentials as the determining factor of different quantities of value created would imply circular reasoning.

Notice that unskilled, or simple, labour is not a-historically given. Rather, the notion of simple labour is both socially and historically determined. Different societies might consider the same type of concrete labour either as skilled or as unskilled while the same society might consider the same type of concrete labour at first as skilled and then, at a different level of development of the productive forces, as unskilled.

4.3 Joint Production

Much fuss has been made about the law of value's supposed inability to determine the value and thus the price of two products jointly produced, that is, produced by a single production process. The reason for this, it is submitted, is that it is impossible to determine how much labour goes into each of the two joint products. In the case of joint production then, the law of value would break down. But is it really so?

4.3.1 The Marxist approach to joint production

Let us call a production process PP and let us indicate the commodity it produces by a lower letter in parenthesis. PP(a) then indicates the production process producing *a* as its only output and PP(b,c) indicates a production process which produces *b* and *c* jointly (e.g. wheat and straw). We should distinguish two cases.

The first case is straightforward. If *a* is produced both by PP(a) and by PP(a,b) and PP(a) is the modal process, then PP(a) determines the price of production of *a*, and thus also of the *a* produced by PP(a,b). The *individual* value of the *a* produced by PP(a,b) cannot be determined, but this is not a problem since its *social* value is determined by the *a* produced by PP(a). The social value of *b* is determined by subtraction.

In the second case, either *a* is produced both by PP(a) and by PP(a,b) and now it is PP(a,b) which is the modal process or *a* and *b* are produced only by PP(a,b). Again, the individual values of *a* and *b* cannot be determined separately. But this is not a problem as long as, as we have just seen, the social value can be computed. However, since, tendentially, the capitalist must realize the average rate of profit on both products, any combination of the prices of *a* and *b* which satisfies this condition is viable. Thus in this case the social value of *a* and *b* would seem to be indeterminate as well. But this is not so.

When some capitalist first introduces PP(a,b), s/he tries to charge as much as possible for both products, the prices being determined by the capitalist's assessment of the maximum feasible prices in that particular situation. That capitalist soon notices whether the prices are too high or too low. S/he also compares the rate of profit s/he makes with what the other capitalists make (and the same comparison is made by the other capitalists). This prompts both price adjustments and capital movements to and from that branch. It is this real process which warrants the assumption that the market for both *a* and *b* is cleared at a price at which that capitalist tendentially realizes the average rate of profit on both products. Under this tendential assumption, both *a* and *b* have a social value (price) separately, even though their individual value cannot be separately determined. There is no indeterminacy here.

Suppose there is now a strong change in social demand. If the demand for *a* increases, its price increases too. If the price of *b* increases, remains unchanged or does not decrease enough for that capitalist to realize the same rate of profit, the higher rate of profit causes a movement of capital to this branch, a change in the structure of production, a new distribution of social demand and thus a new set of relative prices. Again, there is no indeterminacy.

Suppose, however, that the price of *a* increases and that that of *b* decreases just enough for the rate of profit on both products to remain unaltered. This is the only case where the production prices of the joint products would seem to be indeterminate. This is an oddity, the result of pure chance, which hardly has any practical relevance. Thus nothing serious would happen if we did not address it.[6] However, since this is the case on which the critics base their argument, let us consider it.

The social demand for a certain use value refers to the need for a specific quantity of that use value and to the purchasing power allocated to satisfy that need. This applies also to the quantities of *a* and *b* wanted by the purchasers. If these quantities change, the purchasing power allocated to each one of them changes, given that the proportions in which *a* and *b* are supplied are fixed. The social demand (want and purchasing power) for these goods taken separately has changed, even if the total purchasing power allocated to the two products jointly has not. In short, *the prices of the joint products have changed because social demand has changed.* This is perfectly in line with the theory of prices submitted in chapter 3. There, we have seen that the price of production per unit of output is determined both by the structure of production (time needed by the modal producer) and by the distribution of social demand (and consequently by changes in that distribution) under the $D = S$ condition. Strong changes in social demand need not affect modal techniques but they do affect production prices through capital movements, changed surplus value produced and changed average rate of profit.

The specificity of the case under consideration is that now different patterns of social demand for the joint products result in different pairs of prices even if the social demand for the two products taken jointly and for all other products does not change. Since neither modal productivities nor the distribution of social demand among branches change, no other prices change. But, aside from this aspect, the principle that changes in social demand affect prices applies here too. To solve the pseudo-problem of joint production one only needs to consistently apply the Marxist price theory, to recognize that the realization of the average rate of profit by the capitalist producing joint products can be ensured by different patterns of social demand for the joint products. There is no price indeterminacy here. Price determination under joint production becomes problematic only if social demand is denied a role. But then, as we shall see in more detail in 4.7.1, we slip into the (neo-)Ricardian problematic and we leave the realm of Marxist price theory.

4.3.2 The neo-Ricardian approach to joint production

The debate on joint production has been spurred by Sraffa's influential work (1960) and has been used by the neo-Ricardian school to reject the labour theory of value (see, e.g., Steedman, 1977; for an introduction, see Howard and King, 1985, ch. 9). This school's central claim is that joint production leads to the possibility of negative values and surplus value.

Here it is not necessary to entangle ourselves in the neo-Ricardian argument. Suffice it to point out that the notion of negative value is fanciful, to say the least. Negative labour (value) has no economic meaning because it does not exist in reality, neither as a realized nor as a potential phenomenon. It does not arise in the Marxist value theory, it arises in the neo-Ricardian one. It is thus rather peculiar to claim that negative value deals a serious blow to the Marxist value theory. The neo-Ricardian approach, in trying to avoid this problem of its own making, falls into further difficulties. If the number of joint products is equal to the number of processes (as in the above-mentioned example), this approach solves the "negative value problem" by redefining the social value as the value produced by the most productive technique and by defining the value of the joint products along the lines of marginal analysis. One of the results of this approach is that the value of the total output is not necessarily equal to the sum of constant and variable capital plus surplus value.

The number of equations, however, can differ from that of the outputs. To understand the difficulty here, it must be recalled that in the Sraffian system, each commodity is produced by one production process, which is expressed in the form of an equation. Prices are thus determined by a system of simultaneous linear equations, where the number of equations must be equal to the number of unknown (prices) to be determined. But

136

once we drop the assumption that each commodity is produced by a separate industry, or once we assume joint production, there are more prices to be determined than there are equations. This problem is solved by Sraffa by treating all industries as joint-product industries so that "the system of single product industries is ... subsumed as an extreme case in which each of the products, while having a positive coefficient in one of the processes, has a zero coefficient in all the others" (Sraffa, 1960, p. 45).

There are many assumptions on which this approach rests and which have obviously nothing to do with capitalist reality (see Mandel and Freeman, 1984). Here I shall mention only one. There is something strange about a theory which, in order to explain reality – joint production as a sub-case of single-product production – has to turn it upside down. But even stranger is the way Sraffa deals with fixed capital. Take a machine entering a certain production process as fixed capital. In Sraffa's words "at the end of the year, the partly worn-out, older machine which emerges from the process will be regarded as a joint product" together with the final products (Sraffa, 1960; p. 63). Here not only reality has been turned upside down: all ties with reality have been lost. As Sekine puts it, "A capitalist who employs a one-year-old machine for one more year ends up with a two-year-old machine whether he likes it or not" (Sekine, 1982–3, p. 441).

The notion of negative values is probably the distorted perception of a real process, the destruction of value. Let us then turn to this case.

4.4 Destruction of Value[7]

By and large, value theory is used to study the production and distribution rather than the destruction of value. Yet in capitalism, and thus in value theory, the destruction of value is as important as its production and distribution. For example, as we shall see in the next chapter, the analysis of economic crises is the analysis of how the destruction of value (constant capital) makes possible a jump in the rate of profit and thus makes possible the next period of economic boom. The purpose of this section is to consider three cases of destruction of value, the understanding of which refines our understanding of the law of value and of the reality it depicts.

4.4.1 Wasted labour

Under capitalism, the exchange value of a product is realized when the product is sold. Its use value, on the other hand, is realized when the product is used. Since, under capitalism, use values are used by the buyers, rather than by the producers, their sale is a condition for their realization as use values. Thus the sale of the commodity is both the realization of its exchange value and at the same time the condition for the realization of its use value. If a commodity is not sold, neither its use value nor its exchange value can be realized. In this case labour has been wasted and less value is realized than the value which has been produced.

It should be stressed that this case is different from the transformation of individual into social values. There, the value which is not realized by capitals with lower OCC is realized by capitals with higher OCC. There is no waste of use values and no loss of exchange value for the economy as a whole. Here, there is both waste of use values and loss of exchange value which cannot be realized because the "use values" are useless. As long as products are exchanged, or as long as society deems them to be of some use, the value they realize can be equal, greater or smaller than their individual value. But if the products are not sold, neither the producers nor the consumers realize any of the value incorporated in those products.

4.4.2 Value-destroying labour

In *The Political Economy of Growth*, Paul Baran considers the example of a bakery in which one of the workers is given the task of adding chemicals to the dough in order to increase the bread's perishability (Baran, 1968, p. xx). If the result of that worker's labour is that the bread becomes totally useless, loaves of that bread cannot be exchanged (do not have an exchange value) since they do not satisfy society's needs in any measure, and therefore the bread's exchange value disappears as well. If, however, the result of that worker's labour is that there is only an increase in the bread's perishability, or a partial destruction of that bread's use value, assuming that society's needs have not changed, within a certain period of time that bread now satisfies a smaller proportion of society's total needs. Consequently, there is a proportional decrease in the exchange value of the product as well. Here less value is realized not because that value has been appropriated by other capitalists (UE) nor because some value has been wasted (the product has not been sold) but because some value has been purposely destroyed. I have called elsewhere (Carchedi, 1987a, p. 228) this type of labour *value-destroying labour* (from now on, VDL). Any addition of this type of labour does not increase the value of a commodity but rather destroys it.

At least two points should be made in this connection. First, it is clear that VDL is irrational for a capitalist unless the partial destruction of a commodity's value has the effect of restricting supply under monopolistic conditions. This can allow a capitalist to realize higher profits. Second, VDL is more than a theoretical curiosity. There are types of

VDL which are of great practical importance for present-day capitalism. A few examples are: the planning and execution of shutting down enterprises;[8] the planning and execution of restricted reproduction (less capital is invested than in the previous production process); the planning and execution of built-in obsolescence, and the planning and execution of moving a plant (inasmuch as this implies scrapping means of production which are still adequate in terms of technological competition).

4.4.3 Technical obsolescence

The planning and execution of built-in perishability, obsolescence, etc. mentioned above would seem to be similar to the planning and execution of the scrapping of machines which have become obsolete, that is, which are still operational but which must be replaced by new and more efficient ones, due to technological competition. But this is not so. The former is labour which destroys value during the production process, during a production process which is both production and destruction of value at the same time.

In the case of technical obsolescence, the old machines must be replaced before they have exhausted their usefulness. In this case there is destruction of use value, of that part of the machine's use value which has not yet been consumed by physical wear and tear. Consequently there is also a proportional destruction of exchange value. The labour which plans and carries out technical obsolescence is labour which destroys labour after the production process has been completed and the product (e.g. the machine) has been sold and has realized its social value. This type of labour destroys value after it has been produced and realized – by preventing part of the value of the machine being transferred to the value of the outputs of which the machine is an input.

To sum up, the important differences between these three types of labour are: value-destroying labour destroys value during the production process; wasted labour corresponds to destruction of value after value has been produced, the reason being that this value cannot be realized – and the labour which plans and carries out technical obsolescence destroys value after it has been produced and realized, in the next production cycle.

4.5 Okishio and the Fall in the Rate of Profit

In Table 3.5 capital BI increases its OCC to $90c/10v = 9$. This calls for a new tendential situation, a new price of production per unit of capital for that economy (117.3) and a new average rate of profit (17.3%). The average rate of profit has fallen from 20% to 17.3%. It is the investment in more productive techniques (techniques with higher OCCs) within branches, and thus the production of less (surplus) value per unit of

139

capital, which explains the fall in the equalized rate of profit between branches. The objection has been made, however, that technical innovations must increase the general rate of profit unless this increase is sufficiently offset by an increase in the real wage rate. Okishio (1961) is the author most frequently mentioned in this connection.

Okishio starts from the premiss that capitalists introduce new techniques not necessarily because these techniques save labour (the productivity criterion) but because they reduce costs (the cost criterion). His argument is that "if the newly introduced technique satisfies the cost criterion and the rate of real wage remains constant" the rate of profit must increase (Okishio, 1961, p. 92).

It is true that capitalists aim at reducing costs rather than the labour needed to produce commodities and that they introduce new techniques only if costs are reduced, or if their profits are increased. It is also true that, by doing so, they increase their individual rate of profit. These points, by the way, are not a discovery of Okishio but belong to the foundations of Marx's theory and are repeatedly stressed by Marx. But what Okishio does not see is the effects of the introduction of new techniques on the *creation of value* and thus on the average rate of profit. He only sees the reduction in costs, not the reduction in value produced. Thus he does not see that, if less value is produced, the increase in the realized rate of profit of the innovative capitalists must imply both *appropriation* of value from other capitals (branches) and a decrease in the average rate of profit.

For Marx too new techniques reduce the individual value of commodities. However, the specific way this is done under capitalism is by introducing more productive means of production, by purposely increasing the quantity of output per unit of capital invested while unknowingly decreasing the quantity of exchange value newly produced per unit of capital invested. This decrease is due to the increased OCC, to the replacement of people by machines. This means that the *decrease in the value per unit of output* (for BI it decreases from $115/50 = 2.3$ in Table 3.4 to $110/60 = 1.83$ in Table 3.5) is accompanied by a *decrease in the value produced per unit of capital* (from 115 to 110), and thus by a *fall in the average rate of profit* (from 20% to 17.3%) while the rate of profit of the innovative capital (BI) tendentially increases from 0 to 17.3%. The production of cheaper products and of less value per unit of capital are two sides of the same coin. By disregarding this essential linkage, Okishio loses sight of the way in which costs are reduced under industrial capitalism and of the tendency of the rate of profit to fall.

The source of Okishio's difficulty in properly assessing the effect of technological innovations on the rate of profit is the affinity of his views to neo-Ricardianism. In the neo-Ricardian view, the economy produces a physical output valued in money terms. Given certain inputs expressed in money terms (prices and money wages), a new technology is introduced by capitalists if it increases output (and thus its money expression), thus decreasing unit costs (again in money terms). Alternatively, given a certain output (in money terms), a new technology is introduced if it simply decreases unit costs, if fewer or less costly inputs are needed. In both cases unit costs must decrease and, other things being equal, the rate of profit must increase.

This is indeed the way the individual capitalist looks at reality. If one takes the point of view of the individual capitalist (whether s/he knows it or not), this is as far as one need go. In this view, capitalists react to prices and costs and the capitalist system is simply a generalization (aggregation) of the behaviour of individual capitalists. If the effect of the introduction of a new technique for the individual capitalist is a rise in his or her rate of profit, then, the argument goes, a generalization of this technique will lead to a rise in the general rate of profit, unless wages increase.

But this is not the way the capitalist system works. Once one leaves neo-Ricardianism and steps into the Marxist dimension, the way is open to the realization that what holds for the individual capitalist does not necessarily hold for the whole of the capitalist class, that the tendency towards the lower average rate of profit is the unintentional result of conscious attempts to achieve higher individual rates of profit. Under capitalism a new technology does not simply reduce unit costs, it does this by replacing people with more productive machines, or by increasing the OCC. Lower costs and less surplus value produced are two sides of the same coin. This is the specific way unit costs are reduced under capitalism.

By considering how the capitalist system works through the action of individual capitalists, how social laws affirm themselves "behind the back" of individual capitalists, Marx can explain what is an obvious absurdity from the point of view of the individual capitalist, the fact that "the rate of profit does not fall because labour becomes less productive, but because it becomes more productive" (Marx, 1967c, p. 240). Okishio, on the other hand, goes no further than the view of the individual capitalist for whom increases in labour's productivity mean increases in the rate of profit and who cannot understand why, if everybody "produces more value", the average rate of profit can fall.[9]

4.6 Productivity, Exploitation and Redistribution of Value

In economic literature, increased productivity is often confused with increased exploitation and this latter is often simply equated with a simple redistribution of value. Both differences and similarities between these concepts should be spelled out.

4.6.1 Productivity and exploitation

The previous section has argued that an increase in productivity – by requiring a higher OCC – decreases the new value produced and thus the average rate of profit. But there is a case in which – contrary to the thesis submitted in this work – a productivity rise would seem to increase the new value produced and thus the average rate of profit. Take the following example:

80c + 20v + 20s = 120V   Output = 100 units
Working day = 10 hours

In this case, each hour produces 10 units for which 8c of past labour and 2v plus 2s of new labour are needed. Or, each hour of work transfers 8 units of past value to the product (10 use values) and creates 4 units of new value. The 10 units of output thus have a value of 1.2 each. The OCC is 80c/20v = 4, the rate of exploitation is 20s/20v = 100%, the rate of profit is 20s/(80c + 20v) = 20% and the output/capital ratio, or the rate of productivity, is 100 units/ (80c + 20v) = 100%.

Suppose now that the capitalist can force the labourers to work one extra hour without compensation (what follows applies just as well to the case of intensification of labour). In this extra hour 8c are transferred and 4 new units of value are produced. However, this new value is all surplus value. This extra 12V takes the concrete form of 10 extra use values. The situation is now

88c + 20v + 24s = 132V   Output = 110 units
Working day = 11 hours

Now the OCC is 88c/20v = 4.4, the rate of surplus value is 24s/20v = 120%, the rate of profit is 24s/(88c + 20v) = 22.22% and the output/capital ratio (productivity) is 110/(88c + 20v) = 101.85%. It would seem that here we have both an increase in productivity and an increase in the total value produced, and thus in the average rate of profit. But this is not so. What we have here is *an increase in the rate of exploitation*, from 100% to 120%, *not an increase in the rate of productivity*. Or, the technique of production has remained the same and thus productivity has not changed.[10] The OCC increases either because of increased efficiency, and in this case the rate of profit falls, or because of increased exploitation, and in this case the rate of profit rises.

142

Contrary to the case of technical change, the value of commodities (0.8 units of old value plus 0.4 units of new value) does not change if the rate of surplus value increases. If that rate is 100% (i.e. 20/20), the value produced is 120, the output is 100 and the value per unit is 120/100 = 1.2. If the rate of exploitation is 120% (24/20), the value produced is 132, the output is 110 and the value per unit is still 132/110 = 1.2. In short, the OCC increases either because productivity increases, and in this case the value per unit of output falls, or because the rate of exploitation increases, but in this case the value per unit of output remains unchanged.

It should be stressed that it is the *value* of the commodities which either falls (in case of increased efficiency) or not (in case of increased exploitation). The *cost* per unit of output for the capitalist decreases in *both* cases. In fact, in the case of increased exploitation, the value remains 1.2 but the cost falls from (80 + 20)/100 = 1 to (88 + 20)/110 = 0.98.

A similar reasoning holds for a decrease in the rate of exploitation which is perceived as a fall in productivity growth. The following is just one of the many examples: "Low productivity gains aren't unusual in the beginning of a recession because demand and output drop faster than companies can cut payrolls and work time" (Cooper and Madigan, 1991, p. 14). In this case the output/capital ratio falls because of a fall in the rate of surplus value, not because of decreased efficiency. The cost per unit of output increases.

There are then two related reasons why orthodox economics confuses increases in productivity and in exploitation. They derive from accepting the point of view of the individual capitalist. First, the output/capital ratio increases both in the case of increased efficiency and increased exploitation. Since this movement is severed from that of the value per unit of output, it becomes impossible to distinguish between increases in productivity (increase in the output/capital ratio accompanied by a falling value per unit of output) and increases in exploitation (increase in the output/capital ratio accompanied by a constant value per unit of output). Alternatively, the capital/output ratio (unit costs) falls in both cases. Again, if this movement is severed from that of the value of commodities, it becomes impossible to distinguish between a fall in this ratio due to increased efficiency and a fall due to increased exploitation. For the capitalist it is a matter of relative indifference whether the output/capital ratio increases (or the capital/output ratio decreases) as a consequence of increased efficiency or of increased exploitation.

Second, increases in exploitation can be an effective means for less efficient capitalists to compensate for their technological backwardness. There is thus, from the point of view of increasing the individual capitalist's rate of profit, no difference between increases in exploitation and in productivity (efficiency). But the economics of the labouring classes should make this distinction, as the next chapter will make clear.

4.6.2 Exploitation and redistribution of value

The case of an increase in the rate of exploitation due to longer working days or more intensive work is different from the case in which the rate of exploitation rises because wages fall below the value of labour power. Suppose that, in the example at the beginning of 4.6.1, 80c represents one machine and 20v represents one worker. The OCC is $80/20 = 4$. If now that worker is paid 10v, the OCC rises to $80/10 = 8$. However, this increase indicates neither an increased productivity nor an increased exploitation associated with a larger volume of value produced (as above). Rather, now there is simply a redistribution of value from the worker to the capitalist. Since the volume of value remains the same and wages fall from 20 to 10, surplus value rises from 20 to 30. Again, here an increased OCC does not reflect increased productivity, only an increased rate of exploitation. The value composition of the product will be

80c + 10v + 30s = 120V   Output = 100 units
Working day = 10 hours

Here an increase in the rate of exploitation indicates a redistribution of a fixed quantity of value only in case wages change. The rate of profit rises from 20% to $30/90 = 33\%$ while the total value produced does not. If it is the length of the working day or the intensity of labour which change, then a change in the rate of exploitation indicates a redistribution of a *changed* quantity of value.

To sum up, the following three cases should be distinguished:

1. An increase in productivity is mirrored in a higher OCC (within branches). If the rate of surplus value does not change, the new value produced falls. The average rate of profit and the individual value of the commodities fall too.

2. An increase in the rate of exploitation due to longer working days or higher intensity of labour is also reflected in a higher OCC. Here, however, on the assumption that wages (and thus redistribution) and techniques do not change, the new value produced rises. The average rate of profit rises too, but the value per unit of output does not change.

3. An increase in the rate of exploitation due to lower wages (the techniques, length of the working day and intensity of labour remaining constant) is also reflected in an increase in the OCC. This affects neither the total value produced nor the value per unit of output. However, the average rate of profit rises.

In short, an increase in the OCC implies a fall in total value produced if it denotes technological change; a constant total value produced if it denotes a simple redistributional change; and a rise in total value produced if it denotes an increased intensity of labour or longer working days. An increase in the rate of surplus value denotes a greater quantity of value produced if it is due to longer working days and higher intensity of labour; it denotes an unchanged quantity of value produced if it is due to a simple redistribution between variable capital and surplus value.

4.6.3 Productivity, exploitation and the rate of profit

It was mentioned in the previous section that the ultimate cause of the fall in the average rate of profit is increased productivity. There are alternative theories which are based on the opposite notion that the average rate of profit falls because productivity falls, and thus that it rises when productivity rises. Okishio's theory is a case in point (see 4.5). I shall discuss more of these theories in chapter 5. Here I shall only point out that all these theories have Ricardian rather than Marxist roots.

In fact, for Ricardo "profits depend on higher or lower wages, wages on prices of necessaries, and the price of necessaries chiefly on the price of food" (Ricardo, 1966, p. 119). But due to decreased productivity in agriculture, an increased quantity of food can only be produced at rising unit costs in terms of labour, so that "the natural tendency of profits is to fall" (Ricardo, 1966, p. 120). Ricardo does mention that "this tendency ... is happily checked ... by the improvements in machinery ... as well as by discoveries in the science of agriculture" (Ricardo, 1966, p. 120), but these factors play only a secondary role.

Thus if productivity decreases in agriculture, wages rise relative to profits and the rate of profit falls. Conversely, productivity increases in agriculture lead to a rise in the average rate of profit. If, by extension, the same applies to all other branches, the rate of profit falls because productivity falls and rises because productivity rises.

This contrasts with Marx's thesis that the ultimate cause of the fall in the average rate of profit, as pointed out in 4.5 above and as argued in detail in chapter 5 below, is the increase in the OCC which accompanies technological innovations both in manufacturing and in agriculture and thus the fall in the value and surplus value produced per unit of capital. Decreasing surplus value and increasing physical productivity go hand in hand.

Under normal capitalist conditions, there can be decreasing produc*tion* (in periods of crisis) but no decreasing produc*tivity*. Productivity can remain stationary, or increase in some branches and not in other branches, or increase more in some than in other branches[11] but cannot decrease, except in marginal cases as for example when, due to increased demand for some minerals or oil, less efficient mines or oilfields are brought (again) into production. What can decrease is the rate of exploitation and this factor does indeed lower the rate of profit. But, as has been argued in 4.6.1 above, productivity and exploitation are not the same and actually a rise in these two factors has opposite effects on the rate of profit.

4.7 Abstract Labour versus Standard of Value

To close this chapter, a related issue should be considered: the neo-Ricardian claim that the Marxist transformation problem has been correctly solved by Sraffa's standard commodity. Put in these terms, the issue is hopelessly confused. To clarify the issue, the Ricardian measurement problem should be separated from the neo-Ricardian one.

4.7.1 Ricardo's measurement problem

According to Ricardo, prices are not uniquely determined by labour time; they are affected by a number of other factors as well. Therefore labour time cannot be a reliable measure of the value and thus of the prices of commodities. It is this difficulty that moves Ricardo to look for a standard commodity, a "perfect measure of value", which can replace labour time. Let us first consider which cases are regarded by Ricardo as invalidating the thesis of price determination by labour time.

First of all, Ricardo holds, relative prices can change due to the different proportions of fixed (constant, in Marx's terms) and variable capital. Take the case of two producers, A and B. Producer A invests £5,000 as variable capital and produces a machine which, given a rate of profit of 10%, must be sold at £5,500. Producer B also invests £5,000 as variable capital and produces corn which, given the same rate of profit, must also be sold at £5,500. Consider now the next production period. In it, two other producers, C and D, produce corn. C invests £5,000 as variable capital and realizes £5,500, as before. D invests the same variable capital, on which he must realize a profit of £500, plus £5,500 to buy a machine, on which he must realize 10%, or £550. Thus, D, "to be on a par" with C, or to realize the same rate of profit as C, must sell his product at £5,500 + 550 = £6,050 (this, by the way, assumes that no part of the value of the machine is transferred to the value of the product). Ricardo concludes,

146

> Here then are capitalists employing precisely the same quantity of labour annually on the production of their commodities, and yet the goods they produce differ in value on account of the different quantities of fixed capital, or accumulated labour, employed by each respectively. (Ricardo, 1966, p. 34)

It is immediately clear that neither this notion nor this computation of value bear any resemblance to the notion and measurement of value in Marxist theory.[12] In this latter theory value is measured by abstract labour and social value is given by the price of production. If two modal capitalists employ the same amount of constant and variable capital but in different proportions, they produce different individual values, but realize the same social value, or price of production per unit of capital, due to the equalization of the profit rates. However, since they produce different use values, they also produce different quantities of use values per unit of capital. Therefore the prices of production per unit of output will differ. But this, far from being a problem as in the Ricardian price theory, is a logical outcome of the Marxist theory of prices.

Ricardo's mistake resides in presupposing the average rate of profit, or production prices, and then examining how different quantities of "fixed" capital alter these production prices, thus invalidating the law of value. By presupposing, instead of inquiring into, the tendential equalization of the profit rates, Ricardo fails to see that different proportions of constant and variable capital affect the value and thus the surplus value produced and that it is these different amounts of surplus value which must tendentially be equalized. Instead, Ricardo first postulates equalized rates of profit and then considers how these equal rates of profit are changed by what in Marxist terms are different OCCs. This procedure creates a problem in Ricardo's theory, not in the Marxist one.

Second, Ricardo submits that prices vary due to the different turnover periods, even though the labour time necessary to produce them does not change. He provides the following example. Producer A needs two years to produce a certain commodity and £2,000. Of this, £1,000 must be invested in the first year and £1,000 in the second year. Each time that £1,000 is used to employ 20 men. At the end of the second year he sells the product and, assuming an average rate of profit of 10%, realizes £2,310. In fact, Ricardo holds, that producer has invested £1,000 in the first year on which he should realize a profit of £100. However, this sum is "frozen" so to speak in the uncompleted production process. In the second year he again invests £1,000 but at the end of the second year he should get 10% not only on this sum but also on the £1,100 which he could not realize at the end of the first period, that is, he must realize 10% of £2,100, or £210. In total he realizes a profit of £310, and that commodity must be sold at £2,310.

Take now producer B. He invests the same quantity of money (£2,000) and the same number of men (40) but all in the first year. At the end of that year he sells that product for £2,200. These two commodities, then, have "the same quantity of labour bestowed on them" and yet their prices differ.

Ricardo is wrong in attributing these values to the two commodities. This mistake reveals the mentality of the financier who invests £1,000 in the first year and gets a rate of *interest* of 10% on them and who reinvests that £1,100 plus an extra £1,000 in the second year. But this is not how the value of the commodities should be computed. To know these values, we must know the proportions in which the £1,000 is invested in constant and variable capital as well as the rate of surplus value. Marx provides the following example (Marx, 1968, p. 179). Suppose

I $\quad 80c + 20v + 4s = 104$
II $\quad 20c + 80v + 16s = 116$

where the rate of surplus value is 20%. The average rate of profit is 20/200 = 10%, which is Ricardo's assumption. Each of the two branches realizes tendentially a value of 110. If we now suppose that branch I needs two years to complete its production process and branch II needs only one year, in two years branch I produces s = 4 and branch II produces s = 32. The new average rate of profit is then 36/300 = 12% and the prices of production are 112 for both capitals. Ricardo would conclude that a change in the turnover time, rather than a change in labour time, causes a change in prices. Again, Ricardo's mistake resides in postulating the average rate of profit and then considering how this average rate is changed by different turnover times instead of considering how different turnover times affect the quantity of value and surplus value produced and then equalizing these differences in an average profit rate. Again, the different lengths of the production process pose a problem in Ricardo's theory, not in Marx's.

Third, prices change when distribution changes. Suppose, says Ricardo, that wages rise. Profits then must fall and this would have to leave prices unchanged. Yet in the case of producers C and D mentioned above, if profits fall from 10% to 9%, producer D adds 9% of £5,500 (the price of the machine), or £495, to £5,500 (the value of variable capital plus 10% on that value). Producer C, on the contrary, keeps selling his product at £5,500. In this case, concludes Ricardo, the goods "in which more fixed capital was employed, would fall relatively to ... any other goods in which a less portion of fixed capital entered" (Ricardo, 1966, p. 35). It will be noticed that Ricardo is inconsistent in applying the lower rate of profit (9%) only to constant capital. But this is not the real problem.

The problem is that, once more, Ricardo first postulates the average rate of profit and then considers the effects on this rate due to distributional changes. But once more, the fact that distributional changes can affect the average rate of profit is not a problem in Marxist price theory. Consider first a change in the distribution of value between capitalists and workers, e.g. a wage rise. Consider two producers, one with high OCC and the other with low OCC. If wages increase and if the rate of surplus value remains the same, the high OCC producer loses less than the low OCC producer (since the former employs less variable capital than the latter). Other things being equal, capital moves from where losses are bigger (low OCC capital) to where they are smaller (high OCC capital), thus tendentially equalizing the two rates of profit into a lower average rate. Consider now distributional changes caused by shifts in demand for the different products. As argued above, in the Marxist price theory, prices are determined not only by the structure of production, and thus by the level of productivity in each branch, but also by the distribution of social demand, under the $D = S$ assumption. It will be recalled that this assumption means that we disregard weak changes in social demand. However, strong changes in social demand do change the production prices per unit of output, given that they cause capital movements across branches with different OCCs, thus changing the average rate of profit. Differently from Marx, Ricardo theorizes the socially necessary labour time as the labour time socially necessary *to produce* a commodity, thus disregarding the effects of strong changes in social demand on production prices.

In both cases of distributional changes, the technically determined labour time necessary to produce commodities does not change (since productivity does not change) but production prices per unit of output do change. The fact that a change in the value of labour power or strong changes in social demand can affect profits, capital movements and ultimately production prices is consistent with the Marxian, but not with the Ricardian, approach.

It is on the basis of these mistakes that Ricardo concludes that labour time is not the only determinant, and thus not the perfect measure, of value and prices. Within Ricardo's frame, there is only one option left. Since labour time is not a suitable measure of value, could not a commodity fulfil that role? The problem here is, as Ricardo points out, that such a standard would have to be produced under an immutable production technique. Only in this case would we be able to ascertain when the price of a commodity changes, because what has changed is the labour time socially necessary to produce it rather than that needed to produce the standard commodity. Since all commodities, including gold, are subject to variations in the labour necessary to produce them, it is impossible to find a standard measure of value, or standard commodity (Ricardo, 1966, p. 43).[13] This is true, but once more it is a Ricardian problem; it arises only if one needs a commodity as a measure of value. In Marx's system this is not the case. It is abstract labour, and not a commodity, which is the measure of value and it is the production price which is the social value, rather than only the socially necessary labour as given by technical conditions.

4.7.2 The neo-Ricardian measurement problem

The neo-Ricardian measurement problem differs from Ricardo's in that it is couched in terms of *use* values. In the neo-Ricardian world, production relations are technical relations which produce use values. Theirs is truly a world of production of commodities by means of commodities. It is this that explains their need for a standard commodity. In fact, the basic magnitudes of analysis, surplus, social product and real wage "consist of heterogeneous bundles of commodities". But these magnitudes must be "added to, and subtracted from, one another" (Eatwell, 1974, pp. 286–7). There is thus a need for a standard of value which can serve as a standard of measurement, a homogenizer so to speak.

Gold and socially necessary labour time will not do for the reasons mentioned above by Ricardo. Moreover, the neo-Ricardians reject abstract labour, given the belief that the capitalist economy can be analysed without the complications arising from the Marxist value theory (or, the transformation problem). Thus, just as in Ricardo's theory, the need arises for a standard commodity. But this standard cannot be any actually existing commodity (and this is why Ricardo could not find any). There seems to be, then, no other way out than an imaginary standard commodity as the homogenizer. This is precisely the reason behind Sraffa's construction of an imaginary commodity, the standard commodity. This is a

> set of multipliers which, if applied to several equations or industries composing the [real, G.C.] system, will have the effect of rearranging them in such proportions that the commodity-composition of the aggregate means of production and that of the aggregate product are identical. (Sraffa, 1960, p. 26)

It is not necessary to go into the intricacies of the construction of Sraffa's standard commodity. Rather, only one point will be stressed. It is sometimes argued that the Sraffian standard commodity is also the solution of Marx's transformation "problem". However, both the search for an invariable standard of value and its Sraffian solution are a neo-Ricardian problem, totally "meaningless within Marxism" (de Brunhoff,

1974–5, p. 481). They arise from the belief that abstract labour cannot be used as the measure of value (because of the transformation problem)[14] and from a conception of the economy as producing use values. Both claims are wrong.

Notes

1. For some arguments similar to the ones that follow, see Ehrbar and Glick, 1987.
2. This point is dealt with in detail in chapter 7, section 7.
3. I submitted for the first time the notion of value required in Carchedi, 1975.
4. For a detailed analysis of this point and of the importance for a theory of the new middle class, see Carchedi, 1977.
5. Authors of a Sraffian or neo-Ricardian persuasion accept the validity of von Böhm-Bawerk's critique and offer a solution to the reduction "problem" in the form of a system of simultaneous equations for the production of physical goods and of the complex labour of different types needed to produce those goods. For these equations, the physical inputs, the quantities of complex labour of different types, and a certain quantity of simple labour are needed. This system of equations is sufficient to determine an equal number of unknowns, namely the quantity of simple labour directly and indirectly embodied in a unit of each commodity (and which is deemed to be its value) and the coefficients of reduction of complex to simple labour (see Roncaglia, 1974; Rowthorn, 1974).
This approach accepts the validity of von Böhm-Bawerk's critique and thus is open to the objections submitted in 3.6 above. For a criticism of the neo-Ricardian solution to this "problem" see Tortajada, 1977.
6. Notice that what is argued here is not that joint production is irrelevant. Rather, the irrelevance of this case depends on the assumption of opposite price changes in a and b such that the rate of profit on both products is not affected.
7. A longer version of this section first appeared in Carchedi, 1987a, pp. 225–32.
8. According to the *International Herald Tribune* of March 26, 1986, there is a new managerial career developing called "director of plant closings".
9. For a review of some of the formulations of the law of the tendential fall in the rate of profit, see Christiansen (1976). For an approach partly similar to the one submitted here, see Shaikh (1978). For two good complementary discussions and critiques of the "Okishians", see Fine, 1982; Weeks, 1982a.
Some authors do not challenge the correctness of Okishio's critique of Marx but consider it to be not very relevant because of the assumption of constant real wages. This assumption greatly weakens the relevance of Okishio's theorem "because the characteristic pattern of capital accumulation involves increases in real wages at the same time as the value of labour-power falls and the rate of exploitation rises" (Foley, 1986, p. 139). While not taking away from the importance of this critique, the approach submitted here stresses the inconsistency of Okishio's theorem with, rather than its irrelevance for an understanding of, capitalist reality.
10. P. Chattopadhyay distinguishes between *technical change*, or qualitative change, and *organizational change*, or quantitative change. The former indicates increased productivity, the latter increased exploitation. Of course, often these two types of change occur together.
11. Productivity in branch A can increase more than in branch B in the sense that in A it increases by, say, 20% compared to *its* previous level of productivity and in B by 10%, also compared to its previous level. This is not the same as saying that some branches have become more productive than others.
12. Marx engages in the correct computations; see Marx, 1968, pp. 180 ff.
13. Moreover, as Marx comments,

Even if there were such a commodity, the influence of the rise or fall in wages, the different combinations of fixed and circulating capital, the different degrees of durability

151

of the fixed capital employed and the [different] length of time before the commodity can be brought to the market, etc. would prevent it from being "a perfect measure of value". (Marx, 1968, p. 202)

14. Abstract labour, unlike the Sraffian standard commodity, is a theorization of a real phenomenon. The standard commodity, on the contrary, is a mental construction with no element of reality corresponding to it.

========== 5 ==========

Growth, Crises, Inflation and Crashes

5.1 The Fall in the Rate of Profit: Cause and Nature

The previous chapters have examined the capitalist system of production (chapter 2) and distribution (chapter 3). Part of the surplus value produced and appropriated through the price mechanism is reinvested in additional constant and variable capital, in what has been called expanded reproduction (see 3.8.5), or capital accumulation. However, this process of growth is far from being smooth. Under capitalism, periods of economic growth are followed by crises, as Table 5.1 shows.

This table does not cover the last crisis which broke out in the last quarter of 1990, after a year and a half of recession, and which was not yet over at the time of writing. In February 1991, industrial production in the US had fallen for the fifth consecutive month by 0.8% to give a twelve-month decline of 2.6% and a three-month decline of 10.8% (*The Economist*, March 23, 1991, p. 123). In March 1991, business failures were "up by a staggering 38% since last year" (M. J. Mandel, 1991).

Table 5.1 Percentage decline in industrial production and investments in the US, 1948–1980

Crises	Duration (months)	Industrial production	Investment in production	Investment in housing
1948–49	15	9.2	16.0	17.8
1953–54	8	10.0	3.9	4.2
1957–58	14	14.3	14.9	5.6
1960–61	12	7.3	4.5	12.6
1969–70	13	6.8	7.0	15.3
1974–75	9	15.3	17.8	48.0
1979–80	10	9.0	....	26.0

Source: Rapos, 1984, p. 246, table 39

153

5.1.1 The ultimate cause of crises

The first question to be tackled, then, is: what determines crises? The thesis submitted here is that crises are basically determined by the process of technological innovation, by the consequent growth in the OCC and thus by the decreasing quantity of surplus value produced. The result of this movement is the tendential fall of the average rate of profit. Consider the following example:

A $80c + 20v + 20s = 120V$ Output $120a$
B $60c + 40v + 40s = 140V$ Output $140b$

where sector A produces means of production and sector B produces means of consumption. The average rate of profit is 30%. If we assume partial external exchange and simple reproduction (see 3.8.4), $40a$ are exchanged for $60b$, or both capital and labour in A get $30b$ each. Assuming now that B increases its productivity and thus also its OCC,

A $80c + 20v + 20s = 120V$ Output $120a$
B $70c + 30v + 30s = 130V$ Output $260b$

The new average rate of profit is 25%, which is lower than the previous one. However, the quantity of the means of consumption available to both capitalists and labourers has doubled. Now $70c$ is represented by $140b$ which are exchanged for $40a$. This means that both capital and labour in A now receive $70b$ instead of $30b$ each. Capital and labour in B now receive $60b$ each instead of $40b$.[1] Finally, let us assume that it is sector A which increases its productivity; then

A $90c + 10v + 10s = 110V$ Output $220a$
B $60c + 40v + 40s = 140V$ Output $140b$

Again, the average rate of profit falls to 25%. The quantity of means of consumption available to capital and labour in both A and in B has not changed. However, the quantity of the means of production available for internal use in A has doubled.

Why should the rate of profit fall, if the quantity of use values, including the means of consumption, has increased? Given that the fall in the rate of profit causes a crisis, this is tantamount to asking why a period of prosperity is followed by an economic crisis. The answer can be found only if we recall that value is first of all a social relation (see 3.7.3). Value is labour performed by the labourers for the capitalists: the latter appropriate a part of this labour for themselves. Or, capitalism is a system based on the appropriation of labour. If this is so, if a sector (capitalist) introduces labour-saving technologies, it employs fewer labourers and produces at the same time both more use values and less value (and surplus value). The total amount of surplus labour left available for redistribution through the price mechanism is then smaller, and with it the average rate of profit. *For a system based on the appropriation of labour, what is determinant is an increased expenditure and appropriation of (abstract) labour rather than an increased production and appropriation of use values.* The use values produced might increase but, if the labour appropriated (surplus value) decreases, a crisis is in the making.

Crises are the expression of the contradiction inherent in capitalist production, which is at the same time production of use values and of value, and of the fact that an increased production of the former is at the same time a decreased production of the latter. This contradiction, in its turn, is an expression of the social, and contradictory, nature of value, of the fact that value is not simply (abstract) labour but labour performed for one class by another class. Only class analysis can reveal the ultimate cause of economic crises.

5.1.2 The two determinants of the rate of profit

Up to now, the discussion has focused on the relation between productivity and the rate of profit. Other things being equal, if a capital increases its organic composition of capital, or OCC, its own realized rate of profit increases too (due to its increased productivity and appropriation, rather than production, of value), but the average rate of profit decreases (due to that capital's decreased production of value and surplus value). In this and the following chapters, when reference will be made to "the rate of profit" without further qualifications, it is the average rate of profit which will be meant.

The rate of profit, however, is also determined by the rate of surplus value in the sense that the higher the rate of surplus value, the higher the rate of profit. Let us denote the rate of profit (surplus value divided by total capital invested) as p, the rate of surplus value (surplus value divided by variable capital) as s', and the organic composition of capital (constant capital divided by variable capital) as OCC. Then we have

$$p = s/(c + v), s' = s/v, \text{ and } OCC = c/v$$

By dividing both the numerator and the denominator of the rate of profit by v, we obtain

$$p = (s/v)/[(c + v)/v] = s'/[(c/v) + (v/v)] = s'/(OCC + 1)$$

or, the rate of profit varies directly with the rate of surplus value and inversely with the OCC. This means that, whenever it is said that the rate of profit tendentially falls due to an increase in the OCC, it is the rise of the OCC relative to a certain rate of surplus value which is meant.

More specifically, the two determinants of the rate of profit can either move in opposite directions or in the same direction. If they move in the opposite direction, the rate of profit rises if the OCC falls and the rate of surplus value increases; and it falls if the OCC rises and the rate of surplus value falls. If they move in the same direction, there are four possibilities: the OCC can increase more or less than an increase in the rate of surplus value, or the OCC can decrease more or less than the decrease in the rate of surplus value. The effect of each of these four possible combinations on the rate of profit depends in each concrete case on the actual percentage increase or decrease of each of the two variables.

At any given moment, the upward (or downward) movement of the average rate of profit depends on whether all the factors which push the rate of profit upward (or downward) are stronger than all the other factors which push the rate of profit downward (or upward). However, tendentially the rate of profit falls due to a higher increase in the OCC than in the rate of surplus value. Let us see why.

5.1.3 The tendential nature of the fall of the profit rate

The hypothesis that the rate of profit has a tendency to fall implies that the rise in the OCC is the tendency and that the rise in the rate of surplus value is the counter-tendency.

Notice that the increase in the OCC is itself a tendency with its own counter-tendencies, for example the decreased value of the means of production due to increased productivity. The same applies to the increase in the rate of surplus value, which can be checked by, say, rising wages in periods of recovery and boom. The question then is why, *within this context*, the increase in the OCC is given the role of the tendency, or why we assume a tendential fall in the average rate of profit. There are two reasons. First, while the rise of the OCC is practically unrestrained, the rise in the rate of surplus value is limited by workers' resistance and by the fact that the higher the rate of exploitation, the more difficult it is to increase it further. As Marx puts it, "the greater the surplus labour, the less can an increase in productive force perceptibly diminish necessary labour" (Marx, 1973, p. 340).[2] Second, the history of capitalism clearly shows that crises are unavoidable. As we shall see in 5.4, the thesis of the tendential fall in the average profit rate due to increases in the OCC is the only one which allows us to explain that unavoidability.

It is this interplay of tendency and counter-tendency which makes of the fall of the average rate of profit a dialectical law. To quote Marx again, "the same influences which produce a tendency in the general rate of profit to fall, also call forth counter-effects, which hamper, retard and partly paralyse this fall" (Marx, 1967c, p. 239).

However, this should not suggest an image of a constant, even though fluctuating, fall. If this were the case, capitalism would have collapsed a long time ago. Rather, a tendential fall can be depicted as follows. A fluctuating, downward movement causes an economic slowdown and depression. When economic depression turns into an economic crisis, the violent destruction of constant capital and the drastic increase in the rate of surplus value make possible a rise in the rate of profit. For a while the rate of profit will remain high. But at a certain point it will start falling again, thus repeating the same pattern which will lead to a crisis again (see 5.5.1 and 5.5.2 below).

Is there empirical evidence supporting the thesis of the tendential fall of the rate of profit? Empirical research on this issue is greatly hampered by the fact that the available statistics have not been collected according to categories consistent with the value theory. However, in spite of this difficulty, recent serious empirical work does indeed back up this thesis. This is indicated by Chart 5.1 below, where OCC means organic composition of capital, s' means rate of surplus value and p indicates the rate of profit.

Chart 5.1 illustrates three important points. First, it illustrates the fluctuating nature of the fall in the rate of profit. The rate of profit falls dramatically in one year, from 41% in 1949 to 37% in 1950; it then steadily climbs and reaches 40% in 1955; it falls again to 37% the following year, but starts climbing again afterwards and reaches 46% in 1964 where it stays until 1966; it then starts falling once more in the following nine years until it reaches 33% in 1975.

Second, this chart illustrates the long-run movement of the rate of profit. In fact, there seems to be no secular tendency for the average rate of profit to fall. Rather, there seem to be relatively long periods (25 to 30 years) of increasing rates of profit followed by more or less equally long periods of falling rates of profit, of which the period starting in the late 1960s is the last one. Within each of these long-run periods, there are smaller short-run periods of depression and recovery. I shall return to this point in 5.5.1 and 5.5.2.

Third, the chart indicates that the decline in the rate of profit is caused by a greater increase in the composition of capital than in the rate of surplus value. This is a contested point. For example, E.N. Wolff also reaches the conclusion that, over the entire 1947–76 period, the US rate of profit does indeed fall. However, Wolff concludes that this "decline in the value rate of profit is due to a steeper drop in the rate of surplus value than in the organic composition, rather than to a rising organic

Chart 5.1 The US rate of profit (Moseley's estimates)

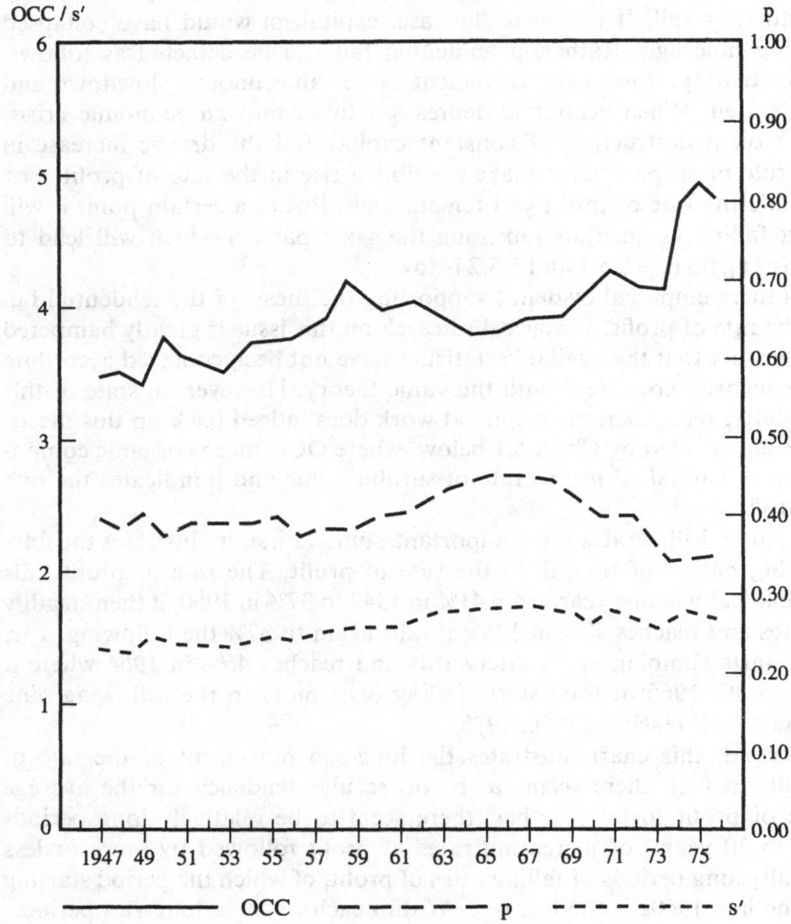

Source: Moseley, 1988 (a), p. 300

composition". This is illustrated in Chart 5.2.

Reati too (1989) reaches the conclusion that the fall in the rate of profit is caused by a decline in the share of profit with the organic composition of capital being essentially trendless (even though there are important differences among countries). However, Moseley is quite right in pointing

158

Chart 5.2 The US rate of profit (Wolff's estimates)

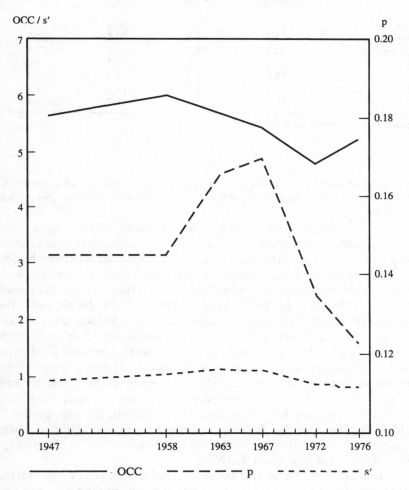

Source: Wolff, 1986, p. 95

out that both Wolff's and Reati's estimates are not rigorous tests of Marx's hypothesis because they do not take into account the distinction between productive labour (which produces surplus value) and unproductive labour (which does not). Variable capital should encompass only capital paid to productive workers. If it encompasses both categories of labour,

159

Table 5.2   Rates of return in manufacturing

	1960s average	1970s average	1982	1983 estimate
US	22.2	16.8	10.6	12.9
Japan	36.5	26.4	21.5	22.2
Germany	20.9	15.7	11.7	12.9
France	15.6	16.0	9.5	9.9
UK	13.6	8.1	5.5	6.4
Italy	18.3	15.3	16.1	14.5
Canada	15.2	13.1	6.7	8.4

Source: Chan-Lee and Sutch, 1985, p. 8

the rate of surplus value (s/v) falls more than it should and the OCC (c/v) increases less than it should. This is so because of two interrelated reasons.

First, the denominator (v) is estimated as being bigger than it really is, since it should not encompass the "variable" capital paid to unproductive workers. If this correction is carried out, both ratios become bigger. Second, the numerator is smaller than it should be since the part of "variable" capital paid to the unproductive workers is surplus value and should thus be added to s in the s/v ratio and because, in the c/v ratio, the costs of the means of circulation and supervision are not added to constant capital (the numerator). Again, if this correction is carried out, both ratios become bigger. Moseley shows that, if the distinction between productive and unproductive labour is taken into account in Wolff's estimates, "the trends in these variables are essentially as predicted by Marx: the rate of profit declined because the composition of capital increased faster than the rate of surplus-value, not because the rate of surplus-value declined" (Moseley, 1989a, p. 5).[3] In short, a correct reworking of the available statistics provides strong evidence for the tendential fall of the average rate of profit due to a rise in the OCC.

It is interesting to note that the same trend emerges from non-Marxist estimates. Table 5.2 gives data on the rate of return, or the gross operating surplus as a ratio of gross capital stock. The same picture emerges from Table 5.3, which provides data on rates of return for the total business sector. These show a widespread trend decline.

Finally, further indirect evidence can be provided if the stock of capital per employed person is taken as a proxy for the OCC. These data are presented in Table 3.1, where EUR 10 stands for the ten countries of the European Community and where the impact of the increased OCC on unemployment can be easily read.[4]

Table 5.3 Rates of return in total business sector

	1960	1973	1982	Trend
United States	16.2	14.5	10.9	−2.1
Germany	24.3	17.2	14.5	−2.0
France	21.7	22.9	19.3	−1.9
United Kingdom	13.3	11.0	10.1	−1.9
Canada	13.3	13.6	9.7	−0.8

Source: Chan-Lee and Sutch, 1985, p. 22

5.2 The Fall in the Rate of Profit, Crises of Profitability and of Realization[5]

Having argued for the tendential fall in the value rate of profit, we must now deal with the question as to how the fall in the *average value* rate of profit (a non-observable phenomenon) is the result of an *unequal* fall (but for some capitalists there will be a rise) in the *realized* rates of profit of the *individual* capitalists in *money* terms (the level at which economic phenomena are observable). To this end, we cannot abstract from money any longer.

Suppose that each branch in Table 3.3 is made up of ten capitals with the same productivity. By definition, these are modal capitals. Suppose also that in the same table each unit of modal capital produces ten commodities (since there is no relation between OCC and productivity in different branches, for ease of computation we can just as well assume that the different branches have the same output per unit of capital; but any other outputs per unit of capital would do). Then, Table 3.3 becomes Table 5.4, where N indicates the number of capitalists, c is constant capital, v is variable capital, s is surplus value, V is value produced, O is output, VTR is value tendentially realized, and p is the rate of profit tendentially realized.

Let us call a unit of money M and let us assume that there are 300M in circulation. Then, each unit of output costs 300M/300 = 1M, each unit

Table 5.4 Value tendentially realized by modal capitals

	N	c	v	s	V	O	VTR	p
Branch I	10	800	200	200	1200	100	1200	20.0
Branch II	10	900	100	100	1100	100	1200	20.0
Branch III	10	700	300	300	1300	100	1200	20.0
Total	30	2400	600	600	3600	300	3600	

Table 5.5 Value tendentially realized by modal and non-modal capitals

	N	c	v	s	V	O	VTR	p
Branch I	10	800	200	200	1200	100	1122	12.2
Branch II (modal)	8	720	80	80	880	80	898	12.2
(above mode)	2	190	10	10	210	40	448	124.4
Branch III	10	700	300	300	1300	100	1122	12.2
Total	30	2410	590	590	3590	320	3590	

of value is expressed as 300M/3600 = 0.0833M, each capital invests 100 × 0.0833 = 8.3333M and realizes the modal output, or 10M. The money profit is 10 − 8.3333 = 1.6667 and the money rate of profit is 1.6667/8.3333 = 20%. These 30 capitals invest 3000V × 0.0833 = 250M and realize the total output, or =300M. Their profit is 300M − 250M = 50M and the average rate of profit in money terms is 50M/250M = 20%. This is equal to the average rate of profit in value terms. The modal commodity (the only commodity considered here) realizes 3600/300 = 12V.

Suppose now that in branch II two capitals introduce a more efficient technique which requires a higher OCC (95c and 5v) and which allows them to double their productivity. This is shown in Table 5.5.

Consider first what happens at the level of value. The total value produced has fallen to 3590. The average rate of profit is 590/3000 = 19.67%. The price of production per unit of output is 119.67/10 = 11.967 for all three branches. Branches I and III realize 11.967 × 100 = 1196.7 each but branch II must realize 11.967 × 120 = 1436.04. The total is 3829.44, which is higher than the value actually produced, 3590. A distributional ratio equal to 3590/3829.44 = 0.9375 must be applied. Prices fall to 11.967 × 0.9375 = 11.22. The ten modal capitals in I then realize 11.22 × 10 = 112.2 each, a rate of profit of 12.2%, and the branch as a whole realizes 11.22 × 100 = 1122. The same applies to the ten modal capitals in branch III. In branch II, the eight modal capitals realize the average rate of profit and 11.22 × 80 = 898 together. The two above-mode capitals realize 11.22 × 20 = 224 each and a rate of profit equal to (224−100)/100 = 124%; together, they realize 448. While the rate of profit realized by modal capitals falls, the rate of profit realized by innovative capitals rises.

If we now consider what happens at the level of money, these results do not change. On the assumption (to be discussed shortly) that the quantity of money remains the same, a unit of value is expressed as 300M/3590 = 0.0836M so that each unit of capital invests 100V × 0.0836 = 8.36M. Each unit of output realizes 300M/320 = 0.9375M, on the assumption that all commodities realize equally less, so that each modal capital realizes

$10 \times 0.9375 = 9.375$. Now each modal capital invests 8.36 and realizes 9.375, thus tendentially realizing a profit of $9.375 - 8.36 = 1.015$; the rate of profit is $1.015/8.36 = 12.2\%$. Above-mode capitals realize $0.9375M \times 20 = 18.75M$ and a profit equal to $18.75 - 8.36 = 10.39M$, a rate of profit of $10.39/8.36 = 124.4\%$. The 30 capitals invest $3000V \times 0.0836 = 250.6962M$. They realize 300M, a profit equal to 49.3038M and a rate of profit equal to 19.67%. If the increase in the OCC ceases, both the average rate of profit and the rate of profit of modal capitals stop falling. If it continues to increase, these rates must continue to fall.

Prices do not necessarily have to fall equally in all branches (from 1M to 0.9375M). If they do not, there is a transfer of purchasing power to the branch(es) whose prices fall less. Which prices fall, and by how much, depends upon the distribution of social demand between branches. This means that there will be a fall in the rates of profit for some or perhaps all capitals, except for the innovative ones. On the assumption that the quantity of money does not change, the more technological competition is a general phenomenon, the more generalized will be the fall in prices.

To sum up, a decrease in the production of (surplus) value, and thus a *general crisis of profitability in value terms*, is caused by increased productivity (and OCC) by some capitals. This manifests itself as a *crisis of realization* (difficulty selling all the output at the old prices) and, through it, as a *crisis of profitability in money terms for some, or perhaps all, capitals except the innovative ones*. This, of course, does not take into consideration those factors which positively affect the average rate of profit, as for example lower real wages and higher rates of exploitation.

Up to the Second World War, crises of profitability manifested themselves as crises of realization and thus as massive overproduction of commodities. While this might not necessarily be the case any more (see 5.3.6 below), many authors have been misled into thinking that the cause of crises is overproduction and/or lack of purchasing power, instead of seeing these latter as forms of manifestation of the fall in value and surplus value produced due to the rise in the OCC. We shall see below (5.4.1 to 5.4.3) why this approach is erroneous.

5.3 Crises, Inflation and Stagflation

Up to now the assumption has been that the quantity of money remains unchanged when there is a fall in the total value produced (from 3600 to 3590 in the above example) following an increase in productivity (from 300 to 320). The average rate of profit therefore falls from 20% to 19.67%

in money terms and the modal capitals' money rate of profit falls from 20% to 12.2%. But could the fall in the average rate of profit (and thus in the rate of profit of the modal capitals) not be stopped by simply increasing prices through an increase in the quantity of money? The objection which immediately arises is that this would lead to an increase in prices (inflation) rather than in profit rates. To ascertain whether this objection is valid or not, we must first inquire into the relationship between increases in the quantity of money and in prices. This, in its turn, requires that we briefly discuss the quantity theory of money.

5.3.1 Marx's critique of the quantity theory of money[6]

As is well known, the quantity theory of money holds that money prices are determined by the quantity of money in circulation and that the latter "depends on the quantity of the precious metals in a country" (Marx, 1967a, pp. 123–4). Marx's critique is based on the assumption of commodity money, that money is a certain commodity, gold or silver. This critique is threefold. First, the quantity of money circulating in a country is not the same as the quantity of money in that country. Being itself value, money is a store of value and can thus be hoarded and dehoarded.

Second, Marx rejects the hypothesis that "once in circulation, an aliquot part of the medley of commodities is exchanged for an aliquot part of the heap of precious metals" (Marx, 1967a, pp. 123–4). In fact, commodities in different branches have different tendential values. Thus the percentage of the total quantity of commodities produced by a certain branch is exchanged for a different quantity of money than the same percentage produced by another branch.

Third, and most importantly, the quantity theory of money is based "on the absurd hypothesis that commodities are without a price, and money without a value, when they first enter into circulation" (Marx, 1967a, pp. 123–4). For Marx, on the other hand, money prices are the expression of the fact that both commodities and gold have a value when they enter into circulation. By applying the results of chapter 3, we see that the quantity of money needed for commodities to circulate, and thus money prices, is determined by the social value of both gold and the other commodities.[7] The money price of a certain commodity is then given by the quantity of bullion which incorporates the same social value incorporated in that commodity.

This explains the role of money in the exchange of commodities. A certain commodity (C) can be sold for a certain money price (M) and with this money a fraction (or a multiple) of another commodity (C) incorporating the same social value can be bought. This is the C–M–C metamorphosis. In it, money serves as a medium of exchange only because it is a measure of value (because it measures the value of the commodity sold, or C–M, as well as of the commodity bought, or M–C). In short, money prices are determined not by money as a means of circulation but by money as a measure of value (Marx, 1967a, p. 117). This is, in a nutshell, Marx's critique of the quantity theory of money.

So far we have assumed commodity money. Once we introduce convertible paper money, the essence of Marx's theory of money does not change. But there are two important differences. First, under a regime of commodity money, money must have an intrinsic value in order to be a measure of value, just as a metre must have a length in order to be a measure of length. But when convertible paper money replaces commodity money, a "symbol" of value (Marx, 1967a, p.127) replaces real value. A symbolic measure of value with no intrinsic value replaces a real measure of value with intrinsic value. This symbolic measure is sufficient for money to perform its role as a measure of value, just as a real one-metre-long rod is not needed any more, but could be used to measure distances. Here too, money prices are determined by this (symbolic) measure of value and not by the quantity of paper money in circulation. The value of money, or its purchasing power, is given by the value of the precious metal of which paper money is a symbol. Second, it is now possible to overissue paper money. Inasmuch as this extra paper money is not saved, a general price increase follows. In this case, "the nominal price of commodities would rise, but the real relation between their value would remain unchanged" (Marx, 1967a, p. 161).

Under modern conditions, however, money is both inconvertible paper money with no intrinsic value and credit.[8] The question then is, if money prices are determined by the social value both of commodities and of gold (either present in circulation in its bodily form or represented by paper money), how are money prices determined when gold disappears as the general equivalent and is replaced by inconvertible paper money with no intrinsic value? Again, the convertibility of paper money is not a necessary condition for it to be a symbol of social value, a symbolic measure of value. The fact that, originally, money as a measure of value had an intrinsic value is a feature typical of a historical period, not an absolutely necessary feature, as the introduction of convertible paper money shows. In the same way, convertibility is a feature of another historical period and not an indispensable prerequisite for money to function as a symbol of value. To return to the analogy with the measure of length, it is possible to measure distances (e.g. between celestial bodies) in metres while actual recourse to a material one-metre-long rod is impossible.

The fact that money has no intrinsic value, however, does not mean that paper and credit money are valueless. Their value is their purchasing power, or the value newly created plus the value of the means of production transferred to the product (which, as we have seen in 3.7, is their cost of reproduction at the time their output is sold) less the value either destroyed or wasted (see 4.4). The purchasing power of one unit of money is then derived by dividing this total by the total quantity of money in circulation, in coins, paper money and credit money. Notice that the total quantity of money serves as a measure of value and thus as a means of circulation of all commodities, whether capitalistically produced or not. As we have seen in 4.1.3, some commodities are not produced capitalistically and yet have a value and thus a money price (while others might have a price without having a value). The total quantity of money serves to express these commodities as well.[9]

A change in the quantity of paper money, inasmuch as it is not (de-) hoarded or as it serves for the circulation of a changed quantity of value (commodities), does affect money prices. However, this effect is not due to money as a means of circulation but to money as a measure of value, given that the value – purchasing power – of money changes. The difference between the monetary and the Marxist view is not that the latter denies that an increase in the money supply can have an (inflationary) effect on money prices. The difference is that in the Marxist view this effect is due to money as a measure of value, rather than as a means of circulation. This is far from being a pedantic point. If, as in the quantity theory, money is simply a means of circulation, money prices are not a symbol of value prices. This theory, then, severs the link between production of value and money prices. But if, as in Marx's theory, money is a measure of value (even though an inconvertible, symbolic measure), money prices express the value prices of commodities and the link between production of value and money prices is retained. Marx's theory of money prices is thus still fully valid.[10]

5.3.2 Crises and quantity of money

As we have just said, present-day economies are based on inconvertible paper money with no intrinsic value and on credit.[11] Given the low costs of printing bills, of increasing or decreasing credit, of engaging in open market operations, etc. (as opposed to the costs of producing commodity money), it is technically feasible for the monetary authorities to supply money practically at will. Thus money supply can be increased not only when the value produced increases but also when it decreases, that is, when, due to a rise in productivity in a certain branch, more commodities (use values) are produced while the total exchange value has decreased. In short, money supply can increase when prices tend to fall. This opens the way for the monetary authorities to try to cope with the realization problem by manipulating money supply.

Increased availability of bank notes or credit money makes it possible for both capitalists and consumers to increase their borrowing from banks and other institutions in order to increase their purchases. If there is a sufficient and properly distributed demand and if the supply of money is also sufficient and properly distributed (two extremely strong assumptions), all products can be sold at the old price. In the example above (Table 5.5), an increased output (from 300 to 320) due to increased productivity implies a fall in the money price per unit of output from 1.00 to 0.9375M. The monetary authorities can try to cope with the crisis of realization by increasing the supply of money, in this example from 300M to 320M; all products can then be sold at the old price, 1.00M.

Let us look now at what happens to profits. Suppose we have a succession of production processes, Table 5.4 depicting the first of these. Each modal capital invests 8.33M, sells its output at 10M and tendentially realizes a rate of profit equal to 20%. In the following production process, two capitals introduce above-mode techniques, so that the total output increases to 320, as in Table 5.5. At the beginning of this process, modal capitals invest 8.33M. At the end of the process, the quantity of money is increased to 320M to avoid realization problems, that is, to sell all the 320 units of product at the same price. Modal capitals invest 8.33M and realize 10M, the same money rate of profit of 20%. Above-mode capitals have invested 8.33M, sell 20 units at 20M and realize a profit rate of 140%. While the value rate of profit for modal capitals has fallen from 20% to 12.2%, the money rate of profit has remained the same. It would seem that the crisis has been avoided. But let us look at the third production process, which we assume to be the same as the second one.

At the beginning of this process, a total value of 3590 is represented by 320M; or, each unit of value is expressed as $320M/3590V = 0.0891M$. The innovative capital invests 100V, which in money terms is equal to $100 \times 0.0891 = 8.91M$. It sells each unit of output at 1M and realizes 20M, a profit equal to $20 - 8.91 = 11.09M$ and a money rate of profit equal to $11.09/8.91 = 124.4\%$. The non-innovative capitals invest 8.91M, realize 10M, make a profit of $10 - 8.91 = 1.09M$ and a money rate of profit equal to $1.09/8.91 = 12.2\%$. The increase in the money supply has not changed the money rates of profit of either the modal or of the non-modal capitals.

Put differently, in the second production process more use values are produced. If some of them remain unsold, the crisis of realization and thus the crisis of profitability reappear. If, as it is assumed here, all products are sold thanks to the increased quantity of money, at the beginning of the third production process capitalists and labourers buy *more* means of production and of consumption at the *same* unit price (1M). The money capital invested in the inputs increases (from 8.33M to 8.91M). However, at the end of the third production process the modal yield is the same as at the end of the second production process, that is 10M. It follows that the modal money rate of profit falls from (10 − 8.33)/8.33 = 20% to (10 − 8.91)/8.91 = 12.2%. The crisis of realization has been averted through an increase in the quantity of money (all products have been sold and can continue to be sold at the same prices) but the crisis of profitability has only been postponed from the end of the second to the end of the third period, given that the sale of the second period's greater output at the same unit price requires a greater money capital to be invested at the beginning of the third period. The price paid for this postponement is money's loss of value (purchasing power).

We have seen that crises follow from: (a) failure to increase the quantity of money; (b) from such an increase which fails to stimulate demand; or (c) from such an increase followed by the sale of all products (means of production and of consumption), on condition that the output of the next production process remains the same (which means that those extra inputs remain unused). There is, however, another possibility: the extra means of production can be employed to enlarge the scale of production and the extra means of consumption can be used to hire the necessary extra labour power. In this case, at the beginning of the third period a modal capital invests 8.33M to produce an output of 10 which realizes 10M (that is, a money rate of profit equal to 20%) and 8.91 − 8.33 = 0.58M to produce an extra output which, if the quantity of money is properly increased to make its sale possible, can also yield a money rate of profit equal to 20%. In this case, the increased quantity of money does hold back the crisis. More specifically, it can prevent the money rates of profit from falling but can at most keep them at their previous level. The reason, however, does not reside in the increased quantity of money but in the fact that such an increase makes possible the creation of *more* (surplus) value through the productive employment of the extra means of production and of consumption, so that the value rate of profit rises again to 20%, that is to the level of the money rate of profit.

For example, a unit of capital in branch I of Table 5.5 invests 8.33M with which it buys 80c + 20v; this capital produces a surplus value of 20s. With the extra 0.58M, it can buy (0.58 × 100V)/8.33 = 6.96V which is divided into (6.96 × 80)/100 = 5.57c and (6.96 × 20)/100 = 1.39v. The employment of this extra capital produces 1.39s. In terms of value, the total capital invested is 85.57c + 21.39v = 106.96; and the total surplus value is 21.39s. The value rate of profit is 21.39/106.96 = 20%. In terms of money the result is the same. If with 8.33M I make 10 commodities, with 8.91 I make (8.91 × 10)/8.33 = 10.7 units, which are sold for 10.7M. The money rate of profit is $(10.7 - 8.91)/8.91 = 20\%$. Similarly, all other capitals will produce proportionally more value and surplus value, so that the rates of profit, both in value and in money terms, both before and after equalization, remain the same.

Only if all the means of production and of consumption are sold and productively used in the same proportion of constant and variable capital can the rates of profit remain the same. However, after a while, rising employment leads to higher wages, lower rates of surplus value and thus to lower rates of profit. Capitalists react either by increasing productivity (and thus decreasing employment, value produced and profits) or by lowering wages, thus causing realization problems in the wage sector. This hampers the demand for consumption goods and thus causes a fall in the orders for production goods. At this point, the system's tendency towards crises of realization and of profitability becomes manifest. The more the means of production and of consumption remain unsold, or are sold but remain unutilized, the lower the realized money rates of profit. In short, the decreased production of (surplus) value due to increased productivity is the tendency, and the increased production of (surplus) value due to the productive employment of the extra means of production and of consumption is the counter-tendency. While in periods of crisis the tendency is stronger than the counter-tendency, in periods of prosperity the situation is reversed.

5.3.3 Crises and inflation

There is another way the increased quantity of money can counter crises: through inflation. In this way, the money rates of profit can not only be maintained at the same level, they can actually be increased. To understand this, it should be stressed that up to now the assumption has been that all prices rise proportionally, so that relative prices are not affected. But this is only fortuitously the case. The question thus revolves around the relative rates of increase of different prices, or the different market prices in money terms.[12]

In this connection, particularly important is what happens to the prices of wage goods. If these prices increase more than money wages (the price of labour power) or if their rise precedes the rise in the price of labour power, higher prices mean lower real wages, higher rates of exploitation, and thus a higher money (and value) rate of profit. This increase in the rate of exploitation, due to a redistribution from wages to profits, is the way inflation can counter the crisis of profitability. But this result is far from being automatic (it depends on the level of combativeness both of the working class and of the middle class) and can rekindle difficulties of realization, at least as far as wage goods are concerned. Moreover,

Table 5.6 Competitive and monopoly prices (changes in price indices from cyclical peak to trough, i.e. in contractions)

Dates of cycles peaks and troughs	Changes in competitive prices (%)	Changes in monopoly prices (%)
November 1948 to October 1949	−7.8	−1.9
July 1953 to August 1954	−1.5	+1.9
July 1957 to April 1958	−0.3	+0.5
May 1960 to February 1961	−1.2	+0.9
November 1969 to November 1970	−3.0	+5.9
November 1973 to March 1975	+11.7	+32.8

Source: Hunt and Sherman, 1986, p. 543, table 37.2

the rate of inflation must be moderate in order not to endanger foreign markets (ideally, it has to be less than other nations' rates of inflation) and not to undermine the national and international public's confidence in the national currency, something which would disrupt the normal functioning of the economy. In short, there are limits to the postponement of the fall in the money rates of profit for non-innovative capitals. Yet inflation can have a positive effect on profitability. *Modern inflation*, then, is a *rise in prices due to the increase in the quantity of money as a means of postponing and countering profitability crises.*[13] Again, the decreased production of the surplus value due to productivity increases (higher OCC) is the tendency, while the increased production of surplus value due to higher rates of expoitation is the counter-tendency.

Another function of inflation is that of redistributing value among capitalists, rather than from labour to capital. The redistribution between the free competition and the oligopolistic sector is a particularly important example which becomes evident in times of crisis. Table 5.6 provides a vivid example.

The effects of this redistribution are contradictory. Inasmuch as value is appropriated by oligopolies, that is, by high OCC production units, and reinvested on the basis of high OCC, the average rate of profit falls. However, inasmuch as oligopolies sell their products on the international market, this appropriation of value gives them the opportunity to increase their profits vis-à-vis foreign competitors. The national average rate of profit increases, while the international one decreases. This point will be elaborated on in chapter 7.

In spite of the dangers inherent in inflation as an anti-crisis measure, in the long term, the difference between what is really produced and its monetary expression can be huge. The extent to which governments resort to increases in money supply to try to cope with crises is indicated by Chart 5.3. This chart shows great difference between percentage

Chart 5.3 Percentage growth of GNP and M2 (1955–1987)

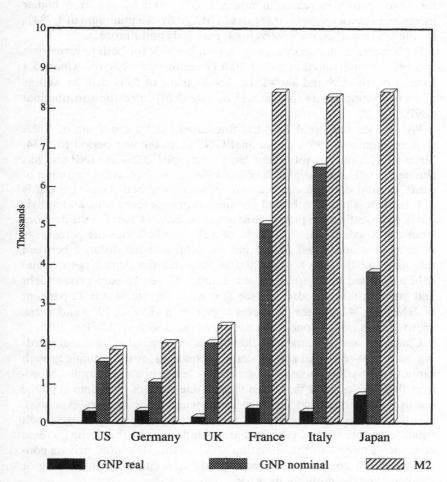

Source: Own computations from IMF, 1988(a). Data for the US are for the 1950–87 period and for France for the 1950–82 period. M2 (i.e. currency, demand deposits and time, savings and foreign currency deposits of resident sectors other than central governments) has been chosen as a measure of money. Line 351 of IMF, 1988(a) provides time series of M2 for each country. For the UK, Italy and France the data are for GDP, rather than for GNP

increases in real GNP among nations in the 1950(55)–87 period. They go from a modest increase of 115% for the UK to a large increase of 830% for Japan. But even Japan's increase in real GNP is dwarfed by the skyrocketing increases in nominal GNP and by the even higher increases in money supply. Increases in M2 go from a minimum of 1,784% for the US to well above 8,000% for Japan, Italy and France.

Such increases in money supply make it possible for both governments and private (individual and corporate) consumers to borrow. Chart 5.4 focuses on the US and shows the development of total debt as well as of its two components (public and private debt) in relation to nominal GNP.

We can see that total debt has fluctuated from a minimum of 172% to a maximum of 195% of nominal GNP from the war period to 1984. Since 1985, however, total debt has overstepped 200% of GNP and has climbed to unknown heights (241% in 1988). If we look at the two components of total debt we can see that, while in wartime about two thirds of total debt is public debt and one third is private (corporate and individual), in peacetime the proportions are reversed. In Chart 5.4 the distance from the X-axis to the "PD as % of TD" line indicates the percentage of total debt accounted for by private debt, and the distance between this line and the 100 horizontal line indicates the percentage of total debt accounted for by public debt. Finally, if we compare private debt and gross national product we see that while private debt is 72 per cent of GNP in 1944, it rises to a level higher than GNP in 1960 and keeps growing to more than one and a half times the amount of GNP in 1988.

Charts 5.3 and 5.4 thus show that over a long period of time, disregarding both long-term and shorter-term fluctuations, real economic growth cannot be separated from much greater increases in money supply. Moreover these tables show that, even though one-third of total debt is public (and this is also needed for huge disbursements for military expenses), it is the stimulation of individual and corporate demand through credit which accounts for the greater share of inflation. In short, the increase of money supply and thus inflation serve to stimulate both private consumption and government-induced production either by postponing or by alleviating the profitability crisis.

5.3.4 Crises and stagflation

The monetary authorities are thus faced by an insoluble problem deriving from the management of money supply with no intrinsic value. Following productivity increases, if the quantity of money is not increased, difficulties of realization appear; the increased quantity of commodities must be sold at lower unit prices and the non-innovative capitals must realize

Chart 5.4 US total debt (TD) and private debt (PD)

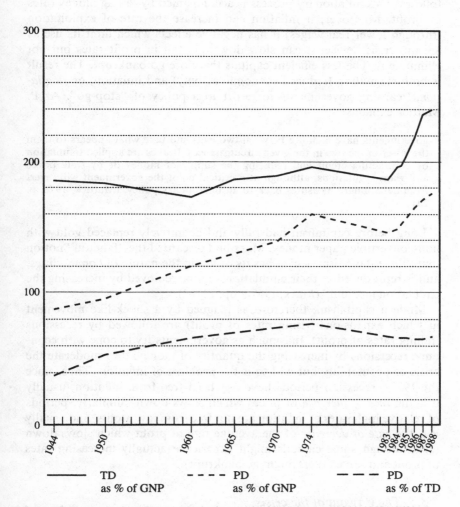

Source: Own computations. Data: (a) total private and public debt: years 1944, 1950, 1960 and 1965: Economic Report of the President, 1970, p. 248; years 1970 and 1974: Survey of Current Business, July, 1975, p. 10; years 1983 to 1988: Federal Reserve Bulletin, May 1989, p. A44 (these last figures are a summary of credit market debt outstanding which is comparable to total private and public debt as computed for the previous years). (b) GNP: Economic Report of the President, 1988, table B-76

173

a lower rate of profit. A crisis of profitability then follows. If it is increased, production is stimulated. However, if the increased quantity of money fails to stimulate either production or the sale of the extra output, inflation follows. This inflationary process is accompanied by falling money rates of profit. Moreover, if inflation can increase the rate of exploitation (through lower real wages) it has negative effects which limit its use as an anti-crisis device; it can slow down the fall in profit rates but not eliminate it. The less efficient capitals therefore go bankrupt. The result is both stagnation (reduced economic activity) and inflation, or *stagflation*,[14] causing governments to resort to a policy of "stop-go". As P. Mattick explains,

> governments have a choice between two evils and take what appears to them the lesser of the two in the given circumstances. Brakes are applied to inflation by contracting credit and reducing the supply of money or by state prices and wage regulations, although at a critical point the government will revert from deflationary measures back to an inflationary policy. (Mattick, 1978, p. 23)

Long before capitalism had fully and definitively replaced gold with non-convertible paper money, Marx had discarded the "fanciful" notion that "the antagonism, which has its origin in the nature of commodities, and is reproduced in their circulation, can be removed by increasing the circulation medium" (Marx, 1967a; pp. 121–2).

Modern capitalism, therefore, is plagued by a shock-like movement in which expansions (rising rates of profit) are followed by recessions (falling rates of profit). Inasmuch as governments try to cope with economic recessions by increasing the quantity of money, they moderate the crisis of profitability but add to it the problem of inflation. Thus, since the 1970s, recession periods have not been free from inflation; usually it is the *rate of increase* of prices which slows down. Similarly, periods of relative high rates of inflation are not free from low profits, and usually it is the *rate of decrease* of the average rate of profit which slows down (even though some capitals might experience actually increasing rates of profit and some others might go bankrupt).

5.3.5 The way out of the crisis

We have seen that if difficulties of realization and lower profit rates are dealt with by the monetary authorities by increasing the supply of money, an inflationary process is started. But as with all distributional measures the redistribution of value (income) from the labourers to the capitalists inherent in inflation cannot solve a problem which is caused by a lower production of value. If, in the midst of a recession, wages are reduced, surplus value rises but cannot be realized because the demand for wage goods has fallen. If, on the other hand, wages rise in order to create more demand, profits fall even more. Alternatively, the rate of surplus value and thus the rate of profit can be increased by increasing the length of the working day or the intensity of labour. But this method too runs into difficulties of realization, given that to an increased output there would not correspond greater purchasing power.

If, however, the way out of the crisis cannot be found in redistributional measures, it cannot be found in increased productivity either. An increase in productivity does not lead to an increase in general profitability, but only to the increase of the profitability of the innovative capitals at the expense of the profitability of the other capitals and of the general rate of profit. An increase in productivity is only a temporary solution to the innovative capitals' (nation) crisis of profitability but is at the same time a factor aggravating that crisis for the national (international) economy as a whole.

Within the context of a nation, an increased productivity (OCC) results in less value produced, a lower average rate of profit and lower money rates of profit except for the innovative capitals. However, once we assume an international economy and a tendential international price of production, if a capital in a nation increases its productivity, it appropriates international value from other nations' capitals as well. In this case, there is an increase in the total value appropriated by that capital and thus by that nation and thus a higher value average rate of profit and possibly also higher money rates of profit for the non-innovative capitals in that nation. Exclusive focus on that nation, or disregard of the international flows of value, creates the illusion that an increased productivity (OCC) has created more value, whereas that extra value has been appropriated from other nations' capitals. The crisis of profitability is shifted abroad, to other nations, and manifests itself on a world scale. This will be one of the basic themes of chapter 7.

The real way out of depression and economic crisis is an abrupt grinding of the economy to a halt, the destruction of large quantities of constant capital and the brute reduction of real wages and salaries. This spurs large new investments (production of value) when real wages are low and thus the rate of surplus value is high. These new investments (contrary to "labour saving" investments) generate *high levels of employment* of both means of production and of labour power, so that the conditions are created not only for a higher level of output but also for the demand and purchasing power for that output, and *high levels of profitability*. This is the twofold long-term condition for capital to come out of economic crises.

5.3.6 Has capitalism overcome the crisis of realization?

It has been submitted above (5.2) that, under certain conditions, profitability crises can manifest themselves as crises of realization. But this thesis
seems to lack credibility in the present crisis when, in spite of individual
capitals' difficulties, capital as a whole does not seem to suffer much
from realization problems. Is the theory submitted here then not in line
with modern empirical reality?

The theory submitted here stresses both the inevitability of the tendential fall in the rate of profit and the several forms taken by it. But this
theory does not submit that each of these forms is either inevitable or
equally likely. In line with what was said in chapter 1, the empirical
form taken by a certain phenomenon depends on the conjunctural interrelation and reciprocal modification of all realized social phenomena.
There is thus no inevitability in the form taken by a certain social phenomenon. For example, as we shall see in section 5.6, for many years after
the Second World War financial crises seemed to have disappeared. Now,
under specific conditions, they have reappeared (the first one dates back
to 1966) and have again become a permanent feature of capitalist empirical
reality.

The same applies to the crisis of realization. As with the financial crisis,
the crisis of realization is just one of the forms taken by the tendential
fall in the average rate of profit. This form is not inevitable and can
appear only under specific conjunctural circumstances. To understand
what these circumstances are, we must first try to find out why problems
of realization have not yet appeared on a massive scale in the postwar
period. There are at least five reasons.

First, capitalists, when confronted by falling sales, can reduce the rate
of capacity utilization, thus decreasing supply and increasing unemployment. This element is not new but it has a much greater significance
now than in Marx's times because of the oligopolistic nature of capitalism.
Chart 5.5 exemplifies this point.

Second, we have seen in 5.3.3 that an increase in money supply can
and does play a role in alleviating (if not eliminating) realization problems.
This is an important new element, compared with Marx's time when,
as a rule, money was either commodity money or convertible paper money.

Third, while increases in money supply affect purchasing power, the
willingness to purchase (demand) must be stimulated as well. This is the
function of advertising.

Fourth, the crisis of realization is countered through the appropriation
by the state of a part of the societal value (purchasing power) which
is then used to stimulate production through government commissions.
The realization of this production is then guaranteed. Particularly import-

Chart 5.5 Capacity utilization rate in the United States, 1948–85 (%)

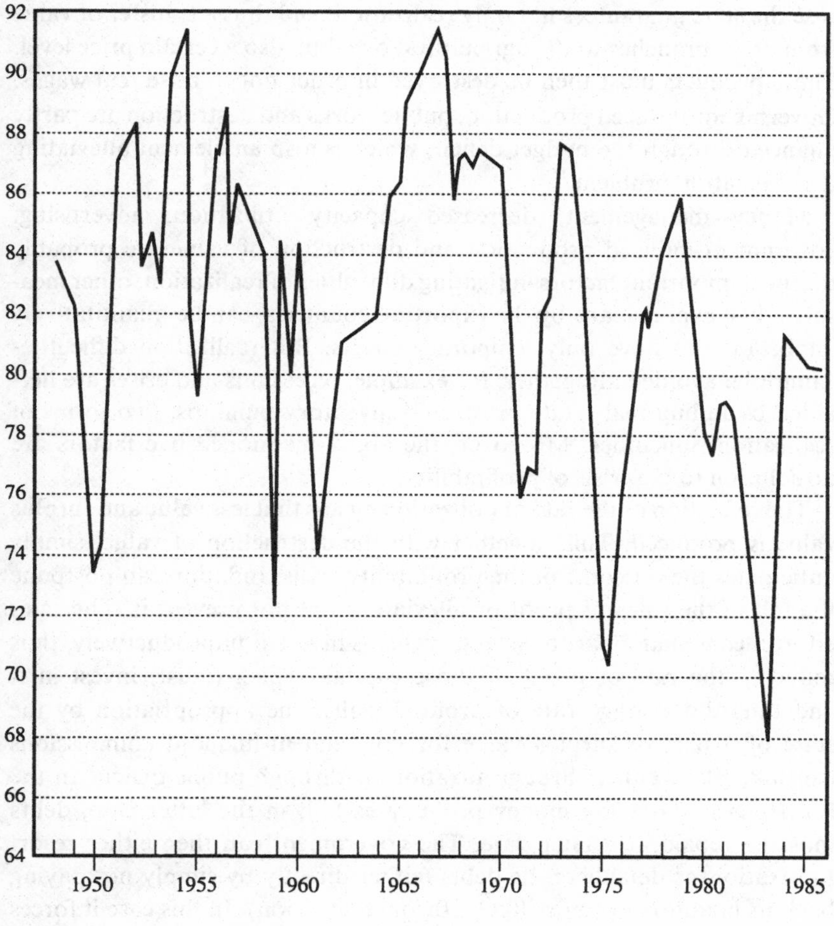

Source: Joint Economic Committee, 1986, p. 29

ant in this connection are public works and production of weapons (see 5.5.6 below).

Fifth, the state can appropriate purchasing power and use it to buy commodities which it then destroys. The EEC's "butter mountains" and "milk lakes" are a recent, but by no means the only, example. In this case the state guarantees not only realization, and thus a transfer of value from other branches to the agricultural one, but also a certain price level. These products must then be destroyed in order not to raise real wages. Government-induced production, public works and destruction are partly financed through the budget deficit, which is also an element alleviating the realization problem.[15]

Money management, decreased capacity utilization, advertising, government-induced production and destruction of value are probably the most important factors mitigating difficulties of realization; other measures, like export loans by the exporting countries, can be quantitatively important but have only temporary effects. But realization difficulties cannot be avoided altogether; for example, recessions and crises are heralded by falling real estate prices and inventory buildups, two forms of realization difficulties. Moreover, the above-mentioned five factors are no solution to the crisis of profitability.

The reduction of the rate of utilization means that less value and surplus value is produced. This, together with the destruction of value, simply anticipates the outcome of the profitability crisis. Inflation can postpone the fall in the rates of profit or alleviate it but not prevent it. The sales effort means that a part of surplus value is invested unproductively, thus reducing the rate of profit of those capitals which (must) invest in it and thus the average rate of profit. Finally, the appropriation by the state of a part of surplus value for government-financed commissions can take place either through taxation or through public deficit. In the former case, after tax money profit rates fall; in the latter case, debts must be repaid at a later date. The government can then either resort to taxation or default on its debts (either directly by simply not paying back its creditors or, more likely, through inflation). In this case it forces capitalists to accept a lower rate of profit and/or labourers to accept lower wages *post festum*.

The smaller role played by realization problems neither dents Marx's crises theory nor excludes the possibility that these problems might again reappear on a massive scale. Trade wars are a real possibility in the (near) future (Frank, 1988). In that event, realization would emerge anew as one of capitalism's major economic issues.

5.4 Alternative Marxist Interpretations of Crises

There are alternative Marxist crises theories. In what follows, I shall only emphasize some basic differences with the thesis submitted here.

5.4.1 The disproportionality thesis

As explained in 3.8.4, for the production cycle to begin anew a certain quantity of means of production, produced by sector A, must be exchanged for a certain quantity of means of consumption, produced by sector B. There, it was implicitly assumed that the technology in the sector producing means of consumption is such that it technically needs all the means of production offered for external sale by sector A and that the technology in the sector producing means of production is such that it technically needs all the means of consumption offered for external sale by sector B. On this assumption, the question tackled concerned the value at which these two types of goods are exchanged.

However, there is no reason to assume that the quantities offered for external as well as for internal sale are actually needed on the basis of the two sectors' technological requirements. The same holds if all branches of production, rather than only two sectors, are considered. The disproportionality thesis submits that the root of crises lies in the difference between the technologically determined demand for specific use values as inputs of some branches and the technologically determined supply of the same use values as outputs of other branches.

The author most commonly associated with this interpretation is Hilferding (1981).[16] In his theory, proportional relations are maintained by the price mechanism (p. 257). However, a variety of factors can cause disturbances in the price structure and these, in their turn, upset the proportional relations. A glut arises in some branches and then expands itself, through a credit crisis, to the rest of the economy. The value produced cannot be (fully) realized and the rates of profit fall. The line of causation, then, goes from price disturbances, to disproportionality, to realization crises (overproduction of commodities), to financial crises and to profitability crises. Strictly speaking, disproportions are not the cause of crises. Rather they are the catalyst, precipitating crises of realization and causing the fall in the rates of profit.

A first point of critique is that, according to this theory, in periods of economic growth, proportionality is the realized (rather than a potential) state of affairs (Hilferding, 1981, p. 297) and production prices are the realized (rather than the potential) prices. Therefore price disturbances are market prices deviating from production prices (ibid., p. 266). This implies that in periods of economic growth supply corresponds to demand (both demand and supply being technologically determined) at prices at which all (modal) capitalists realize the average rate of profit. But, as argued in chapter 3, this is mistaken. Production prices are potential prices. Therefore, in reality there are only price "disturbances" and thus a continuous state of disproportionality. However, there is no reason to reject this theory on this basis, since there is no incompatibility between this more realistic view and the disproportionality theory.

What then is the relevance of price-determined disproportions for economic crises? Marx's answer is that those "price fluctuations, which prevent large portions of the total capital from replacing themselves in their average proportions ... must always call forth general stoppages", due to "the general interrelations of the entire reproduction process as developed in particular by credit". However, these are only "of a transient nature" (Marx, 1967c, pp. 483–4).[17] To see this, let us suppose that an increased demand for computers leads to a price rise and to overproduction. First, prices fall and then supply is reduced. This causes a reduction in the production of, say, chips and this, in its turn, has a negative effect on the inputs needed to produce chips. This movement can (but does not necessarily) branch itself out in a part of the economy big enough to cause a "temporary stoppage". But the target can be overshot and, in this case, the supply of computers is smaller than their demand. An excess demand can also arise in other sectors. In these and other cases, the chain reaction starts again, but now in the opposite direction. Price-determined disproportions for large portions of capital, then, explain self-correcting disturbances in the working of the economy but cannot explain crises, or "paralysed consumption" and stagnation in the reproduction process. The credit system can (and usually does) postpone, and thus aggravate, the fall in those branches' rate of profit, but does not change the self-correcting nature of the process.

However, if crises are not determined by self-correcting disproportions, could they not be explained by non self-correcting disproportions, by the inability, which can be observed in periods of stagnation, both of capitalists to replace their capital and of workers to purchase all consumption goods? Put in these terms, this is tantamount to asking whether crises are the result not of disproportions but of lack of purchasing power. Thus disproportions can either be determined by price fluctuations, and in this case they are self-correcting and cannot explain crises, or by lack of purchasing power, and in this case it is the latter, rather than disproportions, which explain crises.

To conclude, in Hilferding's theory crises are first of all realization crises (Hilferding, 1981, p. 243) and profitability crises are logically derived from difficulties of realization. Disproportions, by hampering the realization of use values, hamper the realization of exchange value as well and cause profit rates to fall. This approach, besides being vulnerable to the above-mentioned critique, has two drawbacks. First, as we have seen in 5.3.6, realization crises are not the necessary form of manifestation of crises. This approach then loses relevance in periods of crises in which realization difficulties can successfully be held in check. Second, if crises are due to the impossibility of realizing the value produced rather than to the decrease in the value produced due to technological innovation, the latter loses its central position in the theory of crises.[18]

However, it is the disproportionality theory, and not the analysis of disproportions, which should be discarded. This analysis has the merit of emphasizing self-correcting disturbances in the reproduction cycle associated with overproduction of commodities which can emerge in the absence of technological change. Moreover, this analysis allows us to inquire into how the crisis of profitability manifests itself first in some branches and then spreads itself among other branches with different intensity, speed and duration, due to the disproportions thus originated. This analysis is therefore a useful complement to the theory of crises submitted in this work.

5.4.2 The Marxist underconsumptionist thesis

What has been said above would seem to imply that the ultimate cause of crises is lack of purchasing power. This is the basic idea behind the underconsumptionist theory[19] which usually adduces, as textual evidence, the following quotation:

> The ultimate reason for all real crises always remains the poverty and restricted consumption of the masses as opposed to the drive of capitalist production to develop the productive forces as though only the absolute consuming power of society constituted their limit. (Marx, 1967c, p. 484)

Two points must be clarified right away. First, this thesis usually refers only to the working class's lack of purchasing power while it should refer to the capitalists' lack of purchasing power as well. This holds for the inability to purchase not only means of production (see above) but also luxury goods.[20] This point will be disregarded here because it is of no essential importance for the present purposes. Second, the thesis cannot refer to an absolute impossibility to sell all the use values and thus to realize all the value produced. This is not a Marxist, but a populist theory, as criticized by Lenin (1967).[21] The discussion of Marx's reproduction schemes has shown this clearly. Even if production and social demand could be manipulated in such a way that all value produced could be realized according to the technological requirements of the reproduction schemes and to the $D = S$ assumption,[22] less and less value would be produced, and thus realized. Crises would occur anyway, due to the fall in the average rate of profit.

There is therefore no inherent impossibility for the social demand for wage goods to be brought in line with their supply, but there is a constant attempt by each capital to reduce the wages, and thus the purchasing power, of its own workers. This is a source of realization problems for the producers of wage goods. But if lower real wages were simply determined by capital's attempt to increase profits, the concomitant decrease in purchasing power for wage goods would be tendentially self-correcting. Realization problems in the wage goods sector would cause lower profit rates in that sector and eventually capital movements to other sectors. The reduced supply of wage goods would thus be tendentially brought in line with their social demand. Like disproportions, underconsumption, seen as the ultimate cause of crises, cannot explain paralysed consumption. This conclusion is certainly consonant with the Marxist framework in which the basic laws of movement of the economy are to be found in production rather than in distribution and realization, of which underconsumption is a case. How then can we explain this phenomenon?

The phenomenon can be explained only if we recall that lower production of (surplus) value and higher productivity (of use values) are two sides of the same coin. The higher the productivity, and thus the quantity of use values, the lower the value rates of profit. In the absence of inflationary movements, prices must fall. If this movement continues, some capitalists start operating at a loss. The increasingly lower prices would make this state of affairs apparent. Thus capitalists refuse to sell at those prices, that is, at a loss. Of course they can hold on only as long as their reserves allow it, after which time they go bankrupt. On the other hand, wages cannot be raised because this would raise costs and reduce profits. Prices are too high and wages are too low. It would seem that the obvious thing to do would be to reduce prices and/or raise wages, but the logic of the system excludes this option. This creates the illusion that the cause of crises is underconsumption and that this is caused by low wages, whereas underconsumption is a consequence of the fall in the (surplus) value produced and thus in the average rate of profit.

This interpretation seems to clash with the above-mentioned quotation identifying in insufficient purchasing power "the *ultimate* reason for all real crises". But this quotation can support an underconsumptionist view of crises only if taken out of its context. This quotation is taken from Marx's discussion of the relation between commercial credit and real crises. Marx argues that, in periods of crises, markets are glutted and yet credit is contracted (Marx, 1967c, p. 483); or it is just when commodities cannot be sold that credit is contracted. It is thus clear that Marx refers here to realization crises, to the impossibility of selling all commodities at an unchanged price.[23] It follows that the above-mentioned quotation should be read to mean that "the ultimate reason for all *realization crises* is lack of purchasing power". This is a fairly obvious conclusion which agrees with the following quotation explicitly rejecting underconsumptionism:

> It is sheer tautology to say that crises are caused by scarcity of effective consumption, or effective consumers ... But if one were to attempt to give this tautology the semblance of a profound justification by saying that the working class receives too small a portion of its own product and the evil would be remedied as soon as it receives a large share of it and its wages increase in consequence, one could only remark that crises are always prepared by precisely a period in which wages rise generally and the working class actually gets a larger share of that part of the annual product which is intended for consumption. (Marx, 1967b, pp. 410–11)

Some authors, aware of the apparent contradiction between this and the previous quotation, as well as of the pivotal role played by the increases in the OCC in Marx's theory of crises, prefer to speak of overproduction, of production growing more quickly than social demand, rather than of underconsumption (Rapos, 1984, p. 55). From the point of view of the present work, this is only a terminological choice which entails no significant theoretical differences. However, for the overproduction thesis, this shift in emphasis is important because it links the growth in the OCC to overproduction. In fact, it is held, an increase in the OCC, or a higher increase in constant than in variable capital, means that production grows more quickly than people's purchasing power (Rapos, 1984, p. 51). Clearly, the increase in OCC (no matter how important it can be) is evoked here as a theoretical support for overproduction and this argument remains basically underconsumptionist. Moreover, similarly to what has been said about the disproportionality theory, overproduction loses relevance in those periods of crises when it is only conspicuous by its absence. One could admit, in order to save the theory, that there are branches experiencing underproduction (scarcity) even in periods of crises (Rapos, 1984, p. 251). But this amounts to an admission that overproduction cannot be the cause of crises and that both overproduction and underproduction are forms of manifestation of a common cause. This, as submitted above, is the fall in the (surplus) value produced due to technological competition.

5.4.3 Disproportions, underconsumption and decreasing production of value

The disproportionality and underconsumption theories cannot account for the inevitability of crises; but, as we have seen, these theories do account for the inevitability of temporary and self-correcting disturbances. Only the approach linking insufficient production of (surplus) value with technological innovations can provide such an explanation.

In all three theories capitals move to where they can realize higher rates of profit. But capital movements caused by disproportions between branches (the protagonists in the disproportionality theory) and by a lack of balance between supply and purchasing power within branches (the protagonists in the underconsumption approach) tend towards a proportional and balanced situation, to where there is insufficient production and away from where there is insufficient purchasing power. In the falling average rate of profit theory on the other hand, capital moves to the innovative (and thus high-profit) branches, to where more use values but less exchange value (and thus less purchasing power) are created. *These are those branches where the higher output of use values has upset technical proportions and where less exchange value (and thus purchasing power) is being produced.* Capital movements aggravate disproportions between branches and reduce purchasing power. Disproportions and lack of balance between supply and purchasing power cause self-correcting capital movements around non self-correcting capital movements. The former, isolated from the latter, cannot explain the inevitability of crises; this can only be explained if we consider money as the expression of value and value as labour under capitalist production relations. It then becomes possible to understand why an increased production of wealth (use values) due to an increased OCC is followed by a fall in money profits.

Notice that the branches where the crisis first appears are not the same branches in which it first originates (where the OCC has increased). This would be the case only if the distribution of social demand remained the same after technological innovations in those branch(es). In this case, prices would have to fall only in the innovative branches. But, as emphasized in 3.3.2, technological innovations change not only the structure of production but also the distribution of social demand. Therefore, prices might fall precisely in those branches where the structure of production has not changed.

5.4.4 *The Monthly Review school*

An influential underconsumption theory is that associated with P. Sweezy and the Monthly Review school. In his 1942 work, Sweezy distinguishes between two forms of crises: crises associated with the falling tendency of the rate of profit and realization crises. Let us first of all see how Sweezy's conception of these two forms of crises differs from the one submitted in this work.

As for profitability crises, for Sweezy capitalists stop investing when the average rate of profit falls below a certain level or range. They resume their activities when "either the rate of profit is back in the usual range or they have reconciled themselves to a new and lower norm for the rate of profit" (Sweezy, 1942, p. 142). But, as argued above, capitalists do not know what the average rate of profit is and if they did know it they would be interested in making the highest possible rate of profit rather than the average one. The fall in the average rate of profit sends capitalists out of business not because they are unwilling to accept a lower norm but because this fall is the consequence of the innovative capitalists having produced less value while realizing higher profits at the expense of other capitalists: these latter have to stop their activities because they have lost money and after their reserves have been used up.

As for realization crises, according to Sweezy, they break out because of "capitalists' inability to realize the full value of the commodities which they produce" (Sweezy, 1942, p. 156). But, as seems likely, if by "full" value Sweezy means either their individual value or their production price, chapter 3 has shown that commodities usually realize neither the former nor the latter. As shown in 5.2, a crisis of realization breaks out because of another reason, namely the inability to sell commodities at their former price which derives from the reduction in the production of value and surplus value due to an increase in the organic composition of capital of the innovative capitalists.

Having specified the meaning Sweezy attaches to these two forms of crises, let us see how he relates them to each other. In 1942 Sweezy still has a place for the falling rate of profit in his theory. He submits that both the falling rate of profit and underconsumption should be treated as "parallel tendencies of capitalist development" (Sweezy, 1942, p. 197). However, in that work the fall in the profit rate is more an appendix to the tendency towards underconsumption than an integral part of a theory in which both aspects are essential. By 1968 the fall in the rate of profit has been removed and replaced by the law of the increasing surplus and by the tendency towards stagnation (Baran and Sweezy, 1968). J. Morris summarizes the argument as follows:

> the poverty of the masses and the consequent underconsumption produces poor consumers' markets but so much capital accumulation and productive capacity in relation to these markets that a lot of the productive capacity must remain unused. The existence of large unused productive capacity is the main thing which inhibits further investment. (Morris, 1983, p. 325)

In other words the line of causation is underconsumption, overaccumulation of capital, unused productive capacity and tendency towards underinvestment (stagnation).

According to this school, the underconsumption of wage goods can be offset by high levels of investment, as it has been in the early stages of industrialization. Usually, however, this is not the case for mature economies. The two ways to stave off stagnation are luxury goods production and waste; or, "in our time, the main constraint of the system is not the generation, but the absorption, of potential surplus product" (Bellamy Foster, 1985, p. 169). The increasing production of "surplus" (either surplus product or an unspecified surplus) and the concomitant increasing difficulty of realizing it replaces the tendential fall in the rate of profit as the main law of monopoly capitalism.

The specificity of this approach is that it assumes a permanent underconsumption of wage goods. The previous section, however, has shown that underconsumption is either self-correcting (thus not permanent) or not. In this latter case though it cannot be the ultimate cause of crises but must be explained, in its turn, by a decreasing production of value, that is, of purchasing power. In the absence of such an explanation, underconsumption cannot but be self-correcting. In fact, if value and thus purchasing power do not diminish in the economy as a whole, if purchasing power is simply taken away from the wage goods sector (and thus from the labourers), underconsumption in that sector simply means lower profits there but higher profits in other sectors. The result is a restructuring of the economy rather than stagnation.

The approach just criticized has the merit of having identified the need to develop a Marxist theory of oligopoly (rather than of free competition) capitalism and to analyse new and important aspects of modern capitalism, for example waste and the economic role of advertising. However, the same aspects can be analysed within the framework of a theory of capitalism and crises in which the tendential fall of the average profit rate remains the central law and in which the Marxist categories of analysis, including value and surplus value, retain their central role.

5.4.5 The regulation theory[24]

This theory stresses the decline in the rate of profit and analyses its causes. On the face of it, the differences with the approach submitted here would seem to be small. In reality, however, the opposite is true. The point is that the Regulation Theory accepts orthodox economics' notion of rate of profit as "rate of return", that is, as the ratio of operating surplus (P) to capital stock (K), or P/K. Let us disregard the difficult question as to whether (and in what measure) statistics of P/K can be used as a proxy of the Marxian rate of profit, $p = s/(c + v)$. Let us assume they can. Let us also disregard Moseley's appropriate objection that this view does not separate productive from unproductive capital and that this is a serious lacuna with important consequences for a theory of crises (see 5.1.3 above). Let us assume this correction has been carried out.

The real objection is that this theory operates with a notion of average rate of profit which is the generalization of the individual rate of profit. In this it follows orthodox economics and is thus drawn into orthodox economics' theoretical terrain, and therefore becomes unable to see the proper relation between productivity and profit rates. To understand this, it is necessary to recall that both orthodox economics and the regulation theory decompose the rate of return (their rate of profit) into the product of the profit share (P/Y) and capital productivity (Y/K). In other words if Y indicates both income and output and if both the numerator and the denominator in P/K are divided by Y,

$$P/K = (P/Y) \cdot (Y/K)$$

where P/Y is the profit share and Y/K is capital productivity.

The point to be stressed is that the division of both the numerator and the denominator by Y (total income, or output) makes it possible to find a *direct* rather than *inverse* relation between the rate of profit (P/K) and an increase in productivity, as indicated by the output/capital ratio (Y/K).

This formula thus expresses the view that an increase in productivity increases the average rate of profit. As we have seen above, this holds for the innovative capital, but not for the economy as a whole. An increase in productivity (as indicated by an increase in the OCC) *decreases* the average rate of profit while *increasing* the rate of profit of the innovative capital through appropriation of surplus value, that is, through the redistribution of surplus value inherent in the price mechanism. The extension to the economy as a whole of the view that higher productivity means higher profitability indicates that once more what holds on a micro-level has been mistakenly applied to the macro-level, to the level of the system as a whole.

At times it seems that authors subscribing to the regulation theory agree with the view submitted here. For example, Lipietz speaks of crises occurring "through a fall in the rate of profit due to a rise in the organic composition of capital" (Lipietz, 1986, p. 16). However, since Lipietz considers the output/capital ratio (the index of productivity) to be approximately the inverse of the OCC (Lipietz, 1986, p. 22), a rise in OCC is necessarily a fall (rather than an increase) in productivity. A fall in the rate of profit therefore is caused by a rise in the OCC, that is by a fall in productivity; vice versa, an increase in productivity causes an increase in the general rate of profit. This is exactly the opposite of the theory submitted here. As 4.6.3 above has argued, if abstraction is made from some industries (e.g. the extractive sector), there can be no question of product*ivity* (as opposed to product*ion*) decreases under capitalism. This is a Ricardian, rather than a Marxist, concept. Capitalism is based on constant technological innovations and these raise, rather than lower, productivity.[25]

5.4.6 The profit squeeze theory

An alternative view in left-wing writings is the profit squeeze theory of crises. As Glyn and Sutcliffe put it, "We conclude that the basic reason for the decline in the profit share was the squeezing of profit margins between money wage increases on the one hand and progressively more severe international competition on the other" (Glyn and Sutcliffe, 1972, p. 65). This means that, for the rate of profit to fall, real wages must increase more quickly than productivity (Shaikh, 1983, p. 14; see also Weeks, 1979). Therefore the problem is that wages are too high, rather than, as in the underconsumptionist view, too low.

For the profit squeeze theory, increased productivity causes an increase in the general rate of profit. For example, Glyn and Sutcliffe define the rate of profit as $P/K = P/Y . Y/K$ (Glyn and Sutcliffe, 1972, p. 54); thus productivity increases cause the rate of profit to rise unless real wages increase more than productivity. This implies that the profit squeeze theory, as well as the regulation theory, wrongly maintains that a productivity rise increases the general rate of profit, both approaches mistaking exploitation for productivity.

For example, the basic element of the theory submitted by Bowles, Gordon and Weisskopf maintains that the primary cause of crisis in the 1966–73 period was a decline in productivity due to the narrow difference between the workers' standard of living while working and that obtainable without working. This made the workers less afraid of losing their jobs and caused a decline in their incentive and motivation (Bowles, Gordon and Weisskopf, 1985). However, inasmuch as workers are less afraid of losing their jobs and thus work less (hard), what declines is not productivity but exploitation.[26] This mistake is thus shared by Okishio, the regulation theory and the profit squeeze theory.

It is true that, as we have seen above, Marx points out that periodic crises are preceded by rising wages. However, a chronological sequence is not necessarily a logical explanation. In fact, Marx is explicit on this question: "The rate of accumulation is the independent, not the dependent, variable; the rate of wages, the dependent, not the independent, variable" (quoted in Foley, 1986, p. 154).

It is also true that a decrease in real wages is a powerful force counteracting the fall in the rate of profit and that an increase in real wages aggravates that fall. However, the profit squeeze theory inverts the chain of causation. During recoveries and booms, wages increase and thus reduce the rise in the rate of profit. But when profits begin to fall, followed by realization problems and mounting unemployment, wages become "too high" relative to profits (and not relative to the labouring population) and are wrongly perceived as being the cause, rather than a symptom, of falling profitability.

5.5 The Cyclical Nature of Production Crises

Crises are not only recurrent but also cyclical. Let us now briefly analyse these patterns of cyclical recurrence and the anti-cyclical measures adopted by governments.

5.5.1 Long waves and production cycles

Time series seem to support the hypothesis of the existence of not only relatively short-term cycles but also of longer (50-year) cycles.[27] These are the succession of long expansionary waves (of 20–25 years) due to a long-run rise in the average rate of profit and of long periods of depression (of approximately the same length) due to a long-run fall in the average rate of profit. During long depressive waves, crises are longer and deeper while during long expansive waves crises are shorter and less violent. Mandel identifies the following periods: 1826–47 (depressive wave); 1848–73 (expansive wave); 1874–93 (depressive wave); 1894–1913 (expansive wave); 1914–39 (depressive); 1940(48)–67 (expansive); 1968–? (depressive) (Mandel, 1980, p. 2).

The estimates of the average rate of profit shown in Charts 5.1 and 5.2 and Tables 5.2 and 5.3 above clearly indicate a downward trend whose starting point coincides with the turn of the 1960s. The effects on production are shown in Table 5.7 below. These data can be related to the data on inflation given in Table 5.8. It can be seen that on the whole the big inflationary jump started at the end of the 1960s or the beginning of the 1970s. This agrees with the theory of inflation submitted in 5.3.3. A long expansionary wave follows the introduction on a massive scale of innovations which create the need for qualitatively new investments, often producing qualitatively new commodities. This creates the conditions for high levels of employment and thus the social demand for new products. If the effects of such innovations, if the need for massive new investments radiate throughout society, long periods of growth follow. A massive destruction of capital following a war can also have the same effect of propelling the economy into a new long period of sustained

189

Table 5.7 Growth rates of world output, by region, 1960–86 (%)

Region/country group	1961–73	1974–80	1981–86
World output	5.5	3.6	2.7
Developed market economies	5.0	2.5	2.2
United States	4.0	2.2	2.4
Western Europe	4.8	2.4	1.5
Japan	9.8	3.8	3.6
Developing countries	6.3	5.1	1.5
Africa	5.5	4.4	−0.9
Asia	5.1	6.0	4.8
Middle East	8.2	3.9	−0.9
Developing Europe	5.5	6.4	2.9
Latin America and the Caribbean	6.7	5.2	1.0
Centrally planned economies of Europe	6.6	4.6	3.3
China	3.8	5.6	8.8

Source: UNCTC, 1988, p. 17, table 1.1

Table 5.8 Consumer prices in selected countries (1980 = 100)

	US	UK	Germany	France	Italy	Canada	Japan
1950	29.2	13.4	39.2	15.6	13.9	28.4	16.4
1960	35.9	18.6	47.2	26.8	18.9	35.3	24.2
1970	47.1	27.7	61.0	39.9	27.1	46.1	42.3
1980	100.0	100.0	100.0	100.0	100.0	100.0	100.0
1981	110.4	111.9	106.3	113.4	119.5	112.4	104.9
1982	117.1	121.5	111.9	126.8	139.2	124.6	107.8
1983	120.9	127.1	115.6	139.0	159.5	131.8	109.9
1984	126.1	133.5	118.4	149.3	176.8	137.5	112.3
1985	130.5	141.6	121.0	157.9	193.0	143.0	114.6
1986	133.1	146.4	120.7	161.9	204.3	148.9	115.3
1987	137.9	152.5	121.0	167.3	214.0	155.4	115.4

Source: IMF, 1988(a)

growth. However, as these effects peter out, a long period of decreasing profitability sets in.[28]

However, technological innovations are not the cause of a long expansionary wave. As seen above, technological innovations push up the rate of profit of the innovators, but they do that at the expense of other capitalists and of the economy as a whole. A generalization of that innovation pushes down the average rate of profit because, inasmuch as it increases the OCC, it *destroys employment*, that is, it expels labour power which is the only factor creating value and surplus value. But in an expansive long wave the generalized introduction of new technologies takes place together with new investments which not only replace on an extended scale capital previously destroyed but also produce a whole range of new commodities thus creating new fields of investment. These investments therefore *create employment* and thus more (not less) value. Moreover, given the relatively high rate of surplus value inherited from the previous long depressive wave, the surplus value and thus the rate of profit are high too. This creates the illusion that high rates of profit in the long period of recovery are due to the introduction of technological innovations, whereas it is the new, employment-creating investments (using new technologies), together with high rates of exploitation, which have that effect on profitability.

As the OCC increases and the rate of surplus value decreases, the average rate of profit falls, thus ushering in a new period of low (or perhaps negative) growth. Again, it is not the lack of basic innovations in the depressive long wave which explains it. In fact, "clusters of basic innovations occurred in the 1820s, 1880s and 1930s exactly during stagnating long waves" while investment outlays massively applying these innovations "generally occurred ten years later, after the turn from the depressive long wave to the expansionist long wave had already taken place" (Mandel, 1980, p. 40). This holds also for the present period. New and powerful technologies (basically, computers and biotechnology, including genetic engineering and manipulation) have already been introduced into the capitalist production process but their effect has not been to lead the capitalist world out of the present long-term crisis. On the contrary, the introduction of computer technologies has massively increased unemployment and aggravated the crisis.

The way out of this crisis will thus come only after new and massive opportunities for job (and thus value) creating investments, which of course will operate on the basis of these new technologies, arise. This can be the result of a range of possibilities. The more traditional ones are either a devastating war or an economic crisis on the scale of 1929. However, this time there seems to be a new factor which might retard the explosion of a crisis: the reintegration into the capitalist system of the production, distribution and consumption of the so-called communist world, a historical phenomenon of major proportions which is now taking place at an accelerated pace.

The extent to which this reintegration will have a positive effect is uncertain. Short-term opportunities for capital investment in the wage goods branches of those countries will be greatly limited by low wage levels. However, Western capital might find an outlet for the realization

of surplus value through the sale of investment goods to the newly priva-
tized enterprises, through the guaranteed absorption of infrastructural
goods commissioned by governments of the "ex-communist" countries,
and through the sale of luxury and consumption goods to the emerging
bourgeoisie. On the other hand, to the extent that Western commodities
penetrate those countries, they destroy, through lower prices and better
quality, local production.[29] Thus, they destroy at the same time the possibility for those countries to become trading partners and consequently the
possibility to find in those countries a channel through which to lessen
realization difficulties. The reintegration of the "ex-communist" countries
into the world of private capitalism as *dependent* capitalist countries might
give private capitalism a new lease of life. But this solution will in all
probability be only a short-term one.

A more long-lasting solution would be the integration of those countries
into the world capitalist system as members of the imperialist centrum.
This option, inasmuch as it is realistic, is open only to the Soviet Union.
This could indeed attract Western and Japanese capital in measures sufficient to give the world capitalist system a new impulse. This is one (but
an important) reason for the insistence by Western politicians on the
need for the Soviet Union to retain its "territorial integrity", without
which this country could not become a powerful imperialist centre. At
this stage, however, this option is merely hypothetical and cannot offer
any solution to the more immediate problems. In any case it would only
displace the inner contradictions of capitalism to a new phase of its development.

5.5.2 The cyclical pattern

Within each long wave, several shorter-term cycles can be distinguished.
Let us then sketch the general features of these industrial cycles. As the
economy emerges from a crisis, two basic features make *recovery* possible.
First, real wages are low and rates of exploitation are high, due to the
high level of unemployment forced upon the working class in the crisis
period and to the weakening of the trade union movement. Second, the
demand for new means of production increases and these are built and
put into operation. This is due to the fact that some means of production
have been physically destroyed in the crisis period and must be replaced.
Moreover, the prices of the means of production have fallen (or have
risen less than other prices), thus spurring capitalists to replace obsolete
means of production with new and more modern ones. Also the less
competitive capitals have disappeared, and their place has been taken
by the surviving ones which, at the first signs of recovery, increase their
investments in order to increase supply. Often these stronger capitals

have taken over the assets of the weakest capitals at liquidation prices, a fact which contributes to the lowering of the OCC. The result is both a large *mass* and high *rates* of profits.

As recovery proceeds, the amount of wage goods going to the working class increases, even though initially the proportion of total value going to the working class might increase less or even decrease. This is so because of the increased productivity of the sectors producing wage goods, so that more wage goods, with a lower exchange value, go into the wage basket and because unemployment decreases and the strength of the unions increases.

As both real wages and technological competition keep growing, while resistance to high rates of exploitation increases, capitalists start replacing people with means of production. Since the new means of production are more modern and efficient, the rate of productivity increases together with the OCC. In this phase then, capitalists can afford to pay relatively high real wages while attempting to increase, at the same time, the level of productivity (OCC). The *boom* has set in. The demand for capital goods increases too, due not only to high rates of profit but also to a great mass of profits. These goods have no difficulty in finding an outlet, and given that the new machines are capital intensive, this increases the OCC. In this stage the demand for investment goods increases more rapidly than the demand for wage goods.

As long as a large mass of profits can be made (even if the average rate of profit might have already started to fall, given the increase in the OCC), capitalist production will go on. But when the level of new value (and thus surplus value) production decreases and, in spite of anti-cyclical measures (see below), difficulties of realization appear, money rates of profit decrease and some capitals make either insufficient profits to compete or no profits at all. A period of *recession* has started. These capitals must reduce production, cut new investments and dismiss part of their work force. The demand for capital goods slows down. Depression strikes first the branches producing capital goods and then extends to the other branches. The demand for wage goods falls too, due to increased unemployment, but less rapidly than the demand for capital goods. The fall in the average rate of profit eventually pushes some enterprises out of business (both in the productive and in the financial sphere) thus starting a spiralling and self-reinforcing movement of closures and unemployment. A new *crisis* has erupted. Wages fall. In periods of depression and crisis, any call for higher wages is met by fierce opposition from the capitalists, since they know that such a rise only aggravates the crisis. At the same time the strength of the working class and of their institutions is weakened.[30]

This same process, however, also generates the possibility of a new upswing. Some constant fixed capital (e.g. machines), usually the less efficient, lies idle and is eventually destroyed (due to both the action of nature and to technological depreciation). Constant circulating capital (e.g. inventories) is also depreciated if it has to be sold at new, lower prices. At the same time the increased rate of surplus value which can be imposed upon the working class in a period of crisis increases the average value rate of profit, and thus the money rate of profit first of some branches and then of others, thus starting again a period of economic *recovery*. New means of production are put into use and the mass of surplus value produced expands. A new level of average productivity contained in the new techniques and organization of the production process emerges and, with it, a new level of production and realization of surplus value.

The production cycle has been described as a succession of recovery, boom, depression and crisis. This is the form the cycle seems to have taken since the 1970s. In its classical form, the cycle was a succession of recovery, boom, crisis and depression. There are also at least two other differences. First, since the 1970s, prices have risen, instead of falling in periods of depression and crisis due to inflationary policies which have resulted in stagflation (see 5.3.4). Actually, for the oligopolies, prices have stopped falling in crises since the early 1950s (see Table 5.6). Second, in a period of recovery and growth, unemployment has fallen but to a level higher than the level of the previous recovery and boom (see Table 3.1).

The production cycle intertwines itself with the financial cycle, to be analysed in 5.6 below. A fuller description of the capitalist crisis must thus await an analysis of the financial crisis.

5.5.3 Anti-cyclical measures: management of private demand

Faced by economic depression, governments resort to anti-cyclical measures. Of these, the management of private demand through fiscal and monetary policies is of paramount importance.

During an expansion, governments can increase taxes and decrease money supply, to hold down inflation. The argument is that increased taxes decrease both profits, and thus the demand for investment goods, and disposable income, and thus the demand for consumer goods. Reduced money supply too decreases demand and increased interest rates have the same effect mainly by discouraging loans. These measures can indeed slow down economic growth. However, their impact is limited and depends upon the conjuncture. In the middle of an expansionary period, when enough profits are generated, enterprises will draw upon internal reserves for investments and will tend to borrow even if interest rates are high, since prospects for profits are good. Consumers will increase purchases (even if the burden of loans increases due to higher interest rates) because wages are increasing. At the end of the recovery, when the economy is ripe for a downturn, these measures can precipitate a recession. However, they do not cause it. They are only its catalyst. Thus these measures have a limited impact which depends on the underlying state of the economy (production of value) and are only the catalyst, not the cause, of an economic downturn.

In the case of recession governments can decrease taxes, in order to increase demand both of investment goods (due to higher retained profits) and of consumer goods, due to higher disposable income. Money supply can be increased and interest rates lowered in order to stimulate demand, loans and investments. But, again, much depends on the conjuncture. If the economy is not ripe for an upturn the enterprises' higher retained profits will not be invested, since the prospects of a recovery are still far away. The extra demand for consumer goods, stimulated by this extra money supply and higher disposable income, will be absorbed by reducing existing inventories or by temporarily increasing utilization rates. But this boost can only be short-lived since, if levels of profitability are still low, no incentives to investment will follow this shot of demand. As for the supposed increase in national income due to the government multiplier, it will be shown in 5.7 below that this argument is fallacious. It is only at the end of the depression period that these policies can trigger an upturn. And again they are of limited effectiveness, are dependent on the production of value and are not the cause of the change in the direction of the business cycle.

Particularly important is the effect of counter-cyclical measures on real wages. We have seen above that higher real wages increase demand (alleviate the realization problem) but reduce the surplus value produced (thus aggravating the profitability problem). Lower real wages, on the other hand, increase the surplus value produced but worsen difficulties of realization. This is an essential point in order to understand the unsolvable problem faced by demand management. Having understood this, there are a few qualifying statements which must be made.

First of all, lower wages do not decrease demand in general, they decrease the demand for wage goods. Higher profits, on the other hand, can increase the demand for investment and luxury goods. Thus, inasmuch as this shift in demand is met by a corresponding shift in supply, that is, by a decreased production of wage goods and an increased production of investment and luxury goods, lower wages can restore profitability (in the sense of both production and realization of profits). However, more means of production will produce, sooner or later, more consumption goods, thus confronting the capitalist system with the same, and intensified problem. Inasmuch as these means of production produce other means of production, the problem is merely postponed.[31] As for the increased production of luxury goods, it transforms the problem from one of insufficient production of (surplus) value to one of excessive consumption of use values (the same holds also for the production of means of destruction, as we shall see shortly). This too is incompatible with capital accumulation, as will be shown in the following subsection.

There remains the option of exporting the goods which cannot be absorbed by the internal market; at the same time, however, this exports the realization problem to other countries.

5.5.4 Anti-cyclical measures: government-induced production of weapons

Fiscal and monetary policies, and their effects on real wages, are attempts to deal with economic crises by increasing or decreasing private (personal and corporate) consumption. An alternative is for the state to become the consumer, that is, for demand to be stimulated or discouraged through government-induced production.

Governments can finance their purchases through taxation, by expanding the money supply and through public deficit. In all three cases, these purchases are financed by government appropriation of value (whether it is surplus value or variable capital). This is most clear in the case of taxation. When money is printed, the government appropriates a value equal to that quantity of money's purchasing power. In the case of public deficit, the government must eventually either pay at a future date, and in this case it will have to either levy taxes or print money, or it must default on its debt (either totally or partly), and in this case it will have appropriated value.

Governments can stimulate the production of different types of commodities. To stimulate the production of means of production would worsen the realization problem, once these means of production start producing consumption goods. To stimulate the production of wage goods would imply an increase in real wages (through the redistribution of these goods). One of the alternatives to this dilemma is to stimulate the production of weapons. Table 5.9 shows the extent to which this option has been resorted.

5.5.5 Is the production of weapons productive of value?

The answer is positive. The contractors deliver goods (weapons) which are paid for by the government by appropriating value (either present or future). These goods are new use values which have been made under

Table 5.9 World military expenditure, in constant figures

	US	UK	Germany	France	Italy	Canada
1978	189,071	21,371	20,974	25,076	10,104	5,832
1979	190,747	22,027	21,255	25,646	10,744	5,652
1980	194,479	23,497	21,550	26,104	11,241	5,944
1981	210,873	23,076	21,808	26,737	11,316	5,877
1982	222,650	25,142	21,527	27,287	12,103	6,428
1983	240,091	26,408	21,707	27,753	12,372	6,961
1984	251,355	27,583	21,485	27,656	12,737	7,419
1985	269,157	27,603	21,529	27,641	13,196	7,635
1986	282,935	27,304	22,127	28,459	13,463	7,780
1987	275,190	27,019	22,447	29,038	13,885	7,794

Source: Stockholm International Peace Research Institute, 1988, table 6A.2. Figures are in US $millions, at 1986 prices and exchange rates

capitalist conditions of production. The labour producing them, therefore, is productive of value and surplus value.

It has been submitted that this type of labour is unproductive (see e.g. Rapos, 1984, p. 224). Often the reason is adduced that weapons are not reproductive, that they do not re-enter the next production process either as means of production or as means of subsistence of the working class. But the same reasoning can be applied to the production of luxury goods which Marx never considered to be unproductive, and rightly so. In this case too the labour thus employed begets new value because it transforms use values into new use values under capitalist relations of production. It is irrelevant whether the capitalist gets his money (value) from other capitalists or from the state and whether he sells his products to other capitalists or to the state.

There is also another possibility. As with all commodities, weapons have a use value: this is their ability to destroy other use values. It could then be submitted that the labour producing them is value destroying labour (VDL), as analysed in 4.4.2 above, and that this labour cannot be productive. During the production of weapons, however, old use values are transformed into new ones and thus exchange value is produced. This is realized at the moment of sale. Their use value, on the other hand, is realized after they have been sold (similarly to all other material commodities). It is the labour of those using the weapons which is VDL, not the labour of those making them.

While being productive of surplus value, the production of weapons is not reproductive and thus threatens the reproduction of society. Their production restricts the volume of *use* values which can be employed for reproductive purposes. This point has been stressed by Marx in relation to the production of luxury goods but can be safely extended to all goods which do not re-enter the production process. Consciousness of this problem is beginning to make its way through in the American ruling class under the impact of the gigantic US military budget and consequent budget deficit. As the *International Herald Tribune* reports,

> the slowdown in productivity growth, combined with chronic budget deficits and growing foreign debt, has weakened US leadership of the non-communist world. A bipartisan group of former American military and economic officials has ... found that the rate of growth in military spending of the early 1980s is no longer possible.

In the view of this "bipartisan" group, the US must, in order to revitalize its economy, "cut back military outlays and divert resources, human, material and technological, to the civilian economy" (Silk, 1988). Similar reasons are certainly an important element explaining perestroika and glasnost in the Soviet Union.

5.5.6 Is the production of weapons an effective anti-cyclical device?

Let us now consider the production of weapons as an anti-crisis factor. First, there are the effects on the realization crisis. This production counters the crisis of realization because, as pointed out in 5.3.6 above, its sale is guaranteed.

Second, its effects on the profitability crisis are contradictory. On the one hand, increased investments in this high OCC branch push down the average rate of profit, even though the realized rate of profit in this branch might be very high. In fact, since modern weaponry has to incorporate leading-edge technologies, arms production has a high OCC. In the words of J. Lovering, "the internationalization of high-technology arms production in the West is taking place around a NATO axis, and a small set of advanced-technology companies" (Lovering, 1987, p. 130). On the other hand, the average rate of profit is pushed up by the redistribution of value inherent in this type of production. In fact, the state appropriates a share of societal wealth (value) not only from the capitalists but also from the labourers. It then redistributes it to the producers of weapons. The state thus operates a gigantic redistribution of value from the labourers to the capitalists, thus increasing *a posteriori* the capitalist class's rate of profit. It is in this sense that the production of weapons can be an anti-cyclical device. This is why a "decline of military spending has set off several recessions, while increases in military spending have encouraged recoveries from several recessions" (Hunt and Sherman, 1986, p. 503).

Such is the "rationality" of arms production. Value is redistributed, and thus crises of realization and of profitability are alleviated, by producing means of destruction, that is, by making use values which are either not going to be used (so that ultimately their own value has been wasted) or are going to be used (so that their own as well as other value is destroyed).

5.5.7 Is the production of weapons inflationary?

It is often held that this production is inflationary, again because of the non-reproductive nature of the goods. After what has been said in 3.8.6 concerning the production of luxuries, it is now easy to see that this is not the case. A similar reasoning applies to the production of weapons, the difference being that this sector buys means of production and means of consumption but sells neither to these two sectors nor internally: it only sells to the state. The state must appropriate sufficient surplus value for it to be able to pay the (modal) producers of weapons the average rate of profit, in accordance with the requirements of the reproduction schemes.

Let us take two branches A and B, producing means of production and means of consumption respectively. Let us add a third branch, W, producing weapons. This is exemplified in Table 5.10 where O stands for output, VTR for the value tendentially appropriated before taxes, VTR* for the same value after taxes and UE for unequal exchange.

Let us assume simple reproduction. In this case, sector A sells 440a internally, 110a to B in exchange for 385b and 110a to W. W does not sell anything to A. Sector B sells 385b to A in exchange for 110a, 165b internally and 165b to W. Again, W does not sell anything to B. Finally, W sells 110w to the government for a value with which it can buy 110a and 165b.

Since the total surplus value is 285, the average rate of profit is 285/1200 = 23.75%. Thus, tendentially, A must realize 550 + (550 × 0.2375) = 680.625, that is, it must gain 20.625. B must realize the same and thus lose 34.375. W must realize 100 + (100 × 0.2375) = 123.75 and thus gain 13.75. These are the VTR and UE columns. This implies that one

Table 5.10   The production of weapons

	c		v		s		V	0	VTR	UE	VTR*
A	440	+	110	+	110	=	660	660a	680.625	+20.625	628.27
B	385	+	165	+	165	=	715	715b	680.625	−34.375	628.27
W	90	+	10	+	10	=	110	110w	123.750	+13.75	114.23
Total	915		285		285		1485		1485.000	0.0	

unit of a is sold at $(220 + 20.625)/220 = 1.09$, one unit of b is sold at $(550 - 34.375)/550 = 0.9375$ and one unit of w is sold at $(110 + 13.75)/110 = 1.2375$. The state must appropriate value from A, B and W with which to buy weapons, under the condition that after this appropriation all sectors realize the same, but lower, rate of profit. For example, if the state taxes 9.5195 units of value for each 100 units of capital invested, it gets $12 \times 9.5195 = 114.23$. This is the sum sector W is left with after taxation $(123.75 - 9.5105 = 114.23)$. The state has appropriated sufficient value for it to be able to pay for weapons, after sector W has been taxed. Sector W realizes an after-tax rate of profit equal to 14.23%, and this is also what A and B realize. In fact, they realize after taxes $680.625 - (5.5 \times 9.5195) = 628.27$ each, which is a profit of 78.27, or a rate of profit of 14.23%.

More generally, if one branch produces weapons which are bought by the state rather than by other producers, simple or expanded reproduction can continue and the rates of profit are tendentially equalized without there being any need for inflation; the fact that weapons are non-reproductive is irrelevant in this context. Weapons are stored and then possibly destroyed without being used. The reason why this type of production might be inflationary is another. In a situation of (near) full employment, the production of weapons increases the demand for means of production and labour power and thus their prices. But this (1) applies to the production of other goods as well, (2) has nothing to do with the fact that weapons do not enter the next production process and (3) applies to a situation of (near) full employment.

If the production of weapons is not inflationary, the appropriation of value by the state with which to stimulate that production can be inflationary. If the state appropriates value through fiscal measures (e.g. taxation) or through some monetary measures (e.g. by selling state bonds) the impact need not be inflationary.[32]

5.5.8 Demand management and value theory

Subsections 5.5.3 to 5.5.7 have discussed some of the most important devices governments rely on in their attempt to ward off crises. They all have their theoretical roots in the fact that orthodox, and in particular Keynesian, theory perceives difficulties of realization as deriving from demand simply being smaller than supply. In this view, the "fine-tuning" of demand should ensure steady and crises-free economic growth. Needless to say, recent history shows that no demand management schemes have managed to ward off crises. Only an analysis in terms of production and realization of value can explain why, even in the case in which demand equals supply, or more precisely, even in the tendential case in which all products are sold (at a price at which all modal capitals realize the average rate of profit), the average rate of profit still tends to fall and crises cannot be avoided.

5.6 Financial Crises and Stock Exchange Crashes

The analytical framework submitted here allows us to deal with the ways in which production crises manifest themselves in the financial sphere as financial crises and with the interrelation between these two types of crises.

5.6.1 Corporate debt and financial crises

The swelling quantity of money capital in the expansionary period is partly used to repay debts contracted in the previous recession and crisis, partly used to purchase extra constant and variable capital,[33] and partly deposited in banks and other credit institutions. These institutions must, in their turn, find outlets for profitable investments of this money. One important source of demand for the money is given by those capitalists who, under the pressure of competition, finance their expansion by issuing private bonds or through bank loans and other forms of debts. But debts must be either paid back or rolled over. This requires a stream of profits such that not only debts can be paid but also reserves can be replenished and thus, if debts must be rolled over or new debts are needed, the lenders' confidence in the borrowers' financial soundness is strengthened. This, as shown above, requires inflationary processes which, however, must be kept within limits in order not to disrupt the normal functioning of the economic system.

Inflationary policies can, however, at most postpone and limit the fall in profit rates. When profits start declining, capitalists must not only keep borrowing to face their financial obligations; they must actually borrow more. In fact, at first capital expenditures keep rising both because of the lag between commitments to invest and actual investment expenditures (these are called *involuntary investments*) and because the financially sound and trustworthy capitalists initially react to increased competition and falling profitability by introducing new production processes in order to gain a competitive advantage. Also, to face increased competition, capitals might resort to forms of concentration and centralization which need external financing, like leveraged buyouts. This further raises the burden of borrowing. It is only at a later stage that capital expenditures begin to fall if, for example, increased borrowing forces companies to cut capital expenditures and thus damage long-term competitiveness.

However, this increasing demand for loans is met by a decreasing supply of finances. Internal reserves decline, due to a smaller stream of profits, the re-financing of debts becomes more difficult because of the lenders' dwindling confidence in the borrowers' financial soundness and, last but not least, the monetary authorities – afraid that inflation might run out of control – decide to intervene by both reducing the quantity of money and credit and by increasing the interest rate. This increase, in its turn, represents a considerable worsening of the borrowers' ability to meet their obligations.

Some non-financial institutions, confronted by a credit crunch and financial difficulties, become unable to pay their debts; and the first signs of a financial crisis emerge. But financial institutions too run into difficulties. These latter are put under pressure to finance an increasing demand for loans in order to avoid their clients' bankruptcies while at the same time having recourse to less reserves and having to charge higher interest rates. As the economic situation deteriorates, some capitals go bankrupt, their debts are not paid due to these bankruptcies, and the crisis extends to the financial and credit system.

This seems to indicate a definite sequence of events. As a recent study has found out, in the United States, in the post Second World War period,

> in every crisis period, a particular timing relationship has – with only one exception – occurred. Peaks have been reached in profit and investment variables for the nonfinancial corporate sector, in relation to the financial crisis, in the following order: (1) the profit rate, (2) new contracts and orders for plant and equipment (in constant dollars), (3) investment in plant and equipment (in constant dollars), (4) the financial crisis, and (5) the financing gap. (Wolfson, 1986, p. 144)

The relevant table, Table 5.11, should be read as follows. Take the first line. The fourth column indicates that the first post-Second World War financial crisis occurred in the third quarter (Q_3) of 1966. The profit ratio peaked in the second quarter (Q_2) of 1965, or five quarters earlier (see first column). After that it started to fall. Investment orders as well as investments peaked when the crisis erupted (see the second and third columns). The *financing gap*, the amount by which internal funds fall short of investment spending, reached its maximum level one quarter after the financial crisis occurred, in the fourth quarter of 1966 (see the fifth column), and one quarter later investment orders reached their lowest level (see last column).

This movement is further strengthened by the fact that, in times of financial difficulties, capital flees into speculative adventures (one of which is investment in the stock exchange market, see 5.6.3 below). This, of course, is no solution. The problem is merely postponed and aggravated, given that speculation implies over-extension of credit. The financial sector

Table 5.11 Chronological sequence from the fall in the rate of profit to trough of investment orders through the financial crisis

Peak of profit ratio	Peak of investment orders	Peak of investment	Date of crisis	Peak of financing gap	Trough of investment orders
$65Q_2$ (−5)	$66Q_3$ (0)	$66Q_3$ (0)	$66Q_3$	$66Q_4$ (+1)	$67Q_1$ (+2)
N.A.	$69Q_2$ (−4)	$69Q_3$ (−3)	$70Q_2$	$70Q_3$ (+1)	$70Q_4$ (+2)
$73Q_1$ (−5)	$73Q_4$ (−2)	$74Q_1$ (−1)	$74Q_2$	$74Q_2$ (0)	$75Q_1$ (+3)
$77Q_3$ (−10)	$79Q_1$ (−4)	$80Q_1$ (0)	$80Q_1$	$80Q_1$ (0)	$80Q_2$ (+1)
$81Q_3$ (−4)	$81Q_2$ (−5)	$81Q_4$ (−3)	$82Q_3$	$81Q_3$ (−4)	$82Q_3$ (0)

Source: Wolfson, 1986, p. 144. Figures in parentheses indicate the number of quarters by which the particular variable leads (−) or lags (+) the quarter in which the financial crisis occurred

thereby becomes increasingly vulnerable. Under these circumstances, the bankruptcy of only a few or perhaps only one major financial institution can ignite a crisis in the financial sector which then extends to the real economy.

One example will suffice. In 1984 Continental Illinois Corporation, the eleventh largest bank holding in the US, was threatened by bankruptcy, due to bad loans. The consequences of a possible failure of Continental would have been extremely upsetting for the economic and financial system. Given the growing interdependence of the banking system, almost "2,300 small banks had nearly $6 billion at risk in Continental; 66 of them had more than their capital on the line and another 113 had between 50 and 100 per cent" (Wolfson, 1986, p. 111). No wonder the American authorities thought that Continental's failure could have triggered a major national, if not international, disaster. In the event, Continental was bailed out through an assistance programme which practically amounted to its nationalization.

As recovery sets in, the need for loans decreases due to the ability of non-financial capitals to draw on their own internal reserves. Also, initially, production is expanded not so much by increasing investments but through higher utilization rates; this leads to more favourable balance sheets. But when recovery turns into strong expansion, loans and other forms of debt increase too, and the stage is set for the next financial crisis.[34]

203

5.6.2 Public debt and the financial crisis of the state

The large amount of money borrowed and spent by the state on weapons and other anti-cyclical devices leads to large state debts and, given the cumulative effects of high interest rates (themselves an effect of inflation) to the difficulty, or perhaps impossibility, of the state to pay back its debts. This is the financial crisis of the state. Chart 5.6 shows this very clearly; in it, W stands for world, IC for industrial countries and DC for developing countries.

As the chart shows, the world's public deficit jumps in 1975 to 4.26% of GDP from where, after a few years of decline, it again shows a tendency to increase. For some countries the situation is far more dramatic than this average suggests. For example, in 1984 the percentage was 15.19% for Italy, and in 1983 it was 12.75% for Belgium, 12.54% for Ireland and 10.41% for Sweden (IMF, 1986).

The figures in the chart, however, do not express the full magnitude of the public deficit. If the Gross Domestic Product is very large, these percentage figures express a huge absolute amount of public deficit which the state finds increasingly difficult to pay back. Table 5.12 shows this clearly.

However, the real magnitude of the problem is not given by the public deficit but by the total debt accumulated through the years. An estimate of the US total debt is given in Chart 5.4, which shows that in 1988

Table 5.12   Public deficit (−) or surplus (+) for selected countries

	US[1]	UK[2]	Germany[3]	France[4]	Italy[5]	Canada[6]
1950	−2.2	339	−0.74	−5.7	−401	+.6
1960	.3	−307	−1.90	−4.2	−382	−2.5
1970	−11.4	923	+6.94	+3.7	−3.222	−9.9
1980	−76.2	−10.961	−26.91	−1.0	−37.017	−10.73
1981	−78.7	−12.381	−35.86	−85.6	−53.296	−8.43
1982	−125.7	−9.126	−32.02	−111.4	−72.653	−20.81
1983	−202.5	−13.515	−32.95	−142.4	−88.604	−25.16
1984	−178.3	−10.182	−32.29	−132.6	−95.353	−28.87
1985	−212.1	−11.832	−20.26		−121.353	−28.68
1986	−212.6		−16.34		−109.418	
1987	−156.0				−113.899	

[1]billions of US dollars; [2]millions of pounds; [3]billions of Deutsch marks; [4]billions of francs; [5]billions of lire; [6]billions of Canadian dollars.
Source: IMF, 1988(a), pp. 276–7; 358–9; 370–1; 436–7; 714–15; 720–21

Chart 5.6 Public deficit (% of GDP)

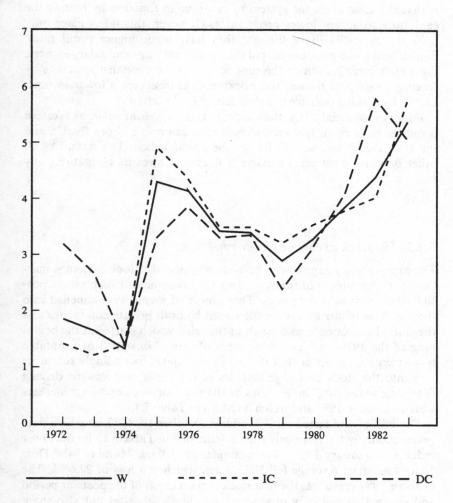

─────────── W ──────────── IC ─ ─ ─ ─ ─ DC

Source: IMF, 1986, p. 68

total debt was 241% of GNP. These figures reveal the *de facto* bankruptcy of the state.

If the creditors whose debt has turned sour are capitalists, their rate of profit is lowered *a posteriori*. Or, their higher rates of profit, which

205

had been made possible by the anti-conjunctural state policies, turn out to have been fictitious. Ultimately, the significance of the whole operation is that the state helps the system to continue to function by forcing the capitalists to accept lower profit rates. However, this takes place only after the capitalists have thought they have made higher profit rates. Similarly, if those who lose part of their credit are wage and salary earners, the state's contribution to the functioning of the capitalist system is by forcing, again *post festum*, the working class to accept a lower income, that is, by making possible a higher rate of exploitation.

Faced by financial crises, the state can resort to *privatization*, as Western countries have recently done following the example of both the US and the UK. This is one way to reduce the public deficit. The state, like all other debtors, must sell its assets if it cannot meet its obligations any more.

5.6.3 The stock exchange and crashes

The excess money capital also finds its way into the stock exchange markets. It is this supply of funds looking for investments which makes possible the boom in stock prices. This supply of money is channelled into the purchase of stocks and bonds issued by both private enterprises and the state. For example, as a result of the crisis which started at the beginning of the 1970s, an increasing mass of capital in search of profitable investments built up in that decade. This capital increasingly found its way into the stock exchange markets in the 1980s and was the driving force behind the surge in the index of all the major stock exchange markets which started in 1982 and which is shown in Table 5.13.

The bull period lasted until Monday, October 19, 1987, at which date prices suddenly fell ruinously (this is indicated in Table 5.13 by the lower indexes of January 1988). For example, on "Black Monday" the Dow Jones Industrial Average fell 508 points, which is a loss of 22.68%. The October 1987 crash was the first stock market crash of the postwar period and shows that not only production and financial crises but also stock market crashes are endemic to capitalism. We must thus briefly analyse the reasons for these crashes.

First of all, we must introduce the concept of *fictitious capital* (Marx, 1967c, ch. 29). This concept refers to government bonds, stocks, etc.; here, however, it will be applied only to shares. Contrary to what is commonly believed, these are titles of ownership on real capital rather than being real capital themselves. By issuing shares, an enterprise does not create capital, it only issues the lender's title of ownership on real

206

Table 5.13   Stock exchange indexes in major industrialized countries (1985 = 100)

	US	Canada	Japan	Germany	France	UK	Italy
1979	55.3	56.2	45.1	53.4	47.4	38.6	27.5
1980	64.7	76.6	47.6	50.0	54.9	41.3	34.9
1981	69.4	74.6	55.3	50.2	48.4	46.5	52.9
1982	64.3	58.8	55.1	49.5	47.0	53.9	43.0
1983	86.9	85.4	64.9	66.8	64.4	68.1	53.4
1984	87.2	84.5	81.9	75.2	85.6	81.0	59.8
1985	100.0	100.0	100.0	100.0	100.0	100.0	100.0
1986	126.2	111.0	132.9	135.2	153.3	123.8	232.8
1987	159.2	131.5	196.4	124.5	177.6	162.2	224.6
1988 Jan.	138.8	112.7	183.5	89.3	126.1	142.7	165.7
Dec.	153.6	125.0	231.0	117.3	202.5	144.7	202.5

Source: Banca d'Italia, 1988, tav. aA10, p. 26

capital. The illusion that titles of ownership on capital (shares) is real capital derives from the fact that these titles become "commodities" (they are bought and sold on the stock exchange market). But it is only an illusion, that "capital" is only fictitious capital. This is just another example of the "insane forms" generated by interest-bearing capital, so that a debt can appear as a commodity (real value).

The important point for the present purposes is that fictitious capital can be further increased without creating new titles of ownership. Let us suppose that an enterprise's capital is equal to $100 million and that this capital is represented by 1 million shares. The *nominal value* of each share, i.e. "the invested sum originally represented by this share" (Marx, 1967c, p. 467) is thus $100m/1m = $100. However, the nominal value of a share is not necessarily equal to its *market price*.[35] Suppose the enterprise pays $10 as dividend for each share. In this case the shareholder realizes 10% on his/her investment. However, investors are interested in the highest rate of profit they can get,[36] so, in deciding whether to invest in shares or in bonds, they compare the highest feasible dividend with the highest feasible rate of interest. If the former is lower than the latter, they invest in bonds, and vice versa. Suppose this rate of interest is 10%. In this case one is willing to pay up to $100 for each share of that enterprise. That share's market price is $100. In this case, the nominal value of that share and its market price are equal. If, however, in order to attract capital, that enterprise decides to double the dividend, each stock gives right to $20. For the investor, 20 is 10% of 200 so that investors will be willing to pay up to $200 for each of those shares; the market price therefore has doubled. More generally, the market price is equal to the dividend multiplied by the nominal value and divided by the rate of interest, or ($20 × $100)/$10 = $200.

If *capitalization* is the number of shares multiplied by their market price, the nominal value of that enterprise ($100m) and its capitalization on the stock market coincide if each share's market price is $100 (1m shares multiplied by $100 gives $100m). However, capitalization is $200m if the market price is $200 (200 times 1m shares, or $200m). This "value", the price this enterprise has on the stock market, is now $100m higher than its nominal value. Or, an extra fictitious capital equal to $100m has been created simply by increasing dividends. Thus, in the process of outbidding each other, companies can create huge amounts of fictitious capital above that which represents real capital.

In general we can say that during an expansionary period high profits allow enterprises to pay high dividends. This creates extra fictitious capital. However, this does not worry the investors. In fact, those looking for high dividends get them and those looking for capital gains get them too, given that prices keep rising (this means that investors can buy stocks and sell them later at a higher price, that is, at a profit). But as contraction sets in, enterprises find it increasingly difficult to keep paying high dividends, and the first financial difficulties appear. The stock market operators know that stock prices are inflated and that the enterprises' real financial situation is far from being the one depicted by their capitalization figures. They worry that stock prices might fall suddenly. Therefore they are constantly and anxiously on the alert, trying to anticipate any such fall. When they think they see indications of such a fall, they sell precipitately. This, given certain circumstances of a conjunctural nature (statements by government officials, economic and financial statistics, etc.),[37] starts a snowball effect the result of which is a stock exchange crash. This is what occurred on October 19, 1987.

In a regime of fiduciary money, governments can and do resort to the injection of money at times of acute financial crises (as the October 1987 stock exchange crash shows) and this helps debtors to pay their debts. A part of social wealth is thus used to allow debtors to pay their debts. This transfer of value creates some breathing space for the system but the bill must be paid later in the form of inflation:

> Many economists see the emergence of inflationary pressures as an almost inevitable consequence of the past year's vigorous growth in Western Europe, fueled by easy-money policies after the October 1987 stock price collapse. (Dale, March 2, 1989)

The reason why a crash starts is purely contingent; but it is only an expression of the fact that the artificial inflation of prices cannot go on indefinitely. The crash destroys fictitious capital and brings the prices of stocks more in line with their real value. Sometimes, as in 1929, if the crash is very severe, the price of stocks might fall way below their real value and might even drop to zero.[38]

Contrary to the opinion of many authors (including Marxist authors), the crash does not destroy real capital, it does not destroy real wealth. It only destroys titles of ownership on that wealth. Suppose I buy a company's stock for $100. If subsequently the stock market collapses and the price of that stock falls to zero, has there been a destruction of value equal to $100? No. There has simply been a transfer of value from me to that company for which I get nothing in return. The mistake usually made lies in assuming that the financial ruin of some stockholders is also the destruction of part of society's wealth. There might be a real destruction of value if the financial crisis forces that enterprise to close down so that (a part of) constant capital is lost either because of the action of nature or because of technological depreciation. But this is not what people mean when they argue that stock price falls are destructions of value.[39] Stock exchange crashes are not violent destructions of wealth; they are violent redistributions of wealth.

Having briefly outlined the general cause and dynamics of stock market crashes, a few words should be said on the specific features of the crash of October 1987.[40] The 1979–82 crisis was characterized by high inflation, high interest rates and low stock prices. In the period which followed, the 1982–87 boom, inflation and interest rates dropped. This favoured investment in stocks. But this was also the period of "Reaganomics", of a tremendous redistribution of wealth from the poor to the well-to-do. This too had a favourable effect on the demand for stocks. Deregulation and the revaluation of the dollar (60% in the 1981–85 period) also played a role. The dollar's revaluation diminished US capital's international competitiveness, especially in the machinery, oil, steel, rubber, car and chemical industries, so that mergers and takeovers rather than "greenfield" investments became the channel through which to invest surplus capital. This increased the demand for existing stocks. Deregulation dented investment banks' profits in their traditional activities. The banks thus turned to the financial backing of leveraged buyouts and of corporate raiders' acquisitions, which often inflated the stocks' market price. This process reinforced itself. The profits made on the stock exchange market were reinvested there and investors started to buy stocks of potential targets of corporate raiders, in order to benefit from the rise in those stocks' prices.

Investors had become interested mostly in capital gains, rather than in dividends. This does not mean, however, that the financial health of the enterprises quoted on the stock market had become unimportant for investors. As more and more money found its way into the stock market, capital became less and less competitive. Investors began to fear the worst and became very jumpy. The first signs of the coming problems came in the autumn of 1986 when the insider trading scandal shook the investors' trust. This episode took place amidst a changing economic scenario, featuring, since 1985, the fall of the dollar's rate of exchange, inflation and higher interest rates. The devaluation of the dollar did not affect the US trade deficit since it failed both to boost exports and to dampen imports. Continuing high imports, at higher prices due to the dollar's devaluation, started an inflationary process which, in its turn, caused interest rates to rise. It is this combination of high interest rates and of stubborn trade deficits which formed the background of the 1987 crash. The immediate reason for it was the publication of new data on a high balance of trade deficit and the disagreement between the US and Germany on interest rates.

The October 1987 crash did not have the catastrophic effects most economic commentators thought it would have: it did not usher in a major production crisis, as in 1929. The reasons for this are basically two. First of all, the fall in the stock market indexes was relatively limited. Second, while many investors lost money, the bulk of the loss was borne by relatively few big investors and institutions. The next crash, however, might have a different outcome.

5.7 The Fallacy of the Multiplier

The theory submitted above allows us to reveal the fallacious nature of the Keynesian multiplier. As is well known, the multiplier states that, if the state or the private sector autonomously increase spending, income increases more. The assumption is that the initial autonomous expenditure becomes income which induces further spending which, in its turn, increases income and spending: in short, the ultimate change in income is greater than the initial expenditure.

An autonomous expenditure can come either from the private or from the government sector. Consider first the case of private autonomous expenditure. This can be money previously saved, either by capitalists or by workers. In this case, the money has been deposited in a financial institution from which it is borrowed either by the same or by other capitalists and workers. But this presupposes some previous situation in which commodities have been produced but not sold because money has been saved instead of being spent. If now this money is spent, those capital and wage goods can be sold. What we have here is the realization of previously produced value and not an increase in national income; or, the creation of new value. That is all there is to it. If there is no production of value, there cannot be an increase in national income.

The same reasoning holds if the private sector disposes of extra money due to monetary expansion or to fiscal policies (e.g. lower taxes).

Consider now the case of money being spent by the state. If this money has been previously withdrawn from the economic system via taxation, and if the state buys commodities, then again, all we have is the realization of previously produced commodities. The same applies if the state increases the quantity of money (it appropriates purchasing power from other economic agents through the creation of money) and if it borrows money from the private sector (it helps to realize commodities now but it increases these difficulties in the future). There is no multiplier, no increase in national income.[41] If the money accruing from this sale is productively employed, there will be a production of value and surplus value. *This* is the real increase in income, the real "multiplier" (of value).

It follows that any multiplier–accelerator theory of business cycle is vitiated. This becomes even clearer if the accelerator is considered: investments are basically determined not by increases in aggregate demand but by profits and rates of profit.

Notes

1. I disregard here the internal redistribution in each sector of the extra means of consumption between capital and labour as well as the proportionality requirements.

2. This is tantamount to assuming not only that the OCC increases more than the rate of surplus value (s') but that it increases sufficiently more for the rate of profit (p) to fall. For example, if OCC = 1 and if s' = 1, p = 1/(1 + 1) = 50%. If now s' rises by 20%, to 1.2, the OCC must rise by more than 40%, to more than 1.4, for p to fall. If the OCC rise by more than 20% but less than 40%, p rises, instead of falling. For example, if the OCC rise by 30%, p = 1.2/(1.3 + 1) = 52%.

3. These estimates are not free from methodological critique. They relate to individual countries, under the implicit assumption of no transfer of value between countries. In this case, an increased OCC indicates less surplus value produced. Then, if the rate of surplus value increases sufficiently less, the rate of profit must fall. But once we allow for a transfer of value between countries, it is possible that an increase in the OCC sufficiently higher than an increase in the rate of surplus value for the rate of profit to fall, is accompanied by an increased rate of profit. This is the case if an increased OCC in that country, or an increased productivity, is higher than a similar increase in other countries. Surplus value is gained from other countries. This can lead to an increased rate of profit even if the rate of surplus value falls, that is, if the surplus value appropriated internationally (through the higher OCC) more than compensates the surplus value lost through a lower rate of exploitation internally. Similarly, an increase in the OCC of that country more than compensated by an increase in the rate of exploitation can be accompanied by a decreased rate of profit if the other country's OCC increases more than this country's. This will become clearer in chapter 7, where it will be argued that the national rates of profit are national manifestations of an international rate of profit.

These remarks are not meant to argue against the usefulness of the results already reached. Rather, they are meant to be a methodological contribution to further studies in this field, knowing very well that the difficulties of carrying out research on the rate of profit, both tendential and realized, on a global level are enormous. Moseley accepts this critique but argues that what is affected is the accuracy of the estimates rather than trends over time (see Moseley, 1989b, pp. 63–4). In this regard, it is certainly no coincidence that estimates made from a non-Marxist perspective (see Tables 5.2 and 5.3 below) point to a downward trend in the realized rates of profit.

4. These data do not tell the whole story. For example, those who lose their jobs as a result of technological innovation can become self-employed. In England, "the number of self-employed workers rose by 31 per cent between 1979 and 1984 to give a total of 2.5 million people or 9.2 per cent of the total working population" (Watson, 1987, p. 269).

5. In this chapter I shall deal with the theory of crises in the developed countries. Chapter 7 will briefly deal with some specific forms taken by crises in the so-called less developed countries.

6. On Marx's theory of money, see de Brunhoff, 1976.

7. It is not necessary to explore here whether the social value of gold is its price of production, its market value or its monopoly price, nor is it necessary to consider how gold prices change when the production and productivity of gold and of commodities change. Suffice it here to mention two points.

First, if the quantity of commodities in circulation increases, gold must be de-hoarded or its production increased. If this does not happen, unit prices fall. This is an element contributing to the "stagnation of production and circulation" (Marx, 1967a, p. 122). In this connection, it should be mentioned that "a fall in general prices expressed in terms of precious metals indicates a revaluation of the metal and an incentive to explore for it ... It is remarkable how the discoveries and the opening of the mines coincided in time over enormous distances" (Vilar, 1976, p. 328).

Second, in the setting of the international economy, an increase in the productivity of commodities in a nation causes an increase in the quantity of gold (international money) circulating in that country, due to the influx of gold paid by the foreign importers to the national exporters. Of course, we presuppose a redistribution of social demand in favour of those commodities. This is why Marx says that the ratio money/value increases in the more productive nation so that the relative value of money is less in the nation with a more developed capitalist mode of production than in the nation where the capitalist mode of production is less developed (Marx, 1967a, p. 560).

8. There is no reason to assume that coins and paper money are indispensable for the circulation of commodities. An accounting system through which the monetary authorities distribute purchasing power by allocating credit would be sufficient, as the widening use of "plastic money" indicates. But this does not change matters in any radical way.

9. Foley (1986, p. 14) arrives at the value of non-convertible paper money by dividing new labour, or value added, by value added expressed in dollars. But as chapter 2 has stressed, the production of new value (value added) is inseparable from the transfer of value of the means of production. Thus Foley does not measure the value of (one unit of) money but only of that money which represents new value. Moreover, Foley does not take into account the destruction and waste of value: that a part of new labour should be subtracted from total new labour before being divided by value added expressed in dollars. Finally, even if these two corrections were carried out, we would not have the purchasing power of paper money, given that purchasing power is divided between paper money and credit money.

10. Hilferding is thus mistaken in conceding that "the quantity theory, then, holds good for a currency with suspended coinage", a situation which he equates with inconvertibility (Hilferding, 1981, p. 55).

11. This is not to suggest that fiduciary paper money did not exist in pre-capitalist systems. It did, as shown by the wealth of examples provided by Vilar, 1976. What I want to explore in what follows is the movement of crises in a capitalist system based on fiduciary, non-convertible paper money, the norm under capitalism.

12. If some prices rise and others fall, an inflationary process in some branches is accompanied by a fall in money prices in others. This, however, does not mean that the money rates of profit fall in the latter branches. In fact, if these are the branches where productivity

212

has increased, the lower prices are the other aspect of increased productivity (and thus production of use values) and thus can yield higher rates of profit. In other words, these prices are lower but still not as low as they would have been for profit to remain the same. If the level of inflation is high, even the prices in those branches experiencing technological progress might rise, but less than the prices of other commodities.

13. In this work I focus almost exclusively on the imperialist nations and only briefly consider inflation in the so-called "under-developed" nations (see chapter 7). The so-called "ex-communist" nations are here disregarded. This will be the topic of my next work.

14. These are only very general remarks holding for the system as a whole. They must be applied to the concrete conditions of each specific country which, however, must always be seen in its international context. For example, in the two Reagan terms, the US managed to avoid high rates of inflation as well as major economic recessions, except the 1979–82 one. This, however, has been possible thanks to a massive appropriation of value by the US from other countries, through the importation of goods and services financed by loans often made by the exporting countries to be paid back by the US with heavily devalued dollars. Only the dominant imperialist country can postpone (but not avoid) the crisis by such means. See also chapter 8 for some of the issues associated with the challenge to the dominant role of the US in the world economy.

15. These measures as well as money management originated in the 1929–33 crisis, in which realization problems took their most virulent form.

16. For a lucid exposition of this theory in the contemporary setting, see Clarke, 1990–91.

17. Marx seems to distinguish between price fluctuations which cause disproportions in large quantities of total capital and which cause general but temporary stoppages, and price fluctuations which cause less important disproportions. The former are possibly those affecting the leading sectors.

18. Changes in the OCC do play a role in Hilferding's theory. Suppose first a lack of technological change. Hilferding submits that, given a certain level of technique, discrepancies between demand and supply affect prices differently because the high OCC branches are slower to respond to demand than the low OCC branches. The former can then raise the price of their products more than the low OCC branches (Hilferding, 1981, pp. 262–3); disproportionalities then follow. The objection to this argument is that this might be, but is not necessarily, the case. Suppose now technological change. Hilferding submits that, if the OCC rises as a result of this change, value and surplus value fall and with them the rate of profit (Hilferding, 1981, p. 260). This is consistent with the theory submitted in this work. However, in Hilferding's theory, this is only one of the many possible causes of the fall in the profit rate and is mentioned almost in passing.

19. There is a vast array of underconsumptionist theories. For a good review, see Altvater, 1981. Notice that authors subscribing to either the underconsumption or to the disproportionality theory often mix elements of both theories.

20. "Every crisis at once lessens the consumption of luxuries" (Marx, 1967b, p. 410).

21. This theory held that not all surplus value can be realized and thus that external markets must absorb what cannot be absorbed by internal markets. But if external markets are an inherent necessity of capitalism, this is so because of capitalism's inherent drive to expand itself and not because of the theoretical impossibility for the internal markets to absorb all surplus value.

22. This is the illusion of so many reformist schemes. See on this point Carchedi, 1987b.

23. I disregard here inflationary policies, which are not relevant to the present discussion.

24. There is no room here for an assessment of the regulation theory. Here suffice it to mention that the concept, as well as the theorization, of "regulation" focuses on reproduction and disregards supersession. As Aglietta writes, "To speak of the regulation of a mode of production is to try to formulate in general laws the way in which the determinant structure of a society is reproduced" (Aglietta, 1979, p. 13). Aglietta does incorporate the principle of qualitative transformation in his theory but this is a change from a stage (e.g. Fordism) to another (neo-Fordism) *within* capitalism rather than a change from a capitalist to another type of system. Therefore, different modes of production become different modes of reproduction of capitalism, rather than different determinant structures of different social systems.

The regulationist discourse is thus encapsulated within capitals' ideological boundaries. This becomes clear in this school's theorization of a post-Fordist use of new technologies. Computerization, it is held, can be beneficial both to capital (it increases productivity) and to labour (it makes possible the democratization of work and upskilling of functions). Actually, the former is not possible without the latter and it is thus irrational for managers to resist the democratization of the work place (see, e.g., Mathews, 1989). This position boils down to yet another form of reformism, not because it argues for a more humane use of the new technologies but because it does that from the perspective of objective common interests between capital and labour, that is, from the perspective of collaborative class relations. For a critique of this school and for the thesis of its affinity with the disproportionality view, see Clarke,1988, and Mattick, Jr., 1990.

25. Of course, if productivity is confused with exploitation (see e.g. Aglietta, 1979, p. 55), the decrease in "productivity" does lead to a lower average rate of profit (see 4.6.1 and 4.6.3).

26.It should also be mentioned that the empirical evidence of the thesis of a decline in the intensity of labour (decline in "productivity") submitted by Bowles, Gordon and Weisskopf has been seriously challenged by Moseley (1986).

27. In what follows I shall only sketch some of the basic features of long waves. The interested reader can consult Mandel, 1975 and 1980, where an extensive bibliography can be found.

28. For some authors, usually referred to as the "monopoly capital" school, falling long-run profitability can be explained by increased monopolization (since monopolies lead to stagnation). They associate monopolies with lack of competition. In chapter 7 we shall see that indices of concentration do not indicate lack of "competition" but a shift from free to oligopolistic competition. For a critique of the "monopoly capital" school, see Auerbach and Skott, 1988.

29. At the time of writing, the reintegration of the Eastern European countries seems to have had no positive effect on the developed capitalist world, while it is having an increasingly disastrous effect on those countries' economies in terms of closures and unemployment.

30. These are general remarks. But crises hit different branches at different times and with different force. Within a cyclical downturn, some branches might fare fairly well. For example, at the beginning of November 1989, the manufacturing industry in the West Midlands seemed to be heading towards a recession. However, the automotive industry continued "to defy gravity" (Tomkins, 1989). Even within the same branch the reaction of different capitalists is different. All cut their labour force. But some react aggressively by investing in new machinery in the hope of reducing costs and thus of being able to sell their product at lower prices, while others are more passive and defer the replacement of equipment. Usually the former option is open only to those who have a financially sound position.

31. This is not an underconsumptionist view. Here, I do not submit that there is a necessary disproportionality between the value of wage goods and labourers' purchasing power. What I do submit is that there are limits to the increase in the average rate of profit through a reduction of wages.

32. The US financed (at least partly) the Vietnam war by printing paper money. It is probably due to this fact that the production of weapons is (mistakenly) assumed to be inflationary. Inflation derived from the specific way to appropriate value by the state (value which, under the circumstances, was used to purchase weapons) and not from the specific type of production the state stimulated. Also, the Vietnam war does not explain the cause of inflation; rather, that war was the conjunctural expression of, the historically specific form taken by, the capitalist system's need to counter the crisis of profitability and thus to generate inflation.

33. In Japan, "big corporations used the booming markets of the late 1980s to remove debts from their balance sheets and go on an unprecedented capital-spending binge, sharply improving their efficiency" (Sterngold, 1991).

34. As these pages are being written, clear signs of a possible major financial crisis are springing up in the US (and across the world economy too). In the US the "financial

excesses" of the 1980s will have to be paid for in the 1990s. The junk bond market, which "played a major role in financing computer-industry expansion in the 1980s" (P.C. Roberst, 1990, p. 7), has collapsed. Estimates of the savings and loans industry bailout vary from $500 billion to $1.369 trillion over 40 years (Silk, 1990).

The banking system "today is the weakest it has been at any time since the Depression" as a result of losses on real estate, corporate buyouts and Third World debt. Growing bank failures "will leave the already depleted deposit insurance fund with less than $10 billion, a relatively small amount to protect $2 trillion of deposits in US commercial banks" (Mufson and Knight, 1990). More recent projections estimate that, by the end of 1992, the fund will have a deficit of $4 billion and that by 1995 the shortfall will be $23 billion (Labaton, 1991). From January to November, 1990,

> the 55,000 companies that declared bankruptcy . . . listed $64.1 billion in debts they cannot pay. That sum is equal to 1.1 percent of the US gross national product. Not since the Depression has the level even approached 1 percent. (Uchitelle, 1990)

A US treasury proposal would give the strongest banks freedom to expand into new ventures and success would be rewarded with lower deposit insurance premiums. It is not difficult to argue that

> the very same solution was offered half a dozen years ago as the sure cure for ills of the thrift industry. The thrifts got their additional powers and immediately used them to leap into risky new ventures in which they had no experience and promptly lost their shirts. (Mufson and Knight, 1990)

Of course, these financial difficulties are due neither to unethical behaviour nor to mismanagement, even though these two factors did play a role. Rather, they are the result of an attempt to postpone the realization and profitability crisis through deregulation and through a gigantic redistribution of value from the working class to the bourgeoisie. Sooner or later the bill had to be paid.

35. Marx uses the expression "market value", probably to stress the difference from "nominal value". However, since in chapter 3 "market value" has been used to indicate the value tendentially realized under conditions of capital immobility, and "market price" has been used to indicate the value actually realized under conditions of capital mobility, I prefer to replace "market value" with "market price".

The market price of securities

> rises and falls inversely as the rate of interest. If the rate of interest rises from 5% to 10%, the securities guaranteeing an income of £5 [and previously representing a capital of £100, G.C.] will now represent a capital of only £50. Conversely, if the rate of interest falls to 2.5%, the same securities will represent a capital of £200. Their value is always merely capitalized income, that is, the income calculated on the basis of a fictitious capital at the prevailing rate of interest. (Marx, 1967c p. 467)

36. I disregard for the sake of simplicity those investors who purchase shares either for takeover purposes or because they are interested in capital gains (speculative gains).

37. Fluctuations in the prices of stocks and bonds are usually explained in terms of economic and financial developments, as expressed by data on unemployment, inflation, balance of payments, budget deficit, and by the impact these developments might have on the financial situation of enterprises. But it should be stressed that these macro-economic trends do not influence stock prices through objective, economic relations. For example, it would be wrong to assume that, say, an increase in employment determines an increase in stock prices because of the higher level of economic activity it indicates. Rather, these trends influence prices by influencing the operators' expectations and speculative behaviour. Favourable employment figures might therefore (but do not necessarily) create the expectation in stock market operators that the higher level of economic activity it indicates might cause a higher demand for loans. If the operators know that the monetary authorities

are worried by too high a rate of inflation, the expectation of a restrictive monetary policy and thus of an increase in interest rates might become generalized. This might cause a massive sale of fixed-interest rate bonds, since speculators do not want to be stuck with those bonds when the rate of interest rises, and an increased demand for (and thus prices of) stocks. This depresses bond prices, that is, it increases the real interest rate on those bonds. At this point speculators sell stocks and shift their resources to those fixed-interest bonds; stock prices then fall. In other words the first, short-term reaction to data indicating an increase in employment figures might be a decrease, rather than an increase, in stock prices. If, however, other investors – less interested in short-term speculative gains and more interested in longer-term investments and profits – expect discounted future dividends to be bigger than present speculative gains, stock prices might increase.

38. In the crash of October 19, 1987, "all the record losses . . . only brought stock market prices down to the levels of 12 or 18 months" earlier (Grahl, 1988, p. 30). On the contrary, in the 1929 crash, the price of many stocks dropped to zero.

39. Unless this depreciation reflected an actual stoppage of production and of traffic on canals and railways, or a suspension of already initiated enterprises, or squandering capital in positively worthless ventures, the nation did not grow one cent poorer by the bursting of this soap bubble of nominal money-capital. (Marx, 1967c, p. 468)

40. Each crisis has its own specific aspects. The reader should consult Coakley, 1988, Evans, 1988, Glyn, 1988, Grahl, 1988, Freeman, 1988 and *Rapporti Sociali*, 1988. However, what follows relies mostly on Guttmann, 1988.

41. The fact that the receipt of the sale of commodity A can be stored away before commodity B can be bought is the basis of Marx's critique of Say's law. This states that, since the sale of a commodity is equivalent to the demand to purchase another commodity, supply creates in the aggregate its own demand. But, given the interval between the sale of one commodity and the purchase of another, Say's law does not hold. As submitted in chapter 3, Marx too assumes $D = S$, that is, that all commodities are sold at a price at which all modal capitals realize the average rate of profit. He assumes $D = S$ in order to find the tendential prices. He thus disregards, at this level of analysis, the cyclical movement of the economy and thus the fact that demand might not be equal to supply. However, once we introduce saving, the theorization of tendential prices, or prices of production, cannot rest on the $D = S$ assumption any more. It is not necessary to pursue this point further here.

(Neo-)Ricardian and (Neo-)Marxist Views of International Prices, Specialization and Exploitation

6.1 Ricardo and Comparative Advantages

As argued in the previous chapters, Marxist price theory is indissolubly tied to the transformation of individual into social values. This transformation has been examined from the point of view of production and distribution of value within a nation. In this, this work has so far followed Marx who focused on the formation of national prices. Marx only occasionally discusses the extension of the law of value to the international setting. But today's economy is worldwide. It would then seem reasonable to expect that a sustained effort has been made in the Marxist camp to examine the working of the law of value within an international context. This, however, is not the case. Marxists have dedicated comparatively few studies to this topic.

Perhaps the most important reason for this lacuna is that the attack on Marx's transformation procedure, and thus on his price theory, has been so virulent that comparatively little attention has been paid to develop, rather than just defend, that procedure and theory. Consequently, aside from a few exceptions, those authors who have attempted to research the international dimensions of the law of value have accepted, more or less implicitly, the validity of Ricardo's theory of comparative advantages and the theory of international prices inherent in it. This is unfortunate. There seems to be little awareness that Ricardo's comparative advantages cannot be integrated into Marxist theory. Let us see why.

In chapter 7 of his *On the Principles of Political Economy and Taxation* Ricardo provides his famous example which is reproduced in Table 6.1. In terms of *absolute advantages*, that is, in terms of a comparison for each commodity (wine and clothing) between the labour time needed to produce it in each country (Portugal and England), Portugal is more productive in both branches: it takes Portugal fewer men per year to produce both one unit of wine and one unit of clothing than it takes

Table 6.1   Ricardo's comparative advantage

Men needed per year to produce one unit of:	Portugal	England
Wine	80	120
Clothing	90	100

England. If capital and labour were mobile across national boundaries as they are within a country, Ricardo holds, Portugal would specialize in both wine and clothing, that is, specialization would be dictated by absolute advantages.

Since, in Ricardo's theory, there is no such mobility, there will be specialization in terms of *comparative advantages*. In Portugal the labour time needed to produce wine related to (divided by) the labour time needed to produce clothing (80/90 = 0.8888) is less than the time needed to produce clothing related to (divided by) the time needed to produce wine (90/80 = 1.125). Thus labour is saved in Portugal if clothing producers invest in wine, that is, if Portugal specializes in wine. The opposite holds for England, where the cost in labour time of producing clothing related to the cost of producing wine (100/120 = 0.8333) is less than the cost of producing wine relative to the cost of producing clothing (120/100 = 1.2). In England labour is saved if wine producers shift to clothing production, that is, if England specializes in clothing. In short,

In Portugal 1 gallon of wine costs 0.8888 yards of clothing
1 yard of clothing costs 1.125 gallons of wine

In England 1 gallon of wine costs 1.2 yards of clothing
1 yard of clothing costs 0.8333 gallons of wine

where the cost is computed in labour time, possibly expressed as prices in arbitrary monetary units.

But once we introduce foreign trade, does England have an objective interest in buying Portuguese wine and does Portugal have an objective interest in buying English clothing? Or, will international prices bring about this pattern of specialization? They will, says Ricardo. To see this, we must first of all determine these prices.

Ricardo's theory allows us to find only the upper and lower limits of international prices, rather than the prices themselves. Consider Portuguese wine first. In Portugal one gallon of wine costs less than (0.8888 times) one yard of clothing, or the Portuguese wine producers get 0.8888 yards of clothing for each gallon of wine. They will be willing to export

Portuguese wine if they get more than 0.8888 yards for each gallon. The English wine consumers (who, in this model, are the English clothing producers) must pay 1.2 yards for each gallon of English wine. They will be willing to buy Portuguese wine if it costs less than 1.2 yards. For a price higher than 0.8888 yards per gallon, the Portuguese wine producers will be willing to export their wine and for a price lower than 1.2 yards per gallon the English clothing producers will be willing to import Portuguese wine. Thus for Portuguese wine to be exported to (sold in) England, its price must lie between 0.8888 and 1.2 yards.

A similar reasoning allows us to find the upper and lower limit of the international price of English clothing. In England, clothing producers get 0.8333 gallons for each yard. To export their clothing to Portugal, they must get more than 0.8333 gallons per yard. The Portuguese wine producers must pay 1.125 gallons of their wine for each yard of Portuguese clothing. To buy English clothing, they must be able to pay less than that amount. For a price higher than 0.8333 gallons per yard, the English clothing producers are willing to export. For a price lower than 1.125 gallons per yard, the Portuguese wine producers are willing to import. Thus for English clothing to be exported to (sold in) Portugal, its price must lie between 0.8333 and 1.125 gallons.

Let us now fix a price ratio within these limits, say 1 gallon = 1 yard. The English clothing producers can then either pay 1.2 yards of clothing for each gallon of English wine or only one yard for one gallon of Portuguese wine. The choice is clear. The Portuguese wine producers can either pay 1.125 gallons of wine for one yard of Portuguese clothing or only one gallon for one yard of English clothing. Again the choice is clear. International prices do bring about a pattern of production specialization based on comparative advantages.

To sum up, the principle of comparative advantages leads to saving universal labour[1] and to the specialization of both countries in the branches in which they are more efficient. It is difficult to imagine a more powerful argument in favour of England's specialization in manufacture and of Portugal's "specialization" in agricultural (raw material) products.

Ricardo might have lived in an "era when no one had heard about 'underdeveloped countries'" (Söderston, 1970, p. 15) and he might have been a "courteous Englishman" who chivalrously assumed that Portugal was more efficient than England across the board. However, that chivalry seems to be nothing more than false humility since, well versed as he was in the practical (as well as in the theoretical) aspects of economic life, he must have been well aware that in reality Portugal was not more efficient than England in the production of manufactured goods.[2]

As is well known, Ricardo's theoretical courtesy was hardly matched by his countrymen's practice. In the words of A.G. Frank,

Since the destruction of the Spanish Armada by the English in 1588 and the economic colonization and de-industrialization of Portugal by means of a series of commercial treaties which culminated in the Methuen Treaty of 1703, Great Britain had virtually eliminated the Iberian countries from participation in world capitalist development. The process was exemplified by the exchange of English textiles – an industrial product – for Portuguese wine – an agricultural product: this trade agreement was made famous by Ricardo, who used it to justify the exploitation of Portugal by England on the basis of a supposed natural law of comparative advantages. (Frank, 1972, p. 46)

Let us then closely examine the theory of comparative advantages. Elsewhere I have shown that, even in Ricardo's own terms, it is possible to show that his theory (1) hides the existence of unequal exchange, and (2) hides the greater advantage which accrues to the dominant capitalists in the imperialist countries from the reproduction of technological "under-development" of the dominated countries (Carchedi, 1986a). Here I shall focus on the fundamental critique, its inconsistency with capitalist reality.[3]

The fact that, *in terms of labour*, in Portugal the production of wine costs less than (0.8888 times) the production of clothing while the production of clothing costs more than (1.125 times) the production of wine is a matter of indifference to the capitalists who reason in terms of profitability. Capitalists move to different branches not to save social labour but to increase their profitability. Since there is no reason to assume that, when *different branches* are compared, labour-saving techniques beget higher profitability, there is no reason either to assume that Portuguese cloth producers will become wine producers. A similar point can be made for the English producers.

Ricardo's mistake resides in comparing productivities *between* branches. Portugal, it is said, is more productive in wine than in clothing. This is why it specializes in wine production. The opposite holds for England. But productivity differentials can be compared only within branches. In this case they do reflect profitability differentials. Such a comparison is meaningless between branches (see 3.4.5.7). It is the comparison of the productivity of wine producers both in England and in Portugal which can be taken as an indication of profitability differentials (and thus of specialization), not the comparison between the relative productivity of wine and that of clothing in Portugal.

Ricardo's comparative advantages can explain neither international specialization nor international prices. This theory is a non-starter.[4]

6.2 Marx on International Market Values

Marx viewed capitalism as a worldwide phenomenon. However, he never went any further than giving some indications of how the law of value should be applied to the international economic context. Undoubtedly this is a consequence of the limited development of international production relations at the time *Capital* was written. There is thus reason to think that, had he embarked upon the task of extending his theory to the international context, he would have done so on the basis of presuppositions which corresponded to the economic reality of his time but which have become at least partly obsolete. Let us see why.

In discussing international wage differentials, Marx points out that the law of value "in its international application" is subject to a double modification. The first modification concerns the *intensity* of labour. On the national plane, Marx argues, labour mobility causes the formation of an average labour intensity. Thus within a country only labour with an intensity *above the* national *average* produces more value and, conversely, labour with below average intensity produces less value. On the international plane, on the other hand, labour is immobile. Therefore, there does not emerge an international average intensity of labour. Rather, the different national intensities "form a scale, whose unit of measure is the average unit of universal labour" (Marx, 1967a, p. 560). It follows that a country's more intense national labour produces *more* value in the same time *than the less* intense national labour of another country. The next chapter will argue that the assumption of international labour immobility has become partly obsolete.

The second modification regards the *productivity* of labour.

> But the law of value in its international application [says Marx] is yet more modified by this, that on the world market the more productive national labour reckons also as the more intense, so long as the more productive nation is not compelled by competition to lower the selling price of its commodities to the level of their value. (Marx, 1967a)

Here, Marx's argument seems to be that, within a nation, the relative ease with which capitalists within the same branch can adopt new technologies leads to the bulk of them using the same technology. The relative capital immobility between nations, on the other hand, prevents capitals moving to where technologies are more advanced, that is, it prevents the quick spreading of technologies: nations have to rely on their own means to develop (including copying) new techniques. It follows that there does not arise an average international productivity and that therefore the more productive labour counts as the more intense relative to the less productive rather than to an international average. Again, as the next chapter will argue, the assumption of relative capital immobility between nations has become obsolete.

6.3 Emmanuel's "Narrow" Unequal Exchange

The most influential attempt to reject the theory of comparative advantages and to extend Marx's law of value to the modern international context is A. Emmanuel's *Unequal Exchange* (1972). This work is based upon the conceptualization of the world economic system as characterized by a great mobility of commodities and capital and by labour power immobility. According to Emmanuel, the logical corollaries of these presuppositions are: (a) capital mobility brings about an international equalization of the rates of profit; (b) labour power immobility prevents an equalization of the wide national differences in the value of labour power, and (c) the transfer of value implicit in the international equalization of the rates of profit depends both upon differences in the levels of productivity of the national capitals and upon differences in wages and rates of exploitation. Another name for this transfer of value is unequal exchange (UE).

More precisely, Emmanuel separates what he calls *broad unequal exchange*, the UE due to differences in organic compositions of capital, from *narrow unequal exchange*, or the UE due to differences in wages and rates of exploitation (Emmanuel, 1972, p. 161). It is this latter which Emmanuel considers to be typical of foreign trade. On this basis Emmanuel argues that, given two countries, say India with low wages and England with high wages,

> if India were to specialize one day in metallurgy and engineering, to the neglect of her textile production, Britain would find no difficulty in taking up the latter branch again. By exchanging fabric and yarn for steel, looms and spindles from India, Britain would achieve the same super profit as she achieves today with the reverse pattern of trade. Whatever she makes and whatever she sells, she must realize the advantage that comes to her from unequal exchange and that corresponds to the difference between British and Indian wages. (Emmanuel, 1972, p. 146)

In short, in the process of transformation of values into prices the low wage countries, which also have the highest rate of exploitation, lose part of the value their labourers produce to the high wage countries, – both to the labourers and to the capitalists of these latter countries. This is, in essence, the meaning of Emmanuel's narrow UE.

To show this, Emmanuel provides the following example. He assumes two countries, country A – a developed country – with high wages (v = 100) and country B – an underdeveloped country – with low wages (v = 20). Both countries employ a constant capital (K) equal to 240 but use, in a certain production period, only 50 of it (c = 50). Both countries produce the same value (V = 170) but wages are different so that the rate of surplus value (s') must be different too. In A it is 20% and in

Table 6.2 Emmanuel's narrow unequal exchange

Country	K	c	v	s	V	PrPr	OCC	s'
A	240	50	100	20	170	210	2.4	20%
B	240	50	20	100	170	130	12.0	500%

B it is 500%. Then the average rate of profit (p) is 25% and the two prices of production (PrPr) are 210 for A and 130 for B (Emmanuel, 1972, p. 63). This is summarized in Table 6.2.

We shall see in a moment how Emmanuel arrives at these two prices of production. Let us first elucidate the reasoning behind this example. In this table, techniques are supposed to be equal, in order to show only the transfer of value due to different wages and rates of exploitation. Emmanuel indicates this by assuming that both countries use 240K, of which only 50c is consumed in a certain production period. Presumably the labour power employed must also be the same. The value produced is also equal for both countries (170). If wages differ, the quantity of surplus value must differ too: the lower wages are, the higher is the rate of exploitation. If now the price of production is computed, there must be a transfer from the high rate of exploitation (low wage) country (B) to the low rate of exploitation (high wage) country (A). As Emmanuel concludes, "It thus becomes clear that inequality of wages as such, all other things being equal, is alone the cause of inequality of exchange" (Emmanuel, 1972, p. 61). This approach has been criticized on several grounds. Here I shall consider only two points of critique.[5]

First of all, the method Emmanuel develops in order to separate the effects of "broad" UE from those of "narrow" UE is wrong. Emmanuel computes the rate of profit as the summation of s (surplus value) divided by the summation of K (constant capital invested), or 120/480 = 25%. He then adds 25% of K, or 240 × 25% = 60, to (c+v) in order to get the prices of production. Therefore 150 + 60 = 210 and 70 + 60 = 130. But these mathematical manipulations have no economic significance.

The correct computation is carried out by recalling from 3.8.3 that, in case only part of constant capital is used in a certain production process, each branch (represented by a modal capital and here representing a nation) tendentially realizes the sum of the constant and variable capital it uses plus the product of the average rate of profit (computed by dividing the total surplus value by the sum of the total constant capital invested plus the total variable capital) times the units of capital invested in that branch. Here the average rate of profit is 120/(480 + 120) = 20% and the units of capital invested by A and B are 3.4 and 2.6 respectively.

Table 6.3 Production prices: labour immobility

	Value produced	Production prices	UE
A	$50c + 100v + 20s = 170$	$50 + 100 + (20 \times 3.4) = 218$	$218 - 170 = +48$
B	$50c + 20v + 100s = 170$	$50 + 20 + (20 \times 2.6) = 122$	$122 - 170 = -48$

Table 6.4 Production prices: labour mobility

	Value produced	Production prices	UE
A	$50c + 60v + 60s = 170V$	$(50c + 60v) + (20 \times 3) = 170$	0
B	$50c + 60v + 60s = 170V$	$(50c + 60v) + (20 \times 3) = 170$	0

Then, with different wages and rates of exploitation, the production prices are given in Table 6.3.[6]

These results can now be compared with the situation in which labour is mobile, that is, when wages are equalized. Both capitals invest K = 240 and v = 60, or 3 units of capital. The production prices then change as in Table 6.4. The average rate of profit remains the same (20%) irrespective of whether labour is mobile or not. But the prices of production and thus UE do change. When there is labour immobility A appropriates 48 from B, while when labour is free to move from B to A there is no appropriation of value because now both capitals have equal OCC (240/60 = 4), and equal wage rates (60) and rate of exploitation (100%). There is thus a tendential appropriation of value due to the fact that the conditions of exploitation in one country are worse than in another. Is this then Emmanuel's "narrow unequal exchange"? The answer is no.

Aside from the computational mistakes (revealing conceptual mistakes) stressed above, "narrow unequal exchange" means a transfer of value from the capitalists *and* labourers of one country to those of another. And this is the fundamental point of critique: Emmanuel substitutes countries for capitals. But even if we can assume equal technologies and different wage rates and rates of exploitation (as in the case of oligopolies investing advanced technologies in the dominated countries), the transfer of value associated with the equalization of the rates of profit differentials due to different wages and rates of exploitation goes *from the capitalists* in the dominated countries *to the capitalists* in the imperialist ones. Lower wages in country B mean higher profits for B's capitalists and, if the rates of profit are to be equalized, a loss (transfer) of value to A's capitalists.

The equalization of the rates of profit (and thus the process of price formation) redistributes the *surplus value* produced *among capitalists*, either from capitalists with lower OCC to those with higher OCC or from capitalists with higher to those with lower rates of exploitation. But contrary to Emmanuel's thesis, in neither case is there a redistribution of value *among workers*. In short, there is no such thing as a "narrow unequal exchange".

In spite of these deficiencies Emmanuel must be given the credit for having drawn to Marxism's attention the obvious fact that wages and rates of exploitation cannot be taken to be the same in different countries. Emmanuel's thesis that, if they are not the same, there might be advantages involved in imperialism for the working class of the imperialist countries is correct. In fact, if labour in the dominated countries is not mobile, its wages cannot be equalized with those of the countries where wages are higher. It is also possible that part of the extra surplus value appropriated by the capitalists of the imperialist countries through unequal exchange is redistributed to the labourers of these countries. This is one aspect of imperialism which cannot be dealt with here and which, in any case, depicts a redistribution of surplus value which is not that considered by Emmanuel.[7]

6.4 The Neo-Ricardian Production Prices and Unequal Exchange

Another influential attempt to apply the notion of UE to the international economy and thus to determine international prices is the Sraffian approach. As an illustration, let us consider the work of S. Amin. According to this author, the choice of the Sraffian model is justified by the fact that Marx's solution to the transformation problem does not take into account the general interdependence of all commodities and thus of their inputs. This is the von Bortkiewicz, or circularity, critique. The price paid for this wrong choice is that the way is barred to the analysis of the value dimension. As Amin says, "in order to take this general interdependence into consideration, we need to stay at the level of immediate appearances, of prices, as Sraffa does" (Amin, 1976, p. 150). This, however, does not seem to be a decisive objection for Amin. Following Oscar Braun (Braun, 1973, ch. 1), Amin provides a numerical example (reproduced in Table 6.5) to show how the Sraffian system can be used to theorize and measure UE. He assumes two commodities, iron and wheat,

Table 6.5   The neo-Ricardian unequal exchange

13 tons of iron + 2 tons of wheat + 10 man-years = 27 tons of iron
10 tons of iron + 4 tons of wheat + 10 man-years = 12 tons of wheat

produced with the production technologies in countries A and B depicted in Table 6.5.

If the rate of profit, r, is uniform,

$$(13p_1 + 2p_2)(1 + r) + 10w = 27p_1$$
$$(10p_1 + 4p_2)(1 + r) + 10w = 12p_2$$

in which p_1 represents the price of one ton of iron which is set equal to 1 (that is, iron is taken as the numeraire), p_2 is the price of one ton of wheat, and w is the wage paid per man-year. It is also assumed that iron is produced in country A (the advanced country) and wheat in country B (the dominated country). On this basis Amin compares two situations which I shall call S1 and S2. In S1 he assumes that wages are equal in A and B (0.56). In this case the rate of profit is equal to 20% and the price of wheat is 2.44 (the price of iron being equal to 1). In S2 he assumes that wages in A are 0.70 and in B are 0.12. In this case, with the same rate of profit equal to 20%, the price of wheat falls to 1.83. This implies a worsening of country B's terms of trade (the prices of export goods relative to the prices of import goods), since B exports wheat and imports iron. This deterioration of the terms of trade is taken to be equal to UE.

But first, the terms of trade (TT) are far from being equal to, or a reliable indication of, UE. The transfer of value inherent in the exchange of commodities produced at different levels of OCC may or may not be reflected in the TT. Suppose that a country increases the productivity of a certain branch. If that branch manages to export its higher output at the same price level, export prices do not change and – disregarding for a moment the fact that TT are weighted averages – the TT do not change either. Yet UE has increased in favour of that country. An improvement in the TT in favour of that country indicates an even greater transfer of value to that country, but a deterioration of the TT might still hide a favourable UE.

Second, the neo-Ricardian procedure for the theorization of UE is similar to, and shares the same drawback as, the Ricardian method as discussed in 4.7.1 above, namely the setting – rather than the determination – of the average rate of profit. Ricardo first sets the average rate of profit and then inquires into how certain factors (e.g. distributional changes) modify that rate. The neo-Ricardian procedure too first sets the average rate of profit, and thus the distribution of value inherent in it, and then introduces wage, or distributional, changes to inquire into how these variations affect that redistribution of value.

Finally, if S2 depicts a situation of UE due to wage differentials, S1 must, by contrast, depict a situation of equal exchange. In fact, for O.

Braun, the "natural production prices" are those which would result if the wage rate and the rate of profit were equal worldwide. This is S1. UE then derives from forcing production prices to a level higher than the natural one in one country and lower in the other country (Braun, 1973, p. 108). The banality of this notion of UE is the necessary outcome of an analysis carried out exclusively at the level of distribution. In other words, movements in the TT (caused by a change in wage rates or by any other factor) are simply an expression of movements in international market prices. The "explanation" of movements in the TT as the result of movements in relative prices is simply a tautology. What we need is a theory which explains movements in relative prices (and thus in the TT) as a result of movements in absolute prices due to changes at the level of production (production prices). In other words we must provide a theory of international production prices, around which international market prices fluctuate. But this is precisely what the neo-Ricardian approach cannot do.

There is thus little that can be learnt from Ricardo's theory of comparative advantages, Emmanuel's theory of "narrow" UE or from the neo-Ricardian theory of UE. Marx's own approach to international prices, while methodologically valid, rests on obsolete assumptions. A Marxist theory of international prices of production must start from Marx's theory of price formation as expounded in chapter 3 but must go further than the national limits. It must develop, rather than ignore or misunderstand, the internal logic of Marx's theory of production prices on the basis of presuppositions which reflect modern international reality. This will be the task of the next chapter.

Notes

1. Even though, as I show in Carchedi, 1986a, more could be saved in the case of specialization in terms of absolute advantages.
2. Modern treatments of Ricardo's example often reverse the roles: England becomes the more efficient and Portugal the less efficient country. There are two variations on the theme. One (see e.g. Feiger and Jacquillat, 1982, ch. 3) considers England, the imperialist country, as more productive across the board than Portugal, the dominated country. However, both countries are still more productive in relative terms in different branches: it is in those branches that they will specialize as a result of foreign trade.

The other (see e.g. Samuelson, 1970, p. 648) considers America not only as more productive than Europe across the board; now both countries are more efficient in the same branch in terms both of absolute and of comparative advantages computed as above. The critique of the Ricardian procedure also holds for these two variations.

Usually the assumption is made that only different use values exchange on the market. This is the heritage of the Ricardian theory: Portugal exchanges wine for English cloth. Yet the nature of international trade is such that often the same country exports and imports the same commodities (Altvater, 1969, p. 11 and UNCTC, 1988, p. 92). Thus even if the Ricardian theory were correct, it would apply only to a part of international economic reality.

This is something which the neo-classical version of comparative advantages, as formulated in the Heckscher-Ohlin theorem, recognizes and attempts to deal with. However, this theory holds only if factor abundance is defined in terms of factor prices (a circular definition) but does not necessarily hold if factor abundance is defined in physical terms. Moreover, empirically, the theory shipwrecks against the Leontieff paradox, that is, the finding that capital-rich countries export labour-intensive goods. All subsequent attempts to reconcile the theory with these empirical findings are, to say the least, unsatisfactory.

Explanations in terms of perverse demand effects make the theorem useless since the principal cause of patterns of trade would then become the various countries' demand functions. An appeal to national differences in labour productivity conflicts with the assumption of the identity of the productive functions. How can US labour be more productive than foreign labour if the techniques of production are the same in both countries? The theory of investment in human capital cannot help since higher levels of skills (supposedly a feature of US labour) are useless when applied to techniques requiring lower levels of skills (since these techniques must be adaptable to foreign labour too). And the introduction of factor reversal is of little help either. If factor reversals are only a theoretical curiosity, Leontieff's empirical findings still have to be explained. If they are quite common, Leontieff is vindicated but the relevance of the Heckscher-Ohlin theorem vanishes.

3. Usually it is the unrealistic nature of the assumptions in Ricardo's model which is challenged, that is,

two countries, two commodities, two factors, perfect competition in product and factor markets, international immobility and national mobility of factors, identical production functions and qualitative similarity of production factors between countries. (Kiljunen, 1986, p. 99)

However, its inconsistency with capitalist competition (perfect or not) is not challenged.

4. If the Ricardian theory is a non-starter, what can we conclude about price formation in the absence of capital and labour mobility? Some Marxist authors (e.g. Shaikh, 1979 and 1980) have opted for a rehabilitation of absolute advantages. In Table 6.1 above, Portugal would specialize in both branches. Whether this is the case or not is a question which does not depend on a comparison between the live labour contents of each commodity, as in the Ricardian approach. A Marxist approach to this question would have to develop a theory of international market values. But this is an obsolete problem, given that capital is now internationally mobile. The important point to be stressed is that not only comparative advantages but also absolute advantages are alien to a Marxist theory of international prices, if only quantities of living labour are considered.

Notice that this section deals with foreign trade only inasmuch as this is necessary in order to discuss the Ricardian theory of comparative advantages and international prices. Foreign trade does have some advantages but these too should be seen in the proper perspective. As Marx says, "two nations can engage in mutual exchange, according to the law of profit, in such a way that both gain and yet one constantly exploits and robs the other" (quoted in French in Palloix, 1975, p. 169). What Marx had in mind is that it can be advantageous to import goods if they cost less than what they would cost if the importing nation had to produce them itself. At the same time, there is inherent in this exchange "exploitation" and "robbery" in the form, as we shall see, of an international unequal exchange. So far we follow Marx's argument. But even the "saving of labour" argument is far from being clear-cut. This point will be discussed in chapter 8, section 2 where it will be argued that this short-term advantage might be more than offset by a long-term disadvantage, that is, by the perpetuation of economic subordination inherent in the exchange of less technologically advanced for more technologically advanced goods. Moreover, the fact should never be lost sight of that those who gain are not "nations" but capitalists.

5. In what follows I shall stress only what I think Emmanuel does wrong in dealing with the theory of international production prices. However, he should also be criticized because he leaves fundamental aspects of that theory out of consideration. In fact he theorizes international prices of production while not discussing (a) the division of the world economy

into an oligopolistic and a free competition sector, (b) the mechanism of the rate of exchange (including the question as to whether there is a tendency towards an equilibrium rate of exchange) and (c) the "seigniorage" attached to the international currency. These three points will be examined in chapter 7. There are at least two more points which would have to be made, if one aimed for a more encompassing review of Emmanuel's approach. First, it is methodologically unwarranted and undialectical to treat wages as an independent variable (Bettelheim, 1972). Second, Lévai remarks that Emmanuel's scheme can be applied equally well within a country where there are capitals with equal technical compositions of capital but different wages. Should we conclude, he asks, that the better paid workers exploit the worse paid workers? (Lévai, 1983).

6. In this example, assuming labour immobility, the transfer of value seems to go in the wrong direction, from the high OCC nation (B, whose OCC is 12) to the low OCC nation (A, whose OCC is 2.4). But as we have seen in 3.8.7 and 3.8.8, if wages and rates of exploitation are not the same, the transfer of value associated with the formation of production prices is the result of two factors: a transfer from the low OCC to the high OCC branch and a transfer from the high rate of exploitation to the low rate of exploitation branch. In this case the influence of the first factor weighs less than that of the second factor. Shaikh theorizes a transfer of value from low OCC to high OCC regions due to wage differentials. Given a "world average wage" and assuming that the high OCC region pays higher wages than the average (while the low OCC region pays lower than average wages), if the international rate of profit is equalized,

the formation of international prices of production will require a larger transfer of surplus value *into* the high organic composition sector, *but also* a larger transfer *out of* the low organic composition sector. (Shaikh, 1980, p. 52)

The transfer of value is larger because of wage differentials. Siegel distinguishes between "unequal exchange of quantities of labour time on the basis of differing levels of productivity and unequal exchange of values on the basis of equal productivity but different wage levels" which "are phenomena in international trade that complement one another" (Siegel, 1984, p. 68).

7. The recognition of the fact that the working class in the imperialist countries can have a higher level of real wages than if there were a free influx of labour power from the dominated countries by no means implies the acceptance of the thesis that the working class in the imperialist countries has an objective interest in the maintenance of the imperialist system. The objective interest of the working class is simply the abolition of exploitation.

Production and Distribution as Worldwide Processes

7.1 Oligopoly Capitalism versus Free Competition Capitalism

Up to now the discussion has implicitly assumed *free competition*, a situation in which all economic units are in principle free to move to those branches where the rates of profit are higher and to introduce new technologies. Consequently, no capital can attain a dominant position in terms of market shares. This corresponded to the reality of Marx's time but is obviously not the case any more. In Marx's time monopolies did exist but they were not the basic unit of economic life. Typically, they were natural monopolies, based on the exclusive ownership either of some natural resources or of public utilities. This is the traditional notion which still dominates much economic thinking not only on monopolies but also on oligopolies.

This notion stresses barriers to capital entry due to legally protected privileged access to some non-reproducible means of production (e.g. land) or to some technique. In this notion, monopolies neither are subjected to competition from other capitals nor are they typical agents of technological change. If monopolies are not subjected to competition, the value of their product cannot be determined by the law of value. This is the situation to which Marx refers when discussing monopoly prices:

> When we refer to a monopoly price, we mean in general a price determined only by the purchasers' eagerness to buy and ability to pay, independent of the price determined by the general price of production, as well as by the value of the products. (Marx, 1967c, p.775)

Some modern authors believe that today's capitalism is based on monopolies which they perceive as being similar to the monopolies referred to by Marx. Therefore for these authors the source of monopoly profits is located in the monopoly's ability to impose prices higher than what they would be if the obstacles to capital entry or to the introduction of more advanced techniques were removed. But this is an anachronistic view.

Today, pure monopolies do indeed exist, but their influence on the economy is severely limited by three factors. First, they are restricted to certain utilities and patented goods. For example, Genentech, the world's biggest biotechnology company, is the sole producer of the drug TPA "which stops heart attacks as they are going on" (*The Economist*, 4 June 1988, p. 69). Second, they are far from having a relevant position in the economy. If pure monopolies are defined in terms of "market shares at or near 100%, plus effectively blockaded entry, plus evidence of effective monopoly control over the level and structure of prices", their share in US total national income actually declined from 6.2 in 1939 to 3.1 in 1958 and to 2.5 in 1980 (Shepherd, 1982, p. 618). Third, monopolies based on patented inventions are not free from the competition of substitute products so that their monopolistic position in that branch is only apparent.

7.1.1 Modern oligopolies and free competition capitals

While monopolies (in the strict sense) do exist, today's reality is dominated by *oligopolies*, by big, technologically advanced capital units which have gained a large share of the market because of large-scale application of advanced technology. It is the application of these advanced techniques on a large scale (made possible by the scale of the capital invested) which results in a superior competitive and market position for these capitals.[1] Oligopolies do not abolish competition but, as we shall see shortly, engage in both old and new forms of capitalist competition among themselves while being able to restrict competition from smaller and weaker capitals. Some examples are provided in Table 7.1. Also, in 1986 the top 40 European firms accounted for 23.0% of all sales generated by manufacturing, though representing less than 0.6% of manufacturing firms (Commission of the European Community, 1989, p. 41).

As Table 7.1 implies, the market in a certain branch is usually shared by oligopolies with other, smaller capital units. This is not always immediately apparent. Consider, for example, the steel industry. In the US a few large producers share the market with so-called "minimills". In the Japanese and Korean industries, in contrast, the minimill sector is entirely absent (Ferguson, 1988, p. 56). It would seem that in the latter case the steel industry operates only oligopolies while in the former case that industry's market is shared by both types of capital. This is so only if we take the point of view of each individual nation, if we

232

Table 7.1 Share of total sales accounted for by the five biggest European firms in the industry, 1986

Industry	Share
Aerospace	65.6
Motor vehicles	65.5
Computers, office equipment	65.3
Tobacco	43.7
Electronics	42.2
Chemicals	41.5
Drink	34.1

Source: Commission of the European Community, 1989, p. 41, table 5.2

assume no international capital movement and technological competition between the steel industries of the different nations. If, however, we consider international competition, if we take a global point of view, there is just one international steel industry which is made up of (among others) both the US and Japanese oligopolies and the US smaller capitals, the minimills.

The smaller capital units are usually called *free competition capitals.*[2] Actually, it is justified to use this term only in the absence of oligopolies. But in a situation in which oligopolies dominate a branch, small capitals cannot be defined any more as free competition capitals, that is, as capitals which can engage in capital movement and technological competition without being subjected to any restriction. If anything, this is what oligopolies can do. In this case we should speak of *dominant* or *oligopolistic* capitals, and of *dominated* or *restricted competition* capitals. These latter are those capitals which have not achieved a dominant productive capacity, which have not attained a substantial share of the market and thus which cannot pose any limits to capital movement and technological transfer, while being themselves subjected to these limits from the oligopolies.

This allows us to distinguish between two types of branches. The *free competition branches* are those branches in which all capitals can freely engage in capital mobility and technological competition. Here the bulk of the producers use the same (modal) technique and no individual producer has a substantial share of the market. This is the situation theorized in chapter 3. The *oligopolistic branches*, on the other hand, are those branches which are dominated by a few large and technologically advanced capital units which have gained a substantial share of the market. In these branches usually co-exist oligopolies and dominated capitals, even though sometimes oligopolies have the power to exclude the smaller capitals from access to certain branches because of high capital requirements, patented inventions, etc.

One of the characteristic features of modern capitalism is the dominance of the oligopolistic branches. This is why I shall refer to modern capitalism as *oligopoly capitalism*, as opposed to *free competition capitalism* in which the dominant branches, and thus the dominant capital units, were the free competition ones. We can also define the *dominated sector* as being made up of both free competition capitals and dominated capitals (both cannot pose any limits to each other's forms of competition) and the *oligopolistic sector* as being made up of all oligopolies, obviously only in the oligopolistic branches.[3]

The notion of oligopoly submitted here differs from alternative ones because market shares and the ability to restrict competition and to influence prices are not the cause of the monopolies' power. Rather they are the consequence of the oligopolies' strength at the level of production, their high level of productivity combined with large capital investments.

7.1.2 Oligopolies and the equalization of the rates of profit

The question now is: given that oligopolies can restrict competition, and thus the working of the law of value, is this law still valid under oligopoly capitalism? More specifically, can we still assume a tendential equalization of the rates of profit of the different branches into an average rate (and thus the formation of a production price) and its realization by the modal capitals? A few preliminary remarks are needed.

Contrary to what many authors still seem to think, the answer cannot be sought within the boundaries of the individual nation, torn from its international context. Given the international dimension of modern capitalism and thus of capitalist competition, the question as to whether there is competition both within each sector and between the two sectors can only be answered by taking a global view. Thus any attempt to place the law of value within the framework of modern, oligopolistic capitalism must transcend the national boundaries. Or, the question whether the law of value still operates under oligopoly capitalism (and, if so, whether it has undergone modifications) is inextricably tied to the question of whether there is a tendential formation of an *international* rate of profit.

If the question is one of international, rather than national, production and distribution of value, the extension of the law of value to the international context requires that we shift the focus of our analysis to the *internationalization of capital*. This is the process through which capital crosses national boundaries, thus (a) acquiring foreign means of production, (b) incorporating foreign labour power, (c) moving (parts of) the production process abroad and (d) selling its products in foreign markets.[4] But if production has become international, the national labour powers have entered the international production relations, have become part of the *international labour power*. This international labour power now produces *international value* – labour expended by the labourers of the different nations under capitalist production relations and producing material and mental use values – and is expropriated of international surplus value. It is this surplus value which is redistributed among the capitalists of the different nations through the formation of the international production price (to be analysed below).

The question as to whether there is a tendential formation of an international rate of profit, in its turn, immediately raises another one: among whom, or what, would the rates of profit have to be tendentially equalized in order for an international price of production to emerge? The answer is that it is capitals of different nations which compete within the same international branch (thus, if technological competition is sufficiently strong, bringing about an international modal production process in each branch) and between branches, by moving from one branch in a nation to another branch in another nation (thus, if mobility is sufficiently strong, bringing about an international production price). Therefore, a proper extension of the law of value to the international scene requires that national branches are replaced by *international branches*, that is, by branches made up of the several similar national branches and thus cutting across and encompassing different countries.

It follows that the hypothesis of the tendential equalization of the different capitals' rates of profit into an international average and of its realization by modal capitals could be empirically substantiated by time series of profit rates for each international branch, as represented by its modal capitals, showing a pattern in which the modal capitals of the different branches overtake each other in terms of profitability.[5] This statistical material is not available; at most one can find data such as those provided by Table 7.2.

Table 7.2 Ratio of gross value added per capital stock in manufacturing
(1975 exchange rates; US = 100)

	1950	1960	1970	1980	1981	1982
United States	100.0	100.0	100.0	100.0	100.0	100.0
Japan	11.8	23.7	50.1	81.8	83.5	85.9
Germany	46.1	69.0	91.8	110.9	109.6	110.1
France	45.6	60.8	88.2	111.2	109.9	113.6
UK	42.4	42.8	46.8	47.6	49.0	50.2
Italy	34.8	50.0	75.5	94.5	94.5	94.5
Canada	69.5	83.1	96.2	99.5	98.5	94.7

Source: Chan-Lee and Sutch, 1985, p. 55

If this ratio is taken as a proxy for the rate of profit, these data support the thesis that the national rates of profit in manufacturing have moved much closer to each other in the 1950–82 period.[6] Notice that, in line with the analysis submitted in chapter 3, there is no tendency for the rates of profit to equalize into an average within branches. But manufacturing is not a branch, it is a general name for a number of branches. Table 7.2 can then be taken to support the thesis of the tendential equalization of the rates of profit across these branches. However, these and similar data are partial and use proxies for the rate of profit. Thus their weight as direct evidence for the thesis submitted here is scarce.

If access to sound direct evidence is barred, we can turn to indirect evidence. Suppose we can observe that capitals compete internationally (1) by introducing new techniques, (2) by moving from one country to another within the same branch, and (3) by moving from one country to another across branches. The first two points would allow us to assume the formation of an international modal production process and thus of a modal rate of profit for each international branch. The third point would allow us to assume the tendential equalization of all rates of profit into an average. The three points taken together would allow us to assume the tendential realization of this average by the modal producers.

In what follows I shall focus on whether these three types of capitalist competition can be observed for the oligopolistic sector. If this is the case we can hypothesize an international tendential average rate of profit for this sector, so that the law of value can be assumed to operate here as well as, of course, for the dominated sector.

The interrelated questions as to whether (1) there emerge two different international average rates of profit, one for each sector, or only one international average for both sectors; (2) in the dominated sector there is only one international average rate of profit or many national average rates of profit; and (3) prices in the oligopolistic branches fall less (or increase more) than in the free competition branches (as Table 5.7 suggests), are important but will not be pursued here. The important point is to ascertain whether the law of value is valid also in the oligopolistic sector and thus under oligopoly capitalism.

7.2 The International Equalization of Oligopolistic Profit Rates

Empirical evidence supporting the thesis that technological competition and capital mobility are sufficiently strong to warrant the hypothesis of an international average rate of profit in the oligopolistic sector has been submitted in Carchedi, 1988. Here I shall only highlight the main reasons lending credibility to this thesis and submit some illustrative examples.

7.2.1 International technological competition

Most observers agree that oligopolies compete within branches by developing and introducing new technologies. This thesis is not specific to the Marxist approach. For example, it has been put forward in 1966 by R.Vernon and has since then been developed by the Harvard Business School within the framework of the "product life cycle" theory.[7] As a recent report puts it, "At the present time, TNCs [transnational corporations, G.C.] are at the centre of an accelerating pace of technological innovations" (UNCTC, 1988, p. 6). And,

> TNCs are playing a key role in the development of new technologies. Most technological innovations are the result of either the R & D [Research and Development, G.C.] activities of TNCs or of research undertaken by others, but funded by TNCs. Even in the numerous cases where innovations are made by smaller national firms on their own, those firms are often eventually taken over by TNCs, or sometimes they grow rapidly and become TNCs in their own right. (UNCTC, 1988, p. 21)

An important indication of the extent to which corporations are increasingly committed to technological innovation is given by the size of R & D spending. The data in Table 7.3, on a branch taken at random, are quite explicit.

Of course, oligopolies can buy, instead of developing, new technologies. Sometimes, however, the dividing line between developing and stealing new technologies can be very vague. The world's largest semiconductor producer, NEC of Japan, "entered the microprocessor market by

Table 7.3   R & D spending in US and Japanese semiconductor companies (US$ millions)

Year	Japanese companies		US companies	
------	R & D spending	Percentage of sales	R & D spending	Percentage of sales
1976	164.7	14.7	227.8	6.7
1977	199.8	15.7	303.3	7.7
1978	375.9	15.1	384.3	8.0
1979	427.8	14.6	470.0	7.1
1980	483.8	12.6	624.6	7.4
1981	621.3	14.9	776.0	9.7
1982	725.4	15.5	875.3	10.9
1983	941.5	14.2	943.8	9.7
1984	1,078.0	11.0	1,414.0	10.1
1985	1,314.0	15.0	1,597.5	15.0
1986	n.a.	n.a.	1,581.8	13.9

Source: Ferguson, 1988, p. 61

licensing Intel's design, then by designing Intel-compatible products, allegedly by illegal copying of Intel's microcode" (Ferguson, 1988, p. 60).

But oligopolies not only develop and introduce new technologies, they transfer technologies as well. Among the many ways in which technology is transferred, the following are usually mentioned: (i) foreign direct investments; (ii) joint ventures; (iii) international subcontracting; (iv) licensing; (v) franchising; (vi) management contracts; (vii) marketing contracts; (viii) technical service contracts; (ix) turnkey contracts; and (x) technological co-operation.[8] These and other mechanisms of technological transfer are also powerful forces towards the emergence of modal production processes within international branches.

It is noticeable that if oligopolies produce the bulk of commodities in their branch, it is they which are the *modal* producers, and thus which determine both the modal level of productivity and the price of commodities in their own branch (and therefore also of the commodities produced by dominated capitals in these branches). Seen within this context, the fact that "the largest 600 industrial companies account for between one-fifth and one-fourth of value-added in the production of goods in the world's market economies" (UNCTC, 1988, p.16) becomes a very convincing argument supporting the thesis submitted here. If the oligopolies tend to share the same technique (productivity), the average technique is a tendency of the first type (mode). If no oligopoly is the modal one, if oligopolies constantly overtake each other in terms of productivity, the average technique becomes a tendency of the third type (mean).

Up to now it has been argued that technological competition leads to the emergence of an international average production process in each branch. But this sort of competition has another important effect. It also leads to the introduction of new products. Under modern conditions,

> it is no longer enough to produce low-cost, high-quality items. Product ranges must be renewed constantly to take advantage of the quickening pace of technological change and create distinctive products which can command a niche in international markets. (Leadbeater, 1991)

Therefore, technological competition leads not only to higher levels of productivity for existing products but also to product innovation and thus to the emergence of new branches of production. This implies international capital movements from the old to the new product lines and thus is a factor enhancing the movement towards the international equalization of profit rates.

While product innovation is an essential aspect of competition under oligopoly capitalism it is not unique to this stage of capitalist development. Product innovation is characteristic also of free competition capitalism, even though not in such an accelerated form. The feature to be examined next, however, is specific only to oligopoly capitalism.

7.2.2 International capital mobility

Differently from the assumption implicit in chapter 3, where each capital invests only in one branch, under modern conditions oligopolies invest in several branches and often develop into agricultural, industrial and financial conglomerates. This greatly facilitates, rather than being an obstacle to, international capital movements across branches and thus the tendential emergence of an international average rate of profit. Moreover, when an oligopoly invests in a certain branch it uses capital accumulated from investments in other branches or raises capital through international sources. In this sense an investment in one branch also becomes an investment across branches and the distinction between capital movement within and between branches increasingly loses its significance. Under these conditions a national deal becomes a positive force for the equalization of profit rates internationally. It is in this light that the data provided in Table 7.4 acquire their proper relevance.

In short, the tendency for the rates of profit to equalize across national borders is not only facilitated by the ease with which oligopolies can transfer their capital across branches, it also springs from the fact that capital movements within national branches cannot be separated any longer from capital movements across international branches.

Many are the ways in which oligopolies move across national frontiers. First of all, there are direct investments (either through equity control

Table 7.4. US corporate mergers and acquisitions, 1967–87 (US$ billions)

Year	(1) Total purchase price paid	(2) Total market value of corporate equity	(3) (1) as % of (2)
1967	18.0	824	2.2
1977	21.9	950	2.3
1980	44.3	1,572	2.8
1981	82.6	1,505	5.5
1982	53.8	1,721	3.1
1983	103.2	2,022	5.1
1984	122.2	2,022	6.0
1985	179.6	2,584	7.0
1986	176.6	2,948	6.0
1987	165.8	3,008*	5.5*

*Estimated
Source: Fruhan, 1988, p. 64

or through greenfield investments) and portfolio investments. Mergers are also powerful factors making for a constant movement of capital across national borders. International subcontracting and original equipment manufacturing agreements (where a company produces a good which carries the brand name of the purchasing company) are also an important way in which capital moves across national boundaries.

Of particular importance in this connection is the growth of international financial activity since the 1960s.

One measure of its growth is that, during the period between 1972 and 1985, the funds raised in international financial markets expanded at an annual rate of some 23 per cent. This far outreached the growth in the value of world trade, which rose annually over the same period by some 13 per cent. (UNCTC, 1988, p. 102)

The cause of such growth has been explained above, in 5.6. Among the technological developments which have made this growth possible, the advances in telecommunications and computer technologies are particularly relevant. Due to these developments, virtually instantaneous worldwide trading has arisen in some markets.

Of course takeovers, mergers, joint ventures, equity investments and other sorts of capital movement are often motivated by the desire to transfer or acquire technology. Just as technological innovation and transfer imply capital movements, the latter are often motivated by, and have as an important effect, the acquisition and transfer of technologies.

To conclude, under modern conditions, technological competition not only determines the emergence of modal techniques within international branches but is also a vehicle of capital mobility within and between branches and thus a factor tendentially equalizing the rates of profit into an average one. At the same time, capital movements within branches cannot be distinguished any longer from capital movements across branches and both types of movement not only tendentially equalize rates of profit but also, by contributing to technological innovation and transfer, contribute to the formation of modal techniques within branches. It is through this complex process that a tendential international average rate of profit in the oligopolistic sector arises.[9]

7.3 International Wage Zones

The second question relevant for the extension of the Marxist price theory to the international context is whether we can assume a tendency towards an international equalization of national wages and exploitation rates. Here, contrary to the equalization of the rates of profit discussed above, we can rely on direct empirical evidence.

Table 7.5   Wage rates in the garment industry, 1975 (DM/hour)

West Germany	10.00	Greece	3.25
USA	9.00	Portugal	3.20
France	8.20	Iran	2.10
Switzerland	5.80	Tunisia	1.80
Italy	5.70	Brazil	1.15
England	5.00	Malaysia	1.00
Austria	4.75	Taiwan	1.00
Japan	4.60	South Korea	0.90

Source: Fröbel, Heinrichs and Kreye, 1980, pp. 136–7

Table 7.6   Manufacturing wages, 1987 (US$/hour)

West Germany	13.13	Taiwan	2.12
United States	10.82	Hong Kong	2.04
Sweden	10.57	Korea	1.43
Japan	9.92	Brazil	1.10
France	8.64	Mexico	0.97
United Kingdom	7.69		

Source: Sivanandan, 1989, p. 9

The international tendential equalization of wage rates might become the tendency in the future but does not yet seem to be the tendency at the present stage of capitalist development, at least if the imperialist block and the dominated block are compared. For example, in mid-1975, a capitalist investing in the garment industry would have had to pay the hourly rates shown in Table 7.5. As Table 7.6 suggests, twelve years later the situation as a whole had not drastically changed; on the other hand, there are data confirming a tendential equalization of wage rates for specific groups of countries, as Table 7.7 shows.

The hypothesis which seems to be empirically supported is, then, that there is no tendential equalization of wages and rates of exploitation between the imperialist block and the dominated one (see Tables 7.5 and 7.6) but that there is such a tendency within these blocks for groups of countries, which I shall call *wage zones* (see Table 7.7 for one of these zones). In this case, instead of there being one tendency towards wage equalization, there are several such tendencies, one for each zone. Consequently, the computation of the international production price should be carried out on the assumption of a (relatively limited) number of tendentially separate zonal wage and exploitation rates. As far as wage and exploitation rate differentials are concerned, the computation of the international production price hardly differs from the one submitted in 6.3,

Table 7.7 Gross hourly earning for manual workers in purchasing power standards

	1976	1977	1978	1979	1980	1981	1982	1983	1984	1985
Belgium	3,33	3,75	4,15	4,73	5,60	6,47	7,03	7,44	7,79	8,07
Denmark	3,91	4,31	4,84	5,62	6,19	6,89	7,49	7,77	8,17	8,68
West Germany	3,17	3,62	3,98	4,43	5,12	5,76	6,34	6,84	7,27	7,77
France	2,35	2,67	2,99	3,34	3,90	4,44	4,91	5,46	5,70	6,02
Ireland	2,70	3,08	3,49	3,96	4,48	5,07	5,50	6,02	6,53	7,00
Italy	2,96	3,35	3,72	4,15	4,64	5,38	5,89	6,39	6,56	
Luxembourg	4,04	4,63	4,99	5,45	6,04	6,48	7,01	7,51	7,87	7,99
Holland	3,25	3,71	4,06	4,56	5,13	5,66	6,28	6,77	7,03	7,36
United Kingdom	3,02	3,21	3,59	4,00	4,43	4,87	5,41	6,06	6,48	

Source: Eurostat, *Review 1976–1985*, p. 130, table 3.6.7

the only difference being that wage zones must replace individual countries.

The reason for the emergence of wage zones is not only labour mobility but also capital mobility. However, this is not sufficient to generate a tendential movement towards wage zones. Preliminary observation seems to indicate that this is the case only for areas which have reached broadly similar levels of economic development. Within these areas, increased synchronization of national economic cycles and relatively uniform fiscal, monetary, employment and other policies have relatively uniform effects on wages. In short, the hypothesis submitted here is that a wage zone is formed by capital and labour mobility between countries which have reached broadly comparable levels of development.

The assumption in this chapter, therefore, will be that there are two blocs of countries (the imperialist and the dominated bloc) but more than two zones within which it is reasonable to assume a tendential equalization of wage rates. Since, in what follows, the purpose is not to engage in quantitative estimates of the international price of production, for simplicity of computation I shall work with the hypothesis of equal wages and rates of exploitation, unless otherwise stated. The more realistic hypothesis of tendentially different zonal wages and rates of surplus value would only change the numerical results.

7.4 International Production Prices in Value Terms

Against this background it is now possible to theorize the formation of the international production price per unit of capital and per unit of output in value terms. Consider Table 7.8, where V stands for the individual value produced by each unit of capital, O is the output per unit of capital, VTR is the value tendentially realized by a unit of capital under the D = S assumption (that is, when all commodities are sold and realize the value realized by the commodities produced under average conditions of profitability) and VTR-V is the transfer of value implicit in the formation of the production price.

In this table we assume that two branches (A and B) are common to both countries and that branches C and D are the exclusive domain of Italy and France, respectively. We assume further that Italy is more advanced (has a higher modal OCC) in branch A and that its modal productivity is the modal one on the international level. Thus capital AII is the modal producer not only in Italy but internationally. Capital AIII in France has already introduced that technique which is the most productive in France but which, given France's relative backwardness in this branch, is only the modal one in the international context. France,

243

Table 7.8 The formation of the international price of production: modal, above mode and below mode capitals

ITALY

	I	II	III
Branch A	below mode	modal	above mode
V	$75c+25v+25s = 125$	$80c+20v+20s = 120$	$85c+15v+15s = 115$
O	90	100	110
VTR	112.85	125.4	137.92
VTR−V	−12.15	+5.4	+22.92
Branch B	below mode	below mode	modal
V	$80c+20v + 20s = 120$	$85c+15v+15s = 115$	$90c+10v+10s = 110$
O	50	55	60
VTR	104.48	114.93	125.4
VTR−V	−15.52	−0.07	+15.4
Branch C	below mode	modal	above mode
V	$65c+35v+35s = 135$	$70c+30v+30s = 130$	$75c+25v+25s = 125$
O	50	60	70
VTR	104.48	125.4	146.27
VTR−V	−30.52	−4.6	+21.27

FRANCE

	I	II	III
Branch A	below mode	below mode	modal
V	$70c+30v+30s = 130$	$75c+25v+25s = 125$	$80c+20v+20s = 120$
O	85	90	100
VTR	106.57	112.84	125.4
VTR−V	−23.43	−12.16	+5.4
Branch B	below mode	modal	above mode
V	$85c+15v+15s = 115$	$90c+10v+10s = 110$	$95c+5v+5s = 105$
O	55	60	70
VTR	114.93	125.4	146.27
VTR−V	−0.07	+15.4	+41.27
Branch D	below mode	modal	above mode
V	$60c+40v+40s = 140$	$65c+35v+35s = 135$	$70c+30v+30s = 130$
O	120	130	140
VTR	115.73	125.4	135
VTR−V	−24.27	−9.6	+5

in its turn, is the modal producer of commodity B. The modal capital is BII in France which also represents the international average productivity in branch B. In Italy BIII has already introduced that technique in the production of B but the technique, which is the most productive

in the context of the Italian productive forces, is only the modal one
in the international context. The different OCCs in branches C and D
cannot indicate different levels of productivity, given that they produce
different goods.

In Table 7.8, in line with what was said at the end of 7.2.1, the modal
units are oligopolies, while the non-modal units can be either oligopolies
or dominated capitals. Also, as mentioned at the end of 3.4.2, the average
productivity is supposed to be the mode, that is, we assume the bulk
of the commodities are produced by the oligopolies with roughly the
same technique. The assumption of a mean, rather than a modal, technique, the assumption that neither the dominated nor the oligopolistic
capitals produce the bulk of commodities, would only change the numerical results.

Let us now compute prices. By counting the surplus value produced
and the capital invested, we compute the international average rate of
profit which is 405/1800 = 22.5%. On the basis of this rate of profit,
both countries' modal capitals would tendentially realize 122.5 per unit
of capital. By dividing this figure by the outputs of each modal capital,
we get the prices for each commodity in each country. For example,
the individual value of the modal commodity A is set by capital AII
in Italy and by capital AIII in France, that is, 122.5/100 = 1.225, since
these two capitals use the international modal production process. The
other four capitals producing commodity A would tendentially realize
this value times their outputs. The same holds for commodities B, C
and D. However, the value produced in both countries is 2205 while
the value which would tendentially be realized on the basis of those prices
is 2154. By applying a distributional ratio equal to 2205/2154 = 1.0237
we derive the adjusted price of production per unit of capital, 122.5 ×
1.0237 = 125.4. The adjusted international average rate of profit is thus
25.4%.

If we now divide 125.4 by the modal productivities, we obtain the
prices of production per unit of output. Multiplication of these prices
by each capital's productivity gives us the values tendentially realized
by each unit of capital. This is the VTR line. By subtracting the values
produced by each capital (V) from these figures we obtain the transfer
of value implicit in the formation of the international production price.
This is the VTR − V line.

Now the total value produced is equal to the total value realized and
tendentially all modal capitals realize the international average rate of
profit per unit of modal capital invested (modified by the distributional
constraint), while above-mode and below-mode capitals tendentially
realize respectively more and less than this rate. Also, all modal capitals
with an OCC lower than the international average OCC (1395/405 =

245

3.44) realize less value than the value produced by them and all modal capitals whose OCC is higher than the international average realize more value than the value they have produced. In Table 7.8 there are no capitals whose OCC equals the international average; if there were, they would realize exactly the same value they produce. The same does not hold for non-modal capitals. For example, capital BII in Italy has an OCC = 85/15 = 5.67 which is higher than the international average (3.4) and yet loses value (-0.07).

On the basis of these results and recalling[10] that the value of the means of production and of labour power entering the formation (and thus the computation) of the price of production are their costs of *re*production at the moment the output is sold, we can summarize how the *international price of production per unit of output* is determined. First, the structure of production determines the cost of reproduction (at the moment the output is sold) of the means of production and labour power and thus the international average rate of profit. Second, this average is added to the constant and variable capital of modal capitals. This is the price of production per unit of capital. Third, this quantity is divided by the modal productivity in each branch. These are the production prices per unit of output. Fourth, these prices are adjusted, through the distributional ratio, to the requirement that only the value produced can be realized. Fifth, the D = S condition ensures that all commodities are sold (that is, that all value produced is realized) at prices equal to the prices just determined.

By multiplying these prices of production per unit of output by the individual productivities, we reach the social value of each unit of capital. This allows modal capitals to realize the average (modified) rate of profit and ensures that the more productive and the less productive realize more and less than this average. The price of production per unit of capital is then the social value (VTR) of one unit of modal capital.

7.5 Rates of Exchange and International Production Prices in Money Terms

For reasons which will become clear in a moment, let us work with an abridged version of Table 7.8, one in which only modal capitals appear. In Table 7.9 each international branch is represented by one unit of a modal capital in a certain country. Also, recalling what has been said above concerning Table 7.8, the modal units are oligopolies which operate under conditions of modal productivities. It should be stressed that, in Table 7.9, surplus value is not redistributed among countries as such, but among international branches as represented by a unit of modal capital

246

Table 7.9 The formation of the international price of production: abridged table

	c	v	s	V	PrPr(v)	PrPr(i)	PrPr(n)
West Germany (cars)	80	20	20	120	120	US$ 120	DM 240
Japan (computers)	90	10	10	110	120	US$ 120	Y 220
France (refrigerators)	70	30	30	130	120	US$ 120	FF 260
Total				360	360	US$ 360	

located in one country. For example, the production of cars is supposed to be carried out in different countries while the modal producers (the only ones considered in this table) are supposed to be operating in West Germany. A similar reasoning applies to Japanese computer producers and to French refrigerator producers. Consider then Table 7.9, where V stands for the national modal values (they also represent the international modal values in each branch and together represent the international value produced), PrPr(v) for the international price of production expressed in value terms, PrPr(i) for the international price of production expressed in the international currency, in this case the US dollar, and PrPr(n) for the national price of production expressed in the various national currencies.

The way in which these different types of production prices have been arrived at will be explained shortly. For the time being, suffice it to say that Table 7.9 has an important new feature. By showing that national production prices are expressed in national currencies and that the international production price is expressed in the international currency, this table stresses the need to incorporate a theory of rates of exchange into the Marxist theory of international production prices.

7.5.1 Realized and tendential rates of exchange

The *rate of exchange* is that at which the foreign currencies, including the international one, are converted into the national one.[11] But just as for each commodity there is an international market price which fluctuates around an international price of production per unit of output, so there must be an exchange rate which expresses the market prices (actually realized prices) and another rate of exchange which expresses the international prices of production (tendential prices). Therefore I shall introduce the distinction between the realized rate of exchange (from now on, *RRE*) and the tendential rate of exchange (from now on, *TRE*).

The *realized rate of exchange* is the rate at which at any given moment foreign currencies, including the international one, are converted into the national one. It has been the merit of the "Berliner Schule" of the early 1970s to focus on the rate of exchange in discussing the law of value in its international application. These authors related changes in the rate of exchange to the operation of the law of value on the international market and argued that the monetary crisis, like all crises, is a manifestation of the contradictions inherent in capitalist production (see Altvater, Neusüss and Blanke, 1971; Busch, Schöller and Seelow, 1971; Senf, 1978, and for an assessment see Deubner, Rehfeldt, Schlupp and Ziebura, 1979; Siegel, 1984). This is incontrovertible. However, these authors accepted the hypothesis of international capital immobility; consequently they did not theorize international production prices. But as argued above, this is, in the context of present-day reality, an obsolete approach. Moreover there are other limits to this approach. First, these authors' analysis of depreciation and appreciation seems at times to come dangerously close to a notion of an automatic equilibrium in the balance of payments. Second, the specific aspect of "seigniorage" (to be discussed in the next chapter) attached to the international currency passes unnoticed.

In what follows, therefore, I shall discard the notion that the RRE is determined by the equalization of the national socially necessary labour times in the absence of international capital mobility. I shall also discard the thesis that the RRE is determined by short-term fluctuations in the demand and supply of currencies (since this "explanation" is unable to explain long-term movements in the RRE). Rather, the thesis proposed here is that the RRE moves towards (oscillates around) the TRE.

7.5.2 National and international production prices in money terms

To find the TRE, consider Table 7.9. This table rests on three assumptions: (1) that the three modal producers produce a value of 120 in West Germany, of 110 in Japan and of 130 in France; (2) that the total value produced (360) is expressed as \$360 (but of course any other figures could have been chosen), and (3) that the quantities of *national* currencies which *express* the *international* value *realized* in each country by *modal* producers are DM240, Y220 and FF260 (these quantities of money are double the value produced but again any other figures would do). The international average rate of profit is then 60/300 = 20% – both in value and in dollar terms – so that the international price of production per unit of capital invested is 120 or \$120. Each modal producer (as representative of its branch) tendentially realizes \$120, or a value equal to 120.

This value of 120 is expressed in each country in terms of national currencies according to the quantity of money in circulation. Thus, a value of 120 will be equal to DM240, Y220 and FF260. But since this value is expressed as \$120, the rate of exchange is \$120 = DM240

= Y220 = FF260, or $1 = DM2.0 = Y1.83 = FF2.17. This is the *tendential rate of exchange*, the rate which converts the international price of production expressed in international money into national prices of production expressed in national currencies so that all modal capitals tendentially realize the price of production per unit of capital in value terms. If the international price of production is expressed in international money and if the national prices of production are expressed in national currencies, then the TRE is the necessary link between these two money forms of the average rate of profit in value terms.

At this rate of exchange all three modal producers, who tendentially realize the same price of production per unit of capital expressed in international money, realize the same price of production in value terms but more than, the same as, or less than the value they produce (according to the level of their OCC). For example, France's modal producers contribute 130 units of the total 360 units of international value for which they receive FF260. If these FF260 are exchanged for $120, France can get only 120 units of international value (-10), or the international price of production per unit of capital. Similarly, Japan's computer producers gain a value of 10. This is *international UE*. Producers with above- or below-mode productivity (not shown here) tendentially realize more or less than the international average rate of profit, according to their level of productivity compared to that of the modal producers.

This conceptualization can be summarized in the following five steps:

(a) the formation of levels of modal productivities in each international branch;

(b) the tendential equalization of the value rates of profit of all capitals, due to international capital mobility between branches, and the tendential realization of this average rate of profit only by modal capitals in the several branches; this international average rate of profit allows us to compute the PrPr(v) both per unit of capital and – for each branch – per unit of output;

(c) the expression of this PrPr(v) in international money in accord with the quantity of the latter in circulation; this is the PrPr(i);

(d) the expression of the PrPr(v) in national currencies, in accord with the quantity of national currencies in circulation; these are PrPr(n), both per unit of capital and per unit of output; and

(e) the expression of the PrPr(i) as PrPr(n) through the TRE. This ensures, tendentially, a transfer of international value consonant with differences in OCCs for modal capitals and consonant with productivity differentials for non-modal capitals.

It is crucial to stress that, in this approach, the national prices of production are the expression in national currencies (according to the quantity of money in circulation) of the international price of production in value terms, that is, of the value realized within each nation by modal capitals. It follows that the international price of production is not the equalization of the national prices of production. On the contrary, *it is the national prices of production which are derived from the international one.*[12]

Table 7.9 shows the formation of international production prices per unit of capital. Let us now compute the international production prices per unit of output, or the tendential prices of commodities. Consider Table 7.8. There, the TRE is computed as follows. Suppose that the total value produced by both countries (2205) is expressed as $2205, so that the international average rate of profit in adjusted terms is 25.4% and the international price of production per unit of capital is $125.4. Suppose further that the value realized by a unit of modal capital is expressed in Italy as Lit.125.400 and in France as FF376.2. All three Italian modal capitals (AII, BIII and CII) must therefore sell the output of a unit of capital at $125.4. The same holds for France's modal producers (AIII, BII and DII) who tendentially realize FF376.2. In this way, all modal capitals realize an international value per unit of capital equal to 125.4. The TRE is $125.4 = Lit.125.400 = FF376.2, or $1 = Lit.1000 = FF3.

In this case, 100 units of A, 60 units of B, 60 units of C and 130 units of D will cost Lit.125.400 in Italy and FF376.2 in France. This will determine the prices of the various commodities in the national currencies. For example, 100 units of A cost Lit.125.400 in Italy and FF376.2 in France, so that one unit of A costs Lit.1254 in Italy and FF3.762 in France. Since 100 units is the modal productivity of A, these prices will be the prices tendentially realized by all units of A.

One last point of clarification. We have seen above that the national and international production prices are *expressed* in money terms in accordance with the quantity of national and international currencies in circulation. This does not imply a monetarist approach in which money prices are *determined* by the quantity of money as a means of circulation. In this chapter the quantity of money in circulation has been taken as given and thus the monetary expression of production prices is also taken as given. But price determination does not depend on the quantity of money in circulation, as I have argued in 5.3.1.

7.5.3 Two alternative views of exchange rates

Mainstream economic theory reasons in terms of equilibria, not of tendencies; it thus seeks the *equilibrium rate of exchange (ERE)*. At least two alternative concepts of ERE, both equally unsatisfactory, have been submitted. The first is the *purchasing power parity theory.*[13] This holds that the equivalence between two currencies at the equilibrium level, or their ERE, is that which expresses equality in their purchasing power. Or, the ERE is that rate which equalizes the prices of identical goods in different countries. The difficulty with this approach is that, at least as far as the determination of the rate of exchange is concerned, it presupposes that only the same goods are traded and thus that the trading nations are at similar stages of economic development. The present approach, on the other hand, does not have to make this unrealistic assumption in order to theorize the TRE. It theorizes nations at different levels of economic development trading in both the same goods and country-specific goods.

It should be added that the purchasing power parity theory calculates the ERE by multiplying a chosen previous equilibrium rate by the relative change which has taken place in the price level. Usually, the criticism focuses on the difficulty of finding a previous equilibrium rate of exchange (see, for example, Scammel, 1974, pp. 452–3). This difficulty is perceived as being of a technical nature. But the real difficulty arises from a faulty, empiricist, methodology. The ERE does *not exist*. What does exist is a tendency of the third type, something which does *not realize* itself. No wonder that the choice of the previous ERE is experienced as a most serious defect of the purchasing power parity theory![14]

The second theory is the *parity of covered interest rates theory*. This theory asserts that the rate of exchange will be in equilibrium when the difference between the forward exchange rate and the spot exchange rate is equal to the difference between the interest rates of the two currencies. This is a purely financial theory in which price formation on the one hand and levels of productivity and profitability on the other are irreparably split. Rather than depicting the behaviour of an economy, this theory depicts the behaviour of financial institutions engaged in interest arbitrage. But a theory of rates of exchange, to be in accord not just with Marxism but also with reality, must be able to relate rates of exchange to levels of productivity. The parity of covered interest rates theory relates at best to the redistribution, not to the production, of surplus value.

7.6 Depreciation and Appreciation

What has been said up to now can be thus summarized: the first specific feature of the formation of the international price of production (both per unit of capital and per unit of output) is that the national prices are derived from the international one (and not vice versa) and that, once this formation is seen within the context of the different money manifestations of value, this leads to the notion of the TRE. But there is another feature which is specific to the formation of international prices.

7.6.1 Depreciation, appreciation and technological competition

Let us consider Table 7.9 again. Suppose that each country in the table is represented by ten modal producers in its specific branch; this means that all figures must be multiplied by 10. That is, West German car producers produce a value of $120 \times 10 = 1200$ and tendentially appropriate the same value which is expressed as $1200 and DM2400; Japan's computer producers produce a value of $110 \times 10 = 1100$ and appropriate a value of $120 \times 10 = 1200$ which is expressed as $1200 and Y2200, and France's refrigerator producers produce a value of $130 \times 10 = 1300$ and appropriate a value of $120 \times 10 = 1200$ which is expressed as $1200 or francs 2600. The total value produced is 3600 and the quantity of international money in circulation is $3600. The TRE obviously does not change. Suppose also that in the table each unit of capital in the different countries produces 10 units of output.[15] This means that each (modal) commodity tendentially realizes $120/10 = $12.

Suppose now that two of the ten Japanese producers adopt a new, more efficient technique. They now use 95c and 5v, instead of the modal 90c and 10v. Due to this technological innovation they double their productivity (they now produce 20 units of output each). This calls for the new tendential situation, that is, the new international price of production and the new tendential rate of exchange, which is shown in Table 7.10.

In Table 7.10, N indicates the number of producers and VTR stands for the value tendentially realized. Since its computation has already been carried out in 5.2 (Table 5.5), it will not be repeated here. $p stands for the dollar rate of profit tendentially realized and $TR for the quantity of dollars tendentially realized (both to be computed below). The total value produced has fallen from 3600 to 3590. However, since neither the capitalists nor the monetary authorities are aware of (or care about) the decrease in value they have no reason, on this account, to decrease

Table 7.10 Depreciation and appreciation

	N	c	v	s	V	O	$p%	VTR	$TR
West Germany	10	800	200	200	1200	100	12.5	1122	1125
Japan (modal)	8	720	80	80	880	80	12.5	898	900
(above)	2	190	10	10	210	40	125.0	448	450
France	10	700	300	300	1300	100	12.5	1122	1125
Total	30	2410	590	590	3590	320		3590	3600

the quantity of money in circulation. The new, lower, international value ($V = 3590$) is still represented by US$3600. The quantities of the national currencies do not change either.

The new average rate of profit in value terms is $590/3000 = 19.66\%$. The price of production per unit of capital is $100 + 19.66 = 119.66$. Since in all three branches (nations) the output per unit of modal capital is 10, the price of production per unit of output is $119.66/10 = 11.966$. If all commodities realized this much, the total would be $11.966 \times 320 = 3829$. But 3829 is greater than $3600, the quantity of international money available to express that value; therefore a deflator equal to $3600/3829 = 0.94$ must be applied. Each commodity must then cost $11.966 \times 0.94 = \$11.25$. Now modal capitals tendentially realize $\$11.25 \times 10 = \$112.5$ each, and $28 \times 112.5 = \$3150$ together. This figure is broken down into $112.5 \times 10 = \$1125$ for the ten French modal producers; the same for the ten German producers; and $112.5 \times 8 = \$900$ for the eight Japanese producers. The two above-mode Japanese capitals realize $\$11.25 \times 20 = \$225$ each and $450 together. The total is $450 + \$3150 = \$3600$. These are the figures in the $TR column of Table 7.10.

In dollar terms, each modal producer realizes a rate of profit of $(112.5 - 100)/100 = 12.5\%$ (instead of 20%, the modal rate of profit in Table 7.9) while the innovative capitals realize $(225 - 100)/100 = 125\%$ (instead of 20%). This is the $p column, or the rates of profit tendentially realized in dollar terms in Table 7.10.

What will the new TRE be? Tendentially, the 10 West German producers appropriate $\$11.25 \times 100 = \$1125$. The same holds for France. But Japan appropriates $\$11.25 \times 120 = \$1350$, that is, the Japanese modal producers appropriate $\$11.25 \times 80 = 900$ and the above-mode producers appropriate $450. Since the quantities of national currencies have remained the same, if the three countries have to appropriate these quantities of dollars, the TRE must be such that $\$1350 = Y2200$ and $\$1125 = DM2400 = FF2600$; or, $\$1 = Y1.63 = DM2.13 = FF2.31$.

Let us now compare the two TREs emerging from Tables 7.9 and 7.10:

Table 7.9: $\$1 = Y1.83 = DM2.00 = FF2.17$
Table 7.10: $\$1 = Y1.63 = DM2.13 = FF2.31$

In Table 7.9, one dollar is equal to Y1.83 while in Table 7.10 one dollar is equal to only Y1.63. Or, after technological change, fewer yen are needed to buy one dollar. Similarly, one dollar used to be equal to DM2.00, while now it is worth DM2.13; and one dollar used to be worth FF2.17 and is now worth FF2.31. Or, after technological change, more DM and francs are needed to purchase one dollar. In other words the tendential value of the yen has increased, while the tendential value of

253

the other two currencies has decreased. At these tendential values, the yen is appreciated while the franc and the mark are depreciated.

The theory of exchange rates submitted above allows us to understand the admirable way in which systemic requirements are actualized through the selfish action of the economic agents, or how countries are rewarded in terms of transfers of value through the capitalists' rewards (higher rates of profit) in terms of money. First, the countries' rewards. After technological innovation has been introduced in Japan, France produces a value equal to 1300 but only gets a value equal to 1122 (−178); West Germany produces a value of 1200 but gets 1122 (−78), and Japan produces a value of 1090 but gets 1346 (+256). This is equal to West Germany's and France's combined losses, and is the extra reward for Japan in value terms (it gets a value of 256 instead of 100, as in Table 7.9, on the assumption that there are 10 Japanese producers) for having increased its productivity, the penalty for West Germany (it loses 78 instead of realizing all the value it produces, as in Table 7.9, on the assumption that there are 10 German producers) for not having increased its productivity, and the extra penalty for France (it loses 178 instead of 100, as in Table 7.9 on the same assumption) for the same reason.

Now for the selfish action of economic agents. It would seem that Japanese capitalists have no interest in increasing their productivity since, in the last analysis, before that increase they realize $1200 \times 1.84 =$ Y2200 and after the increase they realize the same quantity of yen, i.e. $1350 \times 1.63 =$ Y2200. But the fact, which by now should be familiar, is that it is above-mode capitals which are rewarded for increasing their productivity.

In the new tendential situation, all modal capitals realize a lower rate of profit (12.5% instead of 20%). This also holds for the Japanese modal producers. They tendentially realize $112.5 \times 1.63 =$ Y183 instead of $120 \times 1.83 =$ Y220 each. Above-mode capitals realize $225 \times 1.63 =$ Y366 each instead of $120 \times 1.83 =$ Y220. Therefore, while the Japanese *modal* capitals tendentially realize a *lower* rate of profit, the *entire branch* producing computers (which here stands for the Japanese economy) tendentially realizes *more* international value than before the technological innovation because the *innovative* capitals realize a *higher* rate of profit. The rewards in money rates of profit (both in national and in international money) for the innovative capitals and the reward for nations in terms of value are but two sides of the same coin.

Of course, Japan can increase the quantity of money by (approximately) the same percentage as the increase in productivity (and thus consonant with the value appropriated from the other nations), thus keeping the level of prices unchanged. For example, "a sharp increase in the money supply" in Japan in 1987 did not worry the Deputy Governor of the

254

Bank of Japan, according to whom "We have to keep a close watch on the money supply but the recent high growth does not necessarily lead us to the risk of inflation in the immediate future" basically because of no "capacity bottlenecks" (Montagnon, 1988).

This is the tendency; but a real movement is the intertwining of tendencies and counter-tendencies. One of the counter-tendencies is that the appreciation of the yen increases the international price (in dollars) of the computers while the depreciation of the other currencies decreases that of French refrigerators and German cars. The demand for computers (and thus for yen) decreases, that for the other two products (and currencies) increases. This may counter the appreciation of the yen and the depreciation of the mark and the franc. It is through the interplay of tendencies and counter-tendencies that the new realized situation tends towards the new tendential situation, without however being able to reach it. It is this real movement which allows us to conceptualize the tendency and it is the latter which allows us to make sense of the apparently random nature of the former.

The theory submitted here is basically a theory of long-term movements of the rate of exchange. The TRE (as determined by changes in productivity) changes only slowly so that the RRE are fluctuations around a relatively stable or slowly changing centre of gravity. Chart 7.1 below provides an example of a long-term depreciation of the currency of a country (the US) whose productivity lags behind and of the appreciation of the currencies of two countries (West Germany and Japan) which are leaders in technological innovation. Notice that Chart 7.1 relies on data operationalizing exchange rates as the ratio of the national to the international currency; thus a fall in the exchange rate indicates an appreciation and an increase a depreciation.

The trends in labour productivity, here defined as real gross domestic product per person employed, are shown in Table 7.11.

Of course, very short-term movements of the RRE are only indirectly related to changes in the sphere of production. They are caused by speculative shifts of currencies due to the activities of (central) banks, security firms and foreign exchange subsidiaries of multinational corporations. The analysis of these shifts and of their effects on the RRE is obviously of a conjunctural nature and lends itself only partly to general rules. One of these, particularly relevant in the present conjuncture, is that the importance of these speculative shifts, and thus of their effect on the RRE, increases as crises deepen. In fact, as seen in chapter 5, as the crisis of capital over-accumulation develops, an increasing mass of money capital finds its way into the financial and speculative markets in search of those higher profits which cannot be realized any longer in the productive spheres. These huge masses of capital overtake the quantity

Chart 7.1 SDR values of US$, Yen, DM (end of period values)

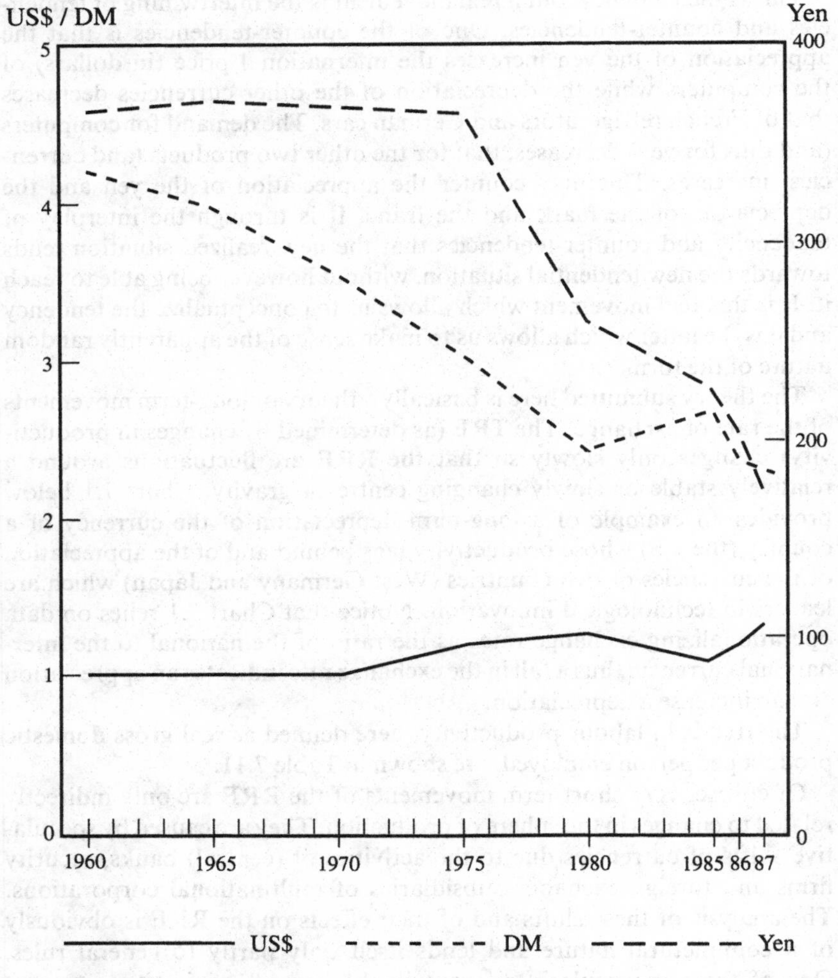

Source: IMF, 1988 (a), pp. 368–9 and 442–3

Table 7.11 Trends in labour productivity (% change)

	US	Japan	Germany
1960–73	2.1	8.4	4.3
1974–82	0.0	3.0	2.2
1983	3.3	9.8	7.6
1984	0.8	8.3	4.8
1985	−0.6	1.3	3.2

Source: Bank for International Settlements, *Annual Reports*, 1984 (p. 23), 1985 (p. 25), 1986 (p. 17).

of capital needed for merchandise trade and are what explain the present volatility of the RRE.

This volatility creates the mistaken impression that rates of exchange are basically determined by ebbs and flows of speculative money. Even such acute authors as Magdoff and Sweezy have succumbed to this mistaken approach. In their words, "Foreign exchange rates which used to be set by trade flows ... are now overwhelmingly dominated by the ebb and flow of money capital in which merchandise trade plays only a minor role" (Magdoff and Sweezy, 1985, pp. 85–6). If this were true, there would be no objective principles regulating the long-term movements of the RRE, only random movements. The thesis submitted here, on the contrary, argues that these movements are not random, as Chart 7.1 clearly shows.

It should also be mentioned that what has been submitted here is a theory of flexible rather than fixed exchange rates. But this theory can be extended to fixed exchange rates. In fact, in the case of rates of inflation differentials between two countries with fixed rates of exchange, price differentials will act upon the balance of trade, possibly on the balance of payments, and thus through an inflow and outflow of foreign money will force realignment. As an example, let us take the Exchange Rate Mechanism, where the rates of exchange of the currencies of the EC's member countries can fluctuate only within a margin of 2.25% around fixed parities (for details, see 8.1.3 below). This is an adjustable, but fixed, system. Since its inception, there have been twelve realignments of these parities but none of them has been a revaluation relative to the DM, the currency of the strongest economy in the EC (see Schinasi, 1989, p. 398).

Finally, this theory relates movements in the rates of exchange to increases in productivity due to technological improvements. It applies thus to countries for which there are no systemic obstacles to technological competition, that is, to the countries of the imperialist centre. However, it is also the first step towards, and necessary prerequisite for, a theory of exchange rates in the so-called underdeveloped countries. We shall see this in 7.9 below.

7.6.2 Rates of exchange and gold

Given a certain value of gold, the devaluation and revaluation of a currency also imply a change in the gold content of that currency. Thus, Stadnichenko defines devaluation as

> the law-sanctioned reduction of the gold content of a national monetary unit, its depreciation, as it were. This means that all the balances in the given currency, no matter who owns them, are simultaneously depreciated. And since a huge part of the media of circulation is represented by liabilities of the central state bank, such a depreciation is simultaneously an admission of the fact that the bank is unable to redeem these liabilities at their former value. Devaluation is partly bankruptcy. (Stadnichenko, 1975, pp. 186–7)

This notion rightly stresses the changed quantitative relationship between national currencies and gold following the appreciation or depreciation of those currencies. But this notion is unsuited to a proper understanding of depreciation and appreciation because it ignores changes at the level of production, or changes in economic strength (productivity), that make these measures necessary. Aside from speculative and other conjunctural phenomena, the rate of exchange as well as its fluctuations can be *described* and *measured* in terms of gold content but are to be *explained* in terms of changes in the levels of technological development, as indicated by changes in the levels of OCC of the different international branches.

7.6.3 International UE, rate of exchange and balance of trade

In Table 7.9 there is international UE since, given a total value equal to 360, when the TRE is applied, France loses a value of 10 and Japan gains a value of 10. In terms of international money, France loses $10 and Japan gains $10.

If we now consider changes in the TRE, depreciation means an impoverishment of West Germany and France, that is, the appropriation of value and thus of the labour of West German and French workers by Japanese capitalists, with the West German and French capitalists as intermediaries. Or, a part appropriated by these capitalists is, in its turn, appropriated by Japanese capitalists. But West German and French capitalists neither know nor care about this; they reason in terms of profits. All they know is that if they increase productivity they increase their money rates of profit and that if they do not their money rates of profit decrease.

However, depreciation and appreciation, while being factors correcting imbalances in the balance of trade,[16] neither automatically eliminate those imbalances[17] nor eliminate international UE because they do not eliminate its cause, that is, different modal OCCs in the international branches and the tendential equalization of all capitals' profit rates into an international price of production.

There is in fact a transfer of value (international UE) also when imports equal exports.[18] The relevance of Marx's value magnitudes, the neo-Ricardian attempts to show the contrary notwithstanding, can again be clearly seen. Only value analysis can show that a balanced trade (equality of exchange at the price level) does not imply equal exchange of international value (equality of exchange at the value level).[19]

7.6.4 Concluding remarks

If the approach submitted here is compared to alternative ones, it can be seen it has are three advantages. First, unlike the purchasing power parity theory, it does not have to assume that two countries trade only in the same goods in order to theorize the rate of exchange. Second, in contrast to the parity of covered interest rates theory, it can relate the movement in the rate of exchange to the level of productivity.[20] Third, unlike Ricardo's and Emmanuel's theories, it does not have to assume that the trade in country-specific products is the norm and that the international trade in the same goods produced by different countries is the exception.

It should also be stressed that, if prices are theorized in a neo-classical fashion, only tradable goods (goods traded on the world market) have an international price; non-tradables do not. If, on the other hand, prices are theorized as tendentially determined by the equalization of profit rates, only those goods produced in branches open to international competition (that is, technological competition within branches and capital movements across branches) have an international production price. These can be both tradable and non-tradable goods. To assume (as some Marxist authors do) that only tradables have an international price reveals the acceptance of a neo-classical theory of international prices.

7.7 Unequal Exchange between Capitalist and Non-capitalist Systems

We can now consider the application of the category of UE to the exchange relations between a capitalist system and a non-capitalist one. This is important since it points to the daily practice of international exchange between capitalist and non-capitalist systems. Here two interpretations have been advanced. On the one hand, Sau points out that the categories of the labour theory of value cannot be applied to a non-capitalist system and concludes that the concept of unequal exchange as formulated by Emmanuel ceases to have any significance (Sau, 1982). I agree on this but I think that the notion of UE submitted in this work (as opposed to Emmanuel's) can be adapted to account for this case, as we shall see in a moment. On the other hand, Caballero (1984) submits that the concept of UE can be applied to the case under discussion (a point on which I agree, on condition that this concept is properly modified) but argues this on the basis that the labour theory of value is also applicable to the non-capitalist system (a point on which I disagree).

This question is best approached by recalling that capitalism is a world system in which capitalist production and distribution relations are determinant. This means that, no matter how the prices of the use values produced in the non-capitalist system have been determined, as long as these use values are sold on the capitalist international market they are sold at international prices which have been determined according to capitalist economic laws. Thus by entering the capitalist *distribution* relations, by being exchanged on the capitalist market, the product (labour) of the non-capitalist producer (a) *counts* as if it had been produced under capitalist production relations, that is, becomes international value, and thus (b) tendentially *fetches* the international production price per unit of output of similar commodities produced under capitalist relations of production.

Suppose now that the non-capitalist producers own their own means of production (as in the case of independent peasants and handicraftsmen). Here, as Marx explains,

we come up against a peculiarity that is characteristic of a society in which one definite mode of production predominates, even though not all productive relations have been subordinated to it. In feudal society, for example, ... relations which were far removed from the nature of feudalism were given a feudal form ... It is exactly the same in the capitalist mode of production. The independent peasant or handicraftsman is cut up into two persons. As owner of the means of production he is capitalist; as labourer he is his own wage labourer. As capitalist he therefore pays himself his wage and draws his profit on his capital; that is to say, he exploits himself as wage-labourer, and pays himself, in the surplus value, the tribute that labour owes to capital. (Marx, 1963, pp. 407–8)

Thus when they sell their products on the capitalist market, these producers act both as capitalists and as owners of their own labour power. Let us look at them as capitalists. If we assume (as is reasonable) higher productivity in the capitalist system, this will appropriate labour (which it will transform into value by pulling it into the sphere of capitalist

260

realization) from the non-capitalist system. If we now look at the same producers as labourers, it is equally reasonable to assume that their "wages", the labour content of their basket of subsistence goods, are lower than the average wage of the workers working in the capitalist sector. This causes an extra appropriation of labour by the capitalists from the non-capitalist producers, as labourers.

This transfer of value can be expressed as profit, as a *capitalist* entity, even if it is the difference between labour expended under capitalist production relations (value) and labour expended under non-capitalist production relations (which, on this account, cannot be considered to be value), because the latter labour counts as value, as labour expended under capitalist production relations, once it is drawn into the sphere of capitalist realization. Moreover, this transfer of value is made up of two components which can only be logically, but not empirically, separated.

This being so, can we talk of UE in this case? We can. But in this case, the notion of UE changes in order to be made to explain a different situation. UE in this case explains neither prices in the non-capitalist sector nor the transfer of *value* from non-capitalist to capitalist sectors. Rather, this notion explains a transfer of *labour* from a non-capitalist to a capitalist sector and its *realization as value* in the capitalist sector. Moreover, contrary to the notion of UE within a capitalist system, it deals with a feature of reality which, important as it is, is not essential for the functioning of the capitalist system. The importance of this notion resides, first, in that it calls our attention to the appropriation of labour from non-capitalist systems and its realization as value, and second, in that it reveals a special case, that of the producers of simple commodities within a capitalist context, in which it is impossible to empirically separate the "capitalist" from the "labourer".

7.8 International (Super-)Exploitation

Different national real wages are often taken to be a measure of the super-exploitation of the workers in the low wage countries. But if we assume different national levels of technology in the production of wage goods, this is not necessarily the case. Actually, the contrary may well be true. The reason for this is that exploitation is the relation between surplus value and the wages of the productive labourers. It follows that exploitation is not only, and cannot be measured only by, the level of wages.

Consider a high technology country, A, and a low technology country, B, both producing corn. In A labourers can produce 18 kg of corn per day, 6 kg of which are wages. The rate of exploitation here is 200%. In B total production is 6 kg, 3 kg of which are wages; the rate of exploitation is 100%. In this case, A has both higher wages and a higher rate of exploitation. If A and B do not belong to the same wage zone, A has higher wages and rate of exploitation than B (as above). If the two countries do belong to the same wage zone, A has higher (and B has lower) wages and rate of exploitation than a tendential average.

So far we have assumed that two countries produce the same wage good by using different technologies. But this is only part of reality. Given the transfer of technology inherent in the internationalization of production, "modern technology in some industries is such that relatively unskilled labour can be combined with fairly sophisticated equipment" so that capital (usually, oligopolies) can take high productivity, modern technology (either entire production processes or parts of them) to low wage, low skill countries (Adam, 1975, p. 91). Under these conditions, if both the length of the working day, the intensity of labour and the technique used are the same, the level of wages is sufficient to indicate the level of exploitation: lower wages also indicate higher exploitation. Or, other things being equal, the country (capitalist) which pays less than the other country or less than the average wage level forces its workers to produce more international surplus value. In this case B's workers are both poorer and more exploited than A's workers, if the two countries do not belong to the same wage zone. B's workers are more exploited, and A's workers are less exploited, than the average if they belong to the same wage zone.

In view both of the possibility of transferring technology and of the huge national wage differentials (see Tables 7.5 and 7.6 above), it is quite clear that such differences are a very important stimulus for the imperialist countries to invest in the dominated ones. Moreover, working conditions (length of the working day and intensity of labour) are often much worse in the low wage (dominated) countries than in the high wage (imperialist) ones. This greatly increases the rate of exploitation, sometimes reaching the limit of the physical reproduction of the working class (Frank, 1981). Of course, other considerations (tax "holidays", export incentives, subsidized credits, duty-free imports of foreign goods for local assembly, environmental control in the imperialist countries, protectionist tariffs in the dominated countries, the "docility" of the local work force due to political repression, etc.) play a role as well but wage differentials and conditions of work are the central and by far the most important item.[21] Unfortunately, examples abound. In the words of an Indian manufacturer-exporter of garments, due to cheap labour, "we can make garments so cheaply that foreign buyers['] ... mark-up is four to five times on their bargains, giving them a huge profit" (Sharma, 1988).

However, it is not only foreign capitalists who profit from low wages in the dominated countries. Local capitalists profit from them too, especially when they import advanced technology from the imperialist countries. Moreover, the higher rates of profit deriving from lower wages and comparable technology allow them to reduce their prices in order to undersell their competitors;[22] thus some capitalists in the dominated countries can become formidable competitors of capitalists in the imperialist countries. Some countries, the so-called newly industrialized countries, can even achieve high, even though temporary, surpluses in their balance of trade. This explains the imperialist countries' grumbling and their calling on the newly industrialized ones to pursue "policies that allow their currencies more fully to reflect underlying fundamentals" (*Financial Times*, June 11, 1987), that is, to increase their prices by appreciating their currencies.[23]

Of course, the capitalists' paradise is a combination of high levels of productivity (appropriation of value produced by other capitalists) and high levels of exploitation (appropriation of value produced by their own labourers). One example of what this "paradise" means will suffice. It pertains to the production of lap-top computers by the Japanese manufacturer Toshiba.

A scarlet sign saying "4 Hours" hangs over the portable computer assembly line at Toshiba's Ome factory ... That means four hours a day of compulsory overtime for the full-time production workers, extending their working day from 8 am to 9 pm, with an hour's lunch break ... White collar engineering and administrative staff ... work even longer hours, often from 7 am to 11 pm. (Cookson, 1988)

7.9 Exploitation, Inflation and Rates of Exchange in the Dominated Countries

The world capitalist system is divided into two blocs which in section 3 of this chapter have been referred to as the imperialist and the dominated bloc. It is now time to specify the meaning which should be attached to these terms.

From a purely economic point of view, the relation which unites the imperialist bloc (of countries) to the dominated bloc is one of determination in the sense that capital accumulation in the dominated bloc is a condition for the extended reproduction of capital accumulation in the imperialist bloc. This is the economic meaning of imperialism, even though imperialism is far from being only an economic phenomenon.

In terms of distribution of value, this means that there is a built-in transfer of value from the dominated to the imperialist bloc. As seen above, transfer of value is inherent in exchange, through price formation, when the same commodity is produced by capitals with different levels of productivity and is sold for the same price. This, in turn, means that even when – as is nowadays usually the case – the dominated countries undergo a process of industrialization (which for a few of them can be considerable), there must be a self-reproducing process which prevents the dominated countries from achieving the same level of technological development as, or from competing technologically with, the imperialist countries. This does not preclude the emergence of new imperialist countries and the decline of old ones. But it does imply that the separation between the two blocs is a permanent feature of the capitalist system.

As mentioned in chapter 1, section 2, the notion of determination implies that the determined instances realize themselves (as conditions of either reproduction or supersession of the determinant one) in the process of their mutual interrelation and thus in the process of their mutual modification. The determined instances thus can (and do) assume a variety of forms. This means that the dominated countries can undergo different levels of industrialization and that this requires different forms of class structure taken in these countries. But the variety of forms taken by "under-development" is what makes it clear that "under-development" is not lack of development but another type, with different forms, of development; that is, that part of the global movement (process of accumulation) determined by accumulation in the imperialist countries. Having said this, only one aspect among the many relevant ones will be touched upon in this section. In what follows, the imperialist countries will be referred to as IC and the dominated countries as DOC.

As just mentioned, if only the IC are considered, the implicit assumption is (as it has been up to here) that there are no objective obstacles which prevent some countries from gaining access to the most advanced technologies and thus from engaging in technological competition. But once we consider the international economy, it is evident that there are countries, the DOC, which cannot engage in the technological race with the IC. What can they do, then, to increase their rate of profit? They can increase the rate of exploitation. By lengthening the working day or by increasing the intensity of labour, that is, by forcing the labourers to make more commodities with the same wage, they can raise their rate of profit. Or, *increased exploitation is the DOC's antidote against technological competition from the IC*. This is the capitalists' side. But, on the labourers' side, when a certain quantity of use values (say, 20 pairs of shoes) produced by a DOC is exchanged for another quantity of use values (say, one computer) on the international market and through the medium of international money (prices), much more sweat, tears and blood are exchanged than when 20 pairs of shoes produced by an IC are exchanged for that computer.

PRODUCTION AND DISTRIBUTION

The DOC's sometimes incredible conditions of exploitation and misery necessary to compete on the international markets can also be created through very high rates of inflation, that is, low real wages. The difference from the case above is that longer working hours and more intensive labour increase output and surplus value while real wages remain the same. Inflation, on the other hand, does not increase output and value but decreases real wages. Of course, whenever possible, the capitalists in the DOC will both increase the intensity of labour and the length of the working day on the one hand and on the other see to it that real wages fall due to inflation. The figures in Table 7.12 below are telling.

This is fine as long as the capitalists of the DOC do not have to sell abroad. But if those goods have to be sold on the international market, the DOC's competitive position is worsened. The remedy is depreciation. Through depreciation, the capitalists in the DOC get less international money, or less international value. Therefore, *inflation is meaningful for the capitalists of the DOC only if accompanied by depreciation*. It is not by chance that whenever a DOC signs an agreement with the IMF it must inevitably combine savage cuts in welfare expenditures – as subsidies for subsistence items – with drastic depreciation.

This is an important aspect of the mechanism which explains both the extreme poverty of the working class in the DOC and the high rates of inflation in those countries.[24] But this is only of indirect concern to the capitalists. Through inflation they rob the labourers of a greater part of the new value produced and through depreciation they can sell their booty at competitive prices (that is, transfer part of the new value they have appropriated from "their" labourers to capitalists in the IC, through unequal exchange). The greater the technological gap between the IC and the DOC, the greater the need to compete through high rates of inflation and depreciation, and the greater the misery of the local populations.

The effects on real wages are grave in the IC but disastrous in the DOC. The effects on the value of the national currencies are the opposite. A country which produces more by improving its productivity tendentially revalues its currency, but a country which produces more through increased exploitation (inflation) tendentially reduces the value of its currency.[25]

Table 7.13 below provides two paradigmatic examples, that of Japan and Germany on the one hand and of Brazil and Argentina on the other. In it, NER stands for nominal exchange rate and CPI for the consumer price index; the values of the Japanese yen, of the West German mark, of the Brazilian cruzeiros and of the Argentinian australes are per US dollar. Again, given that Table 7.13 has been built on data resting on a definition of exchange rates as the ratio of national to international

Table 7.12 Developing countries: changes in consumer prices, 1970–87 (% change from preceding year)

	Average 1970–79	1980	1981	1982	1983	1984	1985	1986	1987
Developing countries	18.1	27.3	25.9	25.4	33.0	38.6	38.9	29.8	40.0
Africa	12.7	16.2	21.2	13.1	18.9	20.4	13.2	15.3	15.8
Asia	9.5	13.1	10.5	6.4	6.6	7.3	7.1	7.8	8.8
Europe	12.3	31.8	23.6	33.1	22.8	25.4	25.4	24.8	30.3
Middle East	11.6	16.8	15.2	12.7	12.2	14.8	12.2	11.4	14.7
Western Hemisphere	34.8	58.3	60.7	66.8	108.6	131.8	143.5	88.3	131.2

Source: IMF, 1988b, p. 15

Table 7.13. Appreciation due to technological superiority and depreciation due to increased exploitation (inflation)

	Japan		Germany		Brazil		Argentina	
	NER	CPI	NER	CPI	NER	CPI	NER	CPI
1950	361.1	16.4	4.1	43.6	n.a.	n.a.	n.a.	n.a.
1955	360.0	22.5	4.2	51.6	n.a.	n.a.	n.a.	n.a.
1960	360.0	24.2	4.2	53.3	n.a.	n.a.	n.a.	n.a.
1965	360.0	32.5	4.0	56.8	n.a.	n.a.	n.a.	n.a.
1970	360.0	42.3	3.6	60.8	n.a.	n.a.	n.a.	n.a.
1975	296.7	72.6	2.4	82.3	.01	13	n.a.	n.a.
1976	296.5	79.4	2.5	85.4	.01	18	.00001	3
1977	268.5	85.9	2.3	87.7	.01	26	.00004	7
1978	210.4	89.5	2.0	88.7	.02	36	.00008	19
1979	219.1	92.8	1.8	93.0	.03	55	.00013	50
1980	226.7	100.0	1.8	100.0	.05	100	.00018	100
1981	220.5	104.9	2.2	107.8	.09	206	.00044	204
1982	249.0	107.8	2.4	114.2	.18	407	.00259	541
1983	237.5	109.9	2.5	115.8	.58	984	.01053	2,403
1984	237.5	112.3	2.8	119.2	1.85	2,924	.06765	17,462
1985	238.5	114.6	2.9	122.1	6.20	9,556	.60181	134,833
1986	168.5	115.3	2.1	119.0	13.66	24,436	.94303	256,308
1987	144.6	115.4	1.7	116.0	39.23	77,258	2.14430	n.a.

Source: IMF, 1988a

currencies, a fall in the rate indicates appreciation of the national currency and a rise, depreciation. The same holds for Tables 7.14 and 7.15.

Between the two paradigmatic cases of the most technologically dynamic countries of the imperialist bloc (Japan and West Germany, whose currencies are revalued because they successfully compete basically through technological innovation) and the technologically backward countries of the dominated bloc (whose currencies are devalued because they compete basically through high rates of exploitation and inflation) there is a gamut of intermediate cases with specific features for which the theory submitted here can only serve as a framework within which those cases can be studied in their specificity. For example, as Table 7.14 shows, a country like Italy which has relied not only on improved technology but also, in order to break a very strong workers' movement in the 1970s and 1980s, on relatively high rates of inflation (compared to those of the other imperialist countries: see Table 5.8) shows a tendency to a moderate depreciation of the lira, starting from the second half of the 1970s.

Up to now I have dealt with nominal exchange rates. A few words are now in order on *real exchange rates*. These are nominal exchange rates corrected for inflation. Suppose that the DM is revalued vis-à-vis the dollar. More value is appropriated by West Germany (and less is appropriated by the US) when fewer DM are exchanged for one dollar. This transfer of value is reinforced if German prices rise (or if US prices fall) and weakened (or reversed) in the opposite case. It follows that the real exchange rate can be conceptualized as the national currency price of a unit of foreign currency multiplied by the ratio of the foreign to the domestic price level.

If RER stands for real exchange rate, N for the quantity of national currency units, F for one unit of foreign currency, CPI(n) for the national consumer price index (which is a measure of inflation) and CPI(f) for the foreign consumer price index, then

$$RER = \frac{N}{F} \cdot \frac{CPI(f)}{CPI(n)}$$

In the case of, say, the real exchange rate between West Germany and the US, this ratio decreases when West Germany appropriates more value, either because the DM is revalued or because prices in West Germany increase (or increase more than in the US). Conversely, this ratio increases when West Germany appropriates less value, either because of a devaluation of the DM or because prices in the US increase (or increase more than in West Germany).

What is the relevance of the RER for a theory of international prices?

Table 7.14 NER of the lira and Italy's CPI

	1950	1955	1960	1965	1970	1975	1980	1985	1986	1987
NER	624	625	624	625	625	652	856	1909	1490	1296
CPI	13.9	17.2	18.9	23.9	27.1	46.4	100.0	193.0	204.3	214.0

Source: IMF, 1988a, pp. 434 and 436

Table 7.15 Real and nominal exchange rates for selected countries

	Japan		West Germany		Argentina		Peru	
	NER	RER	NER	RER	NER	RER	NER	RER
1950	361	643	4.2	3.1	n.a.	n.a.	0.01	0.29
1955	360	520	4.2	3.2	n.a.	n.a.	0.02	0.32
1960	360	534	4.2	3.2	n.a.	n.a.	0.03	0.36
1965	360	423	4.0	2.8	n.a.	n.a.	0.03	0.23
1970	360	401	3.6	2.8	n.a.	n.a.	0.04	0.27
1975	297	267	2.4	2.0	n.a.	n.a.	0.04	0.20
1980	227	227	1.8	1.8	0.00018	0.00018	0.29	0.29
1985	238	272	2.9	3.2	0.60181	0.00057	10.97	0.42
1986	168	194	2.1	2.3	0.94303	0.00048	13.95	0.31
1987	145	171	1.7	1.9	n.a.	n.a.	16.84	0.21

Source: nominal rates, IMF, 1988a; real rates, own computation[1]

1. The RER has been computed according to the formula submitted above, i.e. RER = (N/F).(CPI(f)/CPI(n)). The data have been taken from IMF, 1988a. For alternative formulas of the RER, see Harberger, 1988.

This rate isolates the effects of inflation on the transfer of value implied in the nominal exchange rate. However, this rate does not indicate the actual transfer of value associated with the process of price formation. In fact, different levels of productivity determine, in a contradictory way, different monetary, fiscal, budgetary and other policies (including different levels of inflation) and these policies – as well as a host of other factors – determine capital movements. These latter, in their turn, determine the level of prices and thus also the exchange rate. This is the nominal exchange rate, the rate which emerges as a consequence of capital movements, and thus of the demand and supply of currencies, due not only to different levels of inflation but also to all other factors. If the level of inflation, or of taxation, or of interest rates were to change, capital movements would change too and the nominal exchange rate with them. It is this rate, then, which indicates the actual transfer of value associated with price formation; this, of course, in the case of flexible exchange rates. In the case of fixed rates, the rates of profit would tendentially be equalized on the basis of those fixed rates.

Since it is the nominal exchange rate, rather than the "real" one, which indicates the actual transfer of value inherent in the process of price formation and since these transfers show regular and predictable patterns (that is, an increase in productivity determines an international appropriation of value while the opposite holds for lack of competitivity), we can expect the nominal exchange rates to show regular and predictable patterns, or a trend towards revaluation when productivity increases consistently more than that of the competitors and a devaluation in the case of productivity lags. However, there is no reason to expect the same regular and predictable pattern if the nominal rate is corrected for differences in, say, interest rates. The same applies if the nominal rate is corrected for inflation differentials, that is, in the case of the "real" exchange rate. The theoretical basis of mainstream economics' search for regular and predictable patterns in real exchange rates is thus unclear.[26]

There is perhaps one exception to the point just made. In the imperialist countries (IC), the technological leaders' rate of inflation is usually lower than that of the other countries. In fact, as submitted in chapter 5, inflation is basically a means to counter both the realization and the profitability crisis. The technological leaders (countries) contribute to a decreasing production of international surplus value but realize more surplus value (that is, the capitalists in those countries realize higher profits) at the expense of the other countries. The former type of countries need a lower rate of inflation than the other IC and certainly a much lower rate than most dominated countries (DOC). The appreciation of their real rates of exchange (i.e. a fall in RER as defined above) is basically due to productivity gains rather than to high rates of inflation. However, the movements in the RER of the other IC are much less predictable.

In the DOC, productivity lags cause depreciation of the nominal exchange rate. However, the course of the real exchange rate is unpredictable, given the wide range of fluctuation of the rate of inflation in these countries. If domestic inflation rises more than both foreign inflation and nominal depreciation, the national currency appreciates in "real" terms (i.e. the RER, as defined above, falls); but this latter case is quite different from the appreciation of the IC's currencies due to higher productivity. In such a case, an appreciation of the RER indicates relative economic backwardness rather than greater economic competitivity.

Table 7.15 above provides a few examples. In this table, NER stands for nominal exchange rates and RER for real exchange rates, computed against the US dollar. Japan and West Germany revalue their real rates (with the exception of the 1981–85 period in which the dollar was heavily, but artificially, revalued) because the increase in productivity causes a decrease in nominal rates and because the increase in CPI(f), while being greater than the increase in CPI(n), cannot offset the effects of increased productivity and thus international competitivity (that is, more value is appropriated through increased productivity than is lost through a higher inflationary process abroad than at home). Argentina and Peru experience extremely high rates of inflation, especially in the 1980s, compared to the US rate, which for practical purposes can therefore be considered stationary. These countries' real rates revalue (i.e. their RER, as defined above, fall) when CPI(n) increases more than nominal devaluation (the rise in N/F) and devalue in the opposite case.

What is submitted above is only a first step towards a theory of exchange rates based on Marxist value theory. The four results which have emerged are the following. First, the crucial exchange rate for the Marxist theory of international prices is the nominal one. Second, nominal exchange rates behave in a predictable way, that is, appreciation is the manifestation of sustained productivity growth and depreciation of a sustained lag in such a growth. Third, the tendency of the real rates is clearly predictable only for the leading IC (they tend to revalue relative to the other IC). Fourth, for the DOC, the movements of the real exchange rates are much narrower than the movements of the nominal exchange rates. This last point means for the DOC that, while inflation greatly increases the rate of exploitation, nominal devaluation counters the negative influence of price increases on the international markets so that the purchasing power of the IC's capitals in the DOC is not significantly dented. These are only provisional results which hopefully will be subjected to serious scrutiny by further research. However, the concepts developed in this chapter should provide a solid platform on which further attempts to develop a Marxist theory of exchange rates and international prices can stand.

Notes

1. Given this notion, there is always a certain degree of arbitrariness in the operationalization of the concept of oligopolies.

2. Notice that I refer to "free" rather than "perfect" competition. On the neo-classical, rather than Marxist, assumptions behind conceptualizing oligopolies as opposed to "perfect" competition, one should consult Bryan, 1985.

3. These notions should be considered against the background of the recent debate in *Capital and Class*. See Semmler, 1982, Wheelock, 1983, Bryan, 1985, Wheelock, 1986, Burkett, 1986 and Bryan, 1986.

4. This process is accompanied by the internationalization of the financial funds needed to start the production process (to purchase labour power and means of production): "the loans that finance any country's industry come from many countries (or the stateless international pool)" (Coakley and Harris, 1983, p. 43).

5. This average rate of profit would be an unrealized tendency (an average, or a tendency of the third type). This is one of the reasons why attempts to find actually equalized prices of production per unit of output are bound to fail. For such an attempt, see Andrews, 1980.

6. For a different view, see Gordon, 1988.

7. Vernon, 1971 and 1972. For a critique, see Palloix, 1973; pp. 10 ff.

8. "Even a company as large, as research-oriented and as successful in world markets as IBM has found it necessary to link its efforts with those of other firms" (UNCTC, 1988, p. 60).

9. Many authors still think that international capital mobility is insufficient to justify the formation of an international price of production. For Mandel, for example, the hypothesis of an international price of production would be justified only in the case of a homogeneous world capitalist economy with a world capitalist state (Mandel, 1975, p. 71). But in order to hypothesize an international price of production, we do not have to have an exact replica of the national economic and political situation on the international level. More recently Mandel seems to have partly changed his opinion on this matter. He detects a rising tendency towards international production prices which he links to the rise of the multinationals as the typical form of capitalist enterprise (Mandel, 1983, p. 262).

10. See 3.7.1 point 5 and 4.2.1.

11. Here, I adhere to the British convention of defining the rate of exchange as the ratio of the international to the national currency (the number of units of foreign currencies that one unit of national currency will buy). This is the indirect quotation. But the rate of exchange can also be defined as the ratio of the national to the international currency (the number of units of the national currency which are needed to buy a unit of foreign currency). This latter definition, or direct quotation, will be used towards the end of this chapter, when I shall use empirical data constructed on this definition. An example of indirect quotation in West Germany would be $0.50 = DM1, while the direct quotation would be DM2 = $1.

12. *Computationally*, given the international and the national price of production, the TRE follows. Given the international price of production and the TRE, the national price of production follows. Finally, given the national price of production and the TRE, the international price of production follows. *Chronologically*, it is impossible to establish an order of precedence between the real movements which express the tendency towards national production prices, international production prices and TRE. But *analytically* precedence is given to the international price of production since from the very beginning the various national capitals' surplus value is equalized into an international average rate of profit of which the national rates of profit are a manifestation.

13. M. Dehove (1984) distinguishes three theories: (a) the purchasing power parity theory, (b) the parity of factor costs theory and (c) the parity of covered interest rates theory. He submits these three theories to close scrutiny and underlines their defects. Rather than repeating Dehove's argument, I shall limit myself to pointing out some elements essential for the purposes of this work. Also, in what follows, I confine myself to the discussion of only the first and third theories because, as Officer (1974) has shown, the purchasing

power and the factor cost equalization theories imply each other if factor price equalization is assumed.

14. For a recent admission of the practical impotence of the purchasing power parity theory to "guess" the dollar's "true" rate of exchange, see Stephens, 1988.

15. Since there is no relation between OCC and productivity in different branches, for ease of computation we can just as well assume that the different branches have the same output per unit of capital; but any other outputs per unit of capital would do.

16. These factors have contradictory effects. For example, depreciation is a factor which tends to correct a country's trade deficit since it lowers the export prices in foreign currencies. But at the same time, depreciation raises import prices. If the higher costs of imports more than offset the higher revenues from exports (the J curve), the result is a trade deficit, rather than a trade surplus. Also depreciation, by raising the import prices of raw materials and machinery, can have an inflationary effect on the economy, thus raising export prices. The net effect can be contrary to the one aimed at. For a detailed discussion of four ways in which inflation can be transmitted internationally, see Salant, 1977.

17. In the approach submitted here, the tendency following depreciation and appreciation is not towards equilibrium in the balance of trade or of payments but towards a new axis (the TRE) around which the RRE fluctuates.

18. In this work, depreciation has the same effect as an increase in productivity but it does not increase productivity and the OCC (and thus does not tend to abolish the cause of UE). This thesis is similar to Amin's argument that changes in the rate of exchange cannot correct the imbalance in the balance of payments between dominated and imperialist countries since these imbalances derive from structural, productivity, differences (Amin, 1976, ch. 2). For conventional economics, on the other hand, a fall in the exchange rate has the same effect as a fall in the wage rate. See de Brunhoff, 1978, pp. 88–108.

19. For a good and accessible critique of the balance of payments, one should consult Harris, 1977 in Green and Nore, 1977.

20. Among the very few attempts to relate variations in the rate of exchange to variations in the sphere of capitalist production, the article by Pala (1983) should be mentioned. The author theoretically relates (and finds statistical evidence for this relation between) the variations in the rate of exchange and those in the rate of exploitation.

21. Besides the work by Fröbel, Heinrichs and Kreye, 1980, see also Frank, 1980 and 1981. For Mandel too wage differentials are the main reason for capital movements from the imperialist to the dominated countries (Mandel, 1975, p. 68). Therefore whenever, for whatever reason, the importance of low wages is reduced, the flow of investments to the dominated countries decreases too. This seems to be the case for some transnational corporations (TNCs). The introduction of automated manufacturing has drastically cut the proportion of wage costs to total costs so that some TNCs in the developed capitalist countries reorient the location of their investments away from low wage countries and towards the home market.

22. This is the "secret" of the newly industrialized countries.

23. This case is not the same as that of countries (capitals) with low levels of productivity which must compete through very high levels of exploitation. See below, 7.9.

24. Very high rates of inflation have led in the 1980s to the phenomenon of "dollarization", that is, to the substitution of the dollar (for local currencies in certain countries and for certain products) as a store of value, as a unit of account and also as a means of payment. See Salama, 1988.

25. This allows us to understand why people who have a low standard of living in an IC can have, with the same money, a high standard of living in a DOC. It is of course trivially true that this is possible because of the depreciation of the DOC's currencies vis-à-vis those of the IC. The point, however, is why the IC tends to appreciate and the DOC tends to depreciate, so that not only the capitalists but also all those in possession of the IC's currency can benefit from this mechanism. It is then understandable why a tourist from an IC with modest financial means can have "a rich life" in a DOC.

26. For a review of the difficulties encountered in this enterprise, see Coughlin and Koedijk, 1990.

8

Two Contemporary Problems

8.1 International Production Prices and the Current Monetary Crisis

The theory of international market prices and production prices proposed above is based on the notion that the realized rate of exchange (RRE) tends towards the tendential rate of exchange (TRE) through the mechanism of depreciation/appreciation. This means that the currencies of countries which have fallen behind in the technological race tend to be devalued, thus losing part of the value produced in those countries to those which have adopted more capital intensive techniques. Conversely, the currencies of the latter countries will tend to be revalued, thus appropriating value from the former countries. This applies to all countries, including the dominant imperialist one whose currency is the international money. However, there are three aspects specific to the leading currency.

8.1.1 The causes of the present monetary crisis

First of all, when does a currency become the leading one? In principle, the leading currency is that of the leading, technologically most advanced, country.[1] This is also the country which can produce goods more cheaply than the other countries. Under these circumstances, all other countries will want to purchase the goods of the leading one and thus the currency of that country will be used as a means of international payments. The tendency towards the revaluation of that currency is the result of the appropriation of international value implicit in that country's superior technological position and manifests itself as a sustained demand for that currency. A decline in the technological advantage of the leading country undermines the leading role of its currency as well. This, in turn, under-

275

mines that country's position as the leading supplier of capital and the financial profits deriving from it.[2]

Second, the international currency is not only a means of payments. It is also a reserve currency. The revaluation of its currency increases the other nations' willingness to hold that currency as the international reserve. This situation ensures the stability of the international monetary system. Conversely, a devaluation of the international currency has the effect of reducing other nations' reserves in that currency. If this anomalous situation is not transitory, the system will tend to evolve towards a new situation in which the role of the international currency will devolve to that country which, as a rule, will not have to devalue, which over a long period has consistently higher levels of productivity and a positive balance of trade.[3] These higher levels are principally due to the country's leading technological position.

Third, there is a very peculiar property enjoyed by the international currency. This is the *"seigniorage"* attached to it, that is, the privilege enjoyed by the dominant imperialist country, whose currency is also the key international currency, of being able to appropriate wealth by simply printing paper money. As an economist above all suspicion put it in discussing the role of the dollar,

> the fact that the dollar served as the key currency gave America, in effect, something of the same privilege of creating money out of thin air that the commercial banks enjoy domestically. To a degree, this key position gave America the right to get a certain amount of goods at no real cost. (Samuelson, 1970, p. 630)

More recent history confirms the privileged role of the US dollar: "the US, as custodian of the world's chief reserve currency, was able to impose a de facto default on its Japanese creditors through the halving of the value of the dollar against the yen between Spring 1985 and the end of 1987" (Plender, 1988).

In theory, as long as the dollar is, and is accepted as, the international reserve currency and means of payment it is enough for the US to print dollars in order to pay for imported commodities. But of course there are limits to this mechanism, not the least of which is the inflationary effect of printing large amounts of paper money. Therefore, the advantage of being the leading technological country is to be explained not only in terms of competitive advantages, and thus larger market shares, and in terms of appropriation of value (international UE) but also in terms of greater possibility to make financial profits and in terms of the appropriation of value inherent in the "seigniorage" attached to the role of international currency enjoyed by the currency of the country which has conquered a relatively permanent technological lead (the dominant imperialist country).

These considerations allow us to focus on the essential feature of the *present monetary crisis*. This is the crisis of the international currency, the US dollar, in a period in which the US is losing its technological lead, its dominant economic role. The more the US loses its technological lead, the less is the dollar demanded both as a means of payments and as a reserve currency. The international monetary system, still basically based on the US dollar as the international money, increasingly loses its stability as successive devaluations occur, as they must. Rival economic powers, and thus rival currencies, have emerged but none of the contenders has yet gained the unchallenged leading position. The monetary crisis will be resolved only when a country emerges as the undisputed technological and productivity leader so that its currency will become the undisputed international leading currency.[4] Until then, all proposals to reform the international monetary system can be at best only a palliative.

8.1.2 A concise history of the crisis of the dollar

It is against the background of this interpretative scheme that the case of the US in the post-Second World War period can be assessed.[5] It is useful to separate this period into two sub-periods, with 1971 as the watershed. In the first period (from Bretton Woods in 1944 to 1971) the international role of the dollar was tied to fixed exchange rates and to the fixed parity, and convertibility, of the dollar with gold. The dollar's international role meant that the US was able to buy commodities and to pay for them with paper money ("as good as gold", given the dollar's convertibility in gold). This was acceptable to other countries both because they could buy with dollars the commodities they needed for their postwar economic reconstruction, and which only the US produced (or produced so cheaply), and because all countries were willing to accept dollars (instead of gold) for international payments (given the very large gold reserves of the US).[6] This gave the US the "seigniorage" of appropriating real value by "paying" with paper money.

The adoption of the dollar as the international means of payment and reserve currency (together with gold) required a system of fixed exchange rates, as agreed upon at Bretton Woods. The dollar, in order to be a true substitute for gold, had to be bound to it, thus being the anchor through which other currencies were fastened to gold (through fixed exchange rates). But this meant that the dollar's exchange rate was prevented from adjusting to the level corresponding to the degree of US productivity once, with the passage of time, the US competitive position began to deteriorate (see Table 7.11). An indication of this process of deterioration is given by the percentage shares of the US, Japan and

Table 8.1   Percentage shares in world industrial production

	US	Japan	Western Europe
1950	47.8	1.6	33.3
1960	41.9	4.8	35.9
1970	37.8	9.5	34.2
1980	36.9	10.2	32.1
1985	39.3	11.5	31.2

Source: Institut für Internationale Politik und Wirtschaft der DDR, p. 14

Western Europe in world industrial production, as shown in Table 8.1.

Decreasing productivity meant that the US would have had to devalue the dollar (see chapter 7). Devaluation would have been consonant both with the motivations of US exporters, since it would have decreased the price of US exports in foreign currencies, and with the functioning of the system, since it would have redistributed part of the surplus value produced in the US to other, more productive, countries. But this was practically impossible due to the role of the dollar as international money. A devaluation would have seriously undermined the "international community's" confidence in the dollar and thus the dollar's privileged position. American capital would have been deprived of a powerful instrument of economic expansion abroad and of an easy way to cover the deficit in the American balance of payments.[7]

A "crisis of the dollar" thus developed, that is, the decrease in US productivity gave rise to a contradiction in the role of the dollar. On the one hand, devaluation was undesirable because of the dollar's role as the international reserve currency; on the other hand, devaluation was needed in order to improve US competitivity. As US productivity kept diminishing, due to the necessarily uneven development of the capitalist international economy, the US progressively lost the real basis upon which rested its international appropriation of value through "seigniorage" and its capacity to penetrate foreign capital. The need to devalue the US dollar increased. Moreover, the pressure to devalue was strengthened because "the flood of dollars grew, responding *not* to the need for more reserves but to the requirements of the United States as the hegemonic power" and in particular to the need to finance the Vietnam war (Sweezy and Magdoff, 1983, p. 11; see also Sweezy, 1981, p. 82). In this way, the dollar's devaluation became inevitable. In the words of Parboni, the US "chose the tempo and the form of the crisis, and thus managed to effect a devaluation of the dollar that would not compromise its dominant position as an international means of payments" (Parboni, 1981, p. 8).

Basically, this meant a shift to a system of flexible exchange rates and a "soft landing" – a gradual devaluation – for the dollar. With the suspension of dollar convertibility in 1971,[8] the US "managed on the one hand to obtain freedom to devalue" and "on the other hand fully to maintain mastery over the world supply of the means of payment" (Parboni, pp. 37–8). In this way the US managed to retain the advantage for the dollar of being a reserve currency (which practically meant no balance of trade constraints and appropriation of value through seigniorage) while at the same time being able to devalue the dollar freely by flooding the world with dollars, or, to use jargon, through the "dollar overhang". This, in turn, fuelled international inflation.

However, the US could achieve this only by dealing a severe blow to the dollar as the international currency. The abandonment of the Bretton Woods agreement meant the beginning of a loss of a privilege, the possibility of appropriating value through "seigniorage", and successive devaluations only reinforced this trend. These devaluations created a crisis of confidence (based upon real losses by those who held reserves in dollars) and imperilled the dollar's role as international money. Indeed, currency rivals (the DM and the yen) have emerged, thus challenging the dollar's position and claiming a share of the privilege attached to that position. The "seigniorage" attached to the dollar remains, but what is now taking place is a redistribution of that "seigniorage" among competing imperialist countries through the convulsions of the international monetary system.

The 1980s have witnessed a sharpening of the inter-imperialist struggle for financial supremacy and the partial success of the US in retaining this supremacy not on the basis of real economic power (greater productivity) but through financial, budgetary and monetary policies. The extent to which the US economic lead had been weakened by 1984 can be gleaned from the following passage:

> America's five leading exports to Japan are corn, soybean, wheat, cotton and coal. Japan's leading exports to the United States are autos, trucks, videorecorders, oil-well casings and motorcycles. What is worse, the United States is repeating this same pattern of exchanging raw commodities for sophisticated finished products with other newly industrialized countries around the world. (Lewis, 1984)

A recent study reveals no change in this trend and concludes that "a wide spectrum of evidence, ranging from world market-shares to patent statistics, suggests a fundamental technological decline" in the US (Ferguson, 1988, p. 56).

Against the background of the increasing deterioration of US economic strength, the supremacy of the dollar was retained in the first half of the 1980s basically through huge budget deficits and the concomitant high interest rates and rates of exchange.[9] The overvaluation of the dollar which resulted from this state of affairs had been estimated at 40% in 1985. This way of re-establishing the financial supremacy of the dollar, however, was based on quicksand. The disruptive effects of these deficits on the US economy, on US international performance, on the indebtedness of the "less developed countries", etc. eventually forced another devaluation of the dollar, starting in 1985.[10] In September of that year, at New York's Plaza Hotel, the finance ministers of the major industrial countries launched a plan to drive down the dollar. Since then the dollar has fallen by more than 40% and continues to fall, in spite of the Paris accord of February 1987. But no amount of devaluation will restore the USA's leading position. What the US is presently doing is to trade a limited and temporary improvement in the balance of trade for a further weakening of the dollar as the international currency.[11]

8.1.3 *The crisis of the dollar and the European Monetary System*[12]

It has been submitted above that neither Japan nor West Germany has managed to replace the US as the main imperialist country and that this is the main reason why neither the yen nor the DM has replaced the US dollar as "the" international currency.[13] However, both the yen and the DM are becoming powerful rivals of the dollar. The process of emergence of these rivals is of course different in each specific case. In this subsection I shall examine one of the features characterizing the emergence of the DM as a powerful international currency, its being the currency of the strongest nation within the *European Economic Community (EEC)*. More specifically, since the Community has adopted a *European Monetary System (EMS)*, the struggle for the DM to become one of the few truly international currencies has been strongly influenced by its role as the dominant currency within the EMS.

It is not by chance that it was at the end of the 1970s, when the dollar's position was very weak, that the EMS was introduced. As G. Gaveau rightly remarks,

the EMS was established during a period of persistent weakness of the dollar. From 1978, European monetary authorities had been able to bring about a rather exceptional situation implementing a policy relatively independent of that of the United States. (Gaveau, 1983, p. 34)

The European monetary authorities are, however, to paraphrase one of Marx's expressions, warring brothers and resent the fact that the EMS is actually reinforcing the dominant position of the DM within the EMS and consequently West Germany's dominant position within the EEC. They therefore resent the fact that the Deutsche Bundesbank in a way plays the role of a European central bank. This role was initially accepted by all member countries, given the Bundesbank's "adamantine" resistance to inflation, but is increasingly challenged especially by France and in a more contradictory way by England. To see this, let us consider the *Exchange Rate Mechanism (ERM)*, an essential part of the EMS.

One of the main features of the ERM is that its member countries have pledged to allow their exchange rates to fluctuate only within narrow bands above or below a fixed parity; these bands are called parity limits. Suppose that West Germany has a low rate of inflation and, say, Italy wishes to pursue a highly inflationary economic policy. In this case Italy's prices will quickly rise, thus jeopardizing her international competitive position. The relative fixity of the exchange rate between the DM and the lira rules out a large depreciation of the lira as a means to restore Italy's competitive position. Consequently, Italy must bring down her own rate of inflation. In this way the strongest country, that is, the country which, because of its higher productivity, appropriates surplus value from other countries and has thus less need to resort to inflation as a means to "stimulate the economy", indirectly sets limits to the rate of inflation of the other countries. Or, suppose that the rate of interest in West Germany is much lower than in Italy. Inasmuch as interest rate differentials play a role in capital movements, financial operators will sell DM and buy lire. This will tend to revalue the lira and devalue the DM. If this process threatens to send the lira through the parity limit, Italy will have to lower her interest rate.

In short, the weaker countries surrender some of their freedom to determine their own economic policy. This might not be a problem if all countries were to share the same objectives. However, strains will emerge if different countries have different economic priorities, for example if some countries choose to stimulate employment while others prefer to reduce inflation. To understand this point, we must stress that the DM has a tendency to revalue vis-à-vis the other currencies not only because of productivity differentials between West Germany (the strongest country) and the other EEC countries but also because of its international role outside the EEC. "When there are capital movements out of the United States they tend to go into the D-Mark rather than the other E.M.S. currencies, so that the D-Mark appreciates not only relative to the dollar but also relative to the other currencies" (Corden, 1985, pp. 141–2).

If now

the dollar were to fall steeply, the Deutsche Mark would probably rise faster than other EMS currencies. Traditionally, other EMS countries would then tighten monetary policy to maintain parity with the Deutsche Mark. With unemployment now of greater concern, countries may find this unacceptable and may require Germany to relax monetary policy. Equally, Germany is unaccustomed to allowing an acceleration in its own inflation rate to restrain unemployment elsewhere in Europe. Moreover, it is unlikely to look with equanimity on demands by its partners for greater competitiveness via lower real exchange rates. (Holtham, Keating and Spencer, 1987, p. 24)

The emergence of the DM as an international reserve currency is thus only one side of a complex monetary process, one of the other aspects being its dominant role within the EMS.[14]

The emergence of the DM as a powerful competitor of the US dollar is an unwelcome development for France. Unable to overtake Germany in terms of productivity, she tries to undermine both the role of the DM and the role of the Bundesbank as the supplier of DM. In order to take away at least some of the power the Bundesbank has to supply DM only according to the needs of the West German economy and, at the same time, to limit West Germany's power to indirectly influence other countries' economic policies, France tries to enhance the role of the *European Currency Unit (ECU)*. Up to now the ECU has functioned basically only as a unit of account and as a major currency of denomination of Eurobond issues. France's desire for a greater role for the ECU as a reserve asset and for the creation and distribution of extra ECU can thus be understood in the light of the fact that the ECU is a fixed amount of the EMS currencies (including the DM). Therefore, more ECU would give other central banks an effective holding of DM, thus diminishing the role the Bundesbank has as a supplier of DM.

However, West Germany's role would be weakened much more if the EMS currencies were replaced by a European currency which was not only a unit of account but also a means of national and international payments and a store of value. In this case the national central banks would have to be replaced by a European central bank. This is the reason behind France's urgent need to achieve a full monetary union.

8.2 Is the Theory of Comparative Advantages Compatible with Socialist Development?[15]

The Ricardian law of comparative advantages has been criticized in chapter 6. The thesis submitted there is that that theory is based on premises void of economic significance. As we have seen, there is no reason to assume that capital behaves according to what the Ricardian theory predicts. Thus, if there is a reason for such a specialization, it cannot rest on the "efficiency argument". But there is another reason which is usually put forward to justify international specialization: the "saving of labour argument". It seems undeniable that specialization leads to the saving of international labour. In Table 6.1, in the case of Portugal's

282

specialization in wine and England's specialization in clothing, Portugal uses 160 men per year to produce two gallons of wine (thus saving 10 men per year) and England uses 200 men per year to produce two yards of clothing (thus saving 20 men per year). This is a saving of 30 men-years. Is this argument sound?

8.2.1 Comparative advantages' "rational kernel"

The question can be meaningfully answered only if we ask ourselves: who saves labour, for whom and how? Under capitalism, saving of labour means in fact a decrease in the percentage of variable capital and an increase in the percentage of constant capital per unit of capital invested, due to the introduction of technological innovation. This leads, as shown above, to an increase in profitability which, however, is accompanied by a decrease in employment, and to an increase in the rate of exploitation. The answer to the question of who saves labour, for whom and how is thus unequivocal. For the labourers, the saving of labour tendentially means increased unemployment and exploitation.

As far as international specialization is concerned, history as well as economic reasoning show that the process of international specialization, – the introduction of a new technology in a certain branch and the specialization of a certain country in that branch – leads to an acceleration of unequal development and thus of economic dependence rather than to a more harmonious process of development worldwide. For nations, the saving of labour means UE and unequal (and dependent) development.

This all refers to capitalist conditions of production and distribution. But what about "socialism"?[16] Is specialization in terms of comparative advantages and the concomitant saving of labour not advantageous to "socialist" countries? This is indeed the thesis put forward by the supporters of China's new economic policy. Because of its enormous importance it deserves a separate treatment. A fair picture of this argument can be drawn from two articles in *Social Sciences in China*, the Journal of the Chinese Academy of Social Sciences. Even though the articles "represent the views of the authors and not of the editors", the status of the journal leaves no doubt that the authors' ideas are also those officially accepted. In what follows I shall refer to "the authors" to refer to ideas common to the writers of both articles. The argument can be summarized in the following three points.

1. The international division of labour, which is the basis of trade and of all economic ties between nations, is an outcome of the growth of the productive forces.

2. This international division of labour is an important means of saving

social labour.

3. The expansion of China's foreign economic relations through an international division of labour is a powerful lever for accelerating her modernization (Yuan Wenqui *et al.*, 1980, p. 22).

According to the authors, Ricardo's theory of comparative advantages has a rational kernel. To begin with, the authors accept the validity of Ricardo's theory: "in the international exchange of commodities the decisive factor is the comparative advantages rather than the absolute amount of labour spent on the production of those commodities" (Yuan Wenqui *et al.*, 1980, p. 31).

What does this mean in the case of China? Since China has "huge manpower resources and her wage scales are low . . . it would be to China's advantage if some of her departments are devoted to the export of labor intensive products in exchange for capital intensive and technology intensive products" (Yuan Wenqui *et al.*, 1980, p. 31). In this way, the following two results are reached. First, since the commodities imported are paid with less social labour than the social labour which would be necessary to produce them in China, there is an economy of social labour by means of foreign trade. This makes it possible to distribute among China's production departments the social labour saved through foreign trade, thus increasing the quantity of the various use values. Second, there is an increase in labour productivity due to the introduction of more modern machinery (Sun Xiangjian, 1982, p. 40).

However, the authors argue, this saving of labour can be offset by unequal exchange. To avoid this, commodities should be exchanged according to the principle of equality. By this the authors mean that commodities must be exchanged at their international price of production, which is given by the transformation of the national production prices into the international one (Yuan Wenqui *et al.*, 1980, p. 35), that is, by the equalization of the national average rates of profit.

In this view then, unequal exchange is any deviation from the international prices of production. Particularly important is the case of monopolistic distortions of price formation. As Sun Xiangjian puts it,

> Monopoly capital has subordinated colonial and semicolonial economies to imperialist countries and turned the former into markets or suppliers of raw materials and food grain for the latter . . . As a result of this kind of international division of labour, the economic and trade ties between the imperialist states and colonial countries have never been based on the principle of equality and mutual benefit, but on the ruthless exploitation and plunder of the latter by the former. (Sun Xiangjian, 1982, pp. 28–9)

In short, comparative advantages' rational kernel is that, whenever there is exchange on the basis of international social values, there is equal exchange and mutual benefit. For China, the benefit is saving of labour and increased productivity due to the introduction of foreign, more productive, machines. Under capitalism, the principle of comparative advantages has been misused to justify the trade relations between imperialist and colonial countries. But inherently, one might say, the theory is sound.

8.2.2 What kind of rationality?

Let us consider this argument carefully. To begin with, the principle that, whenever international social values are exchanged, there is equal exchange is simply wrong. There is equal exchange only if those social values have been produced by capitals with both average (modal or mean) productivity and average international OCC. This, however, is neither the common empirical situation nor is it the focus of our attention when the prices of production are considered.

Consider now the two "advantages" accruing to China from international specialization. The first is the saving of labour and the concomitant possibility of specializing in, and exporting, "labour intensive goods". It is quite clear that this view is unable to perceive the real effects of this kind of policy, namely "specialization" in underdevelopment. What else can China achieve if she specializes in, and exports, labour intensive (technologically backward) goods and imports capital intensive (technologically advanced) goods?

The nature of the second "advantage" is less clear-cut. To begin with, it is true that, inasmuch as Western technology is imported and applied, the productivity of labour will increase. Moreover, the authors believe that China's pattern of exports will change gradually as her productive forces develop (thanks to the modernization programme) so that the disadvantage of getting less materialized labour as imports than the labour expended in producing the exported commodities will gradually "give way to advantages" (Yuan Wenqui et al., 1980, p. 42).

However, if international record is any indication, the hopes of the modernization theorists would seem to be ill founded. The Soviet Union and other Eastern countries' increasing reliance on Western technologies has a much longer history than China's, yet there is no indication that, in spite of this industrialization, these countries are ever going to overtake the imperialist ones and become leaders in developing and producing high technology. Of course there has been industrialization in the centrally planned economies, but relations of dependence do not exclude a degree of industrialization as long as this is a dependent (basically, less technologically advanced) industrialization. Modernization, on the other hand, suggests that the transitional societies might reach the same stage of technological development as the capitalist imperialist ones.

Actually, it is possible to argue convincingly either way. One can either argue that the imperialist countries will never consistently export their most advanced technologies (even if, incidentally, this might happen), thus keeping the "socialist" societies in a state of technological dependence. Or, with the Chinese supporters of modernization, one can argue that technological transfers through foreign trade will set in motion a process of self-sustaining technological growth leading to a high technological development.

However, there is another point. It is that the introduction and application of Western technology on the one hand and the integration of the "socialist" societies in the world capitalist market as well as the introduction of capitalist production relations within those societies reinforce each other. The reason for this can be schematically presented as follows.

Low productivity levels and bad product quality are basically the result of a lack of motivation among the labourers which, in its turn, is the infallible symptom of lack of *socialism*, of *workers' self management*.[17] If "technical" rather than political solutions are sought, then on the one hand political repression will be resorted to, and on the other hand "modern" machines, techniques and science will be adopted from the capitalist world. "Modern" machines, however, have built into them a technical division of labour which bears the imprint of the capitalist production relations: this technical division of labour fragments and mutilates the labourers' creative capacity instead of developing all its aspects and thus requires the work of control upon the labourers (for the notion of work of control, see 2.5.2). Both the work of control and the lopsided and caricatured development of men's and women's productive and creative capacity are essential elements of capitalist production relations. Thus, to import Western technology also means to import capitalist production relations, that is, to increase labour's productivity *but in a capitalist way*.

Furthermore, to import technology one needs foreign currency and this means both export of raw materials and of labour-intensive products and credits from capitalist countries (and thus financial obligations and constraints). Inasmuch as these are necessary steps, the country will be integrated in the capitalist market for goods and services and in the capitalist financial markets. As a consequence, the country will experience not only political dependence but also difficulty in planning, which in turn will result in a movement away from central planning and towards a market economy,[18] and will contribute to the strengthening of the capitalist aspect of the country's production relations. This is an important element explaining the development in the so-called socialist countries which resulted in the events of 1989.

This account is necessarily sketchy and schematic but sufficient to drive home the point that modernization, in the sense of the adoption of Western techniques, does indeed increase the level of productivity but in a capitalist way, by hindering at the same time the development of the socialist nature of production relations. But this is exactly what modernization is not supposed to do, or at least this seems to be the intention of its theorists: modernization is supposed to shorten the way to socialism rather than being either a detour or a dead end. What is left, then, of the claim that international trade increases labour productivity (through the introduction of Western technology), saves labour and is of mutual advantage to all nations concerned? Not much. A correct reading of the comparative advantages thesis, as applied to trade between capitalist and "socialist" societies, shows that international trade hides UE (even when commodities are exchanged at their production prices), that the pattern of specialization fostered by this pattern of trade stimulates the "specialization" of "socialist" societies in technological underdevelopment and thus in political dependence, and that the importation of Western technology does increase productivity but that this, instead of being a way to liberate the labouring classes from the yoke of capital, is just the very opposite.

8.2.3 Concluding remarks

I have first put forward these theses in Carchedi, 1986a. Tsang and Woo (1988), while agreeing with many of the above-mentioned points, still maintain that the Ricardian theory of comparative advantages has a "rational kernel". The authors acknowledge that the trade of commodities produced by countries at different levels of productivity implies exchange of different quantities of labour. However, they seem to subscribe to the view that there is equal (and not unequal) exchange if the commodities are exchanged at their international production prices. In their words,

> if it takes country A one labour-day on average to produce one unit of commodity X and country B two labour-days on average to produce one unit of commodity Y; and if both country A's one labour-day and country B's two labour-days equal the same unit of international value, say one day in terms of world necessary labour time, then it will be a perfectly equal exchange for A to trade one unit of X with B for one unit of Y in spite of the fact that one labour-day is swapped with two. (Tsang and Woo, 1988, pp. 25–26)

In this view, there is unequal exchange only when

> due to various factors such as monopoly in the international market and inequality of political power among nations, trade may be carried out in terms deviating from the international value of commodities, e.g. B may have to surrender two units of Y before being able to obtain one unit of X from A. (Tsang and Woo, 1988, p. 26)

Even under these circumstances, however, "B still benefits from trading with A as it is able to acquire X through 4 of its labour days instead of 6 or 5" (Tsang and Woo, 1988, p. 26). As the authors conclude, "although both countries benefit from trade, A *is exploiting* B" due to unequal exchange.

This interpretation is fairly common. However, there are several objections which should be moved to it. First of all it is odd, to say the least, to define the exchange of one labour day for two labour days as equal exchange. This is quite an unusual notion of equality. The condition that "equal quantities of social value" are exchanged does not change matters. Actually, to define this exchange as equal because both country A's one labour day and country B's two labour days are equal to one day of world necessary labour time conceals, rather than revealing, facts as they are. To call this exchange "equal" is to confuse the issue. Even worse: it is to accept the point of view of capital, to be unable to see how capitalist "equality" in fact both presupposes and at the same time hides inequality (in this case, of quantities of labour exchanged). Two different quantities of labour might "count as" the same, but this does not make them the same.

Second, in the authors' view, production prices are formed on the basis of equal exchange and unequal exchange comes in only when actual prices deviate from the international value of commodities, that is, international production prices. But actual (or market) prices always deviate from prices of production due to the fact that the latter are the tendency around which the former fluctuate. Now, if some branches (nations) sell their products at a price higher than the price of production, other branches (nations) will have to sell their products at a price lower than the price of production. Unequal exchange thus loses its theoretical depth and is reduced to the trivial notion of selling dear (cheap) and buying cheap (dear). This concept is thus severed from the laws of motion of capitalism.

On the contrary, as argued in this work, in Marx's theory the exchange of unequal quantities of labour is related to the innermost dynamics of the capitalist system; it is the reward for the capitalists (and branches) which increase their productivity by introducing more efficient (and capital-intensive) techniques. Unequal exchange is inherent in the formation of the price of production and is a redistribution of value at the moment of exchange according to the differences in organic compositions of capital and thus to the constant technological revolutions undergone by the capitalist production processes.

Lastly, the authors seem to agree that unequal exchange is a form of exploitation (Tsang and Woo, 1988, p. 26). However, exploitation is a phenomenon relating the labourers to the capitalists. Unequal exchange, on the other hand, is a transfer of value between capitalists inherent

288

in the price mechanism. Of course once one, either explicitly or implicitly, replaces capitalists with nations, then transfers of value between capitalists are wrongly perceived as transfers of value between capitalists and workers in one nation to capitalists and workers of another nation (see chapter 6, section 3). This might be good "third worldist" propaganda but is bad theory. By collapsing unequal exchange into exploitation, class relations are hopelessly muddled.

The discussion of the conditions under which foreign trade is advantageous to those countries which might want to take a socialist path of development or of the conditions under which the use of Western technology might be a necessary evil is still open. But clarity on these questions can be reached only if the growth of productive forces, of which the international division of labour is an aspect, is not misjudged as an inevitably progressive development and if this international division of labour is seen as one of the forms of the capitalist division of labour inherently bearing the imprint of capitalist production relations. The opposite view finds in the law of comparative advantages an ideal channel to legitimize international exploitation and integration into the capitalist world net.

Notes

1. This is why, *mutatis mutandis*, the leading role reverted to the Florentine florin and to the Venetian ducat in the Middle Ages, to the "piece of eight" or strong peso and to the Dutch negotiepenningen in the seventeenth century (which became veritable world currencies) and to the English pound sterling in the nineteenth century.
2. Thus from 1958, when the British pound became officially convertible, "the City and, under its tutelage, the British state were preoccupied with persuading rather than forcing the overseas holders to continue to hold sterling." The possibility that foreign holders would sell their sterling balances "was seen to be a calamity because it would have overturned London's pivotal role as the supplier of capital and financier of British capital's foreign investment" (Coakley and Harris, 1983, p. 22).
3. In the years immediately following the Second World War it was the US which was in this privileged position. The system of Bretton Woods was built on, and reflected, this situation. Up to 1950 the US balance of trade was positive, something which created a dollar shortage. One of the reasons for the Marshall Plan (1948–52) was precisely the desire to create a line of credit, to increase the supply of dollars for international payments (see Altvater, Blanke and Neusüss, 1971, p. 185).
4. The debate on whether this currency will have to be anchored to the value of gold, that is, whether gold should be demonetized or not, reflects important national interests. The US and UK (debtor countries) refer to money-gold as a "barbarous relic" in order to be able to pay for real goods with increasingly devalued money. The creditor countries and the gold-producing countries, on the other hand, tend to take the opposite view since only gold, and not paper money, has an intrinsic value (see Cochrane, 1980–81). M. Aglietta has a different opinion on this matter. For this author the price of gold can only be fixed arbitrarily (Aglietta, 1986, p. 97) and the demonetization of gold is the condition for a successful international (capitalist) co-operation which, in its turn, will eventually lead to

the institution of the "money of monies" and to "monetary peace" (see, especially, Aglietta, pp. 92–104).

5. What follows is not meant to be a survey of recent developments. My purpose is only to underline some aspects relevant for my thesis. For a useful survey of financial developments since Bretton Woods see Evans, 1985; also Roddick, 1984.

6. Stadnichenko stresses only the US gold reserves during and after the Second World War as the factor determining the ascendancy of the US dollar as the key international currency (Stadnichenko, 1975, pp. 92, 98, 119, 168, etc.). But the accumulation of gold reserves is itself a consequence of other, deeper, economic factors.

7. It is a pity that E.L. Versluysen (1981, ch. 3) does not explore this dimension in his otherwise stimulating book.

8. The collapse of Bretton Woods was, in a way, a recognition that the US had lost its supremacy and that other countries, especially Japan and West Germany, were challenging that position. "Japan's balance of trade changed from a deficit of 480 million dollars in 1964 to a surplus of 5,797 million dollars in 1971, and this clearly contributed to the collapse of the Bretton Woods agreement" (Itoh, 1983, pp. 52–3).

9. This is not the basic reason for the huge budget deficit. They are, basically, a means to counteract the fall in the average rate of profit. For a different view see Medlen, 1984.

10. The US strategy up to 1985 was aimed at retaining financial supremacy (at avoiding devaluation, or delaying it as long as possible) while avoiding at least some of the negative effects of the dollar's overvaluation on US exports. This explains the apparently paradoxical American attempt to increase the role of the yen. In fact, the resulting appreciation of the yen would have satisfied both of the two above-mentioned conditions. Of course this greater role of the yen should not have imperilled the dollar's leading international position.

11. The decline of the US as the hegemonic imperialist power is also the cause of the rise of the Euromarket and of the international debt crisis. Among the many good works on this topic MacEwan, 1986, should be mentioned.

12. This subsection was written before the historic changes in the eastern European countries of 1989. The economic and financial problems of German reunification and their influence on the DM as the leading European currency cannot be tackled here.

13. I am arguing that the inter-imperialist struggle manifests itself, at the monetary and financial levels, as the struggle between the US dollar and other currencies and not between the dollar and gold, as D. Innes holds in his otherwise very good article (1981).

14. For the current and future issues facing the ERM and the EMS, see Gross and Thygesen, 1988.

15. This section was written before China left its "new economic policy" in the wake of the Tiananmen Square massacre. The issue, however, remains topical.

16. The term socialism is put within quotation marks because those countries which used to (and those which still) call themselves socialist or communist were (are) socialist only in name. This point cannot be developed here. All that can be said here is that Cuba would deserve a separate discussion.

17. I refer here to the principle of self-management rather than to the economic system of countries like Yugoslavia which claim to be based on self-management. See Carchedi, 1987a, p. 272.

18. Those countries suffering the worst economic problems are, for the most part, those integrated with, and dependent on, western markets and western capital. In fact ... the most pressing cause of the current economic crisis in a number of smaller eastern European countries is foreign (hard currency) debt combined with peripheral absorption in the western economic system. (Phillips, 1990, p. 21)

Appendix:
The Method of Social Research

A. Dialectics

In this Appendix I return to the concepts sketched in 1.2 and deal with them in a more systematic manner.[1] Let us begin with an example of how Marx applies the dialectical method and let us extract from this application the basic features of that method.

We meet Marx's concept of dialectics as early as in the first chapter of *Capital 1*, where he deals with the relative and the equivalent forms of value. In the expression

20 yards of linen are worth 1 coat

the two commodities play different roles. "The value of the linen is represented as relative value, or appears in relative form. The coat officiates as equivalent, or appears in equivalent form" (Marx, 1967a, p. 48). From the analysis developed by Marx, the following five points can be extracted.

First, "The relative form and the equivalent form are two intimately connected, mutually dependent and inseparable elements of the expression of value" (Marx, 1967a). Second, "The opposition, or contrast existing internally in each commodity between use-value and value, is ... made evident externally by two commodities being placed in such relation to each other, that the commodity whose value it is sought to express, figures directly as a mere use-value, while the commodity in which that value is to be expressed, figures directly as mere exchange-value" (Marx, 1967a, p. 61); or, "The antagonism between the relative form of value and the equivalent form, the two poles of the value form, is developed concurrently with that form itself" (p. 68). Third, "The former [the relative form, G.C.] plays an active, the latter [the equivalent form, G.C.] a passive, part" (p. 48). Fourth, "Whether a commodity assumes the relative form, or the opposite equivalent form, depends entirely upon its accidental position in the expression of value" (p. 49). Fifth, these forms "are mutually exclusive, antagonistic extremes – i.e. poles of the same expression"(p. 48).

What is the relevance of these five points for a theory of dialectics?

1. Point one stresses the mutual existential relationship between the two forms. Each form cannot exist without the other, that is, they are each other's conditions of existence. More generally, all parts of reality are tied by mutual existential interdependence.

2. Point two stresses that both the relative form (which figures merely as a use value) and the equivalent form (which figures merely as exchange value) are potentially contained in both the linen and the coat. In fact, both commodities are already both a use value and exchange value before officiating as either just the former or as just the latter. It is only in the value relation, in the expression of value, that the linen counts exclusively as a use value and the coat exclusively as exchange value. In more general terms, reality is both what has realized itself and what is potentially present.

3. Point three stresses that one form is "more important" than the other, that is, one is "active", the other is "passive". Since Marx, throughout his work, repeatedly uses the terms "determinant" and "determined", a more general way to put this is that some parts of reality are determinant and other parts are determined. This relationship of determination can be expressed by conceptualizing the determined form as being the condition of existence of the determinant form. In the expression of value the linen, which counts only as a use value, determines the coat, which counts only as exchange value. (However, in the creation of value it is the exchange value of a commodity which determines its use value.)

4. Point four stresses the possibility for the relative (more generally, the determinant) form to become the equivalent (or determined) form and vice versa, according to the position they take in the value relation.

5. Finally, point five stresses that these two forms are antagonistic, or mutually exclusive. While the former points are generally applicable, the last point refers only to the specific nature of this particular relationship. Here the determinant and the determined instance are conditions of each other's existence. However, a determined instance can also be a condition of supersession of the determinant instance.

Let us now cast these concepts in a general framework.

A.1 Determination in the last instance

I shall begin by defining three important terms. The first is *instance*. This is a general term which indicates an event which is a part, or element, of a process. The elements of a process are processes themselves. For example, the process of production and distribution is the combination of the process of production and the process of distribution. Thus we can also say that instances are processes which are part of a wider process. The second is *unity*. This term indicates that in reality instances are tied to each other by a relation of existential interdependence, that they exist only as part of the same process. The third term is to *supersede*. This verb means both to preserve and to cause to cease to exist. This statement is only apparently paradoxical. If an instance is superseded, it ceases to exist in the sense that it is its nature, or essence, which ceases to exist. At the same time, that instance is preserved because, having entered into unity with its opposite, it is preserved as something essentially different from what it was before (this is the sense in which capitalism is superseded by socialism[2]). Therefore, to be superseded does not mean to be annihilated; it means to be preserved as something essentially different.

We can now turn to the notion of determination in the last instance. This is based on three postulates.[3]

The *first postulate* is that of the *unity of all instances*. Unity means, as has been said above, a tie of existential interdependence. This is the basic difference between a dialectical and a metaphysical view. The latter considers the objects of analysis taken out of their context and viewed in isolation. The former considers the objects of analysis in their mutual and existential interrelation. An example taken from this work is that of the mutual interrelation of all prices.

The *second postulate* is the *unity of potential and realized instances*. This means that reality encompasses in a unity both instances which have already realized themselves and instances which are only potentially present. The relation between the individual and the social value of a commodity in the process of price formation is a case in point.[4]

The *third postulate* is the *unity of determinant and determined instances*. This means that some realized instances are determinant and some others are determined in the sense that the latter are called into existence as conditions of the former's reproduction or supersession. It is in this sense that the determinant instance is "primary", in the sense that it calls into existence, rather than being called into existence. For example, the determinant instance is the structure of production and the determined instance is the structure of individual values. These, however, are only potentially conditions of reproduction of the economic structure. To become actual conditions of reproduction, they must realize themselves as social values (prices).

If the determinant instance is indicated as A, the determined instance as B and the determination of B by A as $\Rightarrow$, the determination of B by A is depicted as

$$A \Rightarrow B$$

The question now arises as to where the determined instances come from. The answer is that they are already potentially present in the determinant one. This is why the latter can express the former. The determined instances are contained *in nuce* in the determinant one. As such they are formless potentials, possibilities, which realize themselves in their concrete characteristics only in the process of interrelation both with already realized instances and with other newly emerging instances (see A.2 below). These possibilities are not (in a structuralist fashion) different combinations of the same, already realized, elements. They can be truly new and yet be contained in the determinant instance only in a potential state in the sense that they are inscribed in the actual composition, structure or nature of the determinant instance. It is in this sense that they are *real possibilities*.

These three postulates allow us to define *determination in the last instance*. This is a relation between the elements of a process (determinant and determined instances) which are tied by a relation of mutual and existential interdependence in the specific sense that some realized instances (the determined ones) are the actual conditions of reproduction or of supersession of some other instances (the determinant ones) because they were already contained in a potential state in these latter, the determinant ones. As a short-cut, to be determined in the last instance means to be called into existence as a condition for the reproduction or supersession of the determining instance, irrespective of the concrete form taken by both types of instances.[5]

Notice that a determinant instance can, and usually does, determine more than one determined instance, that is, more than one condition of its own reproduction or supersession. However, it would be mistaken to think that each determinant instance has its own "exclusive" determined instances. A determined instance can, and usually is, determined by more than one determinant instance so that it can be at the same time a condition of reproduction of one or more determinant instances and a condition of supersession of one or more other determinant instances. To give just one example, labour mobility determines wage equalization; but wage levels are also determined by other factors, say capital mobility. Capitals move from high wage areas or branches to where lower wages are paid. In short, wage equalization is determined by many determinant factors (in this example, labour and capital mobility), all acting conjointly.

A.2 Concrete realization

In order to be an actual condition either of reproduction or of supersession, an instance must leave the realm of the potential and realize itself, take concrete, specific features. But determination in the last instance does not explain the concrete aspects in which the different instances are realized, their concrete realization. In the example above, the structure of production determines the structure of individual values; but this does not explain the values actually realized which alone can be a condition of reproduction of the economic structure.

In general, if all instances are related to each other, they must realize themselves in a process of mutual interrelation, through their reciprocal interaction. This holds both for the determinant and for the determined instances. Thus, to realize what they potentially are, the determined instances (e.g. individual values) must interact with each other and, in this process, modify each other: they realize themselves (as social values, as prices) in their process of mutual interrelation. At the same time, the social values react upon and modify their determinant instance (the structure of production) in its specific, concrete form. Realization is at the same time modification. This is the *general principle of realization*. Each category of instances, in its turn, also has its own principles of realization.

If, at any given time, all instances realize themselves in the process of mutual interaction and thus mutual modification, they realize themselves simultaneously. Thus, in terms of concrete realization, to determine means "to contribute to shaping the form of". In terms of concrete realization, no instance is primary. In these terms, A determines B because it acts upon B's form of realization, but B determines A because it reacts upon A, thus determining A's form of realization.

A.3 Dialectical relation

The previous two sections allow us to conceptualize the notion of dialectical relation. There are two aspects to it: determination in the last instance (section A1) and concrete realization (section A2). Or, *dialectical relation* is a process in which the determined instances, potentially existing within the determinant one, become its actual conditions of reproduction or of supersession, and thus take on concrete features, through a process of mutual interrelation, and thus modification.

It follows that a dialectical relation is not a relation between dependent and independent variables. From the point of view of determination in the last instance, all variables are dependent upon each other: the determinant depend upon the determined because they need the determined in order to reproduce, or supersede, themselves; the determined depend upon the determinant because they exist only as conditions of the latter's reproduction or supersession. From the point of view of concrete realization all instances are equally dependent upon each other since they realize themselves in the process of mutual interrelation and thus modification. The same applies to the difference between a dialectical relation and a relation of mechanical causation in which some instances are cause and some others effect.[6]

Also, a dialectical relation is not one of simple mutual interrelation: some instances are determinant and some are determined. It is not a relation between the essence, the necessary, and the contingent, that which has to be abstracted from in order to reach the essence: both the determinant and the determined instances are essential. It is not a chronological relation since some determined instances are born together with the determinant one. Even when other determined instances realize themselves after the determinant one has come to life (the determinant instance must constantly create new conditions of reproduction or of supersession), they modify the form taken by the determinant one so that there is contemporaneity in their concrete realization. It is not a relation between something pre-given (the determinant instance) and something-to-be-determined: the determinant instance creates the determined ones in the process of realizing itself in its concrete, conjunctural form. It is not a process of allocation of elements (e.g. social agents) in an already pre-existing structure: the process of "allocation" (e.g. of agents in a social structure) is at the same time a process of reproduction of the structure itself.

A.4 Dialectical movement

We have seen that instances are tied to each other by a dialectical relation, that is, that (a) they are tied to each other by determination in the last instance and (b) they take on their specific and concrete features in the process of their mutual interrelation and simultaneous modification. But there is a logical link still missing between these two concepts. This is the notion of dialectical movement, that is, the movement between one system of simultaneously realized instances tied by a dialectical relation to another system of simultaneously realized instances also tied by a dialectical relation.

Consider again the notion of determination in the last instance, or $A \Rightarrow B$, and suppose B is a condition of reproduction of A. In this case we say that there is *correspondence* between A and B. If B is a condition of supersession of A, there is *contradiction* between the two instances. In other words, correspondence means that the reproduction of B is a condition of the reproduction of A; contradiction means that the reproduction of B is a condition of the supersession of A (a change in the nature of A). Now, a relation of correspondence is not one of harmony. Actually, correspondence implies antagonism. More precisely, a relation of correspondence is *antagonistic* in the sense that in it each instance attempts to reproduce itself by reproducing the other instance but must do so by attempting to change the other instance's *form* of realization, that is, the concrete features that instance takes when it is realized, and/or by attempting to change it from a realized *state* to a potential one, or vice versa. However, and this is the difference with a *contradictory* relation, the two instances do not attempt to change each other's *nature*, to supersede each other.

It is this antagonistic and contradictory nature of reality which explains the internal tension which manifests itself as movement. In the dialectical view, reality is seen not in static but in dynamic terms, as constantly changing. But movement and change do not come from outside; they are inherent in reality because they come from the antagonisms and contradictions inherent in it.

More specifically, *dialectical movement* has three dimensions. To begin with, since reality is the unity of potential and realized instances, movement means change (transformation) of potentially present instances into realized ones and change of realized instances back into a potential state. It is this aspect which allows us, for example, to understand the real nature of the so-called "transformation problem", that is, the constant transformation of individual values into social ones and of these latter back into individual ones (see chapter 3). Second, since all instances realize themselves in the process of their mutual interrelation and thus modification, movement means change in the form of realization of all instances (e.g. variations in prices). Third, since reality is the unity of determinant and determined instances and since these latter can be conditions either of reproduction or of supersession, movement means change of the conditions of reproduction into conditions of supersession and vice versa.

Movement, therefore, is inherent in the antagonistic and contradictory nature of the process of determination in the last instance. It is through this movement that what is potential realizes itself in its concrete form either as a condition of reproduction or as a condition of supersession.

A.5 Dialectics

Dialectics is then the view of reality which explains both the simultaneous realization of all instances at one point in time and their change into a new system of simultaneously realized instances at another point in time in terms of the dialectical nature of the relation binding all instances and of the dialectical movement arising from it.

As applied to the analysis of social life, a *dialectical view of social reality* stresses the relation of existential interdependence and thus mutual interrelation between all social phenomena (both in their realized and in their potential state, that is, as individual phenomena) in which (a) some realized social phenomena (the determined ones) emerge from their potential state to become actual conditions of reproduction or of supersession of other realized social phenomena (the determinant ones); (b) all phenomena are subjected to a constant movement, which can imply a change from a potential to a realized state and vice versa, from a realized form to another realized form, and from being a condition of reproduction to being a condition of supersession and vice versa, and (c) there can be a change from a system ultimately characterized by a certain type of determinant instance to another system characterized by a radically different type of determinant instance.[7]

A.6 Real versus analytical changes

As a final point before closing this section let us distinguish between real and analytical change. Let us first consider the relation between determinant and determined instances. In Marxist analysis, in a social system the production relations are ultimately determinant of all other instances. A change to a different system implies that a determined instance which previously might have been only potentially present (the socialist production relations) and which is contradictory to the present determinant instance (the capitalist production relations) realizes itself as the determinant one and that the previously determinant instance (the capitalist production relations) is first reduced to a determined and then to a potential state before it is completely superseded. In this case, the change of a determined instance into the determinant one indicates a real, historical, and thus chronological movement from one social system to another.

If, on the other hand, we consider the same reality at different levels of abstraction we change the focus of our analysis. This is purely an analytical change. In this case, what is considered to be determined at one level of abstraction can be considered to be determinant at a different level. For example, at a certain level of analysis, the capitalist production relations determine the capitalist production process. If we now engage in the analysis of the capitalist production process, it is justified to assume that it determines a certain technical division of labour, a certain process of deskilling, etc.

The distinction between real and analytical change can also be made concerning the relationship between potential and realized instances. The transformation of individual values into social values is a real change, a redistribution of value. Individual values can realize themselves only as social values but exist before the moment of realization (sale). Here too we have a chronological sequence between two different states of reality. On the other hand, the determination of the individuals' views of reality by production relations is an analytical change. I have submitted above (chapter 2) that classes produce their view of reality through the conception of individual producers of knowledge. In spite of their individual differences, these individual views share a common feature, that of being conditions either of reproduction or of supersession of classes (and this is why they are class-determined). Or, potentially, all individuals carrying the same aspects of production relations share the same view of reality. This is a formless, potential view which can become concrete only through the mental production of each concrete individual.

This does not mean that an undifferentiated class knowledge already exists before it is fragmented into, and appears as, individual knowledge.[8] Rather, it means that all those who objectively belong to the same class (who are carriers of the same aspects of production relations) share a common experience of reality which, by being the determinant one, informs their individual, and different, concrete views. Here too there is no change from one state of reality to another, only a shift in the focus of the analysis of the same reality. Under specific conditions, this common potential view manifests itself as common concrete elements of knowledge shared by the members of the same class.

B. Laws and Tendencies

Particularly important for a method of research stressing the dynamic nature of reality is its laws of movement. These are those social phenomena which regulate the functioning and reproduction of the social system. Social laws can best be understood as natural laws, that is, laws independent of historical determination, which, however, can manifest themselves only in a historically determined, and thus specific, form. For example, "that the product of the serf must here suffice to reproduce his conditions of labour, in addition to his subsistence, is a circumstance which remains the same under all modes of production" (Marx, 1967c, p. 790). More generally, "Natural laws cannot be abolished at all. What can change in historically different circumstances is only the *form* in which these laws assert themselves" (Marx, 1969, p. 419).

It is because they are the specific expression of natural laws that social laws can regulate the functioning of the system, that they can become laws of motion of society.

Figure A.1 The determination of the tendency and the counter-tendency

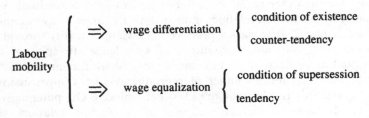

Of particular importance for the present purposes is a specific feature of social laws: their being *tendential*. This means that in them the tendency can only exist in conjunction with its counter-tendencies. Thus, in order to understand the movement of reality, we must understand both the tendencies and the counter-tendencies.

B.1 Tendencies and counter-tendencies

The tendencies are primary in the sense that they are the state towards which the counter-tendencies constantly gravitate while the counter-tendencies are secondary in the sense that they are deviations from the tendency.[9] This means, as we shall see shortly, that the tendency either cannot manifest itself at all or can manifest itself either only partly or only cyclically. Be this as it may, the tendency can only exist in conjunction with its counter-tendencies. The reason for this is that the same determinant instance which determines the tendency also determines the counter-tendencies.

For example, within a nation labour mobility determines both the emergence of a modal wage level for a certain category of labourers (the tendency) and the deviation of some wages from that mode due to the movement of some labourers to areas where, because of, say, labour scarcity, they are paid more for the same job (the counter-tendency). The same determinant instance (labour mobility) determines both the tendency (wage equalization) and the counter-tendency (wage differentiation).

In this example the tendency is a condition of supersession of the determinant instance and the counter-tendency is a condition of existence (reproduction). In fact, if wages are equalized labour ceases to move and if wages are differentiated labour continues to move. However, the tendency is not necessarily a condition of supersession. For example, the introduction of new technologies in the capitalist production process determines both a pressure on existing skilled jobs to be fragmented into a number of unskilled jobs (the tendency) and the creation of new, skilled and qualified jobs (the counter-tendency). In this case, both the tendency and the counter-tendency are conditions of existence of the determinant instance (technological innovation).

B.2 Present and future tendencies

Consider Marx's hypothesis of (tendential) equalization of all rates of profit into an average one. Marx is here interested in the *present tendency*, that is, in the hypothetical present situation which would result if only the tendential forces were operative. Or, to find the present tendency one should ask: what would the situation be like *now* if, given the *present movement*, only the tendency were to realize itself? For example, given the present situation, a constantly changing hierarchy of rates of profit, the present tendential situation is the equalization of those rates of profit to the average of their presently realized level; thus the present tendency is the hypothetical situation in which all branches (as represented by the modal capitalists) now realize the same, average, rate of profit.

Suppose we want to inquire into the tendential course of technological development within a branch. Given that within a branch there is a modal production process (which produces the bulk of commodities) as well as more productive and less productive processes, the present tendency is the adoption by all capitals of the modal process. This is not the tendency at some future point in time, the *future tendency*, which is found by forecasting the future tendential reality on the basis of the present movement. To return to the example just mentioned, since all capitals within a branch would adopt the most profitable technique, the future tendency is the adoption by all capitals of this, the most advanced (because most profitable), technique while the present tendency is the adoption by all capitals of the modal technique.

Future tendencies should not be mistaken for present tendencies. Future tendencies are part of the forecast of the situation towards which the system now moves. Present tendencies are part of the analysis of present reality.

B.3 Three types of present tendencies

Marxist literature has failed to distinguish not only between future and present tendencies but also between different types of present tendencies. This has hampered sharpness of analysis. Since a tendency manifests itself through the real movement of specific events, the different types of tendencies can be discerned by analysing the real movement. More specifically, this work distinguishes between three types of present tendencies.

We have a *tendency of the first type* when the movement shows the tendency as the point or area in which the phenomena of a certain class are clustered; the counter-tendency is then revealed by the phenomena belonging to the same class which deviate from that point or area but which gravitate towards it. As a rule of thumb we can say that a tendency of the first type is indicated by what is usual or typical in a certain empirical situation.

This is the case, for example, of the tendential wage rate. The tendential wage rate is the modal one, the wage rate paid to the great bulk of the labourers, because this is the category of wage belonging to the modal level. However there always are, at any given moment, also counter-tendential forces (e.g. capital competition for scarce labour or capital's movement to low wage areas), and thus wages above or below the modal rate. But all these (lower and higher) wage rates gravitate towards this modal rate.

We have a *tendency of the second type* when the movement shows the tendency only cyclically, that is, when the movement now shows the tendency (e.g. the fall in the average rate of profit) and then the counter-tendency (a rise in the average rate of profit). When the tendency realizes itself, the counter-tendency is present only in a potential state. Similarly, when the counter-tendency realizes itself the tendency is present only in a potential state. Another way to put this is that the tendency reproduces itself within the counter-tendency once this latter has realized itself.

It should be stressed that the notion of *tendency* should not be confused with that of *trend*. In the movement of the average rate of profit, the trend is both downward and upward, according to which period is considered. However, the tendency is only "downward" and the counter-tendency is only "upward". Or, the tendency is always present: in a realized state when the rate of profit falls and in a potential state when it either rises or stays at high levels. More generally, the tendency/counter-tendency hypothesis is a theoretical construction aiming at explaining reality, including the movement of the rate of profit in its upward and downward trends. The trend is a statistical construction which (like other statistics) can be used to verify the usefulness or correctness of a hypothesis (including the tendency/counter-tendency hypothesis).

Finally, we have a *tendency of the third type* when only the counter-tendency, the movement around the tendency (and not the tendency itself), is observable. This is the above-mentioned case of the empirically observable different rates of profit in the different branches which, through their constantly overtaking each other, allow us to hypothesize a tendency

302

towards an equalized average rate of profit. The counter-tendencies too have already been discussed.

In the first type of tendency, empirical reality contemporaneously shows both the tendency and the counter-tendency. The counter-tendency hampers the realization of the tendency in the sense that the latter can realize itself only partially (for example not all, but only the bulk of the workers belonging to a certain category are paid the same, modal, wage). In the second type of tendency, empirical reality alternatively shows either the tendency or the counter-tendency. The counter-tendency hampers the realization of the tendency (e.g. the fall in the rate of profit) in the sense that the latter can realize itself only cyclically. In the third type of tendency, empirical reality only shows the counter-tendency. This is the extreme case in which the counter-tendency completely hampers the realization of the tendency (e.g. the equalization of the rate of profit). In all three cases it is the realized, empirically observable movement which indicates to us the existence of the tendency and the type to which it belongs. The tendency, in its turn, serves to explain that movement.

B.4 Dialectical versus mathematical thinking

The issue is not whether mathematics can be used in economic analysis (of course it can) and to what extent (a question to be answered for each case separately). The issue is one of mathematical thinking versus dialectical thinking in economics. *Mathematical thinking* is exclusively concerned with those economic phenomena which can be expressed mathematically, with the casting of those phenomena in the form of mathematical models, and with the formal consistency of those models. Those aspects of economic life which cannot be expressed mathematically are either ignored or forced into a theoretical straitjacket which reduces dynamic and multifaceted processes to a static and one-dimensional picture of them. Ultimately, one engages in the solution of mathematical problems and loses sight of the economic, or social, content of those models (if they ever had any).

Dialectical thinking, on the other hand, is concerned with real, that is, dynamic and contradictory, phenomena – whether they can be expressed mathematically or not – with the analysis of the real processes of their reproduction or supersession, and with the social content of those phenomena and processes. Ultimately, one engages in the solution of theoretical problems through a dialectical analysis of social reality. From this (the dialectical) point of view, reality is seen both in its potential and in its realized existence, both in its tendencies and in its counter-tendencies, both in its process of reproduction and in its process of radical change (supersession).

B.5 Tendency and verification

A tendential relationship is not a mechanical one. In the latter, a certain cause always has a certain effect. A "counter example", then, is sufficient to disprove the validity of the hypothesized relationship. In the former, the same system which determines the tendency also determines the counter-tendency so that, if both tendency and counter-tendency realize themselves (the first two cases just mentioned), they do that only in the process of their mutual interrelation and modification. In this view, the "counter examples", or counter-tendencies, do not disprove the validity of the tendency but fit in the same explanatory frame. The verification of a tendential relation thus needs a theory of verification other than the empiricist one.[10]

B.6 Static and dynamic analysis

If reality is movement, a static analysis of reality, one in which movement has been banned, cannot by definition be correct. It is possible to hypothesize lack of movement as a hypothetical case useful only for didactical purposes but this is quite different from hypothesizing lack of movement as an essential feature of reality, as the state towards which movement tends (see 3.5). Also, if movement cannot be disassociated from time, an analysis of reality must always include time. It is possible to depict reality at a certain moment in time provided this is a snapshot of elements tied by a dialectical relation and thus tied by a dynamic relation. Thus, a dynamic picture of reality is not the "introduction of time" into a static model. At most, one engages in comparative statics. Once a dead model has been created, it is useless to try to breathe life into it.

However, to assume that reality constantly moves is not to assume that all its elements constantly change. Given a certain time period, some elements might remain the same. This is explained within a dynamic frame of analysis as movement reproducing those elements of reality in the same form and with the same function, that is, either as conditions of reproduction or as conditions of supersession of their determinant instance.

Finally, if movement is not chaotic but guided, so to speak, by tendential laws, and if the tendencies and the counter-tendencies exist only conjointly, an analysis of reality is an analysis of the interplay between phenomena acting as tendential forces and phenomena acting as counter-tendential forces and of what determines both of them. It is possible to isolate the tendency for analysis. But this is not a static analysis, provided the tendency is first of all conceptualized as part of the complex process which determines both tendencies and counter-tendencies. The importance of isolating the tendency is that it allows us to understand the situation towards which reality tendentially moves, the situation which would arise if only the tendential forces were operative, to isolate the system's driving forces, as it were.

Notes

1. This Appendix draws heavily upon Carchedi, 1987a, ch. 2. For a more detailed presentation of the following concepts, the reader is referred to that work.

2. Of course, I do not refer here to the "actually realized socialism" whose economic and moral bankruptcy has been there for all to see at least since the 1960s.

3. Postulates are concepts which (a) are not immediately evident, (b) are conditions of existence of other concepts and (c) can somehow be shown to be true. This last point requires a theory of verification, something which the reader can find in Carchedi, 1987a, ch. 3, Appendix. Axioms, in comparison, are commonly accepted, self-evident notions the truth of which cannot be verified. Each and every theory (social or not) is based on some postulates and to argue the contrary is pure nonsense. Whether the chosen postulates are useful (to understand reality) or not is a question that can be answered only on the basis of a theory (process) of verification. This is the *ex-post* reason for accepting a postulate, and not its *ex-ante* "reasonableness". If we were to reject those postulates which are not immediately evident, the application of the same method (that postulates must be immediately evident) to science would greatly hamper scientific discovery. For example, Einstein would have never discovered his special theory of relativity if he had not turned the "absurd" notion of the constancy of the velocity of light into a postulate (see Zukav, 1979, p. 157).

4. What is potential is something which either has not realized itself at all or which has realized itself at a certain level of analysis but must change before appearing at another level of analysis, the one we are dealing with. In this latter case, what is potential and what is realized depends upon the part of reality we want to consider; thus, when we analyse social values (prices) the values commodities have before sale (realization) is their individual value.

5. In chapter 1, I have used a simpler, but less precise terminology. There, the determined instance *is* a condition of reproduction or of supersession of the determinant instance. Here, the determined instance *is called into existence* as a condition of reproduction or of supersession of the determinant instance. The expression "called into existence" is intuitively acceptable in cases where human agency is obviously involved, as for example when a legislative system needs a certain police force to implement laws. However, this expression would seem to be less suitable in cases where institutions, or more generally, structures are involved (as, for example, when the structure of production determines the structure of individual values). But it is precisely in these cases that "called into existence" is a useful expression. In fact, it indicates that determination always needs human agency. For example, individual values can be determined by the structure of production only because people engage in production and create value.

6. This, of course, does not imply that all variables should be taken into account in order to carry out a certain inquiry. This is obviously an impossible task. What it does mean is that, having chosen our field of inquiry (thus including only some selected variables), we should consider the interrelation among them as one of dialectical relation.

7. This approach aims at making sense of reality without claiming to be a "reflection" of reality in our thought. By "reflection" I mean here a view which is not affected by social reality and especially by the social position of the subject of knowledge. Traditionally, in the "reflection" approach (typical of Second International Marxism) it is the individual, not class, who is the subject of knowledge.

The view implicit here, on the contrary, holds that knowledge is class-determined (it is indeed produced by individuals but they are carriers of ideological class relations) and that a "correct" view of reality is both subjective (it is imbued with the subjectivity of a class) and objective (reality is known in its objectivity). Or, what is known is objective in the sense that it exists independently of our perception of it but is subjective because it can be known only through a class-determined system of knowledge. A "correct" knowledge of reality is then one which finds a correspondence between facts and theory. But it should be immediately added that both the facts (not only the part of reality chosen for inquiry but also our perception of it) and the principles establishing when there is such correspondence (the principles of verification) are themselves part of that theory and thus class-determined.

8. As I have pointed out in chapter 2, this position should not be misread as subscribing to a metaphysical view. One should always be careful not to mistake an analytical change for a real one.

9. The choice of the elements of reality which we define as tendencies reflects our conception of the nature of reality. This conception is in fact a hypothesis which must be subjected to verification. There is no room here to discuss verification within a dialectical approach. Here it is sufficient to stress that verification is a more complex procedure than the simple empiricist comparison of theories with "neutral" facts would have us believe. I deal with this question in Carchedi, 1987a, ch. 3.

10. For such a theory, see Carchedi, 1987a, ch. 3.

Bibliography

Adam, G. (1975), "Multinational corporations and world wide sourcing", in H. Radice, *International Firms and Modern Imperialism*, Penguin Books, London, pp. 89–103

Aglietta, M. (1979). *A Theory of Capitalist Regulation*, New Left Books, London

—— (1986), *La Fin des Devises Clés*, La Découverte, Paris

Altvater, E. (1969), *Die Weltwährungskrise*, Europäische Verlagsamstalt, Frankfurt

—— (1981), "La crisi del 1929 e il dibattito Marxista sulla teoria della crisi", in E. J. Hobsbawm, G. Haupt, F. Marek, E. Ragionieri, V. Strada and C. Vivanti (eds), *Storia del Marxismo*, Einaudi, Turin, pp. 341–88

Altvater, E., B. Blanke and Chr. Neusüss (1971). "Kapitalistischer Weltmarkt und Weltwährungskrise", *Probleme des Klassenkampfs*, 1, 5–117

Amin, S. (1976), *Unequal Development*, Monthly Review Press, New York

Andrews, S.M. (1980), "Unequal exchange and the international law of value: an empirical note", *Economia Internazionale*, Maggio-Agosto, pp. 169–77

Arthur, C. (1986), *The Dialectics of Labour*, Blackwell, Oxford

Auerbach, P. and P. Skott (1988), "Concentration, competition and distribution: a critique of theories of monopoly capital", *International Review of Applied Economics*, no. 2, pp. 42–61

Banca D'Italia (1988), *Assemblea Generale Ordinaria dei Partecipanti*, 31 May, Appendix

Bank for International Settlements (1984, 1985 and 1986), *Annual Report*, Basle

Baran, P. (1968), *The Political Economy of Growth*, Monthly Review Press, New York

Baran, P. and P. Sweezy (1968), *Monopoly Capital*, Monthly Review Press, New York

Bartelheimer, P. and H. Wolf (1985), *Das Einkommen der Lohnabhängigen sinkt*. Unpublished paper

Batchelor, C. (1988), "The Key to Survival", *Financial Times*, May 24

Baumol, W. (1974), "What Marx 'Really' Meant", *Journal of Economic Literature*, March

Bellamy Foster, J. (1985), "Sources of instability in the U.S. political economy and empire", *Science and Society*, vol. XLIX, no. 2, summer, pp. 167–93

—— 1986, *Monopoly Capitalism*, Monthly Review Press, New York

Bettelheim, C. (1972), "Theoretical comments", in A. Emmanuel, *Unequal Exchange*, Monthly Review Press, New York

Betts, P. and J. Wyles (1988), "Pirelli throws a counter-punch", *Financial Times*, 8 March

Bishop, A.J. (1990), "Western mathematics: the secret weapon of cultural imperialism", *Race and Class*, Oct.–Dec., pp. 51–66

Blaug, M. (1974), *The Cambridge Revolution: Success or Failure?*, The Institute of Economic Affairs, London

Böhm-Bawerk, E. von (1973), "Karl Marx and the close of his system", in Sweezy (ed.), *Karl Marx and the Close of His System*, Kelley, Clifton

Bortkiewicz, L. von (1973), "On the correction of Marx's fundamental theoretical construction in the third volume of *Capital*", in P.M. Sweezy (ed.), *Karl Marx and the Close of His System*, Kelley, Clifton

Bottomore, T., G. Harris, V.G. Kiernan and R. Miliband (eds) (1983), *A Dictionary of Marxist Thought*, Blackwell, Oxford

Bowles, S., D.M. Gordon and T.E. Weisskopf (1985), "Two views of capitalist stagnation: underconsumption and challenges to capitalist control", *Science and Society*, vol. XLIX, no. 3, fall, pp. 259–86

Brainard, R. (1988), "Science in the market", *OECD Observer*, no. 151, April–May, pp. 20–22

Braun, O. (1973), *Comercio Internacional y Imperialismo*, siglo XXI, Buenos Aires

Braverman, H. (1974), *Labor and Monopoly Capital*, Monthly Review Press, New York

Brett, E.A. (1983), *International Money and Capitalist Crisis*, Heinemann and Westview Press, Boulder, Colorado

Bryan, R. (1985), "Monopoly in Marxist method", *Capital and Class*, no. 26, pp. 72–92

——— (1986), "Competition and monopoly: a reply", *Capital and Class*, no. 30, pp. 209–14

Burawoy, M. (1979), *Manufacturing Consent: Changes in the Labour Process Under Monopoly Capitalism*, University of Chicago Press, Chicago

Burkett, P. (1986), "A note on competition under capitalism", *Capital and Class*, no. 30, pp. 192–208

Busch, K., W. Schöller and W. Seelow (1971), *Weltmarkt und Weltwährungskrise*, Bremen

Caballero, I.M. (1984), "Unequal pricing and unequal exchange between the peasant and the capitalist economies", *Cambridge Journal of Economics*, 8, pp. 347–59

Carchedi, G. (1975), "Reproduction of social classes at the level of production relations", *Economy and Society*, vol. 4, no. 4, pp. 361–418

——— (1977), *On the Economic Identification of Social Classes*, Routledge and Kegan Paul, London

——— (1979), "Authority and foreign labour: some notes on a late capitalist form of capital accumulation and state intervention", *Studies in Political Economy*, no. 2, autumn, pp. 37–75

——— (1983), *Problems in Class Analysis*, Routledge and Kegan Paul, London

——— (1984), "The logic of prices as values", *Economy and Society*, vol. 13, no. 4, pp. 431–55

——— (1986a), "Comparative advantages, capital accumulation and socialism", *Economy and Society*, vol. 15, no. 4, pp. 427–44

——— (1986b), "Two models of class analysis", *Capital and Class*, no. 29, pp. 195–216

BIBLIOGRAPHY

—— (1987a), *Class Analysis and Social Research*, Blackwell, Oxford

—— (1987b), "Class politics, class consciousness and the new middle class", *The Insurgent Sociologist*, vol. 14, no. 3, fall, pp. 111–31

—— (1988), "Marxian price theory and modern capitalism", *International Journal of Political Economy*, fall, pp. 6–109

—— (1989), "Between class analysis and organization theory: mental labour", in S. Clegg (ed.), *Organization Theory*, W. de Gruyter, Berlin

Carter, R. (1985), *Capitalism, Class Conflict and the New Middle Class*, Routledge and Kegan Paul, London

Castells, M. (1980), *The Economic Crisis and American Society*, Princeton University Press, Princeton, NJ

Chan-Lee, J.H. and H. Sutch (1985), *Profits and Rates of Return in OECD Countries*, Working paper no. 20, Economics and Statistics Department, OECD, Paris

Chattopadhyay, P. (1987), *Economics of Shortage or Specificity of Capital Accumulation? The Soviet Case – A Marxian Perspective.* Unpublished paper

Chew, W.B. (1988), "No-nonsense guide to measuring productivity", *Harvard Business Review*, Jan.–Feb., pp. 110–18

Christiansen, J. (1976), "Marx and the falling rate of profit", *Papers and Proceedings*, American Economic Association, May

Clarke, S. (1988), "Overaccumulation, class struggle and the regulation approach", *Capital and Class*, no. 36, winter, pp. 59–92

—— (1990–91), "The Marxist theory of overaccumulation and crisis", *Science and Society*, vol. 54, no. 4, winter, pp. 442–67

Clegg, S. (ed.) (1989), *Organization Theory and Class Analysis*, W. de Gruyter, Berlin

Clegg, S., P. Boreham and G. Dow (1986), *Class, Politics and the Economy*, Routledge and Kegan Paul, London

Coakley, J. (1988), "International dimensions of the stock market crash", *Capital and Class*, no. 34, spring, pp. 16–21

Coakley, J. and L. Harris (1983), *The City of Capital*, Blackwell, Oxford

Cochrane, P. (1980–81), "Gold, the durability of a barbarous relic", *Science and Society*, vol. XLIV, no. 4, winter, pp. 385–400

Cohen, G.A. (1981), "The labour theory of value and the concept of exploitation", in various authors, *The Value Controversy*, Verso, London

Cohen, S. (1987), "A labour process to nowhere?", *New Left Review*, Sept.–Oct., no. 156, pp. 34–50

Cogoy, M. (1987a), "Neo-Marxist theory, Marx and the accumulation of capital", in P. Mattick Jr. (ed.), "Value, accumulation and crises", *International Journal of Political Economy*, vol. 17, no. 2, summer, pp. 11–37

—— (1987b), "The falling rate of profit and the theory of accumulation", in P. Mattick Jr. (ed.), "Value, accumulation and crises", *International Journal of Political Economy*, vol. 17, no. 2, summer, pp. 54–74

—— (1987c), "The theory of value and state spending", in P. Mattick Jr. (ed.), "Value, accumulation and crises", *International Journal of Political Economy*, vol. 17, no. 2, summer, pp. 75–110

Commission of the European Community (1989), *European Economy*, no. 40, May

Cookson, C. (1988), "The lap-tops that mean business", *Financial Times*, September 14

Cooper, J.C. and K. Madigan (1991), "On recession's battlefield, the economy is losing ground", *International Business Week*, Feb.18, pp. 13–14

Corden, W.W. (1985), *Inflation, Exchange Rates and the World Economy*, Clarendon Press, Oxford

Coughlin, C.C. and K. Koedijk (1990), "What do we know about the long-run real exchange rate?", *Review*, The Federal Reserve Bank of St. Louis, Jan.–Feb., pp. 36–48

Cutler, A. (1978), "The romance of labour", *Economy and Society*, vol. 7, no. 1

Dale, R. (1989), "Echoing U.S. fears of inflation grow in Europe", *International Herald Tribune*, March 2

De Brunhoff, S. (1974–5), "Controversies in the theory of surplus value", *Science and Society*, vol. XXXVIII, no. 4, winter, pp. 478–82

—— (1976), *Marx on Money*, Urizen Books, New York

—— (1978), *The State, Capital and Economic Policy*, Pluto Press, London

Dehove, M. (1984), "Les taux de change et ses modèles théoriques", *Critique de l'Économie Politique*, Oct.–Dec., pp. 81–129

Delaunay, J.C. (1989), "Research on the Marxist theory of the rate of surplus value and the wage-earning class" in F. Moseley (ed.), "Declining profitability and the current crisis", *International Journal of Political Economy*, vol. 19, no. 1, spring

Deubner, Chr., U. Rehfeldt, F. Schlupp and G. Ziebura (1979), *Die Internationalisierung des Kapitals. Neue Theorien in der Internationalen Diskussion*, Campus Verlag, Frankfurt

Dullforce, W. (1988), "Islamabad sets minefield for Gatt unwary", *Financial Times*, October 7

Eatwell, J. (1974), "Controversies in the theory of surplus value: old and new", *Science and Society*, vol. XXXVIII, no. 3, fall, pp. 281–303

Economic Report of the President (1970), Washington, D.C.

—— (1988), Washington, D.C.

The Economist (1988), "Living with smart machines", pp. 81–3, May 21

—— (1988), "A portrait of America's new competitiveness", pp. 69–70, June 4

—— (1988), "Multinational, not global", pp. 97–8, December 24

Edquist, C. and S. Jacobsson (1988), *Flexible Automation. The Global Diffusion of New Technology in the Engineering Industry*, Blackwell, Oxford

Edwards, R. (1979), *Contested Terrains: the Transformation of the Workplace in the Twentieth Century*, Basic Books, New York

Ehrbar, H. and M. Glick (1986–87), "The labor theory of value and its critics", *Science and Society*, vol. L, no. 4, winter, pp. 464–78

Eichenwald, K. (1990), "Housecleaning hits executive suites", *International Herald Tribune*, November 10–11

Eichner, A.S. (ed.) (1979), *A Guide to Post-Keynesian Economics*, Macmillan, London

Eldred, M. (1984), "A reply to Gleicher", *Capital and Class*, no. 23, summer, pp. 135–40

Elger, T. (1979), "Valorization and de-skilling: a critique of Braverman", *Capital and Class*, no. 7

Elson, D. (1979), *Value: The Representation of Labour in Capitalism*, CSE Books, London

Emmanuel, A. (1972), *Unequal Exchange*, Monthly Review Press, New York

Engels, F. (1970), *Anti-Dühring*, International Publishers, New York

—— (1976), *The Dialectics of Nature*, Progress Publishers, Moscow

Ernst, J.R. (1982), "Simultaneous equations extirpated", *The Review of Radical Political Economics*, vol. 14, no. 2

European Commission (1987), *European Economy*, supplement A, no. 4, April, table 1, p. 4

Eurostat (1986), *Review, 1976–1985*, Brussels

Evans, T. (1985), "Money makes the world go round", *Capital and Class*, no. 24, pp. 99–123

—— (1988), "Dollar is likely to rise, fall or stand steady, experts agree", *Capital and Class*, no. 34, spring, pp. 10–15

Federal Reserve Bulletin, May 1989, Washington, D.C.

Feiger, G. and B. Jacquillat (1982), *International Finance: Text and Cases*, Allyn and Bacon, Boston, MA

Fennel, D. (1976), "Beneath the surface: the life of a factory", *Radical America*, vol. 10, no. 5, pp. 21–44

Ferguson, C.H. (1988), "From the people who brought you voodoo economics", *Harvard Business Review*, May–June, pp. 55–62

Financial Times (1987), "Countries in surplus promise action to strengthen domestic demand", June 11

Fine, B. (1982), *Theories of the Capitalist Economy*, Edward Arnold, London

—— (1983), "A dissenting note on the transformation problem", *Economy and Society*, vol. 12, no. 4

—— (1985–6), "Banking capital and the theory of interest", *Science and Society*, vol. XLIX, no. 4, winter, pp. 387–413

—— (ed.) (1986), *The Value Dimension*, Routledge and Kegan Paul, London

—— and L. Harris (1979), *Re-reading Capital*, Macmillan, London

Fishlock, D. (1989), "Spotlights fall on the Cinderellas", *Financial Times*, February 9

Foley, D.K. (1986), *Understanding Capital*, Harvard University Press, Cambridge, MA

Frank, A.G. (1972), *Lumpenbourgeoisie and Lumpendevelopment*, Monthly Review Press, New York

—— (1980), *Crisis: in the World Economy*, Heinemann, London

—— (1981), *Crisis: in the Third World*, Heinemann, London

—— (1988), "American roulette in the globonomic casino", in P. Zarembka (ed.), *Research in Political Economy*, pp. 3–43, Jai Press, Greenwich, Conn.

Freeman, A. (1984), "The logic of the transformation problem", in E. Mandel and A. Freeman, *Ricardo, Marx, Sraffa*, pp. 221–64, Verso, London

—— (1988), "The crash", *Capital and Class*, no. 34, spring, pp. 33–41

Friedman, A.L. (1977), *Industry and Labour*, Macmillan, London

Fröbel, F., J. Heinrichs and O. Kreye (1980), *The New International Division of Labour*, Cambridge University Press, Cambridge

Fruhan, W.E., Jr. (1988), "Corporate raiders: head 'em off at value gap", *Harvard Business Review*, July–Aug., pp. 63–8

Galarza, F.T. (1982), *The neo-Ricardian Theory of Trade and its Critical Evaluation*, Institute of Social Studies, The Hague

Garnett, N. (1988), "The culture shock of automation", *Financial Times*, October 7

Gaveau, G. (1983), "Turmoil in the international monetary system", in *World View*, Pluto Press, London

Gernstein, I. (1976), "Production, circulation and value", *Economy and Society*, vol. 5, no. 3

311

Giussani, P. (1984). "Labour power: the missing commodity", in E. Mandel and A. Freeman, *Ricardo, Marx, Sraffa*, pp. 115–40, Verso, London

—— (1988), *La teoria della caduta del saggio di profitto*, paper presented at the meeting: La teoria economica Marxista oggi, Milan, March 20

Gleicher, D. (1983), "A historical approach to the question of abstract labour", *Capital and Class*, no. 21, winter, pp. 97–122

—— (1985), "Note: a rejoinder to Eldred", *Capital and Class*, no. 24, winter, pp. 147–55

—— (1985–6), "The ontology of labor values", *Science and Society*, vol. XLIX, no. 4, pp. 463–71

Glyn, A. (1988), "The crash and real capital accumulation", *Capital and Class*, no. 34, spring, pp. 21–4

—— and B. Sutcliffe (1972), *British Capitalism, Workers and the Profit Squeeze*, Penguin Books, London

Gordon, D.M. (1988), "The global economy: new edifice or crumbling foundation?", *New Left Review*, no. 168, March–April, pp. 24–64

Grahl, J. (1988), "The stock market crash and the role of the dollar", *Capital and Class*, no. 34, spring, pp. 24–32

Green, F. and P. Nore (1977), *Economics: an Anti-Text*, Macmillan, London

Gross, D. and N. Thygesen (1988), *The EMS. Achievements, Current Issues and Directions for the Future*, Centre for European Policy Studies, Brussels

Guerrero, D. (1990a), "Salario relativo y depauperacion obrera: el caso español", Universidad Complutense de Madrid, unpublished paper

—— (1990b), "Trabajo, capital y redistribucion del estado: la evolution del 'impuest neto' en España (1970–87)", Universidad Complutense de Madrid, unpublished paper

Guerrien, B. (1989), *L'Économie Néo-classique*, La Découverte, Paris

Guttmann, R. (1988), "Il Crollo dell '87: correnti pericolose su Wall Street", *Primo Maggio*, no. 29, Autumn, pp. 32–40

Hampton, J.H. and J.R. Norman (1987), "General Motors: what went wrong", *Business Week*, March 16

Harberger, A.C. (1988), "Applications of real exchange rate analysis", *Contemporary Policy Issues*, vol. VII, no. 2, April, pp. 1–40

Harris, L. (1977), "The balance of payments and the international economic system", in F. Green and P. Nore, *Economics: an Anti-Text*, Macmillan, London

Hilferding, R. (1973), "Böhm-Bawerk's criticism of Marx", in P.M. Sweezy (ed.), *Karl Marx and the Close of his System*, Kelley, Clifton

—— (1981), *Finance Capital*, Routledge and Kegan Paul, London

Himmelweit, S. and S. Mohun (1978), "The anomalies of capital", *Capital and Class*, no. 6, autumn, pp. 67–105

Hobsbawm, E.J., G. Haupt, F. Marek, E. Ragionieri, V. Strada and C. Vivanti (eds) (1981), *Storia del Marxismo*, 3**, Einaudi, Turin

Hodgson, G. (1980), "A theory of exploitation without the labour theory of value", *Science and Society*, vol. XLIV, no. 3, fall, pp. 257–73

—— (1981), "Critique of Wright: Labour and Profits", in various authors, *The Value Controversy*, Verso, London

Holtham, G., G. Keating and P. Spencer (1987), *EMS: Advance or Face Retreat*, CSFB, Boston

Howard, M.C. and J.E. King (1985), *The Political Economy of Marx*, Longman, London and New York

Hunt, E.K. and H.J. Sherman (1986), *Economics*, Harper and Row, New York

BIBLIOGRAPHY

IMF (1986), *International Financial Statistics*, Supplement on Government Finance, Supplement Series, no. 111

—— (1988a), *International Financial Statistics*, Washington, D.C.

—— (1988b), *Annual Report*, Washington, D.C.

Indart, G. (1987–88), "Marx's law of market value", *Science and Society*, vol. 51, no. 4, pp. 458–67

Innes, D. (1981), "Capital and gold", *Capital and Class*, no. 14, summer, pp. 5–36

International Herald Tribune (1986), March 26

—— (1989) March 11–12

—— (1990), November 10–11, "Enimont shares sequestered"

Institut für Internationale Politik und Wirtschaft der DDR (1987), *Die Wirtschaft kapitalistischer Länder in Zahlen*, IPW Forschungshefte, Heft 1/1987

Itoh, M. (1976), "A study of Marx's theory of value", *Science and Society*, vol. XL, no. 3, fall, pp. 307–40

—— (1978), "The formation of Marx's theory of crisis", *Science and Society*, vol. XLII, no. 2, summer, pp. 129–55

—— (1981), "On Marx's theory of accumulation: a reply to Weeks", *Science and Society*, vol. XLV, no. 1, spring, pp. 71–84

—— (1983), "The great world crisis and Japanese capitalism", *Capital and Class*, winter, pp. 49–60

—— and N. Yokokawa (1979), "Marx's theory of market value", in D. Elson, *Value*, pp. 102–14, CSE Books, London

Joint Economic Committee (1986), *Joint Economic Report*, Congress of the United States, Washington, D.C.

—— (1989), *Joint Economic Report*, Congress of the United States, Washington, D.C.

Kay, G. (1979), "Why labour is the starting point of capital", in D. Elson (ed.), *Value*, CSE Books, London

Kehoe, L. (1991), "IBM cuts its computer workstation prices by up to 60%", *Financial Times*, May 8

Kenyon, P. (1979), "Pricing", in A.S. Eichner (ed.), *A Guide to Post-Keynesian Economics*, Macmillan, London

Kieve, R.H. (1988), Review article on *Analytical Marxism*, *Science and Society*, vol. 52, no. 2, summer, pp. 229–32

Kiljunen, K. (1986), "The international division of industrial labour and the core-periphery concept", *CEPAL Review*, United Nations Economic Commission for Latin America and the Caribbean, Santiago, Chile, December

Kliman, A. and T. McGlone (1988), "The transformation non-problem and the non-transformation problem", *Capital and Class*, no. 35, summer, pp. 56–83

Krause, L.B. and W.S. Salant (eds) (1977), *Worldwide Inflation*, The Brookings Institution, Washington, D.C.

Labaton, S. (1991), "U.S. predicts 1992 deficit for FDIC", *International Herald Tribune*, January 28

Leadbeater, C. (1991), "A crackdown on originality", *Financial Times*, April 25

Lebowitz, M.A. (1988), "Is 'Analytical Marxism' Marxism?", *Science and Society*, vol. 52, no. 2, summer, pp. 191–214

Lenin, V.I. (1967), *The Development of Capitalism in Russia*, Progress Publishers, Moscow

Levai, I. (1983), *The Political Economy of the Working Class*, Institute for World Economy, Budapest

313

Lewis, H. (1984), "Coming: a new international economic order", *International Herald Tribune*, January 18

Linder, M. (1977), *Anti-Samuelson*, vol. II, Urizen Books, New York

Lipietz, A. (1986), "Behind the crisis: the exhaustion of a regime of accumulation. A 'Regulation School' perspective on some French empirical work", in various authors, "Empirical work in Marxian crisis theory", *Review of Radical Political Economics*, vol. 18, nos. 1–2, pp. 13–33

Lippert, J. (1978), "Shopfloor politics and Fleetwood", *Radical America*, vol. 12, no. 4, pp. 53–69

Locke Anderson, W.H. and F.W. Thompson (1988), "Neoclassical Marxism", *Science and Society*, vol. 52, no. 2, summer, pp. 215–28

Lovering, J. (1987), "The Atlantic arms economy: towards a military regime of accumulation?", *Capital and Class*, 33, winter, pp. 129–55

MacEwan, A. (1986), "International debt and banking: rising instability within the general crisis", *Science and Society*, vol. L, no. 2, summer, pp. 177–209

Magdoff, H. and P. Sweezy (1985), *Stagnation and the Financial Explosion*, Monthly Review Press, New York

Mandel, E. (1975), *Late Capitalism*, New Left Books, London

—— (1980), *Long Waves of Capitalist Development*, Cambridge University Press, Cambridge

—— (1983), *De Krisis, 1974–1983*, Antwerp

—— and A. Freeman (1984), *Ricardo, Marx, Sraffa*, Verso, London

Mandel, M.J. (1991), "The recession may be over before its work is done", *Business Week*, March 18

Marsh, P. (1987), "Textile industry enters the jet age", *Financial Times*, May 15

Marx, K. (1963), *Theories of Surplus Value*, part I, Progress Publishers, Moscow

—— (1967a), *Capital*, vol. I, International Publishers, New York

—— (1967b), *Capital*, vol. II, International Publishers, New York

—— (1967c), *Capital*, vol. III, International Publishers, New York

—— (1968), *Theories of Surplus Value*, part II, Progress Publishers, Moscow

—— (1971), *Theories of Surplus Value*, part III, Progress Publishers, Moscow

—— (1973), *Grundrisse*, Penguin Books, Harmondsworth

—— and F. Engels (1969), *Selected Works*, vol. 2, Progress Publishers, Moscow

—— and F. Engels (1970), *The German Ideology*, International Publishers, New York

Mathews, J. (1989), *Tools of Change*, Pluto Press, London

Mattick, P. (1969), *Marx and Keynes*, Merlin Press, London

—— (1972), "Samuelson's 'transformation' of Marxism into bourgeois economics", *Science and Society*, vol. XXXVI, no. 3, pp. 258–73

—— (1978), *Economics, Politics and the Age of Inflation*, Merlin Press, London

Mattick, P. Jr. (1981), "Some aspects of the value-price problem", *Économies et Sociétés*, XV, 6–7, pp. 275–81

—— (1986), *Social Knowledge*, Sharpe, Armonk

—— (ed.) (1987), "Value, accumulation and crises", *International Journal of Political Economy*, vol. 17, no. 2, summer

—— (1990), "Contribution to the Critique of 'Regulation Theory'", unpublished paper

Medlen, C. (1984), "Corporate taxes and the federal deficit", *Monthly Review*, November, pp. 10–26

Montagnon, P. (1988), "Japanese growth hits 11%", *Financial Times*, June 17

Morris, J. (1983), "Underconsumption and the general crisis: Gillman's theory",

Science and Society, vol. XLVII, no. 3, fall, pp. 323–9

Mortensen, J. (1984), "Profitability, relative factor prices and capital/labour substitution in the Community, the United States and Japan, 1960–83", Commission of the European Communities, *European Economy*, July, no. 20

Moseley, F. (1986), "The intensity of labor and the productivity slowdown", *Science and Society*, vol. L, no. 2, pp. 210–18.

—— (1988a), "The rate of surplus value, the organic composition, and the general rate of profit in the US economy, 1947–67: A critique and update of Wolff's estimates", *American Economic Review*, March, pp. 298–303

—— (1988b), *The Decline of the Rate of Profit in the Postwar U.S. Economy: Regulation and Marxian Explanations*. Paper presented at the International Conference on the Theory of Regulation, Barcelona, June 1988

—— (ed.) (1989), "Declining profitability and the current crisis", *International Journal of Political Economy*, vol. 19, no. 1, spring

—— (1989a), Introduction, in F. Moseley, (ed.); "Declining profitability and the current crisis", *International Journal of Political Economy*, vol. 19, no. 1

—— (1989b), "The decline in the rate of profit in the postwar US economy", in F. Moseley, (ed), "Declining profitability and the current crisis", *International Journal of Political Economy*, vol. 19, no. 1

Mufson, S. and J. Knight (1990), "US plans overhaul of banking system", *International Herald Tribune*, December 11

National Institute for Economic and Social Research (1987), *National Institute Economic Review*, no. 120, May

Nichols, T. (ed.) (1980), *Capital and Labour*, Collins, Glasgow

OECD, *Economic Outlook*, Various issues, Paris

OECD, *Economic Indicators*, Various issues, Paris

Officer, L.H. (1974), "Purchasing power parity and factor price equalization", *Kyklos*, vol. XXVII, fasc. 4, pp. 868–77

Oiserman, T.I. (ed.) (1979), *Geschichte der Dialektik, 14 bis 18 Jahrhundert*, Berlin, 1979

Okishio, N. (1961), "Technical change and the rate of profit", *Kobe University Economic Review*, 7

Pala, G. (1982), "Forme di valore, denaro, prezzi non concorrenziali", *Note economiche*, no. 1, Monte dei Paschi di Siena, pp. 118–35

—— (1983), "Money, course of exchange and rate of exploitation", *Economic Notes*, Monte dei Paschi di Siena, no. 3, pp. 122–51

Palloix, C. (1973), *Les Firmes Multinationales et le Procès d'Internationalisation*, Maspero, Paris

—— (1975), *L'Economie Mondiale Capitaliste et les Firmes Multinationales*, Maspero, vol. 1, Paris

Parboni, R. (1981), *The Dollar and Its Rivals*, Verso, London

Pasinetti, L.L. (1981), *Structural Change and Economic Growth*, Cambridge University Press, Cambridge

Phillips, P. (1990), "The debt crisis and change in Eastern Europe", *Monthly Review*, pp. 19–27

Plender, J. (1988), "Price of turbulence", *Financial Times*, February 15

Quint, M. (1989), "Japanese banks raise sights to middle market in United States", *International Herald Tribune*, October 6

Radice, H. (1975), *International Firms and Modern Imperialism*, Penguin Books, London

Rapos, P. (1984), *Wirtschaftkrises im Heutigen Kapitalismus*, Dietz Verlag, Berlin

Rapporti Sociali (1988), "Crak di borsa e capitale finanziario", no. 1, February, pp. 9–25

Reati, A. (1989), "The rate of profit and the organic composition of capital in the post-war long wave", in F. Moseley (ed.), "Declining profitability and the current crisis", *International Journal of Political Economy*, vol. 19, no. 1

Reuten, G. (1988), "Value as social form", in M. Williams (ed.), *Value, Social Form and the State*, pp. 42–62, Macmillan, London

Ricardo, D. (1966), *On the Principles of Political Economy and Taxation*, Cambridge University Press, Cambridge

Roberst, P.C. (1990), "Sure, Milken's sentence will serve as a deterrent – to innovators", *Business Week*, December 17

Robinson, J. (1972), "Ideology and analysis", in J. Schwartz, *A Critique of Economic Theory*, Penguin Books, Harmondsworth

Roddick, J. (1984), "Crisis, 'seigniorage' and the modern world system: rising Third World power or declining US hegemony?", *Capital and Class*, summer, pp. 121–34

Roemer, J.E. (1982), "New directions in the Marxian theory of exploitation and class", *Politics and Society*, vol. 11, no. 3, pp. 253–87

Roncaglia, A. (1974), "The reduction of complex labour to simple labour", *Bulletin of the Conference of Socialist Economists*, autumn, pp. 1–12

Rosenberg, N. (ed.) (1971), *The Economics of Technological Change*, Penguin Books, Harmondsworth

Rowthorn, B. (1974), "Skilled labour in the Marxist system", *Bulletin of the Conference of Socialist Economists*, spring, pp. 25–45

Rubin, I.I. (1972), *Essays on Marx's Theory of Value*, Black and Red, Detroit

Ruivenkamp, G., *Biotechnologie: een herstructurering van de mondiale voedselproduktie*, unpublished Ph.D dissertation, University of Amsterdam

Salama, P. (1975), *Sur la Valeur*, Maspero, Paris

—— (1988), *La Dollarisation*, La Découverte, Paris

Salant, W.S. (1977), "International transmission of inflation", in L.B. Krause, and W.S. Salant (eds), *Worldwide Inflation*, pp. 167–227, The Brookings Institution, Washington, D.C.

Samuelson, P. (1970), *Economics*, McGraw-Hill, Kogakusha Company, Tokyo

Sau, R. (1976), "The theory of unequal exchange, trade and imperialism", *Economic and Political Weekly*, vol. XI, no. 10, March 6

—— (1982), *Trade, Capitalism and Development*, Oxford University Press, Calcutta

Sawyer, M.C. (1989), *The Challenge of Radical Political Economy*, Wheatsheaf, Hemel Hempstead

Scammel, W.M. (1974), *International Trade and Payments*, Macmillan, London

Schinasi, G.J., (1989), "European integration, exchange rates and monetary reform", *The World Economy*, December, pp. 389–413

Schwartz, J. (1972), *A Critique of Economic Theory*, Penguin Books, Harmondsworth

—— (ed.) (1977), *The Subtle Anatomy of Capitalism*, Goodyear Publishing Co., Santa Monica, California

Semmler, W. (1982), "Theories of competition and monopoly", *Capital and Class*, winter, pp. 91–116

Sekine, T. (1982–3), "The law of market value", *Science and Society*, vol. XLVI, no. 4, winter, pp. 420–44

Senf, B. (1978), "Politische Ökonomie des Kapitalismus", *Mehrwert*, no. 18

BIBLIOGRAPHY

Shaikh, A. (1977), "Marx's transformation of value and the 'transformation problem'", in J. Schwartz (ed.), *The Subtle Anatomy of Capitalism*, Goodyear Publishing Co. Santa Monica

—— (1978), "Political economy and capitalism: notes on Dobb's theory of crises", *Cambridge Journal of Economics*, 2, pp. 233–51

—— (1979), "Foreign trade and the law of value": part I, *Science and Society*, fall, pp. 281–302

—— (1980), "Foreign trade and the law of value": part II, *Science and Society*, spring, pp. 27–57

—— (1983), "Economic crises", in T. Bottomore, L. Harris, V.G. Kiernan, and R. Miliband, *A Dictionary of Marxist Thought*, Blackwell, Oxford, pp. 138–43

Sharma, K.K. (1988), "India fashion and export boom from backstreet tailors", *Financial Times*, June 22

Shepherd, W.G. (1982), "Causes of increased competition in the US economy", 1939–80, *The Review of Economics and Statistics*, vol. LXIV, no. 4, November, pp. 613–26

Sherman, H.J. (1979), "The Marxist theory of value revisited", *Science and Society*, vol. XXXIV, no. 3, fall, pp. 257–92

Siegel, T. (1984), "Politics and economics in the capitalist world market", *International Journal of Sociology*, vol. XIV, no. 1

Silk, L. (1988), "Economic pressure grows to cut military spending", *International Herald Tribune*, June 4–5

—— (1990), "New long-term estimates on thrifts: $1 trillion", *International Herald Tribune*, June 2–3

Sims, C. (1988), "Polaroid, in restructuring, will sell conventional film", *International Herald Tribune*, July 14

Sivanandan, A. (1989), "The global market-place", *International Labour Report*, November–December, pp. 7–9

Smith, T. (1990), *The Logic of Marx's Capital*, State University of New York Press, Albany, NY

Söderston, B. (1970), *International Economics*, Macmillan, London

Sraffa, P. (1960), *Production of Commodities by Means of Commodities*, Cambridge University Press, Cambridge

Stadnichenko, A. (1975), *Monetary Crisis of Capitalism*, Progress Publishers, Moscow

Steedman, I. (1977), *Marx After Sraffa*, New Left Books, London

Stephens, P. (1988), "Guessing the dollar's true rate", *Financial Times*, January 28

Sterngold, J. (1991), "Japan: most to gain from a short war?", *International Herald Tribune*, January 29

Stockholm International Peace Research Institute (1988), *Sipri Yearbook*, Stockholm

Sun Xiangjian (1982), "The question of the profitability of China's foreign trade to the national economy", *Social Sciences in China*, vol. III, no. 3, September, pp. 35–61

Survey of Current Business (1975), "Public and private debt", July, pp. 9–11

Sweezy, P.M. (1942), *The Theory of Capitalist Development*, Monthly Review Press, New York, 1968

—— (ed.) (1973), *Karl Marx and the Close of his System, by Eugene Böhm-Bawerk and Böhm-Bawerk's Criticism of Marx, by Rudolf Hilferding*, Kelley, Clifton

—— (1981), *Four Lectures on Marxism*, Monthly Review Press, New York

—— (1987), "Some problems in the theory of capital accumulation", in P. Mattick, Jr. (ed.), "Value, accumulation and crises", *International Journal of Political Economy*, vol. 17, no. 2, pp. 38–53

—— and H. Magdoff (1983), "Review of the month", *Monthly Review*, vol. 35, no. 5, October

—— and H. Magdoff (1984), "The two faces of the world debt", *Monthly Review*, vol. 35, no. 8, January

Szymanski, A. (1984), "Productivity growth and capitalist stagnation", *Science and Society*, vol. XLVIII, no. 3, fall, pp. 295–322

Thompson, P. (1983), *The Nature of Work*, Macmillan, London

Tomkins, R. (1989), "A first hint of recession", *Financial Times*, November 1

Tortajada, R. (1977), "A note on the reduction of complex labour to simple labour", *Capital and Class*, no. 1, spring, pp. 106–16

Tsang, S. and T. Woo (1988), "Comparative advantages and trade liberalization in China", *Economy and Society*, vol. 17, no. 1, pp. 21–51

Uchitelle, L. (1990), "Amid signs of US recession, bankruptcies hit a record", *International Herald Tribune*, December 1

UNCTC (United Nations Center on Transnational Corporations) (1988), *Transnational Corporations in World Development*, United Nations, New York

Various authors (1981), *The Value Controversy*, Verso, London

—— (1986), "Empirical work in Marxian crisis theory", *Review of Radical Political Economics*, vol. 18, nos. 1–2

Vernon, R. (1971), "International investment and international trade in the product cycle", in Rosenberg (ed.), *The Economics of Technological Change*, pp. 440–60, Penguin Books, Harmondsworth

—— (1972), "Die grundlegenden Triebkräfte der Multinationalisierung", in Chr. Deubner, U. Rehfeldt, F. Schlupp and G. Ziebura, *Die Internationalisierung der Kapitals*, Campus Verlag, Frankfurt

Versluysen, E.L. (1981), *The Political Economy of International Finance*, Gower Publishing Co., Westmead, Hants

Vilar, P. (1976), *A History of Gold and Money, 1450–1920*, New Left Books, London

Watson, T.J. (1987), *Sociology, Work and Industry*, Routledge and Keagan Paul, London

Weeks, J. (1977), "The sphere of production and the analysis of crisis in capitalism", *Science and Society*, vol. XVI, no. 3, pp. 281–302

—— (1979), "The process of accumulation and the 'profit-squeeze' hypothesis", *Science and Society*, vol. XLIII, no. 3, pp. 259–80

—— (1981), *Capital and Exploitation*, Princeton University Press, Princeton, NJ

—— (1982a), "Equilibrium, uneven development and the tendency of the rate of profit to fall", *Capital and Class*, no. 16, pp. 62–77

—— (1982b), "A note on underconsumptionist theory and the labor theory of value", *Science and Society*, vol. XLVI, no. 1, spring, pp. 60–76

Wheelock, J. (1983), "Competition in the Marxist tradition", *Capital and Class*, no. 21, pp. 18–44

—— (1986), "Competition and monopoly: a contribution to debate", *Capital and Class*, no. 30, pp. 184–91

Williams, M. (1988) (ed.), *Value, Social Form and the State*, Macmillan, London

Wolff, E.N. (1986), "The productivity slowdown and the fall in the US rate of profit, 1947–1976", *Review of Radical Political Economics*, vol. 18 (nos. 1 and 2), pp. 87–109

Wolfson, M.H. (1986), *Financial Crises*, Sharpe, Armonk

Wright, E.O. (1985), *Classes*, Verso, London

Yaffe, D. (1973), "The Marxian theory of crisis, capital and the state", *Economy and Society*, vol. 2, no. 2, pp. 186–232

——(1975), "Values and prices in Marx's *Capital*", *Revolutionary Communist*, 1, 2nd ed.

Yuan Wenqui, Dai Lunzhang and Wang Linsheng (1980), "International division of labor and China's economic relations with foreign countries", *Social Sciences in China*, vol. I, no. 1, pp. 22–48

Zarembka, P. (ed.) (1988), *Research in Political Economy*, vol. 11, Jai Press, Greenwich, Conn.

Zukav, G. (1979), *The Dancing Wu Li Masters,* Richard Clay, Bungay, Suffolk

Index

Adam, G. 262, 307
Aglietta, M. 213 n24, 214 n25, 289, 290 n4, 307
Altvater, E. 213 n19, 227 n2, 248, 289 n3, 307
Amin, S. 225, 273 n18, 307
Andrews, S.M. 272 n5, 307
Arthur, C. xi, 20, 307
Auerbach, P. 214 n28, 307

Banca d'Italia 207, 307
Bank for International Settlements 257, 307
Baran, P. 138, 185, 307
Bartelheimer, P. 129, 307
Batchelor, C. 62, 307
Baumol, W. 122 n32, 307
Bellamy, Foster J. 186, 307
Bettelheim, C. 229 n5, 308
Betts, P. 308
Bishop, A.J. 53 n38, 308
Blaug, M. 308
Blanke, B. 248, 289 n3, 307
Böhm-Bawerk, E. von 90, 126, 127, 131, 308
Bortkiewicz, L. von 90, 91, 308
Boreham, P. 50 n6, 309
Bottomore, T. 308, 317
Bowles, S. 188, 308
Brainard, R. 50 n9, 308
Braun, O. 225, 227, 308
Braverman, H. 15, 17, 308
Brett, E.A. 308
Bryan, R. 122 n29, 272 n2, 272 n3, 308
Burawoy, M. 16, 308

Burkett, P. 272 n3, 308
Busch, K. 248, 308

Caballero, I.M. 260, 308
Carchedi, B. xi
Carchedi, G. 5, 6 n4, 16, 35, 41, 47, 49, 50 n6, 50 n8, 50 n11, 51 n19, 51 n21, 52 n29, 53 n36, 122 n32, 123 n37, 138, 151 n3, 151 n4, 151 n7, 213 n22, 220, 227, 236, 287, 290 n17, 305 n1, 306 n9, 306 n10, 308, 309
Carter, B. 16, 52 n29, 309
Castells, M. 102, 309
Chan-Lee, J.H. 160, 161, 235, 309
Chattopadhyay, P. 151 n9, 309
Chew, W.B. 58, 309
Christiansen, J. 151 n9, 309
Clarke, S. 213 n16, 214 n24, 309
Clegg, S. 50 n6, 309
Coakley, J. 216 n40, 272 n4, 289 n2, 309
Cochrane, P. 289 n4, 309
Cohen, G.A. 126, 309
Cohen, S. 50 n7, 309
Cogoy, M. 120 n3, 309
Commission of the European Community 232, 233, 309
Cookson, C. 263, 309
Cooper, J.C. 143, 310
Corden, W.W. 281, 310
Coughlin, C.C. 273 n26, 310
Cutler, T. 15, 310

Dai Lunzhang 319
Dale, R. 208, 310

De Brunhoff, S. 150, 212 n6, 273 n18, 310
Dehove, M. 273 n13, 310
Delaunay, J.C. 310
Deubner, C. 248, 310, 318
Dow, G. 50 n6, 309
Dullforce, W. 18, 310

Eatwell, J. 150, 310
Economic Report of the President 173, 310
The Economist 60, 69, 70, 153, 232, 310
Edquist, C. 121 n8, 310
Edwards, R. 16, 52 n29, 310
Ehrbar, H. 151 n1, 310
Eichenwald, K. 39, 310
Eichner, A.S. 310
Eldred, M. 126, 310
Elger, T. 15, 310
Elson, D. 310
Emmanuel, A. 121 n17, 222, 223, 308, 310
Engels, F. 5 n2, 52 n35, 310
Ernst, J.R. 311
European Commission 311
Eurostat 242, 311
Evans, T. xi, 216 n40, 289 n5, 311

Federal Reserve Bulletin 173, 311
Feiger, G. 227 n2, 311
Fennel, D. 16, 311
Ferguson, C.H. 59, 232, 237, 238, 279, 311
Financial Times 18, 263, 311
Fine, B. 122 n32, 151 n9, 311
Fishlock, D. 50 n10, 311
Foley, D.K. 122 n32, 151 n9, 188, 212 n9, 311
Frank, A.G. 178, 220, 262, 273 n21, 311
Freeman, A. xi, 122 n32, 137, 216 n40, 311, 312
Friedman, A.L. 16, 311
Fröbel, F. 241, 273 n21, 311
Fruhan, W.E., Jr. 238, 311

Galarza, F.T. 311
Garnett, N. 2, 6 n3, 311
Gaveau, G. 280, 311
Gernstein, I. 122 n32, 311
Giussani, P. xi, 120 n4, 312
Gleicher, D. 126, 312

Glick, M. 151 n1, 310, 312
Glyn, A. 188, 216 n40, 312
Gordon, D.M. 188, 272 n6, 308, 312
Grahl, J. 216 n38, 312
Green, F. 273 n19, 312
Gross, D. 290 n14, 312
Guerrero, D. 130, 312
Guerrin, B. 123 n40, 312
Guttmann, R. 216 n40, 312

Haan, W. de xi, 122 n32
Hampton, J.H. 120 n2, 312
Harberger, A.C. 269, 312
Harris, L. 122 n32, 271 n4, 273 n19, 289 n2, 308, 309, 312, 317
Haupt, G. 307, 312
Heinrichs, J. 241, 273 n21, 311
Hilferding, R. 90, 179, 180, 212 n10, 213 n18, 312
Himmelweit, S. 312
Hobsbawm, E.J. 307, 312
Hodgson, G. 126, 127, 312
Holtman, G. 282, 312
Howard, M.C. 120 n6, 136, 312
Hunt, E.K. 170, 198, 205, 206, 312

Indart, G. 121 n14, 313
Innes, D. 290 n13, 313
International Herald Tribune 45, 51 n22, 68, 151 n8, 198, 313
International Monetary Fund 171, 190, 204, 256, 266, 268, 313
Institut für Internationale Politik und Wirtschaft der DDR 278, 313
Itoh, M. 121 n14, 122 n32, 290 n8, 313

Jacobsson, S. 121 n8, 310
Jacquillat, B. 227 n2, 311
Joint Economic Committee 177, 313

Kay, G. 79, 127, 128, 129, 313
Keating, G. 282, 312
Kehoe, L. 95, 313
Kenyon, P. 119, 313
Kiernan, V.G. 308, 317
Kieve, R.H. 51 n21, 313
Kiljunen, K. 228 n3, 313
King, J.E. 120 n6, 136, 312
Kliman, A. 122 n32, 313
Knight, J. 214 n34, 315
Koedijk, K. 273 n26, 310

Krause, L.B. 313, 316
Kreye, O. 241, 273 n21, 311

Labaton, S. 214 n34, 313
Laibman, D. xi
Leadbeater, C. 238, 313
Lebowitz, M.A. 51 n21, 313
Lenin, V.I. 14, 181, 313
Levai, I. 229 n5, 313
Lewis, H. 279, 314
Linder, M. 314
Lipietz, A. 187, 314
Lippert, J. 16, 314
Locke Anderson, W.H. 51 n21, 314
Lovering, J. 198, 314

MacEwan, A. 290 n11, 314
Madigan, K. 143, 310
Magdoff, H. 257, 278, 314, 318
Mandel, E. 122 n28, 122 n32, 137, 189,
    191, 214 n27, 272 n9, 273 n21, 312,
    314
Mandel, M.J. 153, 314
Marek, F. 307, 312
Marsh, P. 58, 314
Marx, K. 7, 12, 19, 20, 28, 40, 52 n35,
    55, 57, 58, 64, 67, 68, 69, 70, 74, 93,
    101, 110, 118, 122 n31, 125, 128, 130,
    141, 148, 151 n12, 151 n13, 156, 157,
    164, 165, 174, 180, 181, 182, 183,
    206, 207, 212 n7, 213 n20, 214 n35,
    216 n39, 221, 231, 260, 291, 299, 314
Mathews, J. 214 n24, 314
Mattick, P. 122 n28, 123 n39, 174, 314
Mattick, P., Jr. xi, 48, 52 n34, 122 n32,
    214 n24, 314, 318
McGlone, T. 122 n32, 313
Medlen, C. 290 n9, 314
Miliband, R. 308, 317
Mohun, S. 312
Montagnon, P. 255, 314
Morris, J. 185, 314
Mortensen, J. 61, 315
Moseley, F. xi, 120 n5, 158, 212 n3, 214
    n26, 315, 316
Mufson, S. 214 n34, 315

National Institute for Economic and
    Social Research 315
Neusüss, C. 248, 289 n3, 307
Nichols, T. 315
Nore, P. 273 n19, 312

Norman, J.R. 120 n2

Officer, L.H. 273 n13, 315
Oiserman, T.I. 5 n1, 315
Okishio, N. 140, 315
Organization for Economic
    Cooperation and Development 61,
    315

Pala, G. xi, 273 n20, 315
Palloix, C. 228 n4, 272 n7, 315
Parboni, R. 278, 279, 315
Pasinetti, L.L. 60, 315
Phillips, P. 290 n18, 315
Plender, J. 276, 315

Quint, M. 315

Radice, H. 307, 315
Ragionieri, E. 307, 312
Ramer, R. xi
Rapos, P. 153, 183, 197, 315
Rapporti Sociali 216 n40, 316
Reati, A. 120 n5, 158, 316
Rehfeldt, U. 248, 310, 318
Reuten, G. xi, 103, 316
Ricardo, D. 145, 147, 148, 150, 217,
    316
Roberst, P.C. 214 n34, 316
Robinson, J. 96, 316
Roddick, J. 290 n5, 316
Roemer, J.E. 51 n21, 126, 316
Roncaglia, A. 151 n5, 316
Rosenberg, N. 316, 318
Rowthorn, B. 151 n5, 316
Rubin, I.I. 122 n32, 316
Ruivenkamp, G. 63, 316

Salama, P. 122 n30, 273 n24, 316
Salant, W.S. 273 n16, 313, 316
Samuelson, P. 227 n2, 276, 316
Sau, R. 260, 316
Sawyer, M.C. 100, 316
Scammel, W.M. 251, 316
Schinasi, G.J. 257, 316
Schlupp, F. 248, 310, 318
Schöller, W. 248, 308
Schwartz, J. 316, 317
Seelow, W. 248, 308
Semmler, W. 272 n3, 316
Sekine, T. 137, 316
Senf, B. 248, 316

Shaikh, A. 122 n32, 151 n9, 188, 228
    n4, 229 n6, 317
Sharma, K.K. 262, 317
Shepherd, W.G. 232, 317
Sherman, H.J. 49 n3, 170, 198, 312, 317
Siegel, T. 229 n6, 248, 317
Silk, L. 198, 214 n34, 317
Sims, C. 64, 317
Sivanandan, A. 241, 317
Skott, P. 214 n28, 307
Smith, T. 317
Social Sciences in China 283
Söderston, B. 219, 317
Spencer, P. 282, 312
Sraffa, P. 83, 96, 97, 136, 137, 150, 317
Stadnichenko, A. 258, 290 n6, 317
Steedman, I. 136, 317
Stephens, P. 272 n14, 317
Sterngold, J. 214 n33, 317
Stockholm International Peace
    Research Institute 197, 317
Strada, V. 307, 312
Sun Xiangjian 284, 317
Survey of Current Business 173, 317
Sutch, H. 160, 161, 235, 309
Sutcliffe, B. 188, 312
Sweezy, P.M. 90, 120 n3, 123 n39, 185,
    257, 278, 314, 317, 318
Szymanski, A. 318

Thompson, F.W. 51 n21
Thompson, P. 50 n6, 318
Thygesen, N. 290 n14, 312
Tomkins, R. 214 n30, 318

Tortajada, R. 151 n5, 318
Tsang, S. 287–8, 318

Uchitelle, L. 214 n34, 318
United Nations Center on
    Transnational Corporations 60, 190,
    227 n2, 237, 238, 240, 272 n8, 318

Vernon, R. 272 n7, 318
Versluysen, E.L. 290 n7, 318
Vilar, P. 212 n7, 212 n11, 318
Vivanti, C. 307, 312

Wang Linsheng 319
Watson, T.J. 212 n4, 318
Weeks, J. 120 n3, 151 n9, 188, 318
Wheelock, J. 272 n3, 318
Weisskopf, T.E. 188, 308
Williams, M. 316, 318
Wolff, E.N. 120 n5, 157, 159, 160, 318
Wolf, H. 129, 307
Wolfson, M.H. 202, 203, 319
Woo, T. 287, 288, 318
Wright, E.O. 51 n21, 319
Wyles, J. 308

Yaffe, D. 122 n32, 319
Yokokawa, N. 121 n14
Yuan Wenqui 284, 285, 319

Zarembka, P. 319
Ziebura, G. 248, 310, 318
Zukav, G. 305 n3, 319

Printed in the United States
by Baker & Taylor Publisher Services